Counseling Strategies for Loss and Grief

KEREN M. HUMPHREY

AMERICAN COUNSELING
ASSOCIATION
5999 Stevenson Avenue
Alexandria, VA 22304
www.counseling.org

Counseling Strategies for Loss and Grief

10 9 8 7 6 5 4 3 2

American Counseling Association
5999 Stevenson Avenue
Alexandria, VA 22304

Director of Publications
Carolyn C. Baker

Production Manager
Bonny E. Gaston

Editorial Assistant
Catherine A. Brumley

Copy Editor
Elaine Dunn

Cover and Text Design by Bonny E. Gaston.

Library of Congress Cataloging-in-Publication Data
Humphrey, Keren M.
    Counseling strategies for loss and grief/Keren M. Humphrey.
        p.   cm.
    Includes bibliographical references and index.
    ISBN 978-1-55620-246-9 (alk. paper)
    1. Loss (Psychology) 2. Grief. 3. Counseling. I. Title.
    BF575.D35H86 2009
    158'.3—dc22   2008041860

Dedication

This book is dedicated to the women who shaped me with their presence:
my mother, Amy Riser Harrington Humphrey,
and my maternal grandmother, Elberta Riser Harrington.
And to the woman who shaped me with her absence,
my paternal grandmother, Lela Marie Beller Humphrey.

Table of Contents

PART 1 Unique Grief and Unique Grievers

PART 2 Counseling Strategies for Loss Adaptation

Preface

For years my professional colleagues and I have discussed the need for a book of counseling interventions to supplement the theoretical literature on loss and grief. The vast majority of this literature centers on theoretical conceptualizations of bereavement grief and research on distinct topics (e.g., complicated grief, AIDS-related grief) or the characteristics of distinct populations (e.g., bereaved parents, the chronically ill). Although this knowledge base is essential to our understanding of loss and grief, the literature tends to falls short in consideration of the technical aspects of intervention. Most often authors suggest a direction for therapy, such as examining unfinished business or facilitating emotional expression, but the nuts-and-bolts descriptions of what to actually do with clients in therapy are often disappointingly vague or entirely absent. It is the old challenge of translating theory into practice, and it is the reason for this book.

The purpose of *Counseling Strategies for Loss and Grief* is to describe a range of counseling strategies appropriate to the treatment of loss and grief issues in diverse psychotherapy settings. It is based on contemporary understandings on the nature of personal and interpersonal loss and the ways in which people attempt to integrate loss and grief into their lives. The suggested strategies incorporate constructs and procedures from a wide variety of sources, reflecting both time-tested counseling strategies and more recent innovations in counseling theory and practice. Five themes guide this text.

1. Loss and grief are frequently encountered issues in psychotherapy that are inclusive of both death-related and nondeath-related circumstances. Despite substantial attention given to bereavement grief, nondeath-related losses just as often present significant challenges in the lives of clients. "All changes involve loss, just as all losses require change" (R. A. Neimeyer, 2000a, p. 5).
2. The experience of loss and grief is highly individual and intensely personal, reflecting a unique interaction of person, loss event, and the multiple contexts in which that loss and grief occur.
3. The boundary between death-related and nondeath-related loss is permeable so that knowledge associated with each assists understanding of the other. Differences between the two have less to do with the fact of death and bereavement and more to do with the uniqueness of an individual's response to loss and his or her particular grieving journey.
4. The natural extension of appreciating the uniqueness of each person's experience of loss and grief and her or his particular manner of adapting to loss is the importance of tailoring counseling strategies to client needs. If the experience of loss and grief is unique, then counseling interventions that address those experiences must prioritize that uniqueness.

5. It is assumed that counseling professionals regard the strategies described here, like any therapeutic intervention, as inherently adaptable. Sound theoretical conceptualization and a solid working relationship precede selection of interventions, which are then customized to fit the unique needs of clients and the evolving counseling process.

Perhaps it is useful here to point out what this book does not attempt to do. It is not intended as a comprehensive treatment manual in which a set of prescribed interventions from a standardized theory are applied invariably to every client, family, or group. There is no laundry list of goals and objectives from which to pick and choose and no stereotypical list of cultural characteristics that obscures individuality. Instead, this book describes a broad range of counseling strategies that are adaptable across various theoretical orientations and includes practical suggestions for increasing their effectiveness.

Whom This Book Is For

Counseling Strategies for Loss and Grief is intended primarily for counseling professionals and clinical supervisors working in diverse psychotherapy settings. It also provides a valuable, practical resource for graduate trainees in counseling and counseling-related professions, where issues of loss and grief are inadequately addressed (Humphrey, 1993). The counseling strategies outlined here are most appropriate for adolescents and adults and are primarily aimed at individual therapy situations. However, suggestions for using these strategies in group and family therapy settings are provided. Additional resource recommendations specific to certain topics are also included throughout the text.

Terminology in This Book

Sometimes the terminology associated with professional psychotherapy services can be confusing, so the following clarifications apply in this text:

+   *Counseling* and *therapy* refer to psychotherapeutic intervention services provided by qualified mental health professionals. No distinction is made in this text between counseling and therapy as long as services are delivered by a qualified mental health professional.
+   A *qualified mental health professional* possesses at least a master's degree in counseling or a counseling-related field (e.g., psychology, social work) and national certification or state licensure. *Counseling professional*, *therapist*, *counselor*, and *psychotherapist* are interchangeable terms describing qualified mental health professionals.
+   *Grief counseling* and *grief therapy* refer to psychotherapeutic interventions involving both death-related and nondeath-related grief.
+   *Strategies* is the preferred term for counseling interventions described in this book. The word *techniques* implies something done to clients by counselors without input from clients, whereas *strategies* suggests a more respectful and collaborative therapeutic activity, tailored to the uniqueness of clients, that is consistent with effective counseling for loss and grief.

Organization of the Book

Counseling Strategies for Loss and Grief includes two parts. Part 1, Unique Grief and Unique Grievers, orients readers to current thinking about loss and grief and the implications for professional counseling practice. Chapter 1 summarizes the shift from traditional to contemporary grief models in the form of guidelines for conceptualizing loss and grief. Chapter 2 highlights diverse aspects of loss and grief that merit special attention by counseling professionals. Chapter 3 outlines two contemporary grief models—adaptive grieving styles and the dual process model—with suggestions for using these models to enhance counseling services with grieving clients. Part 2, Counseling Strategies for Loss Adaptation, offers detailed descriptions of various interventions appropriate in counseling for issues of loss and grief, distinguishing them by focus or theoretical origins. Chapter 4 provides strategies that focus on cognitive and behavioral interventions, drawing largely from cognitive–behavioral and constructivist therapy models. Chapter 5 provides strategies that focus primarily on emotional processing. Chapters 6 and 7 offer strategies derived from two contemporary therapies arising from postmodern and constructivist thinking: narrative therapy and solution-focused therapy. Chapter 8 describes a number of recommended adjunctive activities that are especially beneficial to grieving clients, their adaptation to loss, and the counseling process. Finally, Chapter 9 addresses the challenges of working with loss and grief for the counselor as a person and a professional.

Acknowledgments

It has been my good fortune to work directly or indirectly with grieving people in a variety of settings over several careers. I remain in awe of those individuals and families who willingly shared their dying and their grief with me so many years ago in my first career as a parish minister. This book began with you.

I am deeply grateful for the clients, supervisees, and students who have taught me so much about doing and teaching psychotherapy. You convinced me this book was necessary.

I thank my friends and professional colleagues for their contributions and encouragement, especially Cathie Barrett, Don Combs, Deb Davis, Liz Doughty, Phyllis Erdman, Sue Metzger, Jan Pattis, and Linda Osborne.

I acknowledge my American Counseling Association editor, Carolyn Baker, whose patience, good humor, and professionalism are deeply appreciated.

My family is always a reliable source of support, especially my stepchildren Patti and Mike, who must have wondered if that darn book would ever be done.

I acknowledge my writing partner, Chief the Black Lab, the ultimate practitioner of mindful attention, who reminds me that long hours at the computer must be balanced with regular Frisbee and cookie breaks.

Finally, I express my deepest thanks to my husband, Jim, whose sustaining love and unwavering support for my endeavors so brighten and bless my life. Our life together is a wonderful adventure.

About the Author

KEREN M. HUMPHREY, EdD, NCC, LPC, LCPC, has more than 25 years experience in the helping professions as a parish minister, probation officer, professional counselor, and counselor educator. In addition to a private psychotherapy practice, Dr. Humphrey has provided counseling, supervision, and consultation services in the corrections field and on college campuses. A popular national and international presenter on grief counseling and counselor preparation, Dr. Humphrey is also the author of numerous journal articles, coauthor of *Problem Solving Technique in Counseling* (CD-ROM), and coauthor with Deborah Davis of *College Counseling: Issues and Strategies for a New Millennium.* She has held various leadership positions in the American College Counseling Association and has been a representative to the Governing Council of the American Counseling Association. She is the recipient of the Outstanding Professional Leadership Award and the Award for Dedicated and Outstanding Service from the American College Counseling Association. Recently retired after nearly 20 years as a counseling professor at Western Illinois University and Texas A&M University–Commerce, Dr. Humphrey is the CEO of 4 Directions Consulting, Rockwall, Texas.

PART 1

Unique
Grief
and
Unique Grievers

Chapter 1

Thinking Differently About Loss and Grief in the 21st Century

The experience of loss is a universal phenomenon that, while frequently challenging and distressing, is often transformational. Most people develop skills and attitudes over a lifetime that allow them to manage the distress and assimilate the losses, even difficult losses, into their lives in a satisfactory manner. Nevertheless, loss and grief appear as familiar themes in the lives of psychotherapy clients in a variety of settings. They may be the primary source of client difficulties or just as often serve as contributing or complicating factors in other areas.

Despite the fact that these concerns regularly occur in psychotherapy settings, counseling professionals sometimes fail to identify the presence of loss and grief. This is particularly common with nondeath-related loss circumstances. Yet the responses to both death-related and nondeath-related losses are in most ways the same: We feel deprived, we experience sadness, we confront and avoid painful emotions, we attempt to reorganize our world, we struggle with connection and disconnection, our new losses trigger material from our old losses, we yearn to return to preloss circumstances, we try to make sense or make meaning of our losses, we are paralyzed, we are transformed, and we struggle to integrate our losses into our lives. In fact, grief reactions to nondeath-related losses can be just as severe, or more so, than those connected to bereavement loss.

> When we think of loss we think of the loss, through death, of people we love. But loss is a far more encompassing theme in our life. For we lose not only through death, but also by leaving and being left, by changing and letting go and moving on. And our losses include not only our separations and departures from those we love, but our . . . losses of romantic dreams, impossible expectations, illusions of freedom and power, illusions of safety—and the loss of our younger self. (Viorst, 1986, p. 2)

It is important that counseling professionals be adept at identifying different forms of loss and recognizing the diverse ways in which loss and grief may influence people's lives. Equally important is the counselor's ability to provide skilled intervention services that promote a functional, healthy process of adapting to loss. Consider for a moment how you would work with the following loss-related client difficulties, including what counseling strategies might be most effective. Later, after you have studied the various counseling strategies detailed in this book, return to these cases and consider what you might do differently.

Kito, a counselor working at an addiction recovery center, noticed the absence of emotion as his client described the terrible toll her husband's gambling had taken on her: "I've stood by him for 14 years; through the gambling, the drinking, the legal hassles, his suicide attempts, not knowing where he was or when he would come home, getting calls from the police in the middle of the night, wondering how long before he lost another job, trying to keep things from the kids and my parents, wondering how I was going to keep body and soul together. I'm glad he has gotten help, but you know this is the third time for him and I just don't know that I expect anything other than failure again. I don't think I can do this anymore." Then, Kito noticed her voice begin to quaver as she continued, "It wasn't supposed to be like this. This is not what was supposed to happen. This is not what I hoped for. It's all gone."

Elena, a school counselor, listened carefully as 15-year-old Robert complained about his mother, her boyfriend, his teachers, the school, and the general injustice of life for adolescent boys. She had seen him off and on for several months now, focusing on the hostile attitude and angry outbursts that had already earned him one school suspension that year. Robert's family life had certainly been chaotic. His parents had split up 2 years ago, then his father went to prison. Soon after this his mother had moved Robert and his younger sister into her boyfriend's apartment in a different school district. Robert did not get along with the boyfriend, and his mother seemed disinterested in her son's school problems. Although he indicated a good relationship with his father, there had been little contact since his father's imprisonment. Elena was pleased that Robert finally found a few boys to hang out with at school, but it appeared that he was on his own most of the time. As she continued to focus on Robert, she suddenly realized that the only person this lonely, hurting, and angry young man had not complained about or even mentioned was his father. Elena held up her hand to get his attention and asked him to take a deep breath. She waited for silence to fill the space then quietly said, "Robert, you've experienced a lot of losses in the last few years and it is clear that one of them is your father. Tell me about losing your father."

Jane sought therapy initially for depressionlike symptoms that had lasted over a year. Her mood was generally low, and she was often irritable, felt helpless, had little energy, and could not seem to summon interest in much of anything. Her physical health was excellent and she reported a solid and supportive marital relationship. The difficulties began around the time she and her husband relocated to a new house across town from the neighborhood where they had lived for 14 years. Jane had lovingly renovated the old house in their former neighborhood and had been deeply involved in community activism, especially in helping others renovate nearby homes. She absolutely loved being part of revitalizing this neighborhood, finding in it a direction and identity that was quite satisfying. Then, a few years ago, a nearby hospital began buying up homes in the area. The community organized and, with Jane in the lead, fought the hospital on every front but to no avail. Neighbor after neighbor bowed to the financial and political pressure to sell, the last few couples avoiding Jane at the end for fear of her disappointment in their "selling out." Finally, only Jane and her husband were left and, admitting defeat, they also sold their home and moved away. Although Jane realized her problems had something to do with the move, she focused more on the difficulty of adjusting to the new situation than the circumstances behind the move. Jane's counselor, on the other hand, recognized that loss and grief were at the heart of Jane's difficulties. She had lost a familiar and beloved place, a home where she had raised her children, built close social relationships, and developed an activist identity. She had lost her expectations about the future, no longer anticipating the visits of grandchildren or growing old with her husband in that special home they created. Perhaps more importantly, Jane had lost certain core assumptions about the goodness of people, the rightness of her ideas, her own invulnerability, and her ability to control what goes on in her world. The counselor realized what Jane was struggling with was not a problem of depression, but a problem of grief.

Billy's wife of 9 years, Lucille, died following a traumatic 2-year battle with breast cancer. During her illness Billy and Lucille both had found great comfort in their conservative faith, and this had continued to sustain Billy when Lucille died. Three years later Billy is struggling to reestablish himself. He ruminates obsessively about Lucille's illness and death; he alternately blames himself or the doctors for not doing enough to save Lucille. Billy has had several uncharacteristic angry outbursts lately on the job and during a church meeting, the anger clearly inappropriate to the situation at hand. Billy recognizes that his problems are related to Lucille's death. He has, with reservations, sought professional counseling at the suggestion of his pastor. As the counselor works with Billy, it becomes clear that a major stumbling block is Billy's insistence that these difficulties would not be occurring if only he was strong enough in his faith. The counselor's assessment is that Billy has not really allowed himself to grieve at all. His rigid interpretation of emotional distress as a sign of insufficient faith makes it very difficult for him to engage fully with Lucille's death. In one session, when the counselor asks Billy to talk about the anger he is experiencing, he blurts out that he is really angry at God for taking Lucille. As the counselor carefully and respectfully encourages Billy to explore this, it becomes clear that Lucille's death has significantly challenged his religious beliefs and he has been unwilling to face this issue. For Billy, the loss of faith might be just as devastating as the loss of Lucille.

Loss and Grief Terminology

The language associated with loss and grief is often confusing, due in part to variations in common expression, culturally specific usage, and professional terminology. For example, some people may associate *grief* only with a death experience, whereas others may apply the term to any experience of loss. The word *mourning* may describe certain cultural practices, a communal rather than an individual reaction to loss, or any outward signs of death-related grief. To confuse things even more, people often use terms interchangeably but not necessarily accurately. For example, grief, mourning, and bereavement may denote the same experience for one person but may carry differences for another. In an effort to provide clarity, the following terms and definitions are applied in this text.

Loss is defined as the real or perceived deprivation of something deemed meaningful. In this text the term refers to both death-related and nondeath-related loss.

Grief refers to (a) an emotion, generated by an experience of loss and characterized by sorrow and/or distress, and (b) the personal and interpersonal experience of loss. Grief is highly unique and multidimensional, reflecting a distinct convergence of responses (i.e., cognitive, affective, physical, behavioral) and contextual influences (e.g., personal, social, cultural, historical). In this text, the terms *grief* and *grieving* apply to both death-related and nondeath-related loss events.

Loss adaptation refers to the process of adjusting to loss and grief. The term *adaptation* is preferred over the term *coping* when speaking of grief, and these terms are not interchangeable. Coping implies a time-limited reaction in which an event is simply endured or momentarily managed with coping skills (e.g., counting to 10, positive self-talk). Adaptation, on the other hand, conveys an active process of modification, revision, reorganization, and assimilation over time that more accurately describes the grieving experience (Corr & Doka, 2001).

Bereavement refers to a period of sorrow following the death of a significant other. Bereavement is always associated with a death.

Mourning refers to socially prescribed practices or outward expressions of grief and can apply to both death-related and nondeath-related circumstances.

Changing Ideas About Loss and Grief

Mental health professionals draw on a variety of theoretical and clinical approaches to understand and explain the nature of loss and grief and the process of loss adaptation. The most influential models focus almost exclusively on death-related loss and bereavement grief. Traditional psychoanalytic theory portrays grief as an abnormal and transient state of psychic trauma in which the griever must detach from the deceased so as to reinvest energy in other things (e.g., relationships, work, and the self). This requires a process of confronting the loss and resolving ambivalence called *grief work*. Failure to detach or sever bonds with the deceased and resolve ambivalent feelings is regarded in this model as pathological. Attachment theory (Bowlby, 1969, 1973, 1980), drawing primarily on the study of parent–child bonding, emphasizes separation anxiety arising from the nature of the griever's attachment to the deceased (e.g., secure, insecure), the disruption of affectional bonds, and the need to emotionally detach from the lost object (e.g., the deceased). Bowlby was the first to propose a progressive or linear course of grieving involving phases. Other phase models followed, most notably those proposed by Parkes (1972) and Sanders (1989). Kubler-Ross's (1969) stage model, based originally on her work with dying patients in a hospital setting, is especially well known to the general public. These traditional models generally conceptualize grief as an internal process in which all grievers endure a common set of predictable phases or stages ending in a final stage of resolution that resembles their preloss level of functioning.

More recently, Rando (1984, 1993) and Worden (1982, 1991, 2002), recognizing the limitations of universal phase/stage bereavement grief models applied to all grievers, conceptualized grieving in terms of overlapping processes or tasks. Rando identified six processes for bereaved persons: recognizing the loss, reacting emotionally to the separation, recollecting memories (of the deceased) and reexperiencing the relationship, relinquishing old attachments and assumptions, readjusting to an altered world, and reinvesting in new relationships. Worden's approach describes loss adaptation involving four tasks that, while implying some progression, can also overlap: accept the reality of the loss, work through the pain of grieving, adjust to an environment in which the deceased is missing, and emotionally relocate the deceased and move on with life.

However, many counseling professionals and grief researchers today recognize significant limitations in many of these bereavement grief models or significant flaws in their interpretation and application (Attig, 1996; Harvey, 1998; Klass, Silverman, & Nickman, 1996; R. A. Neimeyer, 1997, 2000a, 2000b; S. Payne, Jarrett, Wiles, & Field, 2002; Stroebe, Schut, & Stroebe, 1998; Stroebe & Stroebe, 1991; Weiss, 1998; Worden, 2002; Wortman & Silver, 1989). These limitations include

  + Following one-size-fits-all grief models that emphasize universality, predictability, and sameness, thus obscuring the individual griever's unique experience.

+ Overemphasizing grief work and emotional processing to the exclusion of cognitive processes involved in loss adaptation.
+ Viewing grieving individuals and families as passive victims of grief phases and stages.
+ Insisting on the necessity of severing ties or disconnecting one's self from the lost objects.
+ Assuming abnormality, pathology, dysfunction, and disability when dealing with loss and grief.
+ Failing to account for the impact of personal, social, familial, historical, and cultural influences on loss and grief experiences.
+ Assuming that grief ends.

The previous 2 decades have seen a remarkable evolution in the understanding of bereavement grief and loss experiences in general. Historical, conventional, and stereotypical assumptions have given way to new perspectives that emphasize the uniqueness of the griever, the dynamic and adaptive nature of grieving, the role of meaning reconstruction and cognitive processing, and the multiple contexts that shape the experience of loss and influence loss adaptation. Noteworthy contributions to these newer perspectives on loss and grief include cognitive stress theory (Folkman, 2001), constructivism (R. A. Neimeyer, 2001a, 2001b), the social-functional perspective (Bonanno, 2001; Bonanno & Kaltman, 1999), trauma and traumatic loss (Litz, 2004), the two-track model of bereavement (Malkinson & Rubin, 2007), the dual process model (Stroebe & Schut, 1999, 2001a, 2001b), and adaptive grieving (Martin & Doka, 2000). It is interesting that these more recent perspectives on bereavement grief also enhance the understanding of nonbereavement or nondeath-related loss and grief precisely because they recognize that all losses, all grief, and all grievers are not the same. The following guidelines reflect the current shifts in the understanding of loss and grief that are especially important for counseling professionals to consider.

Nine Critical Guidelines for Conceptualizing Loss and Grief

1. Recognize That People, Their Experience of Loss, and Their Grief Are Unique

We grieve like ourselves, not just like others. Our grief is our own, reflecting the particular nuances of ourselves, our world, and our lives. Rather than focusing on how one person's grief is like everyone else's grief (e.g., universal grief stages), it is far more helpful and respectful to focus on the idiosyncratic nature of an individual's grief and his or her particular manner of adapting to loss. In fact, as Attig (1996) suggested, this is exactly what grieving clients want from professionals (i.e., counselors)—an understanding that their grief is distinctly and profoundly their own.

For example, some women may experience menopause as a loss of cherished identity as a woman and mother, whereas other women may regard menopause more as a relief or symbolic of a welcomed life transition. Those differing perceptions about menopause, one focused on loss and the other on gain, reflect the influence of diverse variables (e.g., cultural expectations, personal history) making each woman's response unique. Consider also the couple grieving the death of their child. One parent moves toward others, especially the other parent, finding solace in connection and healing in the open expression of emotional distress. The other parent, instead, moves toward introspection, is reserved about sharing feelings, and finds the resumption of everyday activities most helpful. Despite the commonality of their loss, each grieves differently because each experiences the loss in a unique manner.

Once counseling professionals accept that there are "multiple ways of experiencing, expressing, and dealing with one's losses" (Corr & Doka, 2001, p. 183), then rather than sorting everyone's grief into predictable stages or universal tasks and applying generic counseling strategies, the focus of counseling shifts toward discerning uniqueness—the particular combination of factors and contexts at work for any specific individual and her or his particular experience of loss and grief. "It might prove desirable to teach clients that there are many goals that can be set, many ways to feel, and no set series of stages that they must pass through—that many forms of expression and behavioral patterns are acceptable reactions to loss" (Stroebe, Gergen, Gergen, & Stroebe, 1996, p. 42).

2. *Recognize That Loss and Grief Occur in the Multiple and Fluid Contexts of Personal, Familial, Social, Cultural, and Historical Influences*

Loss and grief do not occur in a vacuum. An individual's grieving involves a continual process of negotiation among the various sociocultural influences specific to that person and to the environments in which she or he lives. These influences include beliefs, values, and assumptions related to meaning; rules and norms for conduct and behavior; attitudes toward helping; coping methods; role and status expectations; support networks and functions; individual or collective orientation; healers and mentors; kinship structure and dynamics; social and cultural identity (e.g., class, sexual orientation, ethnicity); attitude toward suffering; relationship and socialization patterns; religious and spiritual practices and symbols; communication styles; traditions and rituals; level of acculturation and assimilation; and personal, familial, communal, and ethnic history. The counseling professional considers the personal and sociocultural influences at work for a given client, how these influences affect the client's experience of loss and grief, how the client negotiates these influences, and the ways that therapy can facilitate the client's negotiation of these influences for a healthy loss adaptation.

Consider the various sociocultural influences in the loss and grief experiences described below. Then go back over each case, change or add something (e.g., ethnicity, age, gender, family, developmental stage, religion/spirituality, family composition, personality trait), and reconsider what effect those changes may have on the situation.

Teresa and her husband recently separated after 21 years of marriage. For much of that time the couple led essentially separate lives. Philippe had traveled extensively for his work and Teresa had focused on her own job, raising the children, keeping the home, and caring for her aging parents. The children now have moved out and are making their own way. Teresa's father died 2 years ago and her mother, who has Alzheimer's disease, is in a care facility. Teresa tells her therapist: "I feel like everyone is leaving me. My mother hardly recognizes me, the children don't need me, Philippe is gone—no one needs me anymore. I'm not sure what I am supposed to do with myself. I'm no longer a wife and not really much of a mother or daughter anymore—guess I am pretty useless."

Ahmed immigrated to the United States 13 years ago and, although he originally planned to return to Palestine, he has not done so and has no real plans for making that happen. He sees himself as living a temporary life in which he focuses on his identity as a Palestinian and Muslim and idealizes his homeland while at the same time keeping himself separate from American culture. His personal life reflects his limbo status because he has made no lasting attachments even with other Palestinian immigrants, citing always the temporary nature of his sojourn in the United States. Ahmed is isolated, discouraged, and sad. He struggles with anger problems that have cost him several jobs. Although it is clear that Ahmed grieves, he does not see himself as grieving, because acknowledging his losses would mean facing the fact of his continued presence in the United States and the unlikelihood of ever returning to Palestine.

When George and Sherry's son, Bobby, was killed while serving as a soldier in Iraq, the hostility of their 10-year-old divorce was rekindled. Sherry, an Army brat whose brothers and second husband are all career military, wants her son buried at Arlington National Cemetery because that would represent her son's patriotism and love for the Army. George, however, wants a small memorial service focusing on his son's entire life, followed by a scattering of his ashes at his grandparents' farm. As they struggle to settle the funeral plans, George and Sherry face not only the loss of their son but also the differences between them that contributed to the loss of their marriage.

Henry, the child of a White father and Apache mother, had only minimal contact with his tribal culture in his formative years and none at all after his mother died in an automobile accident when Henry was 8 years old. His father rarely spoke of Henry's mother, remarried (a White woman), and had two more children. As an adolescent and young adult, Henry struggled with a bipolar disorder and alcohol abuse. He left home and lived on the streets for a few years before reestablishing a shaky contact with his father. At 19 years old, Henry saw himself as a failure, did not feel he really belonged anywhere, and despaired of ever turning his life around. His first attempt at rehabilitation was marginal. Henry found the medication helpful, but he disliked group therapy and was uncomfortable with the heavy Christian slant and rigid 12-step program of Alcoholics Anonymous. He fared better in his second rehabilitation experience, finding individual therapy and a small, dual diagnosis group particularly useful. During therapy, when discussing his mother's death, Henry for the first time began to think about his other losses, including his mother's family and his Apache identity.

There is an important caution here when it comes to considering the personal, familial, social, cultural, and historical influences on loss and loss adaptation. As counseling professionals, we must beware of blanket assumptions about sociocultural groups that blind us to the uniqueness of the individual (e.g., laundry lists of cultural characteristics). Even in our good intentions to be culturally competent practitioners, we sometimes lose sight of the individual and the differences that exist between and among people. For example, a woman who does not cry in grieving a significant loss, when viewed through the gender stereotype lens, may be judged as avoidant, in denial, or cold-hearted when, in fact, her response may be entirely consistent with an emotionally reserved personality; a man of Asian background may be emotionally expressive despite the cultural stereotype of stoicism. Any one person may not "fit" the general assumptions of his or her social, cultural, familial, or historical background, this being an expression of difference rather than deficiency. People are not caricatures. The challenge for culturally competent counselors is to be aware of and sensitive to multiple and fluid cultural and contextual influences while at the same time respecting the unique manner in which these influences are integrated by a given individual or family.

3. *Nonlinear Grief Models Are Preferred Over Universal Stage/ Phase Models*

Nonlinear or nonsequential approaches are especially useful because they prioritize uniqueness and assume variations in the grieving journey rather than the sameness implied by stage/phase models. In fact, there appears to be little empirical support for a linear model of bereavement grief (Artlet & Thyer, 1998; R. A. Neimeyer, 2000a), and despite statements from proponents regarding the fluidity or adaptability of stages and phases, many professionals continue to interpret them in a progressive, linear fashion. The emphasis on uniqueness found in nonlinear grief models draws attention to the multiple contexts that shape an individual's experience (e.g., personal, social, familial, cultural, and historical), avoids artificial recovery timelines, and accounts for the differential impact of loss and grief immediately and over time. Two excellent examples of nonlinear grief models are the dual process model (Stroebe & Schut, 1999, 2001a, 2001b; Stroebe et al., 1998) and adaptive grieving styles (Martin & Doka, 2000). These models, while specific to bereavement, offer some application to nondeath-related grieving precisely because they prioritize the individual's unique experience of loss and grief. More detailed descriptions of the dual process model and adaptive grieving styles, including treatment recommendations, are provided in Chapter 3, but a brief discussion explaining each model is provided here to underscore the benefits of nonlinear models.

The *dual process model* conceptualizes grieving as a highly individualized movement or "oscillation" over time between two dimensions: loss-oriented coping and restoration-oriented coping. *Loss-oriented coping* involves stressors associated with the loss itself (e.g., rumination, yearning, loneliness), and *restoration-oriented coping* involves stressors associated with changes brought on by the loss (e.g., learning new skills, adjusting to the environment, revising identity). The griever sometimes confronts and at other times avoids the stressors associated with each dimension over the course of loss adaptation, sometimes even within a single day. Oscillation between dimensions is natural and critical to healthy grieving. Stroebe and Schut (1999, 2001a, 2001b) suggested that problems occur when the griever does not oscillate between loss-oriented and restoration-oriented coping (e.g., a grieving woman ruminates excessively about losses associated with a divorce while avoiding adjustments to her postdivorce situation and identity).

Martin and Doka's (2000) model of *adaptive grieving styles* centers on the different patterns exhibited by grieving people as they experience loss and the various strategies people use to adapt to loss. These patterns and strategies reflect the unique manner in which a given individual inwardly experiences and outwardly expresses grief. Three primary styles are visualized along a continuum: the intuitive grieving style at one end, an instrumental grieving style at the opposite end, and a blended grieving style between them. People who exhibit a more *intuitive grieving style* experience grief primarily in terms of intense emotion, express their feelings, and talk about their grief in affective language. Such individuals benefit from adaptive strategies that facilitate emotional processing and connecting with others (e.g., grief groups). In contrast, people who exhibit a more *instrumental grieving style* experience grief more cognitively and behaviorally, are more modulated in their feelings, and tend to express their grief in terms of thought and behavior. They benefit most from adaptive strategies that facilitate analysis and activity (e.g., problem solving). Martin and Doka believe that most people exhibit a *blended grieving style* that combines elements of both intuitive and instrumental styles, but with a greater tendency toward one or the other. There is no ideal or preferred grieving style and no suggestion of pathology attached to any particular pattern. Instead, grieving styles simply reflect the natural differences among individuals that result from personality traits as well as cultural, familial, developmental, and social influences. Problems occur when individuals make ineffective use of a limited range of adaptive strategies or select strategies that are incongruent with their natural grieving style (e.g., a more intuitive male griever represses emotions due to gender socialization).

Both the dual process model and adaptive grieving styles focus on uniqueness and difference rather than universal phase/stages and sameness of experience among individuals in their adaptation to loss. Both models recognize grief as a multidimensional process and invite consideration of the diverse personal and contextual influences that make one person's experience of grief different from another's. Both models suggest grieving as a dynamic process. Both models manage to avoid being overly prescriptive, recognizing wide variations in grieving response while at the same time suggesting potential problem areas.

4. *Promote the Value of "Continuing Bonds" of Connection Rather Than "Broken Bonds"*

The conventional *broken bonds* view that clients must sever their attachments, especially to the deceased, in order to resolve their grief reflects narrow, outdated assumptions of dualism, Freudian psychoanalysis, and a Western overemphasis on self-sufficiency/autonomy rather than connection/interdependence as a determinant of mental health. This view can be damaging to clients and their adaptation to loss. The demand that all grievers "say goodbye," "move on," "let go," "put it behind," or "forget" often says more about the discomfort of others than it does about the real needs of grieving people. After all, how can one expect parents to sever the relationship with their deceased child? Can't a widow continue to love her deceased husband while also loving others, including a potential spouse? A grieving client may resist making new attachments precisely because that would mean (if he or she swallows the broken-bonds demand) a final severance or even a rejection of the relationship with his or her deceased family member. Indeed, an expectation of disconnection following divorce is counterproductive and even harmful, because children benefit from parents who can develop a satisfactory, ongoing relationship with each other in the best interests of their children. Especially disturbing is the way in which the demand for severance of connection abnormalizes culturally based belief systems about communing with the spirits of the dead. The problem here is on the insistence that all grievers must sever bonds with their lost objects and on extreme interpretations of detachment, rather than respecting the uniqueness of each griever's experience and what kind of bond seems most appropriate for that particular person (Stroebe, Schut, & Stroebe, 2005).

Instead of demanding disconnection, a more helpful and humane approach is to assist grievers in revising, redefining, or altering their relationship with their lost objects to allow enduring connection—*continuing bonds* (Klass et al., 1996). Worden (2002), in a revision of his original task model, described this as finding "a way to remember the deceased while feeling comfortable reinvesting in life" (p. 52). The counselor helps clients to configure a relationship with lost objects that allows them to draw comfort from the continued connection while at the same time accepting the reality of the original loss, marking the meaningfulness of the relationship, adjusting to changes, and opening themselves to other attachments. The nature of the bond changes and can change over time, the lost object and the loss being integrated in a way that the lost object "becomes part of us" (J. Murray, 2001, p. 225). Thus, the grieving father redefines his relationship with his deceased child in a way that allows him to feel a sense of the child's comforting presence while also engaging fully with his other children. The widow emotionally relocates love for her deceased husband, invests energy into other relationships, and loves again. The divorced couple alters their relationship to include an ongoing connection as parents while also recognizing the end of a marital union. The grieving immigrant retains important ties to his native land while at the same time embracing his new country.

5. Recognize Grieving as a Normative Response to Perceived Loss That May, Nonetheless, Involve Serious Difficulties

Grief, in and of itself, is neither abnormal nor a disease nor dysfunctional. This is an especially important concept for counseling professionals to maintain in the face of the tendency to see grieving as pathological. Some diagnostic labels (e.g., pathological grief, neurotic grief, abnormal grief, unresolved grief, absent grief, chronic grief, prolonged grief), instead of providing clarity and direction, may obscure the unique nature of a particular griever's experience, ignore resilience, reduce grief to symptomatology, and promote stereotypes about normalcy. For example, an apparent absence of grief following a significant relationship loss may not be evidence of pathology at all but actually reflect resilience, a particular attachment style, a culturally influenced response, or a more instrumental grieving style. Similarly, the "prolonged grief" label implies a magic line between normal and abnormal grieving that allows no circumstantial distinctions.

There is also the very real problem of cultural bias in diagnostic classification, especially when applied to something so culturally defined as grief. Foote and Frank (1999) questioned whether the notion of pathological grief actually just means the griever's attitudes and feelings are at odds with the dominant discourse (of the professional community). The diagnostic labels can also be disempowering descriptions that imply unhelpful and discriminatory value judgments and actually contribute to stigmatization by others (e.g., family members, cultural groups) and even by counselors and grievers themselves (e.g., "Even my therapist says my grief is abnormal!"). Recent efforts to include an Axis I bereavement-specific diagnostic classification in the fifth edition of the *Diagnostic and Statistical Manual of Mental Disorders*, which is targeted for publication in 2012 (Zhang, El-Jawahri, & Prigerson, 2006), have generated intense discussion regarding these labels and the possible "medicalization" (e.g., Is grief a disease?) of this normative aspect of the human condition (Glass, 2005; Walter, 2005). The challenge for counselors is to recognize the normality of grief as a response to loss while at the same time being aware of potential complications in the grieving process.

6. Recognize Grieving Clients as Active Agents in the Process of Adapting to Loss

Phase and stage models encourage passivity because they portray the grieving process as a process largely outside of the griever's control—something that happens *to* grievers that must be endured or coped with (e.g., disorganization phase, anger stage). Task models (Rando, 1993; Worden, 2002) and nonlinear grief models (e.g., dual process model, adaptive grieving styles) offer a more helpful view in this regard because they frame the client as an active participant in a dynamic process of adapting to loss by meeting various challenges in the grieving process. Although one may question the implied universality of specific tasks, the expectation that people are capable of engaging with their grief, making choices, and determining the course and outcome of their grieving is a critical point of view for both counselor and client. The counselor who assumes clients' active participation in their own grieving promotes functionality, survivorship, strength, resilience, potentiality, competence, empowerment, and resourcefulness. Additionally, seeing clients as active agents in their adaptation to loss, along with a primary focus on the uniqueness of the griever's experience, encourages counseling professionals to amend traditional counseling roles to adopt a more collaborative stance with their grieving clients. The collaborative counselor, deferring to the expertness of clients on their own lives, confers and consults with clients about what is helpful, what works, and what is meaningful for them. This respectful approach enhances motivation, provides support, and facilitates change.

7. *Recognize Meaning Reconstruction as a Critical Aspect of Loss Adaptation for Most Grieving Persons*

We humans live our lives on the basis of certain assumptions, beliefs, and expectations that shape our understanding of ourselves, our world, and how the world works. These assumptions and beliefs constitute our *meaning structures* (Gillies & Neimeyer, 2006) or *assumptive world* (Attig, 1996; Janoff-Bulman, 1992; Parkes, 1971) that shapes our understanding of the world via our philosophical and spiritual beliefs, personal and social identities, the nature of relationships, and expectations about how the future will unfold and who will be part of that future. Our meaning structures are highly individualized; they are the truths we believe and the reality we see. Sometimes our losses fit into our meaning structures. For example, the death of an older person, while generating sorrow, is likely consistent with our beliefs about the inevitability of death with advanced age. However, the reality of loss sometimes conflicts with our taken-for-granted meaning structures. For example, the murder of a child, losing a valued job/career, developing a disability or chronic illness, forced migration, natural or human-caused disaster, and experiencing a failed love relationship are losses that generally do not fit the assumptions, beliefs, and expectations we hold about ourselves and our world. In fact, loss sometimes shatters a person's meaning structures, becoming a source of intense distress and a primary obstacle to functional loss adaptation.

In the face of this mismatch with one's preloss meaning structures, grieving persons strive to make sense of their losses, to develop alternative perspectives, to find some benefit, to revise identity, or to create some consistent story that allows them to live with, through, and beyond the losses. Thus, people embark on a process of *meaning reconstruction*, which R. A. Neimeyer (1998) called "the central process of grieving" (p. 338). Attig (1996) conceptualized this process as "relearning the world . . . learning how to be and act in the world differently in the light of our losses" (p. 107). It is, as Attig pointed out, a multifaceted transition that involves revising and reorganizing one's thinking, emotions, behavior, and spiritual beliefs to incorporate loss. This process is less about a search for meaning than it is about discovering, inventing, or creating meaning (R. A. Neimeyer, 2000b). According to Gillies and Neimeyer (2006), the counseling professional's role in meaning reconstruction is to

> facilitate a constructive process in which meanings can be found or developed that help the client reshape her or his shattered world, restore a sense of order, promote new insight and personal growth, guide meaningful actions in response to the loss, and bring some degree of relief from the common and undeniable pain of grief. (p. 60)

An important caveat exists regarding the central role of meaning reconstruction in loss adaptation. It is clear that meaning reconstruction is not a critical element in loss adaptation for everyone. Yet another expression of the uniqueness of each individual grieving experience is the fact that some loss situations may not create dissonance of meaning, and some people may not be personally oriented toward making meaning of their losses. An individual may experience little or no dissonance of meaning if his or her view is that the loss, even with sudden or tragic circumstances, is just part and parcel of the natural unfolding of the universe. Some people are simply not concerned with "why" as much as they are focused on "what" and "how." Or it may be that for all the times when one's spiritual and religious beliefs are challenged by loss, these beliefs just as often provide a sufficient framework for incorporating loss. Counseling professionals must, therefore, never automatically assume a dissonance of meaning structures or demand a focus on meaning reconstruction for their grieving clients. Rather, counselors should evaluate the meaning structures and the role of meaning reconstruction for each individual person to ascertain their relevance to the grieving process.

8. *Recognize That Grief Does Not End, But It Does Change*

Many people operate under the mistaken belief that grief ends. The fact is that while the intensity of grieving usually moderates, grief—as an emotion and as a personal and interpersonal process—changes more than it ends. How that grief is experienced at different points in an individual's life varies according to the person, the contexts, the loss, and the particular life journey. For example, a woman whose father died when she was a child may only experience intensity of grief at meaningful life span transition points, such as graduation, marriage, or the birth of her own children. Many people experience what Rando (1993) termed *STUG reactions* (subsequent temporary upsurges of grief) when unanticipated situations or sensations jog their memories of lost objects. The nature and significance of STUG reactions vary, but the experience clearly points to the long-term aspect of grief.

Counseling professionals must, of course, also understand that grief has no end. Indiscriminately using language that implies the end of grief (e.g., letting go, resolution, recovery) or that all grievers move inevitably through phases/stages to a final point at which grief somehow disappears (e.g., reorientation, acceptance, recovery) is misleading to clients and ignores the uniqueness of the griever and that person's particular journey through grief. The assumption of a concrete ending to grief also implies that there is some magic timeline beyond which grief automatically becomes abnormal. In fact, grief and grieving change as people confront, avoid, accommodate, assimilate, or integrate their losses into their lives over a lifetime, but their grief does not end nor do timelines provide an accurate measure of functionality or normality. It is recommended that counseling professionals use the term *integration* or *assimilation* to describe the process of adapting to loss—the griever's unique journey through grief. The most helpful and hopeful answer, when distressed clients ask "How long will this last?" is the most honest one:

> Your journey here is unique to you so your grief has its own timeline. There will be better and worse times with the worst times probably occurring less intensely and less often as you gradually adapt and integrate this loss into your life. There will always be times when you grieve for X, but the grief itself will change.

9. Tailor Treatment to the Uniqueness of Grieving Clients

Once we assume the uniqueness rather than the universality or sameness of every grieving client and his or her experience of loss and grief, it becomes clear that there can be no one-size-fits-all treatment. Rather, counseling professionals must tailor treatment to the particular experience, needs, goals, and multiple contexts (e.g., personal, developmental, social, familial, cultural) of their clients.

For example, a counseling professional designs a group counseling experience for adolescents who have recently experienced a parental divorce. One adolescent, Shari, is uncomfortable talking about her feelings, but she does share them with one close friend. She admits to sadness about the divorce and wishes her parents would get back together, but she is, for the most part, able to focus on activities with her friends, schoolwork, and plans for the summer. DuWayne is upset about his parents' divorce, has difficulty focusing on school, and ruminates about the divorce situation constantly. He tends to avoid uncomfortable feelings but clearly does experience his emotions deeply, especially anxiety.

A one-size-fits-all counseling intervention would dictate that all adolescents whose parents have recently divorced should be referred to the group counseling experience or that healthy grieving is always accompanied by talking about feelings, especially for girls. This lumps everyone together, stereotypes their responses, and ignores the uniqueness of Shari's and DuWayne's differing loss adaptation experiences. In fact, DuWayne is more likely to be helped by the group, where he can connect with others, share his feelings, receive support, and talk about his experience. Shari, on the other hand, would probably find the emotional tenor of the group experience intrusive and the exclusive grieving focus unhelpful. She is likely to drop out if she attends at all. The counselor who values the uniqueness of each client's loss adaptation experience would refer DuWayne to the group but not Shari. And what about Shari? Support, reassurance, and individual counseling, if she so desires, would be interventions most respectful of her way of adapting to loss. Therefore, effective counseling for loss adaptation means understanding the highly individualized ways that people integrate loss into their lives and providing interventions specifically designed to facilitate that unique integration.

Tailoring treatment to the uniqueness of the client challenges two prevalent assumptions from 20th-century bereavement conceptualizations: the necessity of grief work for all clients and the priority placed on emotional experiencing. Grief work is the traditional view that all grieving persons must review events surrounding a significant loss; confront, express, and overcome uncomfortable emotions; resolve all ambivalence; and detach themselves from their lost objects. Counseling professionals who accept this view typically focus heavily on facilitating grief work with an emphasis on emotional processing. However, the grief work assumption fails to recognize variations of personality, differences in the impact of loss and grief, the idiosyncratic nature of each person's grief journey, and the multiple social, familial, and cultural influences on grievers and their loss adaptation. In fact, there is little empirical evidence in bereavement research that grief work is necessary for all grievers (Stroebe & Stroebe, 1991; Wortman & Silver, 2001). Some bereaved people appear to be quite resilient to loss, experiencing little disruption to their functioning and minimal distress (Bonanno, Keltner, Holen, & Horowitz, 1995; Bonanno, Moskowitz, Papa, & Folkman, 2005; Bonanno, Wortman, & Nesse, 2004; Exline, Dority, & Wortman, 1996). Avoiding traditional grief work may even be healthy for some people (Bonanno, 2001). However, it may be that people experiencing the most severe grief symptoms, which might include those seeking psychotherapy, are those who would benefit from grief work

15

(Bonanno, 2004). It appears that whereas grief work might be helpful for some, it may not be an appropriate loss adaptation strategy for others (Harvey, 1998).

The accompanying assumption that the primary focus of grief counseling should be on affective expression is also problematic with regard to tailoring treatment to the uniqueness of the client. Experiencing and expressing emotion may or may not be helpful, depending on the person and the multiple contexts influencing his or her loss adaptation. For example, a griever with a more instrumental style (according to the adaptive grieving styles model) naturally utilizes cognitive and behavioral strategies more than affective strategies, whereas a griever with a more intuitive style relies on affective strategies. A counselor who automatically attempts to evoke deep emotions from people who show little or no distress simply because the topic is grief is more likely to provoke anxiety than to reduce it (Riches & Dawson, 2000). As R. A. Neimeyer (1998) pointed out, an overemphasis on affect can also mean insufficient attention to other adaptive strategies (e.g., cognitive, behavioral, spiritual) that might be beneficial to clients, ignores the impact of meaning structures, and contributes to pathologizing grievers and grief (e.g., minimal emotional expression viewed as "denial"). The affective bias of Western-based counseling practices also ignores cultural differences (Rando, 2000; Sue & Sue, 1990). At best, a therapist's blind insistence on emotional experiencing and expression for all grievers is unhelpful; at worst such insistence is abusive and counterproductive. Therefore, instead of making universal assumptions, counseling professionals should evaluate the appropriateness of grief work and attention to emotional processing in light of the uniqueness of the client and his or her distinct experience of loss and grief.

Counselors customize treatment via three interrelated dimensions: the Way of Understanding, the Way of Intervening, and the Way of Being (Cheston, 2000). The *Way of Understanding* includes the counselor's theoretical approach (e.g., cognitive, behavioral, constructivist, Adlerian, existential, integrated) informed by knowledge of loss, grief, and loss adaptation. A Way of Understanding that draws on several theoretical approaches that are consistent with each other or a fully integrated theoretical model is recommended because this offers the maximum flexibility for customizing treatment. Theoretical models that encourage exploration of the client's own theory of change and emphasize the client's voice are also recommended because such honoring of the person's expertness on her or his problems further promotes customizing treatment to the uniqueness of the client.

The *Way of Intervening* includes the strategies, techniques, or methods that facilitate client change. Interventions must be consistent with the Way of Understanding and adaptable to the uniqueness of the client. Whether the counselor subscribes exclusively to a single theoretical approach or practices theoretical integration, the focus must be on interventions that serve the specific needs of specific clients. Strategies should fit clients rather than attempting to make clients fit accepted strategies. Counseling professionals who work with loss and grief are encouraged to practice "technical eclecticism" (Lazarus & Beutler, 1993, p. 384), in which interventions are borrowed from diverse theoretical orientations without necessarily subscribing to the approaches with which they most identify. Thus, a counselor working from a cognitive therapy orientation may use an empty-chair technique traditionally associated with the emotional emphasis of gestalt therapy but do so in a way that highlights maladaptive cognitions and facilitates cognitive modification. A counselor working from a more integrated theoretical approach may use a chair dialogue to facilitate both emotional processing and cognitive restructuring. Some counseling strategies are especially well suited for adaptation across theoretical models, and many can serve multiple uses. For example, cinematherapy can be used to enhance emotional experiencing, raise existential awareness, promote restructuring of a family system, or challenge irrational thinking; therapeutic work with photographs can facilitate emotional processing, promote meaning making, assist deconstruction and reconstruction of narratives, support amended family communication, and promote cognitive restructuring; and therapeutic writing can be used to address spiritual, cognitive, emotional, and even behavioral material. Cultural sensitivity suggests that although some counseling interventions might not be appropriate for some people, many other strategies and methods can be amended in suitable ways (e.g., using a nondirective approach) or combined with culture-specific practices, such as incorporating storytelling, music, ritual, and symbols and even consulting with traditional healers (e.g., *curandera*) or tribal and community elders (Aros, Buckingham, & Rodriguez, 1999; Duran, 2006; Kennedy, 2006; Rollins, 2008; Thomason, 1991). Tailoring treatment to the uniqueness of clients requires counseling professionals to think creatively and flexibly—outside the box— about the strategies most likely to deliver preferred outcomes.

The *Way of Being* involves the therapeutic relationship between the counseling professional and client, how the counselor operates, the counselor's use of self, and how this relationship contributes to client change. Obviously, the Way of Being must be consistent with the Way of Understanding and the Way of Intervening. In some approaches the counselor–client relationship is central to the therapy and integral to client change, whereas in others the emphasis is more on establishing an effective working alliance. Counselors may be more or less directive, more or less challenging, or more or less empathetic depending on the theoretical approach, the specific intervention, the client, and the counselor's own distinct counseling style. The Way of Being offers another way of customizing treatment to the uniqueness of the client. The counselor asks: What relationship and what way of working with Client X will most effectively contribute to change? Sensitivity to social, cultural, and personal influences must also inform the counselor in tailoring treatment to the uniqueness of the client. For example, people who are helped in their grieving by emotional expression and sharing are likely to respond to a warm and actively empathetic approach, whereas grieving people who are more emotionally reserved and private might respond better to a problem-solving approach. People with a history of being controlled are particularly sensitive to counselor direction. Some people respond better when time is spent building rapport through social conversation. Cultural background often influences a preference for direct or indirect communication, comfort space, or eye contact. Whereas knowledge of the characteristics and preferences associated with social and cultural groups is helpful, prioritizing the uniqueness of the client means recognizing that individuals vary in the manner in which they incorporate these influences. Professionals must recognize that the counselor–client relationship is always cross-cultural; therefore, it is imperative to avoid automatic assumptions of similarity and to respect difference. Because the most important factor in establishing an effective therapeutic relationship or alliance is *the client*, counseling professionals should intentionally collaborate with their clients in building a relationship that is most helpful to them and continue to monitor that relationship throughout therapy.

Recommended Resources

Bonnano, G. A., & Kaltman, S. (1999). Toward an integrative perspective on bereavement. *Psychological Bulletin, 125,* 760–776.

Brave Heart, M. Y. H., & DeBruyn, L. M. (1998). The American Indian holocaust: Healing historical unresolved grief. *Journal of American Indian and Alaskan Native Mental Health Research, 8*(2), 60–82.

Davis, C., Wortman, C., Lehman, D., & Silver, R. (2000). Searching for meaning in loss: Are clinical assumptions correct? *Death Studies, 24,* 497–540.

Golden, T. R. (2000). *Swallowed by a snake: The gift of the masculine side of healing* (2nd ed.). Gaithersburg, MD: Golden Healing.

Klass, D., Silverman, P., & Nickman, S. (Eds.). (1996). *Continuing bonds: New understandings of grief.* Washington, DC: Taylor & Francis.

Malkinson, R. (2007). *Cognitive grief therapy: Constructing a rational meaning to life following loss.* New York: Norton.

Neimeyer, R. A. (Ed.). (2001). *Meaning reconstruction and the experience of loss.* Washington, DC: American Psychological Association.

Chapter 2

Listening To and Listening For Loss and Grief

Experienced counseling professionals recognize that loss and grief frequently appear as issues of concern in psychotherapy settings. Sometimes clients seek therapy specifically to deal with major losses, such as death, divorce, and relationship breakups. In these cases people usually have some sense that they are not adapting as well as they think they should, they see themselves as stuck in their grieving, or they are worried about the grieving of others, especially family members.

However, loss and grief experiences appear far more often in therapy not as a client's initial presenting problem but as an underlying cause or contributing factor to client troubles. For example, exploration of client anger often reveals core losses that have never been addressed or were inadequately grieved; anxiety problems sometimes originate in loss events and certainly intensify and compound anxiety reactions; people with addictions frequently have a history of loss experiences that contributed to development of their addiction as well as losses resulting from their addictions that complicate their recovery. Traumatic experiences usually include significant loss, although the loss is sometimes obscured by more critical circumstances or crises while grieving lingers in the background. Major life transitions, planned or unplanned, always include loss, yet many times these losses are neither validated nor explored.

Consider the losses associated with the following frequently encountered presenting problems in psychotherapy:

+ divorce, separation, breakups, and estrangement
+ disappearance, abandonment
+ death and dying (e.g., human or animal companion)
+ acquired disability, functional limitations, and chronic illness
+ mental disorders (e.g., depression, anxiety, schizophrenia)
+ addictions (e.g., gambling, drug abuse and dependence)
+ loss of capacity (e.g., sexual dysfunction, infertility)
+ natural and human-caused or human-aggravated disasters (e.g., Hurricane Katrina, tsunamis, earthquakes, fires)
+ job or career changes, unemployment, and financial reverses (e.g., bankruptcy)
+ loss of possessions or home (e.g., foreclosure, homelessness)
+ relocation, immigration, and migration
+ incarceration

- foster care, adoption, child welfare removal
- miscarriage, stillbirth, and abortion
- individual and family developmental transitions
- oppression (e.g., racism, ageism, homophobia)
- violent loss (e.g., abuse, war, genocide, suicide, murder, crime, rape)
- cultural and historical trauma (e.g., loss of language, homeland, self-rule, support structures)
- status and role changes (e.g., social class change, parenting role, provider role, overresponsible role)
- loss of fantasy and illusion (e.g., divorced parents will reunite, mental illness will disappear, parent will nurture and protect, nothing bad can happen)
- loss of assumptive world (e.g., meaning associated with faith, life direction, core beliefs, and worldview)
- loss associated with identity or one's sense of self (i.e., Who am I now that this loss has occurred?).

Counseling professionals must listen carefully *to* and *for* the losses that their clients endure and the grieving that may or may not follow. This begins with expanding one's notion of loss and grief to include nondeath-related circumstances, discerning different types of loss and grief, investigating specific psychosocial factors, and recognizing clues to the presence of loss-related issues.

Types of Loss and Grief

Primary and Secondary Losses

A *primary loss* is a significant loss event, such as death. *Secondary losses* are those losses that are a consequence of a primary loss and vary according to the individual and the contexts in which loss occurs. For example:

- The death of a spouse may bring the loss of companionship, financial security, a predictable future, sexual intimacy, family role, and social status.
- Immigration may bring the loss of personal, social, and cultural identity, as well as the loss of familiarity, place, safety, connectedness, and shared history.
- Menopause may bring the loss of identity, role, and status.
- Siblings of a kidnapped child may also lose trust in their parents' ability to protect them and even lose the continuing presence and attention of an emotionally stable parent.
- Job loss may bring a loss of financial security, family role, self-esteem, sense of future, and opportunity.
- Loss of the family farm may mean a loss of face, identity, a way of life, community, and even loss of family heritage.
- Brain injury may bring a loss of purpose, intellectual capacity, quality of life, sexual function, capacity to love, and income/earning potential (Chwalisz, 1998).
- Childhood sexual abuse brings the loss of innocence, trust, and control.
- Imprisonment (loss of freedom) often brings loss of parenting role, relationships, and hope.

- Chronic illness may bring a loss of abilities, potentialities, and even identity.
- The death of child may bring a loss of faith, of parenting identity, and of presumed future.
- Mental illness (e.g., depression, schizophrenia) may bring a loss of control of emotions and/or cognitions, relationship loss, loss of family role, perhaps loss of freedom, and loss of occupational or income earning future.
- Retirement may bring a loss of status, identity, social connection, self-esteem, and financial security.

Whereas primary losses are usually recognized as loss events, secondary losses are often overlooked or only realized over time. Secondary losses are especially important to identify because they reveal the idiosyncratic meanings that the individual attaches to his or her loss experience and point to potentially problematic issues and concerns. For example, two men, Joe and Sam, were laid off from the factory jobs each had held for 13 years. For Joe the secondary loss of his role as major provider for his family profoundly affected his sense of self as a man and his role as a husband and father. Sam, on the other hand, had more difficulty with the secondary loss of status and identity as a worker than its effect on his male image or family role. Some secondary losses may not be apparent or especially important early on but may arise as important issues later. For example, Tara, serving an 8-year prison term, struggled initially with the loss of freedom, control, and partner relationship, but later the secondary loss of her parenting role emerged as a central concern in her adjustment to prison life.

Multiple Losses

A number of primary losses occurring in a single event or within a constricted time period can be particularly difficult experiences. For example, all family members killed or injured in a single traffic accident; divorce, job loss, and major illness occurring within a 2-year span; children leaving home, marital infidelity, and menopause occurring within a similar time period; or friends killed or injured in a campus murder spree. Multiple losses tend to overwhelm people's coping skills and adaptive capacity, reduce resources, and challenge core assumptions and beliefs. People often numb their feelings in an effort to manage the intense emotions associated with grieving the myriad of secondary losses that accompany multiple primary losses. Kastenbaum (1969) described the overwhelming nature of multiple and concurrent death-related primary losses, especially those common in older age, as *bereavement overload*. Counseling professionals can facilitate functional adaptation with multiple losses by helping clients sort out the implications of each primary loss and grieve each one separately while also managing the distressful symptoms that may overload them.

Ambiguous Loss

Ambiguous loss is a permanent state of dissonance regarding the simultaneous absence and presence of a significant other (Boss, 2001, 2006). There are two types of ambiguous loss situations. The first is when a person is perceived as *physically absent* but *psychologically present*, for example, people missing in natural disasters, genocide, or kidnapping; a child or parent in a divorce situation who is physically missing from the family; a baby put up for adoption; or family members with whom one has no contact after immigration. The second kind of ambiguous loss occurs when a person is *physically present* but is perceived as *psychologically absent* (emotionally or cognitively missing), for example, a person with Alzheimer's disease, traumatic brain injury, or an addiction (e.g., alcoholism). Ambiguous loss is often an immobilizing situation in which people's lives remain "on hold" and the lack of closure can impair family dynamics. Cissy, whose father had Alzheimer's disease, commented:

> I lost my father bit by bit. First he was just a little different, then he developed that vacant look and the paranoia that was so inconsistent with his personality; then, finally, he did not recognize me as his daughter. I grieved the steady loss of the person who was my father as we became strangers to each other.

The uncertainty characteristic of ambiguous loss and long-term dysfunctional coping often contribute to complications in the grieving process.

Obscured Loss

Obscured loss refers to longstanding, unaddressed, and sometimes unrecognized losses that contribute to client difficulties. The losses have often been obscured or overlooked previously by more critical or urgent situations (e.g., addiction, trauma, physical recovery), inadequate adaptive grieving, avoidance, or suppressing one's own needs to serve others. For example, a refugee may only be able to attend fully to her losses once the critical demands of physical safety and survival for self and family are satisfied; a man with a gambling addiction may only realize his losses once he is in recovery because his addiction impaired prior recognition; a sexual assault survivor may be ready to deal with her losses only when she has first addressed the trauma associated with that experience.

Stigmatized Loss

Losses may be labeled by some sociocultural groups, individuals, or families as particularly notorious or shameful events because they reveal some transgression of societal norms. These include, for example, losses related to HIV/AIDS, suicide, violence (e.g., homicide, genocide, and domestic violence), illegal activities, infidelity, divorce, sexual abuse, unemployment, homelessness, and addictions. The stigma may attach blame to victims and survivors alike, implying that the loss situations were preventable or the individual or survivor is responsible and reflecting a kind of fear of contagion from something judged as improper or immoral. As a consequence, people who experience stigmatized loss often struggle with trust, guilt, blame, and shame. Stigmatized loss frequently impairs the griever's support network because these groups (e.g., religious groups, tribe, and family) are often the primary source of stigmatizing judgment. For example, parents whose children commit suicide are exposed to stigma from insurance agents, clergy, medical personnel, police, and even other parents; couples experiencing infertility may be the object of hurtful comments and gender stereotyping (blaming the woman, implying God's will or punishment); people with HIV/AIDS may face discrimination in health care from insurance companies, medical professionals, their communities, and even their own families (Sheskin & Wallace, 1976). The exact nature of the stigma perceived by the individual is unique to that person and the multiple contexts of her or his life. Stigmatized loss adds another level of difficulty to the grieving process.

Sudden, Expected, or Gradual Loss

Sudden loss circumstances usually include natural disasters, accidental or random losses, and sudden illness. Examples of sudden loss include death or impairment from heart attack or stroke, earthquake, tornado, terrorism, acts of war, car crashes, farm accidents, murder, rape, and sudden infant death syndrome. Other losses may qualify as sudden, such as an unexpected estrangement or relational separation, being fired from a job, or sudden relocation or immigration. The apparent randomness of sudden loss circumstances presents particular difficulty. People may experience an increased sense of vulnerability that tends to raise anxiety and intensify emotions; they may react to the loss of control by becoming more controlling or, at the other extreme, very passive. The degree of intentionality and preventability of sudden loss circumstances sometimes create guilt, blame, and anger that may be internalized or externalized. Because sudden death circumstances often occur without the survivor's presence, questions are raised about whether a lost loved one suffered and may become the focus of nonproductive and distressful rumination. A desire for retaliation or fantasies of revenge, particularly in traumatic situations such as murder or war, are common. People struggle with dissonance between what should be and what, suddenly and abruptly, is. The unpredictability of sudden loss frequently challenges assumptions, beliefs, and expectations about the world or self, so that a major task for many grievers is simply making sense of the senseless. The abruptness of sudden loss often leaves people with unfinished business that impairs loss adaptation. Additional difficulties associated with trauma may also complicate grieving of sudden losses.

Gradual or expected loss circumstances such as hearing impairment, prolonged incapacitation (e.g., dementia) or terminal illness, marital decline, loss of the family farm or business, imprisonment, and planned immigration or relocation present unique challenges. Often gradual loss circumstances have cycles of recovery and decline that are emotionally and physically exhausting. There may be a series of losses leading to a final loss event, some of them more difficult than others; for example, a series of strokes with increasing impairment or personality changes and capacity losses with Alzheimer's disease. People may avoid recognizing the circumstance as loss related. They may have to cope with the depletion of interpersonal and financial resources. Feelings of helplessness, lack of control, guilt, ambivalence, and anger are also common in gradual or expected loss circumstances.

Cultural Loss

In an immediate context, cultural loss refers to losses related to relocation, migration, or immigration. These include the loss of a sense of place and community; loss of personal, social, and cultural identity; loss of traditional resources, structures, and advocacy; and loss of predictability. Cultural loss may include loss of expectations and hopes. Relocation, migration, and immigration losses are sometimes accompanied by trauma (e.g., refugee situations). In an historical context, cultural loss refers to contact between European colonists and indigenous people resulting in the loss of cultural memory, loss of language, loss of traditional resources, loss of self-rule, family disruption, loss of economic viability, and involuntary relocation (Stamm, Stamm, Hudnall, & Higson-Smith, 2003). Historical cultural loss is always associated with trauma and oppression.

When working with people who have experienced cultural loss (immediate or historical), counseling professionals must understand that other loss experiences, such as chronic illness, disability, death, divorce, developmental transitions, job loss, infertility, and addictions, are often interpreted within the larger context of these cultural losses. For example, in a study of Latino and Irish American caregivers in Boston, researchers found that the "diagnosis of a family member with dementia . . . links tragedies 'there' with tragedies 'here'. The grief of Alzheimer's disease flows into a greater sea of sadness and tribulations" associated with immigration (Ortiz, Simmons, & Hinton, 1999, p. 494). Modern-day American Indian people endure repeated traumatic losses through alcohol-related accidents, homicide, suicide, domestic violence, depression, and child abuse in a continuation of historical unresolved grief transmitted over generations (Brave Heart & DeBruyn, 1998). Validation of specific cultural losses in the larger context is appropriate. Therapeutic intervention must be culturally consistent, often blending clinical and traditional practices to facilitate loss adaptation (e.g., circle groups, traditional healing ceremonies).

Anticipatory or Preparatory Grief

Anticipatory or preparatory grief describes grieving that begins in anticipation of a loss. The term is most often applied to death-related grief and terminal illness situations. It may occur for both the dying person and those who will be her or his survivors. Mutual recognition of impending death may encourage people to address outstanding interpersonal issues. However, there is a downside to anticipatory grief. It may have an adverse effect on caregivers, and observing the grief reactions (e.g., withdrawal, sadness, anger) of some loved ones can contribute to distress for the dying person. Anticipatory grief does not always occur, and it is important to note that experiencing anticipatory grief does not necessarily ameliorate postdeath grieving.

Disenfranchised Grief

Doka (1989) introduced the term disenfranchised grief to describe grieving a loss that cannot be or is not "openly acknowledged, publicly mourned, and/or socially supported" (p. 4). The disenfranchisement occurs for three reasons. (a) The relationship is not socially recognized; for example, the death of a former spouse or lover in an extramarital affair or a friendship termination. (b) The loss is not socially recognized as a legitimate loss; for example, the loss of a companion animal, abortion and miscarriage, death or absence of someone who has been institutionalized or is comatose, or loss of cultural traditions, history, language, and identity. (c) The griever is not socially recognized; the implication is that this person is not capable of grief, for example, the very old, the very young, or someone who is cognitively disabled because of developmental delay or brain injury. Brave Heart and DeBruyn (1998) pointed out that the historical view of American Indians as stoic and savage created a view that they were not capable of grief; therefore, American Indians have experienced disenfranchised grief.

Disenfranchised grief adds another layer of potential complications to loss adaptation. The lack of social recognition frequently impairs the usual sources of support that assist grievers; for example, the absence of ritual (e.g., divorce, pet death, perinatal loss) or being denied participation in a ritual (e.g., gay partner not included in funeral by blood relatives of deceased or by a religious group). Disenfranchised grief situations may also carry some social condemnation or discrimination; for example, being fired from a job, HIV/AIDS illness and death, elective abortion, or the loss of an abusive parent. Doka (1989) noted that disenfranchised grievers may experience an intensification of common grief reactions, especially isolation, hopelessness, anger, resentment, guilt, self-condemnation, and ambivalence. Validation of the loss, the griever, and the appropriateness of grieving is imperative in helping people who experience disenfranchised grief.

Selected Psychosocial Factors

Recognizing the uniqueness of the griever, the loss, and the multiple contexts in which loss occurs allows the counseling professional to tailor interventions to facilitate functional adaptation to loss. This begins with assessment of various psychosocial factors, such as age, gender, intelligence, mental status, locus of control, self-esteem, self-efficacy, extraversion–introversion, or attributional style. Additionally, there are eight specific psychosocial areas that merit particular investigation when counseling for loss and grief: adaptive strategies, attachments, disruptive meaning structures, personal history of loss, developmental considerations, strengths and abilities, social support, and sociocultural influences.

Adaptive Strategies

Adaptive strategies are the methods people employ to manage transitional events such as grief. These strategies are used both for symptom reduction and to address sources of distress. Adaptive strategies include the following:

- affective strategies (e.g., emotional expression, affective regulation)
- cognitive strategies (e.g., analysis, reframing, cognitive distraction or avoidance)
- behavioral strategies (e.g., problem solving, activity, behavioral distraction)
- spiritual strategies (e.g., prayer, meditation, rituals)

Individuals tend to utilize certain strategies more than others. For example, some people find it helpful to express their emotions (e.g., crying, voicing sadness), whereas others find activity—doing something (e.g., exercising, problem solving)—more helpful in dealing with emotional distress. Adaptive strategies can be used in both positive and negative ways. For example, one person may use self-blame and wishful thinking to manage the distress associated with being "dumped" by a girlfriend or boyfriend, whereas another may rely on reframing (e.g., "I'm better off without that kind of person") and behavioral distraction (e.g., keeping busy). Distraction or avoidance, often used in grief circumstances, occurs as a cognitive, behavioral, emotional, or spiritual adaptive strategy and can be functional or counterproductive depending on the circumstances. For example, avoiding emotional distress temporarily in some cases is a helpful management strategy, but avoiding emotional distress via alcohol use can have negative consequences. A limited range of adaptive strategies, poor skills (e.g., ineffective emotional regulation, poor problem solving), and counterproductive strategies (e.g., drug abuse) can impair the grieving process. Counseling professionals should encourage the use of adaptive strategies consistent with clients' personality and multiple contexts, assist in enhancing skills, and help clients broaden the range of adaptive strategies available to them.

Attachments

Counselors inquire into the nature of a client's attachments to others, especially to a lost person, and how that attachment affects his or her grieving. Healthy attachments generally contribute to more functional loss adaptation. Insecure attachments, highly dependent or codependent relationships, conflictual relationships, and ambivalence about relationships are likely to contribute to grieving problems. Separation from the lost person, by whatever means, can impair self-esteem, contribute to unfinished business, increase interpersonal anxiety, activate dysfunctional schemas, compromise social support, and create feelings of guilt, anger, resentment, abandonment, and helplessness. Counseling professionals should identify clients' current relationships and attachment history to discern potential complications, help clients modify reactivity, and promote functional relationships.

Disrupted Meaning Structures

A major source of distress for grieving persons involves the disruption of beliefs, assumptions, values, and expectations that make up their meaning structures (Gillies & Neimeyer, 2006) or assumptive world (Attig, 1996; Parkes, 1971). These meaning structures constitute the ways in which people explain how things are, shaping reality by delineating basic truths about self and the world. For example, most people go about their lives believing that bad things happen to other people but not to them. Meaning structures are highly idiosyncratic, the product of the uniqueness of people and their multiple contexts, and contribute to differences in the impact of loss and the nature of grief. When loss experiences are inconsistent with one's meaning structures, the dissonance is a source of substantial distress and a major impediment to functional loss adaptation. As one chronically ill woman put it, "The ground shook beneath my feet. I didn't know who I was anymore." An important function of grief counseling is helping clients deal with the disruption of their preloss meaning structures. This process, called *meaning reconstruction* (Gillies & Neimeyer, 2006) or *relearning the world* (Attig, 1996), involves reviewing, reorganizing, and redefining the assumptions, values, beliefs, and expectations that make up one's meaning structures.

Meaning structures shape one's reality in six interrelated areas: daily activities and priorities, perceptions of self and personal identity, interpersonal relationships, outlook on the future, spiritual or philosophical view of the world, and activities in one's social communities (Gillies & Neimeyer, 2006). The chief activities of meaning reconstruction are (a) sense making or meaning making, (b) benefit finding, and (c) identity change (Gillies & Neimeyer, 2006).

Making sense of loss frequently begins with variations of the existential "why" regarding the meaningfulness of the world, the worthiness of people, and the fragility of life. Why did this happen? How could this happen to me or to us? Often sense making involves dealing with disrupted assumptions and beliefs regarding predictability, fairness, and manageability or control (Janoff-Bulman, 1992). It is clear that attempting to make sense of loss may challenge one's deepest spiritual, philosophical, or religious beliefs: If God is in control, then how could this happen? How could such a bad thing happen to a faithful person like me? Where is God's justice and love in this loss? How can God cause or permit such suffering? If this loss shatters my beliefs, then what do I base my life on? How can I ever recover balance and harmony in the face of this loss? My soul is lost, can I ever recover? The process of sense making or meaning making, while often difficult, involves examining the meaning structures that once made one's world comprehensible, then renewing, redefining, or revising them so as to restore balance.

Benefit finding as a process of meaning reconstruction is not about loss being a good thing but about the benefits or personal growth that may arise from an individual's struggle to adapt to loss in life-affirming ways. This is an important distinction. Meaning comes from turning a bad thing into something good. Indeed, grief can be a transformative process (L. Calhoun & Tedeschi, 2001; Tedeschi, Park, & Calhoun, 1998). Benefits may include a strengthening or amending of faith; an increase in self-esteem or self-worth; greater valuing of the present moment; enhanced appreciation of life and relationships; developing competence and independence; relearning ways of connecting with self, friends, family, and a larger community; learning to manage emotions; and increased awareness of resources, abilities, and talents that were previously unrecognized or underdeveloped (Attig, 1996; Davis & Nolen-Hoeksema, 2001; Frantz, Farrell, & Trolley, 2001; R. A. Neimeyer, Prigerson, & Davies, 2002).

Identity change as a process of meaning reconstruction involves rebuilding or reorganizing a sense of self sometimes fragmented by loss. For example, a person who develops a disability may experience impairment in his or her view of self as a whole person, seeing the self instead as partial, perhaps as less able, unable, or even as "damaged goods." An untimely or accidental death may destroy a person's self-view as deserving only of good things, leading a charmed life, or blessed in the eyes of God. Infertility may threaten one's view of self as masculine or "fully woman"; it may disrupt one's self-definition as a potential parent or successful wife or husband. Chronic illness (e.g., fibromyalgia, sickle cell anemia, arthritis) may rob one of a sense of self as capable, functional, independent, in control, or even as a person with potential. The death of a child, sibling, or parent may impair one's evolving identity by removing persons and interactions essential for self-definition. This is especially relevant in early stages of development and within the contexts of family and cultural identity. The challenge of meaning reconstruction is to revise one's self-narrative in a way that maintains continuity of person while also incorporating altered aspects of the self—the person is always *becoming*.

The role of counseling professionals in meaning reconstruction is to help grieving clients identify, explore, and rebuild disrupted beliefs, assumptions, and expectations in ways that promote a functional integration of loss. Diverse theoretical approaches and counseling strategies support meaning reconstruction in loss adaptation.

Personal History of Loss and Separation

Multiple losses and early losses associated with significant others, especially caregivers, are most influential here. However, the key is not how many losses people may experience but the nature and impact of their losses, and the functionality of loss adaptation. Those with a history of numerous and profound losses may have used those experiences to develop resilience that includes excellent skills for managing grief, whereas people with a more limited loss history may be overwhelmed by their first encounter with significant loss. It is an axiom that current losses call up past losses, especially if those losses were unmarked, disenfranchised, or incompletely grieved. Counseling professionals often find themselves helping clients with unfinished business from prior losses rather than the more recent losses that may even have precipitated therapy. Obtaining a loss and grief experiences history for the individual and/or the family is beneficial in this regard.

Developmental Considerations

An individual's developmental history and progress influence the experience of loss and grief, and, in turn, loss and grief affect the individual's developmental progress. For example, adolescents' concerns with fairness and justice, the primacy of peers over family, a strong desire for privacy, a tendency to magnify problems ("No one understands"), self-absorption, mood swings, a sense of invulnerability, and a strong desire to be considered normal influence their reactions to the loss of a parent or sibling (via divorce, illness, death, separation). At the same time, the loss of a parent or sibling in adolescence is likely to have immediate and long-term impact on an individual's developing autonomy, individuation, and identity formation. General psychosocial or life span development models are valuable and should be consulted to aid understanding of the impact of loss and grief on development as well as the impact of development on the experience of loss and grief. Additionally, developmental models specific to certain dimensions should also be considered as appropriate to client and client situation, for example, models of moral development (Gilligan, 1982/1993, 1991; Kohlberg & Hersh, 1977), college student development (Evans, Forney, & Guido-DiBrito, 1998), transition theory (Schlossberg, Waters, & Goodman, 1995), career development (Holland, 1985/1992; Super, 1985), and family development (Carter & McGoldrick, 1999). However, counseling professionals must be cognizant of the limitations of these models, especially their reflection of Western cultural values. The models outlined below are offered as examples of the usefulness of considering specific developmental dimensions when working with issues of loss and grief.

Women's/Womanist Identity Development

Models of women's/womanist identity development (Conarton & Kreger-Silverman, 1988; Gilligan, 1982/1993, 1991; Helms, 1990) emphasize differences in male and female development, especially the ways in which a woman's sense of self is organized within the context of relationships (self-in-relation). Key themes include connectedness, internal versus external self-definitions, balancing autonomy with relational concerns, the demands of traditional roles, loss of intuitive voice, and learning how to care for self as well as for others. Women operating in an early development phase in which their identity is largely derived from external sources (e.g., relationships) and shaped by uncritical acceptance of the traditional role of caring for others to the exclusion of self sometimes have difficulty establishing boundaries, become unnecessarily dependent, and fail to learn appropriate self-care. For these women, loss experiences, especially disrupted relationships, can be devastating and grieving further complicated by this selfless, other-focused identity. However, the process of confronting and adapting to loss may also encourage growth by propelling women to establish a more internally derived self-definition in which they learn to maintain appropriate boundaries and balance care for self with care for others. Helm's womanist identity development model (Ossana, Helms, & Leonard, 1992) describes the movement from external standards of gender identity to internal standards with particular reference to race as well as gender, having special value for women of color.

Racial Identity Development

Cross's (1971, 1991) Black identity development model describes the process experienced by African Americans in developing a positive racial identity. The model outlines five stages: (a) *preencounter*, in which the individual has absorbed many beliefs and values of the dominant White culture; (b) *encounter*, in which the individual acknowledges the impact of racism in one's life; (c) *immersion/emersion*, in which the individual glorifies anything associated with Blackness, denigrates anything associated with White people, and is exclusionary in relationships; (d) *internalization*, in which the individual is willing to establish meaningful relationships with White people who are respectful of his or her self-definition and the individual is also open to building connections with other oppressed groups; and (e) *internalization/commitment*, in which the individual continues to proactively transcend racial identity while maintaining a strong cultural identity. Loss and grief circumstances may propel developmental shifts and influence particular experiences at different stages. For example, an individual encountering a loss event (e.g., divorce, death) while in the immersion/emersion stage is likely to look exclusively to other African Americans for support (e.g., prefer a Black therapist) and may frame the loss in terms of racial and cultural influences. An individual at the internalization or internalization/commitment stage is more likely to include Whites in her or his support network. (*Note.* There is some evidence that Cross's model has value for identity development with other people of color; Phinney, 1989.)

Homosexual Identity Development

Models developed by Cass (1979) and Troiden (1989) describe the formation of homosexual identity and the coming-out process via stages that, while generally linear, can also overlap and be repeated. The Cass model outlines six stages: (a) identity confusion, in which individuals become aware of being different but do not label the difference; (b) identity comparison, in which individuals begin to accept the possibility that their behavior may be homosexual but their identity remains heterosexual; (c) identity tolerance, in which individuals tolerate the probability of being homosexual, try to understand what that may mean for them, and seek out gay and lesbian culture; (d) identity acceptance, in which individuals accept rather than merely tolerate their gay or lesbian identity and begin to explore the homosexual community; (e) identity pride, in which individuals immerse themselves in gay and lesbian culture and limit involvement with heterosexual culture; and (f) identity synthesis, in which individuals embrace a broader and deeper self-definition in which sexual orientation is only one part of their identity. Loss and grief circumstances may impede or propel developmental shifts and influence the particular experiences at different stages. For example, grieving a significant loss during the identity comparison stage may be complicated by the social isolation that is typical of that period.

Faith Development

Models of faith development help counseling professionals understand the ways in which clients experience religious and/or spiritual growth (Fowler, 1981; Genia, 1995; Oser, 1991; Washburn, 1988). There are important limitations with these models that counseling professionals must take into account, most notably their reflection of Western historical and cultural contexts and the inference that higher stages are more mature or desirable than previous stages (Frame, 2003). However, despite these limitations, the models do provide some useful information about the manner in which some people experience religion or spirituality over the course of their lives. Fowler's (1981, 1991) faith development model focuses on the form of faith or spirituality rather than the content or object of faith. According to Fowler, there is a clear progression from one stage to another, although people may remain in one stage for most of their lives. The stages include the following:

1. intuitive-projective faith (early childhood): faith images basically a reflection of relationships with parents and other significant adult figures
2. mythic-literal faith (middle childhood and beyond): one-dimensional and literal beliefs, anthropomorphic concept of God, often see faith in terms of punishment and rewards

3. synthetic-conventional faith (puberty to adulthood): faith based on moral authority of others, conform to community standards regarding beliefs, values, and faith practices
4. individuative-reflective faith (young adulthood): critical examination of faith, assume responsibility for own views and practices, conscious choice to practice faith rather than unexamined conformity
5. conjunctive faith (midlife adult): acknowledge multiple ways of faith practice, open to differences yet grounded in own faith
6. universalizing faith (few people attain this stage): "grounded in oneness," committed to peace and justice as expressions of faith (Fowler, 1991, p. 41)

An individual at the synthetic-conventional faith stage of Fowler's faith development model tends to look to others for moral authority and conform to community standards regarding beliefs, values, and faith practices (i.e., organized religion). Loss experiences, such as those associated with death, divorce, relationship breakup, or acquired disability, often trigger a critical examination of the previously accepted external sources of authority and conventional beliefs, which may be an additional source of distress for grieving persons. An individual may reject this examination and thus remain at the synthetic-conventional faith stage, may reject all consideration of faith (lose faith), or may embrace the examination process in a search for meaning, moving into the next developmental stage, individuative-reflective faith. Here, the individual makes a personal choice to commit to certain values, beliefs, and faith practices (as opposed to unexamined acceptance of the authority of others).

Summary of Developmental Considerations

It is not the purpose of therapy to push people from one developmental phase to the next. Rather, understanding a client's developmental experience helps the counseling professional discern relevant issues and discriminate maladaptive from adaptive behavior. A developmental perspective draws attention to the whole person and places loss and grief in a broader context. Counseling professionals must be familiar with general psychosocial and life span development models and other models related to specific identity dimensions that may be appropriate for their particular client population. Clients often respond positively to information that places their loss and grief experiences in the wider context of development.

Client Strengths and Abilities

Everyone has some strengths or abilities that can be applied to their grieving situation. However, these assets are often overlooked or even denigrated in the face of difficult circumstances, bias, or longstanding problems. Even counseling professionals sometimes focus so much on client negatives that they fail to consider client positives. Strengths and abilities that are particularly useful in loss and grief circumstances include the ability to tolerate emotional distress, a history of endurance and survival, patience, intelligence, agency-thinking ("I think I can"), self-awareness, a sense of humor, adequate social skills, self-comforting skills, a capacity for forgiveness, a capacity for empathy, problem-solving skills, an ability to identify and utilize diverse resources, an ability to access social support, a growth orientation, life-encouraging values, and spiritual commitment. Although these strengths and abilities may exist only to a limited degree, counseling professionals should help clients identify and develop these qualities so that they can be applied to loss adaptation. The following questions are useful in this regard: "What qualities do you have that you seem to be able to tap into when there are troublesome times? What is it about you that allows you to keep going? . . .What would others [e.g., friends, coworkers, family members] say are the qualities you have that keep you going?" (Bertolino & O'Hanlon, 2001, p. 137). Other questions that can be posed to clients to help them identify their strengths may include the following: There have been other difficult situations that could have defeated you but you did not let them. What did you do to get through those difficulties? Given all that has happened to you, how have you managed to keep going? Given all the difficult things that have happened to this family, how is it that you all keep hanging in there?

Social Support

A social support network could include family, friends, quasi-kin, fellow employees, mentors, community members, psychotherapists, social service agencies, support groups, traditional healers (e.g., shaman, *curandera*), and religious/spiritual resources (e.g., pastor, rabbi). The better the quality of a grieving individual's social support network, the more functional is her or his loss adaptation. However, people in grief situations may encounter a reduction in expected support. For example, the griever and the loss may not be recognized (e.g., cognitively disabled person, pet loss), family dynamics may limit or even cut off support, and social groups may withhold recognition of relationships (e.g., gay/lesbian partnerships). Traditional sources of support may be absent or limited because of immigration or refugee movement. Cultural differences and bias may impair delivery of support services. Sometimes grievers endure a secondary loss in discovering that the very people they expected to provide support (e.g., friends, teachers, government) are unable or unwilling to do so. Grieving individuals may also have deficits in interpersonal relationship skills that reduce or impair their support network. For example, a griever's anger reactions may drive people away. While social support is beneficial to grieving clients, grieving persons may find such support more or less helpful at different times over the course of their grieving journey. Counseling professionals must also recognize that some degree of social withdrawal is entirely normal and appropriate as people conserve their energy and focus inwardly at times during adaptation to loss. An important component of grief counseling is helping clients access beneficial sources of social support in ways that are meaningful to them and to their own particular grieving experience.

Sociocultural Influences

Gender, sexual orientation, ethnicity, family, race, class, religion, age, and distinct communities (e.g., neighborhood, deaf community, the military, faith-based affiliation) instill values and beliefs, generate worldviews (e.g., individualism vs. collectivism), influence attachments (e.g., kinship, the nature of relationships), establish behavioral norms and expectations (e.g., emotional expression, gender scripts), create meaning, and may even provide rituals that define and shape a person's experience of loss and grief in significant ways. Counseling professionals must collaborate with grieving clients in exploring the nature of these influences, the particular manner in which clients negotiate them, and their impact on clients' experience of loss and grief. For example:

+ In what ways does gender, ethnicity, or sexual orientation define the primary and secondary losses experienced by a particular individual or family?

+ In what ways do the griever's assumptions about gender roles shape his or her losses and affect his or her grieving?
+ In what ways do this person's cultural influences impact his or her ideas about suffering, the locus of control, and emotional expression?
+ How does this person's orientation toward the individual or the group (e.g., individualism vs. collectivism) affect his or her grieving?
+ How does this person's level of acculturation influence sources of social support?
+ Is this person torn between traditional and mainstream cultures, and how does that affect the experience of loss and grief?
+ How does this person's sexual orientation influence his or her experience of loss and grief, especially the nature of one's social network and family relations?
+ How might social or cultural stigmatization and discrimination affect the experience of loss and grief (e.g., homophobia, ageism, and sexism).
+ In what ways does this person's spiritual or religious affiliation shape his or her response to loss and manner of grieving?
+ What is the impact of estrangement from cultural, social, or familial roots on the grieving of this individual or family?
+ What culturally influenced rules and standards regarding emotional expression and communication affect this person?
+ In what ways, if at all, does this client or family hold values and views that are different from those generally assumed by their identified cultural influences? What impact do those differences have on their experience of loss and grief?
+ How might this person's loss experience fit into a history of familial, communal, or cultural loss?
+ What strengths and challenges flow from this person's cultural, social, and familial background that can help or hinder the process of adapting to loss?

One way of opening up discussion of sociocultural influences on grieving is to engage clients in reflection on the following: What is important to understand about the influence of (gender, race, sexual orientation) on your life? What has it been like for you to grow up as a (woman, Asian American, Latino, gay man) in this world? What challenges have you encountered and how have you managed them? What resources and strengths from your background and meeting those challenges can you draw on now? (Bertolino & O'Hanlon, 2001, pp. 200–201).

Listening for Clues to Loss and Grief in Psychotherapy

During the course of therapy, counseling professionals should listen carefully for clues that suggest that loss is an insufficiently addressed issue or that grief is not being integrated in a functional manner. These clues include the following:

+ Loss as a prominent and repetitive theme in therapy: Such losses are both symbolic and concrete and often are nondeath related. Clients may frame life events, both normative and unusual, only in terms of loss with no regard for gain or growth or may continually report on losses that happen to them or to others.

+ Substantial anger, sometimes to the extremes of rage: Insufficiently addressed loss and grief are often at the core of anger difficulties.
+ Uncontrolled ruminative coping that impairs functioning: Clients who obsessively focus on symptoms of distress and the meaning of such symptoms with no active outcome may be distracting themselves from loss and grief concerns.
+ Preoccupation with revenge fantasies: The desire for revenge often flows from loss and grief experiences as a symbolic way of righting wrongs, getting even, or avoiding distress.
+ Overreactions to events and experiences: Current situations may provoke memories of prior losses, especially those that have been insufficiently integrated.
+ Informational gaps following significant loss events: Sometimes these reflect avoidance of distressful material.
+ Unexplained illness or other physical impairment: Sometimes examination of such difficulties reveals unaddressed loss and grief.
+ Excessive guilt or resentment: Exploration of these emotions, two sides of the same coin, often reveals unaddressed loss and insufficiently integrated grief. Sometimes excessive guilt is a way of avoiding uncomfortable resentment feelings, and excessive resentment is a way of avoiding uncomfortable guilt feelings.
+ Interpersonal relationship problems: Loss, separation, and grief concerns often contribute to and stem from difficulties forming and reforming attachments.

Of course, each of these conditions must be viewed in light of the individuality of grieving clients and the particular multiple contexts that influence their experience of loss and grief.

Diagnosing Uncomplicated and Complicated Bereavement Grief

Researchers and other professionals have long attempted to define the course and characteristics of "normal" or uncomplicated bereavement grief and distinguish this from "abnormal" or complicated bereavement grief. The uncomplicated–complicated terminology is certainly preferred because it avoids the baggage associated with questions of abnormality. The purpose of the distinction is to alert counseling professionals to specific symptoms and levels of human distress that are especially life limiting and to distinguish this disorder from other disorders (e.g., mood and anxiety disorders) so as to optimize appropriate intervention. *Uncomplicated bereavement grief* is generally self-limiting, with a gradual diminishing of common symptoms (e.g., sadness, yearning, confusion, numbing, and loneliness), an increasing acceptance of the reality of death and its implications, and a steady integration of loss into the fabric of life. People experiencing uncomplicated bereavement grief generally recognize their symptoms as normal to grief. The easing of symptoms is evident over the first 6 months to a year. *Complicated bereavement grief* is prolonged, grief symptoms intensify rather than diminish, disbelief regarding the reality of death lingers, and the loss is not integrated.

Worden (2002) described four types of complicated bereavement grief. *Delayed grief* refers to a grief that is put off, perhaps because the person is too overwhelmed, and then reappears at a later time. This resurfacing of grief is often precipitated by a more current loss or stressors. *Masked grief* refers to a grief that is not evident immediately following the death but appears later in the guise of a physical symptom or maladaptive behavior (e.g., chest pains, panic attacks, facsimile illnesses, acting-out or risking-taking behaviors). *Chronic grief* refers to a protracted grief reaction that is never satisfactorily integrated wherein grievers are aware that their grieving is problematic. A persistent yearning and longing for the deceased with fantasies of reunification is common. *Exaggerated grief* refers to the magnification of usual grief symptoms. For example, the depressed mood, anger, or mild anxiety of uncomplicated bereavement grief becomes clinical depression, rage, or agoraphobia in complicated bereavement grief.

The current *Diagnostic and Statistical Manual of Mental Disorders* (4th ed., text rev.; *DSM–IV–TR*; American Psychiatric Association, 2000) specifies a diagnosis for uncomplicated bereavement grief but does not include a diagnosis for complicated bereavement grief. As a V-code, V62.82, bereavement is viewed as a condition that may be the focus of clinical attention but is not considered a mental disorder. The *DSM–IV–TR* points out that the symptoms of V-code bereavement are characteristic of those in a major depressive episode (e.g., sadness, insomnia, weight loss, and poor appetite), but, importantly, they are regarded by the griever as normal grieving experiences. Recognizing the influence of cultural variation, no determination is attempted regarding the duration and expression of symptoms. However, the *DSM–IV–TR* does caution that the presence of certain symptoms, in addition to the bereaved state, suggests the additional diagnosis of a major depressive episode. These symptoms include (a) guilt feelings (other than about actions one might or might not have taken at the time of death); (b) death preoccupation (other than wishing he or she had died with the loved one or would be better off dead; (c) morbid preoccupation with personal worthlessness; (d) marked diminishment of psychomotor activity; (e) functional impairment that is marked and lasts a particularly long time; and (f) hallucinations (other than seeing or hearing the deceased in a transient way). The *DSM–IV–TR* suggests that adding the major depressive episode diagnosis is usually not considered until after the symptoms accompanying the bereaved state last longer than 2 months. Other clinical diagnoses may be used when treating complicated bereavement grief depending on the particular symptoms demonstrated, such as generalized anxiety disorder, posttraumatic stress disorder, or major depressive disorder.

An Axis I diagnostic classification of complicated bereavement grief is currently proposed for the fifth edition of the *DSM* (*DSM–V*), targeted for publication in 2012. The criteria offered by Prigerson and her colleagues emphasizing the duration and degree of impairment appear to be the most widely accepted (Prigerson et al., 1999; Zhang, El-Jawahri, & Prigerson, 2006). The proposed classification, identified as complicated grief disorder, includes the following:

+ Criterion A: Yearning, pining, longing for the deceased. Yearning must be experienced at least daily over the past month or to a distressing or disruptive degree.
+ Criterion B: In the past month, the person must have experienced four of the following eight symptoms as marked, overwhelming, or extreme: 1. Trouble accepting the death. 2. Inability trusting others since the death. 3. Excessive bitterness or anger about the death. 4. Feeling uneasy about moving on with one's life (e.g., difficulty forming new relationships). 5. Feeling emotionally numb or detached from others since the death. 6. Feeling life is empty or meaningless without the deceased. 7. Feeling the future holds no meaning or prospect for fulfillment without the deceased. 8. Feeling agitated, jumpy, or on edge since the death.

- Criterion C: The above symptom disturbance causes marked dysfunction in social, occupational, or other important domains.
- Criterion D: The above symptom disturbance must last at least 6 months. (Zhang et al., 2006, p. 1191)

The proposed inclusion of a complicated bereavement grief diagnosis in the *DSM–V* raises serious concerns that must be carefully considered by counseling professionals. The core symptoms are shared by several other disorders so that distinguishing among complicated bereavement grief, uncomplicated bereavement grief, adjustment disorder, a major depressive episode, and posttraumatic stress disorder is problematic (Zhang et al., 2006). Labeling bereavement grief, a normative life experience, as a mental disorder or mental illness may be so stigmatizing that people will not seek treatment. Walter (2005) pointed out that power brokers (e.g., counselors, managed care, families, researchers) have a vested interest in developing this diagnosis as a means for delineating resources and services, but this may not be in the best interest of the clients who receive the diagnosis. He further noted that this diagnosis, like others, may simply be another way in which society can label people who resist dominant narratives and cultural norms about grieving. According to Foote and Frank (1999),

> Grief, like death itself, is undisciplined, risky, wild. That society seeks to discipline grief, as part of its policing of the border between life and death, is predictable, and it is equally predictable that modern society would medicalize grief as the means of policing. (p. 170)

Counseling professionals should keep current with evolving research on this proposed diagnosis and are encouraged to participate with other professionals in the frank discussion of its potential and limitations.

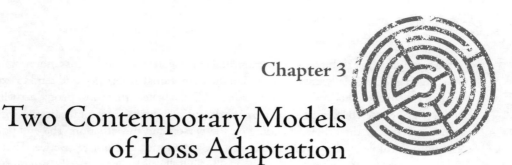

Chapter 3

Two Contemporary Models of Loss Adaptation

This chapter describes two contemporary models of loss adaptation that are highly recommended to counseling professionals: Martin and Doka's (2000) model of *adaptive grieving styles* and the *dual process model* developed by Stroebe, Schut, and Stroebe (1998; Stroebe & Schut, 2001a; Stroebe & Stroebe, 1999). These approaches (discussed briefly in Chapter 1) offer distinct advantages over traditional grief models. Both models (a) centralize the griever and his or her distinct experience of loss and grief; (b) assume the normalcy of variations and difference in each griever's response to loss and particular manner of loss adaptation; (c) emphasize loss adaptation as an active process; (d) invite consideration of diverse cultural, familial, social, contextual, personal, and historical influences; (e) normalize "differential grief" among family members (Gilbert, 1996); (f) suggest potential problems areas for assessment and intervention for both individuals and families; (g) facilitate tailoring treatment to the client and client needs; and (h) address the shortcomings of detrimental assumptions, such as the grief work hypothesis, gender stereotyping, universal stage or phase models, and the bias toward affect in the mental health field. It is important to note that both models were developed specifically to describe bereavement grief. However, they are useful in working with nondeath-related loss circumstances precisely because of their emphasis on the uniqueness of the individual and the individual's distinct experience of loss and grief.

Adaptive Grieving Styles

Martin and Doka's (2000) model of adaptive grieving describes personality-related grieving patterns or styles and how these uniquely influence a person's experience of loss and adaptation to loss. The model centers on (a) specific patterns of grieving emerging from an individual's natural, innate response to loss and (b) the preferred cognitive, behavioral, affective, and spiritual strategies an individual uses to manage that innate response to loss. Martin and Doka's work draws conceptually on Carl Jung's type theory and on research about repressive coping and temperament-based affect intensity.

Martin and Doka (2000) identified three basic grieving styles visualized on a continuum. These styles reflect the unique manner in which individuals inwardly experience and outwardly express their grief. At one end of the continuum is an intuitive grieving style, at the other end is an instrumental grieving style, and in between lies a blended grieving pattern. People who exhibit a more *intuitive grieving style* respond to loss primarily in terms of emotion (affect), tending to feel and express their emotions intensely. For them, "a grief expressed is a grief experienced" (p. 37). In contrast, people who exhibit a more *instrumental grieving style* respond to loss more cognitively and physically than emotionally, are modulated in their emotional experience, and tend to express their grief in terms of thoughts and activity. Martin and Doka believe that most people actually exhibit a *blended grieving style*, combining elements of both intuitive and instrumental patterns, with a greater emphasis on one or the other depending on the person and the situation. The end points of the continuum, intuitive and instrumental styles, are descriptive and not restrictive. That is, people exhibit more or less of a pattern rather than falling wholly and stereotypically into one style or the other. An individual's preference for a specific grieving style can shift some along the continuum but is generally consistent across time. For example, a person whose grieving style is highly intuitive may shift in an instrumental direction but will not suddenly begin using a highly instrumental pattern. A person with a blended style that tends toward the intuitive side of the continuum might shift toward the more instrumental side but would not move to a highly instrumental style. Grieving styles simply reflect and respect the innate differences among individuals that result from personality traits as well as cultural, familial, developmental, and social influences. It is important to note that there is no ideal or preferred grieving style and no suggestion of pathology attached to any one style. Just as there is no correct way to grieve, there is no correct grieving style.

The second element of Martin and Doka's (2000) model focuses on the preferred cognitive, behavioral, affective, and spiritual adaptive strategies used by grievers to help them manage and express their natural responses to loss. Adaptive strategies are learned methods used to deal with transitional events (Silverman, 1986, cited in Martin & Doka, 2000). More than mere coping, adaptive strategies help people adjust immediately and over time to the event itself and also to the experience of transition. The following provides a description of adaptive strategies applied specifically to loss adaptation (adapted from Martin & Doka, 2000, pp. 135–142; Moos & Schaefer, 1986, pp. 13–19):

Affective strategies
+ Emotional expression/discharge: ventilation of feelings, catharsis, crying
+ Emotional connection: sharing, connecting with others on an emotional level
+ Affective regulation: choosing time/place to experience painful feelings and monitor emotional intensity (e.g., expose oneself to distressful feelings incrementally = "dosing").
+ Appraisal of abilities and skills in emotion management (e.g., what are my limits?)

Cognitive strategies
+ Logical analysis: breaking down the loss experience into parts or tasks so as to evaluate and manage it
+ Cognitive restructuring: reframing or redefining loss (e.g., it is natural, it is an opportunity for growth); redefining the relationship with the lost object (e.g., the deceased) to allow for continuing connection/creating inner memory of lost object; meaning making to make sense of the loss and amend previously held assumptions and beliefs about self, self and other, the world, and self in the world
+ Information seeking: obtaining information to help the grievers understand their responses, assess ways of managing their experience and the problems they may encounter
+ Cognitive avoidance or denial: denying, avoiding, or minimizing the loss; selecting times and circumstances to avoid or to focus on loss and grief

Behavioral strategies
- ✦ Physical activity (e.g., running, chopping wood, building a memorial)
- ✦ Seeking out information and support for self or others
- ✦ Problem solving/directed activity to deal with problems, accomplish tasks, pursue alternative rewards (e.g., arrange funeral or ritual, undertake quest or journey, plan a new job search, become a political/social activist in immigration reform or Mothers Against Drunk Driving)
- ✦ Acting-out behaviors (e.g., alcohol and other drug abuse, fighting, overeating, compulsive spending, other risk-taking behaviors)

Spiritual strategies
- ✦ *Note.* Spiritual strategies lend themselves to cognitive, behavioral, and affective interpretations
- ✦ Prayer and meditation: used to express emotion, aid processing of thoughts, and serve as a directed activity
- ✦ Surrender to higher power
- ✦ Meaning reconstruction: revising, reaffirming, or discarding beliefs and assumptions about self and Other, self in the world (e.g., lose one's faith, deepen faith, discover new spiritual depth)

Any of the adaptive strategies can be used by any grieving person at any time to serve her or his particular needs. However, there is a clear preference for those adaptive strategies that are most likely to address a person's specific and unique way of responding to loss—the grieving style. These "go-to" strategies are the primary adaptive strategies for each grieving style. Individuals with a more intuitive grieving style are most likely to use adaptive strategies that help them manage their emotions, express their feelings, and share their experience with others. In contrast, those operating from a more instrumental grieving style are most likely to use adaptive strategies that facilitate analysis, cognitive restructuring, and activity. People exhibiting a more blended grieving style, because it represents a combination of instrumental and intuitive styles, select primary adaptive strategies based on their innate response and distinct needs in a particular situation. If the emotional experience is more dominant for them, then they use affective adaptive strategies; if problems and issues are more dominant than emotion, then they use cognitive and behavioral adaptive strategies.

The same adaptive strategy can be used differently by different grievers. For example, telling and retelling the story of loss, a common activity, helps the more intuitive griever express emotion and connect on an emotional level with others. The more instrumental style griever, however, tells and retells the story of loss in order to gather information, organize a response, or solve problems. Spiritual strategies, especially, serve multiple purposes: The more intuitive style griever uses a spiritual strategy like prayer to focus on the here-and-now experience, for meaning making, and to facilitate emotional expression, whereas the more instrumental style griever uses prayer to aid cognitive restructuring and meaning making as well as to serve as a directed activity. Martin and Doka (2000) noted that even violence can serve multiple functions as an adaptive strategy: assaulting another can facilitate the expression of feelings (affective strategy) and also be a directed activity (behavioral strategy).

It is important to recognize that adaptive strategies, even if complementary to the individual's grieving style, can have their disadvantages (Martin & Doka, 2000). Often this is due to the ineffective use of the strategy. For example, excessive emotional displays can be debilitating and drive others away; cognitive strategies may be used to suppress emotion or avoid reality; directed activity such as physical exercise, although it may help a griever channel psychic energy, can be detrimental if overdone; acting-out and risk-taking behaviors such as drug and alcohol abuse, fighting, or promiscuity are clearly self-destructive. Adaptive strategies that are useful in the short term of loss adaptation may become counterproductive in the long term. For example, accepting an untimely death as consistent with God's will and plan may be comforting early on but later become a source of distress and resentment; intense emoting may be helpful at the funeral but impair necessary decision making later on. Finally, individual differences in grieving styles and selected adaptive strategies may create conflict and misunderstanding with others that further complicates loss adaptation. For example, the more intuitive style griever who cries and talks about her grief may feel abandoned by her more instrumental style partner who is helped by resuming work and avoiding emotional display. They are both using adaptive strategies that are appropriate to their natural grieving styles, but the differences in adaptive strategies make it difficult for them to understand and to help each other.

Descriptions of the characteristics of intuitive, instrumental, and blended adaptive grieving styles are provided below (Martin & Doka, 2000, pp. 31–53):

Characteristics of the intuitive adaptive grieving style
+ Natural grieving response is emotion focused.
+ Emotions are intensely experienced.
+ Outward emotional expression of inner distress is typical (e.g., crying, depressed mood, anger).
+ Psychic energy is channeled into the emotion-focused experience.
+ Grief may be framed as a problem of emotional distress and emotional regulation.
+ Grief may be perceived as a threat; griever may fear being overwhelmed by emotions.
+ Primary adaptive strategy = emotional experiencing and expression.
+ Sharing loss and grief (e.g., grief support groups, counseling) may be helpful.
+ Griever may have difficulty with emotion regulation.
+ Excessive emotional displays may restrict social support.
+ Griever may get lost in emotions and feel unable to resume daily activities and functions.
+ Griever may appear to progress more slowly in loss adaptation.
+ Griever may experience prolonged periods of cognitive dysfunction (e.g., confusion, difficulty concentrating, and forgetfulness) because the emotional experience dominates.
+ Griever may be viewed by others as overemotional, stuck in grieving, disturbed, or crazy.
+ Griever may have difficulty understanding people who do not express feelings or talk about their grief (e.g., instrumental style grievers).

Characteristics of the instrumental adaptive grieving style
+ Natural grieving response is cognitively focused.
+ Thinking is dominant over emotion.
+ Emotional experience and expression are typically modulated and private.
+ Psychic energy is channeled into analysis, organization, problem solving, and activities.

- Grief may be framed as problems and issues rather than as painful emotions.
- Grief may be perceived as a challenge to the griever's ability to master the situation and get through it.
- Primary adaptive strategy = cognitive restructuring, directed activity.
- Griever is helped by thinking and doing, such as problem solving, organizing, completing tasks, or planning activities (e.g., organize memorial/funeral, develop job search strategy, and initiate political/social activism).
- Griever may rely on cognitive strategies to avoid emotion.
- Periods of cognitive dysfunction (confusion, difficulty concentrating, and forgetfulness) are usually brief but may be especially distressful because this impairs the griever's natural cognitive tendency.
- Griever may be viewed by others (e.g., more intuitive style grievers) as cold, insensitive, or in denial.
- Griever may resent pressure from others (e.g., counselor, family member) to show feelings.
- Griever may have difficulty understanding intense emotional focus of other grievers.

Characteristics of the blended adaptive grieving style
- Griever has characteristics of both intuitive and instrumental grieving styles, although one style tends to be more dominant.
- Griever has some ability to shift toward one style or the other as needs and circumstances require.
- Griever demonstrates moderate levels of emotional intensity and repressive coping.

Martin and Doka (2000) suggested that primary adaptive strategies are the best clue to the individual's likely adaptive grieving style because these point directly to one's innate response to loss. However, grievers may utilize other adaptive strategies when the need arises. More intuitive grievers may call on cognitive and behavioral strategies to help them manage problems and issues; more instrumental grievers may call on affective strategies to help them manage emotions. These secondary adaptive strategies are generally less familiar to the griever and more likely to be ineffectively applied. Martin and Doka stated that it is more advantageous to have a greater number of effective strategies, whatever the grieving style, rather than relying on a limited few or ineffectively implemented strategies.

Dissonant Responses: Adaptive Grieving Styles

Consider the following situation and two different outcomes:

Theodore is a college counselor whose natural grieving style is more intuitive, so his primary adaptive strategies for dealing with loss are affective (e.g., expressing feelings, talking about his distress with others). However, when a colleague is killed in a traffic accident, Theodore's initial response is to "put my emotions on hold" and instead begin organizing campus resources to deal with the tragedy. For several days Theodore fields phone calls from concerned parents, speaks to the press, advises campus administrators, and provides counseling services. He is conscious from time to time of feeling sad, tense, and a bit anxious, but he pushes these emotions away, telling himself that he will deal with these them in time and instead stays focused on the job of helping others.

Outcome 1: In the week following the tragedy, Theodore is satisfied that things are working well on campus due in part to his efforts. It has taken more and more effort to avoid his feelings, making him tired and a bit irritable. He feels out of sorts with himself. Theodore decides it is time to attend to his emotions so he sits down with a colleague and begins to fully experience and express his feelings about the tragedy. This helps, and Theodore gradually feels more centered and better able to fulfill his responsibilities.

Outcome 2: In the weeks following the tragedy, Theodore is increasingly irritable with his family and his colleagues. He puts more and more energy into avoiding his emotions, especially his sadness about losing this colleague. Theodore avoids emotional material with his clients and stays focused on everyone but himself. The other day he choked back tears by reminding himself to "be a man" and of the importance of projecting a professional demeanor. He is drinking more than his usual occasional beer.

According to Martin and Doka (2000), the adaptive strategies used to respond initially to a loss are not necessarily indicative of a person's natural grieving style. This is especially so with highly intuitive and highly instrumental style grievers rather than blended grievers. For various reasons, a person may respond initially by using the less familiar secondary adaptive strategies that are consistent with the opposite grieving style. This sets up a discrepancy, as in Theodore's case, between a person's inner experience and his or her outward expression of grief. In most cases this discrepancy is resolved by eventually moving into one's natural grieving style, as noted above in Outcome 1. But sometimes a griever is unable to resolve the discrepancy and remains stuck in that initial response, as noted in Outcome 2. This situation is termed a *dissonant response,* "a persistent way of expressing grief that is at odds with the griever's primary internal experience" (Martin & Doka, 2000, p. 58). Under such conditions, the person whose natural style is more intuitive tries to behave like a more instrumental style griever and the person whose natural style is more instrumental tries to behave like a more intuitive style griever. Factors related to personality, gender role socialization, image management, and cultural norms especially influence emergence of a dissonant response. Martin and Doka believe that an unresolved dissonant response is often the source of complications in the grieving process because it impedes movement and direction.

Dissonant Response: More Intuitive Style Griever

Martin and Doka (2000) suggested that the dissonant response for more intuitive style grievers typically occurs when they try to limit the uncomfortable internal experience of emotional intensity through avoidance and distraction. Usually this means using cognitive and behavioral adaptive strategies, including the following: avoiding people and situations that are likely to create an emotional response; rationalizing or intellectualizing their experience; suppressing their feelings; using alcohol and other drugs (prescription and nonprescription, legal and illegal); overdoing physical exercise, work, or activities; fighting; denying the reality of the loss and its meaning; focusing on everyone but themselves; and severing their emotional connection to the lost object. The discrepancy created by using strategies that are at odds with one's natural grieving style—at odds with one's inner experience—over time can significantly impair healthy loss adaptation. Unfortunately, because avoidance breeds more avoidance, some more intuitive style grievers must devote increasing effort and energy into distraction from feelings and can become stuck in this dissonant response. This often results in emotional and physical exhaustion, estrangement from self and others, disenfranchised grief, and complications from risky and/or self-defeating behaviors.

> Consider Xavier, a man whose innate grieving style is more intuitive. He has been raised to regard his emotional experiences as unmanly and most emotional expression as a sign of weakness (*"Los hombres no lloran,"* men do not cry). When his mother dies, he wants to be strong for his father and for himself, so he suppresses his grief, but this just intensifies his feelings. The bottled-up emotions erupt into angry outbursts, which Xavier tries to control by avoiding others. The isolation then leaves Xavier disconnected, unable to truly mourn his mother, and concerned that he has failed his father at this critical time.

Dissonant Response: More Instrumental Style Griever

In contrast to the intuitive style, the dissonant response for more instrumental style grievers is not about avoiding feelings; it is about *not feeling* in the first place. Martin and Doka (2000) suggested that more instrumental style grievers are particularly susceptible to self-blame and guilt regarding their innate, tempered emotional response to loss. Rather than accept this as simply part of who they are, some more instrumental style grievers may believe there must be something wrong with them because they do not experience or express the emotional intensity that they "should" be feeling under the circumstances. They may use excessive self-criticism or reactively distance from others to punish themselves for being cold, uncaring, and insensitive or simply to avoid the negative judgment of others. They may attempt to "conjure up" feelings (Martin & Doka, 2000, p. 66) from their natural, modulated emotional experience by various means. For example, they may use alcohol or drugs to loosen inhibitions (rather than numb them), they may rely on a screen emotion such as anger to trigger emotional energy and display, they may create crisis situations full of emotional energy through risk-taking or other acting-out behaviors, or they may provoke violence to create an emotional response. It is very likely that the problems created by the dissonant response of a more instrumental griever, rather than the dissonant response itself, will present initially in therapy.

> Consider Paloma, a more instrumental style griever whose husband of 25 years recently died. While she is deeply saddened by his death, she has no urge to cry. Her friends and family have encouraged her to express her true feelings (which they assume she is hiding) and tell her that she really needs to stop holding it all in—to let her feelings out. Paloma regrets that she has no tears, feels guilty that she is not more emotional, and is concerned about the negative impression others must have of her. In the months following her husband's death she begins drinking more, seeking to decrease her inhibitions and force herself to "feel" more and perhaps to cry. Instead, the drinking has impaired her work performance, created problems in relationships with her children, and earned her a driving under the influence citation.

Counseling Intervention With Adaptive Grieving Styles

According to the adaptive grieving style model, optimal adjustment in loss adaptation involves the implementation of effective adaptive strategies consistent with one's natural grieving style. Problems are likely to occur when the client uses a limited range of adaptive strategies, when adaptive strategies are ineffectively applied, and when the client consistently responds in a manner that is incongruent with his or her natural internal experience. Intervention should focus on enhancing the client's strengths and effectiveness according to her or his natural adaptive grieving style. The counseling recommendations outlined below are based on those suggested by Martin and Doka (2000, pp. 125–157) and Martin and Wang (2006, p. 274).

Recommendations for identifying natural grieving styles, adaptive strategies, and dissonant responses include the following:

+ Listen for clues found in client language, descriptions, history, and attitudes.
+ Ask clients to describe themselves and how others would describe them.
+ Ask clients to describe what they find stressful on a daily basis and with their grief.
+ Ask clients about the methods they use for coping on a daily basis and with major as well as minor stressors.
+ Listen especially for words and tone that suggest affect, cognition, or physical/behavior (e.g., "I feel overwhelmed"; "I think I'm confused"; "I was restless").
+ Use open-ended questions that invite description (e.g., How did you respond? How did you react? What is that like for you? What does that mean for you? What was the experience like for you?)
+ Investigate clients' history of loss, especially attending to how they experienced loss, what helped, and what was unhelpful (i.e., adaptive strategies).
+ Find out what has been helpful or unhelpful in clients' current loss experience (i.e., adaptive strategies). Are they helped by expressing their feelings and talking about their loss (intuitive style) or do they find activity (doing something) more helpful (instrumental style)?
+ Would clients rather discuss "issues" related to their loss (instrumental) than feelings about their loss (intuitive)?
+ Do clients perceive loss as more of a challenge (instrumental style) or a threat (intuitive style)?
+ Investigate client goals and motivation for counseling. Are they seeking assistance with emotional expression (intuitive style) or problem solving (instrumental style)?
+ Investigate clients' specific cultural and social influences (e.g., gender, spiritual/religious, and ethnicity). Is there discrepancy between their perception of cultural and social influences and their own experience regarding loss and grief?
+ Investigate clients' spiritual/religious beliefs and how these affect their experience of loss and grief.
+ Ask if there is a difference between what clients think they "should" be doing as a grieving person and what they are doing.
+ Ask if friends or family have indicated that the client should be grieving differently than she or he is.
+ Ask if clients have noticed differences between their way of grieving and that of others, especially family members.

Recommendations for counseling *more intuitive style* grievers include the following:

+ Normalize and validate the primary emotional response to loss.
+ Educate clients regarding adaptive grieving styles.
+ Facilitate the experience of emotion and the expression of feelings. The traditional notion of grief work is most appropriate for more intuitive style grievers.

- Assist development of effective skills for emotion regulation and emotion management.
- Help clients identify strengths and limitations of their more intuitive grieving style and of adaptive strategies.
- Consider referral to grief support groups or group counseling. Groups provide a safe place to experience and express emotional intensity and to share one's grief. Clients also can learn emotion regulation skills from others.
- Enhance skills in less familiar secondary adaptive strategies (e.g., effective problem solving).
- Encourage self-care (emotional focus can be exhausting).
- Identify and investigate any avoidance or distraction from emotion and ascertain effectiveness.
- Facilitate dialogue on existential issues, values clarification, spiritual/religious concerns, and meaning making to help clients process experience and emotion.
- Evaluate and address any evidence of substance abuse, including possible function as avoidance/distraction from emotional intensity.
- Evaluate and address acting-out or risk-taking behavior, including its possible function in creating and maintaining emotional intensity.
- Help clients manage possible negative response of others to their intuitive style (e.g., viewing them as disturbed, overly emotional).

Recommendations for counseling *more instrumental style* grievers include the following:

- Normalize restricted or modulated experience/expression.
- Respect the private, reserved grief experience of the instrumental style.
- Educate clients regarding adaptive grieving styles.
- Facilitate effective decision making regarding activities (e.g., appropriate problem solving).
- Enhance skills for emotional experience and expression as needed. Remember these are less familiar and likely to be less developed for more instrumental style grievers.
- Encourage more instrumental style grievers to use their skills to help others (e.g., problem solving, planning).
- Help clients identify strengths and limitations of their more instrumental grieving style and of their preferred adaptive strategies.
- Encourage more instrumental style grievers to join group experiences that provide socialization, acceptance, respect for reserved emotions, and activity (e.g., sports team, Habitat for Humanity, cultural interest group) instead of referring them to typical grief support groups or group counseling.
- Identify and attend to guilt or penance that suggests dissonant grieving.
- Evaluate evidence of substance abuse and ascertain whether the function of that abuse is to provoke or intensify emotion.
- Evaluate acting-out or risk-taking behavior to ascertain whether the function of that behavior is to provoke or intensify emotion. Help clients manage possible negative responses of others to their natural grieving style (e.g., seeing them as uncaring, cold, insensitive).

More blended style grievers combine the characteristics of both intuitive and instrumental styles while generally favoring one style. Therefore, consider the recommendations for both styles and adjust for such grievers' more dominant style and problem areas. More blended style grievers may benefit from groups and are especially helpful members of group counseling and grief support groups because they often relate effectively to different grief styles.

Recommendations for counseling *dissonant grieving responses* include the following:

+ Help clients using a dissonant response to identify and embrace their own natural adaptive grieving style.
+ Facilitate client exploration of incongruence/discrepancy in their grieving, especially discrepancy between their inner experience and outward expression.
+ Explore possible role of image management (need to control impression on others), especially for intuitive style grievers.
+ Identify helpful ways of resolving discrepancy from their past and apply that to the present.
+ Help clients identify advantages and disadvantages of specific adaptive strategies.
+ Facilitate values clarification to address dissonance.
+ Facilitate meaning making to address dissonance (e.g., exploring beliefs and assumptions associated with the loss).
+ Identify and address cognitive distortions.
+ Identify and address self-defeating or risk-taking behaviors (e.g., alcohol abuse, violence), especially their function in possible dissonant response.
+ Facilitate client exploration of social and cultural influences on dissonant response and adaptive strategies, especially gender role socialization (e.g., men don't show feelings; women are good at emotional expression).
+ Identify and address guilt as an indicator of dissonance for more instrumental style grievers.
+ Identify and address distraction/avoidance as an indicator of dissonance for more intuitive style grievers.

Summary Recommendations

The following items summarize important elements of Martin and Doka's (2000) model of adaptive grieving styles:

+ Do not interpret the grieving styles too rigidly or stereotypically; people fall somewhere between the extremes of intuitive and instrumental, and most people are, in fact, more blended style grievers.
+ It is correct to speak of someone having a *more* intuitive, *more* instrumental, or *more* blended style.
+ People tend to use a particular adaptive grieving style consistently, but they may shift slightly on the continuum according to time and circumstance.
+ Adaptive strategies, even if consistent with one's grieving style, may be effectively or ineffectively applied.
+ Primary adaptive strategies are the best clues to a person's innate grieving style.
+ Recognize that more instrumental style grievers do experience emotions, just less intensely than more intuitive style grievers.

- There is no ideal grieving style and no pathology attached to any of the three basic styles. People just naturally grieve differently because of the influence of personal, social, and cultural factors.
- Adaptive grieving styles are influenced by gender and culture but are not determined by them.
- Having a range of effective adaptive strategies is most helpful in loss adaptation.
- A griever's initial response is not a reliable indicator of her or his innate grieving style.
- Complications in loss adaptation often occur when people consistently use adaptive strategies that are in conflict with their natural grieving style (dissonant response).
- Individual differences in grieving style can be a source of conflict and misunderstanding, especially in families. Such variations should be viewed as "differences, not deficiencies" (p. 160).

Martin and Wang (2006), building on Martin and Doka's (2000) original work, developed a 14-item instrument for measuring intuitive and instrumental grieving styles. Although results are promising, continued research to establish this instrument's reliability and validity is necessary.

The Dual Process Model

An excellent nonlinear, process-oriented grief model is the dual process model of coping with bereavement (Stroebe & Schut, 1999, 2001a; Stroebe et al., 1998). The developers, drawing on cognitive stress theory, coping models, and general theories of bereavement grief, regard their model as an integration of existing ideas and research. Their original focus was on bereavement following the death of a partner, but they suggest that their model may have application for other death-related and perhaps for nondeath-related circumstances.

Loss Orientation and Restoration Orientation

According to the dual process model, loss adaptation involves a fluctuating process of both confronting and avoiding a range of stressors along two primary dimensions: loss orientation and restoration orientation. *Loss-oriented stressors* are those associated with the loss itself, for example, ruminating about the loss or the preloss situation, reacting emotionally to loss, exploring the meaning of loss, missing the absent lost object, experiencing troubled or pleasurable remembering, and reviewing the events surrounding the loss. A primary focus here is the disrupted bond with the object of loss (e.g., the deceased). When in loss orientation, the griever avoids these stressors at times and confronts these stressors at other times. For example, a griever may feel and express sadness and anger with family and friends (confronting stressors) but actively distract herself from those feelings when she is at work (avoiding stressors); a griever may obsessively ruminate about his former lover (confronting) and at other times try to block any thoughts about the situation at all (avoiding). Both avoidance and confrontation are seen as the normal, natural processes of loss adaptation. The dual process model views the primary work of loss orientation to be managing grief work; the intrusion of grief; relinquishing, continuing, and relocating bonds and ties; and denial or avoidance of restoration changes.

Restoration-oriented stressors, alternatively, are associated with the consequences of loss; that is, dealing with the changes that result from the primary loss. These include, for example, revising one's identity, adapting family roles, making meaning-of-life changes, reorganizing plans for the future, adapting family rules and roles, learning new skills, engaging in different activities, dealing with loneliness, and managing emotions related to the changed situation. The confrontation–avoidance dynamic applies in restoration orientation as well. For example, a recently divorced parent with sole custody of her children may avoid the new demands of parenting alone but may also make occasional attempts to provide parenting (confrontation); a man grieving the loss of his job may tell himself it is best to wait for something to turn up (avoidance) or may actively investigate a new career direction or learn new work skills (confrontation). The dual process model views the primary work of restoration orientation to be attending to life changes, doing new things, seeking distraction from grief, denying or avoiding grief, and dealing with new roles, identities, or relationships (see Figure 3.1).

A critical component of the dual process model proposes that loss adaptation normatively involves a dynamic "oscillation," or shifting back and forth, between loss orientation and restoration orientation in a self-regulating manner over the course of time and sometimes within a single day. The rate and timing of oscillation are affected by the nature and meaning of the loss and the unique personal, social, familial, developmental, and cultural influences at work for the griever. For example, in traditional Navajo practice, bereavement grief is expressed publicly over only 4 days, during which discussion of the deceased occurs and some modulated emotional expression is allowed. A shift into restoration orientation occurs after the 4 days when the griever is expected to resume daily life, the name of the dead is never again spoken, and emotional expressions of grief are frowned on (Miller & Schoenfeld, 1973, cited in Nagel, 1988). Consider the following examples.

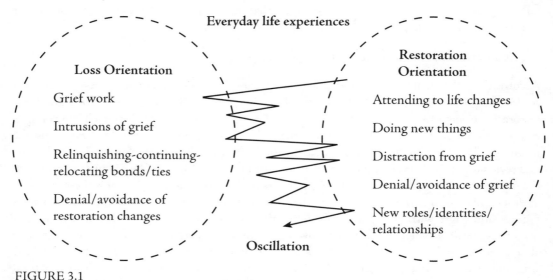

FIGURE 3.1

The Dual Process Model of Coping With Bereavement

Note. From "Attachment in Coping With Bereavement: A Theoretical Integration," by M. Stroebe, H. Schut, and W. Stroebe, 2005. *Review of General Psychology, 9,* p. 51. Copyright 2005 by the American Psychological Association. Adapted with permission. The use of APA information does not imply endorsement by APA.

When Fatima mourns the death of her infant child, she initially engages in loss orientation as she experiences despair and sadness. She confronts these disturbing emotions when she allows herself to feel them, talk about them, and share them with others. At other times she avoids these emotions by distracting herself into anger directed at her husband or by attending to other tasks. She moves also into restoration orientation as she recognizes the need to rebuild the couple relationship around their shared loss. Sometimes she avoids this and at other times she participates in this rebuilding. Fatima shifts between loss orientation and restoration orientation over the course of her grieving.

David was injured by a roadside bomb while he was serving with the Marines in Iraq. He lost his left leg and three fingers on his left hand. During rehabilitation in hospitals back in the United States, David's life is a seesaw in which he swings from despair and resentment to determination and hopefulness. The most constant emotion for David is anger. Sometimes his anger is focused on resentment and a sense of being "damaged goods," at other times the anger is more an expression of frustration at the difficulties of learning to walk and use his hand again. The setbacks in his physical recovery tend to set off anger about the disability. David's counselor sees his anger in restoration orientation as normative and even helpful, because it tends to fuel motivation to acquire new skills and adapt to life changes. However, the counselor is concerned that David's anger during loss orientation is primarily used to distract himself from his feelings of being weak or damaged.

Cho is a freshman at a large university 500 miles from her home and family. She is having difficulty making the transition to college because she is so terribly homesick. She misses her family, the food and routine of her home, and even the oversight of her parents. She feels depressed, cries alone in her room, calls home often, and thinks constantly about what a mistake she made insisting on going away to college. She fears failing and the disappointment of her parents. Academics provide some distraction from the homesickness, but not nearly enough. When she seeks assistance at the university counseling center, Cho's counselor helps her explore her feelings of loss and also helps her develop skills and plan ways to improve her adjustment to the campus environment. Gradually, as Cho learns her way around campus, makes new friends, and feels more in control of her studies, things begin to improve. Occasionally she feels a wave of homesickness that is upsetting and pulls her back into feeling depressed, but she more and more often can get herself back on track. By the middle of the year, Cho is no longer experiencing much homesickness at all. Cho was initially in a loss orientation, moved into a restoration orientation, then experienced some oscillation between the two with increasing alignment in the restoration orientation.

As was discussed earlier in Chapter 1, it is important to note that both loss orientation and restoration orientation are normative and critical dimensions of loss adaptation and that restoration orientation is not just a healthier or preferred dimension. There is a time for loss and a time for restoration in grief. Both can involve positive and negative experiences as the griever sometimes confronts and at other times avoids the stressors associated with each dimension. Avoidance, according to the dual process model, is an expected response to stressors and is not in and of itself necessarily bad. In fact, the choice to avoid the intrusion of loss by distracting oneself from it can be a healthy means of coping. For example, Fritz recognizes that if he allows himself to think about the recent death of his mother, he becomes too upset to work. He begins actively suppressing thoughts of her during the workday, but allows himself to think about his mother and feel the sadness when he is at home after work.

Stroebe and Schut (1999) suggested that problems encountered by grieving clients have to do with the failure to oscillate between loss orientation and restoration orientation. Avoidance of loss orientation by moving solely into restoration orientation implies a continued denial of the reality of loss. Avoidance of restoration orientation by exclusively focusing on loss orientation implies denial of the reality of changes resulting from loss. Thus, by failing to oscillate, the person is stuck in his or her grieving.

> Tonya and Ned's 19-year-old daughter, Jessie, recently shared with them that she is a lesbian. The couple initially entered a period of loss orientation in which they focused primarily on the loss of their assumptions about Jessie, their hopes for her future, and their idea of themselves as parents of a heterosexual child. Their anger, guilt, resentment, disappointment, and confusion brought painful interactions with Jessie. Ned gradually worked through the loss, sometimes allowing himself to fully engage with the negative emotions and sometimes distracting himself with work or other activities. Gradually Ned began revising his assumptions, focusing more and more on the changes the losses have brought, and tentatively trying to rebuild his relationship with Jessie (shift to restoration orientation). Tonya, on the other hand, remains stuck in loss orientation. She ruminates endlessly about the loss of her fantasies about how her daughter's future would unfold and the loss of predictability in her relationship with her daughter. She seems to take Jessie's homosexuality as a personal failure. Occasionally she distracts herself from the painful emotions, but she remains focused on her losses. She resists Ned's efforts to help her consider the present and future relationship with Jessie, angrily rebuking him for not understanding "what this means to a mother." Differences in the oscillation between loss orientation and restoration orientation contribute to relationship difficulties between them and with Jessie, thus complicating loss adaptation for the entire family.

The dual process model provides some important benefits to one's understanding of the grieving process, most clearly in its recognition of the uniqueness of every grieving person's particular journey. Rather than universal and generic phases/stages, the model allows for variations based on personal, cultural, familial, social, and other contextual variables. Another important benefit is the dual process model's recognition of the ebb and flow of grieving as a process of dealing simultaneously with the stressors associated with one's losses and those associated with the changes brought about by the losses, "identifying the need to both come to terms with the loss and adapt to the different environment" (Stroebe, van Vliet, Hewstone, & Willis, 2002, p. 150). The model normalizes both avoidance and confrontation as predictable and even useful strategies for dealing with stressors associated with loss and grief while at the same time pointing out potential complications associated with a failure to oscillate. Furthermore, the dual process model recognizes that clients use diverse adaptive strategies for responding to grief (e.g., cognitive, behavioral) and not just emotion-focused strategies.

Using the Dual Process Model in Counseling

The dual process model provides the counselor with a nonlinear model of loss adaptation that suggests potential problem areas and facilitates tailoring interventions to meet the uniqueness of clients and their needs. The model's developers postulate that oscillation, which is dynamic, flexible, and self-regulating over time, is necessary for optimal adjustment (in bereavement; Stroebe & Schut, 1999, p. 216). The following recommendations are helpful:

+ Identify and explore the client's loss-oriented stressors and the specific avoidance and confrontation responses used to manage these stressors.
+ Identify and explore the client's restoration-oriented stressors and the specific avoidance and confrontation responses used to manage those stressors.
+ Identify evidence of oscillation or failure to oscillate in the current loss and in previous loss experiences. Keep in mind that an initial period of loss orientation is normal before oscillation begins, so consider timing, situation, and context overall.
+ Normalize and validate the functionality of avoidance, confrontation, and oscillation.
+ Explain the dual process model, emphasizing its specific application to the client's situation. Invite client collaboration in understanding its potential relevance for the client's grieving experience.
+ Address any problematic avoidance and confrontation (e.g., alcohol use, extreme denial, excessive or consistent suppression of emotion, acting out).
+ Do not push clients toward restoration orientation. Rather, support management of stressors associated with both loss orientation and restoration orientation and the oscillation process.

Differential Grief in Families

The two contemporary approaches described in this chapter are especially useful when counseling grieving families. While traditional stage, phase, or tasks models imply universal processes and the sameness of grieving experience, these nonlinear models highlight the occurrence of differential grief in families: "the tendency of family members to be dealing with different issues at varied points in their grief process and with sometimes contrasting styles" (Gilbert, 1996, p. 269). The fact is that even when a loss is shared (e.g., death of a family member, loss of home, divorce, wartime separation), family members experience the loss and adapt to loss in different ways. As Gilbert (1996) so succinctly put it: "Families do not grieve. Only individuals grieve. This is done in a variety of contexts, one of which is the family" (p. 273). Multiple factors contribute to these differences, including the particular nature of one's relationship with the lost object, individual ways of making sense of loss, how an individual experiences the impact of the loss on family functioning, relationships with other family members, stages of individual and family development, one's unique history of loss and grief, cultural influences, and characterological features. These grieving style and process differences, through normative, can also be a complicating factor in loss adaptation for grieving families. Consider the following examples.

Michelle and Andrew's 3-year-old daughter, Isabel, developed leukemia and died just 8 months later. The couple had coped relatively well during Isabel's illness but have encountered great difficulty since her death. Andrew, a more intuitive griever who expresses his emotions with intensity, felt supported by Michelle initially, relying on her emotional reserve and practical bent to get them through. Increasingly, however, Andrew experiences Michelle as detached and unresponsive to his need to talk through his grief. Michelle, a more instrumental griever, finds resuming work and daily routines more helpful than the emotional intensity of the early days of grief. At times she allows herself to experience the sadness and anger regarding the loss of her child, even sharing those emotions with Andrew, but once shared she needs to do something else (e.g., focus on restoration). Andrew feels Michelle has let him down by not being more emotionally available and wonders about what he sees as Michelle's indifference. The other day Michelle sought a sexual encounter with Andrew, wanting the intimacy for herself and thinking that Andrew would find it comforting as well. She was surprised by Andrew's angry rejection and stung by his accusation of her being unfeeling and cold when he said, "How could you even think about this when Isabel is dead?"

Anupama and her husband, Partha, both immigrated to the United States from India as young children and maintain strong ties with their Indian heritage. Their social network consists primarily of other families of Indian heritage. Anupama's parents and sister have returned to India; Partha's parents and siblings live nearby. The couple is unable to have biological children together owing to Anupama's infertility. The loss of the possibility of biological children is mourned by them individually, as a couple, and within their large, extended family. Anupama's grief is compounded by the rigid gender role expectations of Indian culture: She feels she has failed as a woman, wife, daughter, and daughter-in-law. The couple feels isolated and stigmatized, mourning a sense of place in society that they assumed would be theirs. They struggle with the intrusive presence of Partha's mother, who is distraught over the loss of expected grandchildren and how that impacts her own place and security in society. She pressures her son to divorce his wife, which he resents, especially at this time when they need family support. Anupama's grieving style is to express her emotions and to find solace in talking about her loss with others. Partha's grieving style is more emotionally reserved; he is not inclined to share his grief with others, even with Anupama, preferring to deal with distressful emotions more privately. The dissonance of grieving styles further affects their ability to help each other. Anupama sees Partha's emotional reserve as rejection, and this contributes to her feeling stigmatized. Partha is at a loss about how to deal with Anupama's emotions or reassure her that his reserve is not rejection.

As these examples illustrate, grieving style and process differences may impair family communication and conflict management, impede mutual support, contribute to misinterpretations and cognitive distortions, promote unhelpful family narratives, negatively impact developmental transitions, and discourage postloss reorganization of family structure. The dual process model and adaptive grieving styles approaches are particularly valuable resources in helping families negotiate these differences.

The following are recommendations for addressing differential grief in families. These suggestions draw specifically from the work of Gilbert (1996), Martin and Doka (2000), and Kissane and Bloch (2002).

1. *Help family members understand that loss and grief are experienced differently by each family member, even when a specific loss is shared.* Explain the dual process model and adaptive grieving styles to families, encouraging them to identify how each family member's experience is reflected in these models. This normalizes difference over sameness, encourages acceptance of variations in grieving response, orients family members to grief as individuals, and reduces blame. Exploring diverse grieving styles and the specifics of loss/restoration processes in the family will often reveal problematic issues that can be explored further (e.g., maladaptive thinking, different assumptions and expectations, unhealthy coping behaviors, dissonance, unfinished business, avoidance, communication difficulties, and problems in emotional processing). As discussed in the next chapter, systemic and thematic genograms and loss experience timelines are useful strategies for exploring grieving styles and loss/restoration processes

in the family of origin. The counselor may also ask family members to identify grieving styles and loss/restoration processes in selected movies (i.e., cinematherapy strategy). Recommended movies for this purpose include *In America* (Sheridan, 2002), *In the Bedroom* (T. Field, 2001), *Marvin's Room* (Zaks, 1999), *Moonlight Mile* (Silbering, 2002), and *Ordinary People* (Redford, 1980).

2. *Help family members negotiate differences in grieving style and loss/restoration processes through functional communication, effective problem solving, and conflict resolution.* Perhaps the single most important element for resolving grieving style and process differences in families is effective communication (Gilbert, 1996; Gilbert & Smart, 1992; Rando, 1984). As family members recognize and accept their differences, they are often more amenable to changing dysfunctional communication practices. Improved communication assists families in reorganizing family structure (e.g., roles, rules, alliances, boundaries) to fit postloss circumstances and encourages mutual support during loss adaptation. Essential communication skills include I-statements, remaining in the here and now, active listening, and empathetic responses.

3. *Assist families in recognizing strengths, resources, and abilities in their differences and the value of multiple viewpoints arising from those differences.* The counselor must frame differences in grieving styles as strengths that contribute to family functioning. Assist family members in exploring the various ways of adapting to loss, examining the advantages and disadvantages of grieving styles, and identifying how members can be helpful to each other in light of these styles. Coaching family members through reenactments of problematic interactions during the session is an especially useful tool for this purpose. For example, the counselor working with Andrew and Michelle, described above, can ask Andrew to talk with his wife about their daughter's illness and death, and then assist Michelle in how to respond most helpfully to her husband's desire to express and share emotionally. Counselors should help family members recognize how the strengths of one style can offset the weaknesses of another. For example, the more instrumental griever who uses activity to avoid emotional distress may be assisted by the more intuitive griever partner who is able to help his or her spouse encounter emotional material. Family members can also support each other as they oscillate between loss and restoration processes, recognizing that there is a time for each over the course of their grieving a common loss. The following are some examples of exploratory questions: What is helpful about the way Insoo handles her emotions? What can you learn from Trevor about getting through the day? What can you borrow from each other? How can you be helpful to each other? The counselor can also emphasize complementarity of function contributing to the whole. For example, Martin and Doka (2000) described a family where the mother, a more instrumental griever, arranges for her teenage daughter, a more intuitive griever, to participate in a grief support group. The counselor might encourage a family to design a ritual that would help them mark transition, resolution, or ending—facilitating each member's contribution in a manner that reflects her or his grieving style.

Questions aimed at uncovering unique outcomes or solutions are often effective in helping family members identify strengths and abilities associated with different styles. These questions focus on uncovering what is working or helping:

- Tell me what your dad does that is helpful as you all cope with Aaron's death.
- What is it about your mother's emotional expressiveness that seems to help the family sometimes?
- Tandor, you said you noticed that your brother was better able to get going again, get involved in a daily routine, than the rest of you. What does he do that might be helpful to you and other family members?
- Elena, you told me the family really pulled together in the early days of your grandfather's illness. What was everyone doing that was helpful? What strengths and abilities do you think each of you contribute to this family, especially at this time of grieving?
- Let's imagine that it is 5 years from now and when you look back at this difficult time you recognize there were some things you all did that were helpful. What would those things be?

Chapter 4

Cognitive–Behavioral and Constructivist Strategies for Loss Adaptation

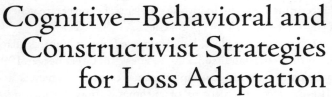

This chapter focuses on counseling strategies that emphasize the centrality of cognitive processes over emotive processes in adaptation to loss. The strategies outlined here derive mainly from traditional cognitive–behavioral therapies (e.g., cognitive therapy, rational emotive behavioral therapy [REBT], schema therapy) and from postmodern constructivist therapies, especially the work of R. A. Neimeyer (2000a, 2000b, 2001a, 2001b; R. A. Neimeyer, Holland, Currier, & Mehta, 2007).

Cognitive–Behavioral Strategies for Loss Adaptation

Cognitive–behavioral therapies, which view emotional and cognitive distress as resulting from and maintained by unhelpful or maladaptive thinking, offer a range of strategies for addressing loss and grief in psychotherapy. Modern cognitive–behavioral therapies focus on altering irrational or maladaptive thoughts, assumptions, and beliefs that impair a functional adaptation to loss. The approach helps people identify and evaluate beliefs as they relate to distressful emotional states and behaviors, consider the origins and sources of those beliefs, then reorganize their thinking to support preferred outcomes. Cognitive–behavioral strategies emphasize self-monitoring; identification of cognitions, emotions, and behaviors and their reciprocal processes; evaluation of the validity of dysfunctional thoughts (e.g., hypothesis testing, disputing, Socratic questioning, guided discovery); and cognitive reconstruction (e.g., developing amended or alternative thinking). A major advantage of cognitive–behavioral strategies is their flexibility and adaptability, allowing the counselor to tailor treatment to the uniqueness of clients and their multiple contexts. Many clients benefit from cognitive–behavioral strategies at one point or another in the therapy process.

It is assumed here that professional counselors who choose to implement cognitive–behavioral strategies are well acquainted with the theoretical approach and basic practices of traditional cognitive–behavioral therapies, including REBT, cognitive–behavioral modification, and cognitive therapy. It is especially important when working with client cognitions to recognize that assumptions and beliefs are strongly influenced by social and cultural experiences. For example, traditional cognitive and cognitive–behavioral approaches tend to emphasize individualistic, Western values of self-sufficiency, personal responsibility, and choice, which may be incongruent with cultural worldviews that value communalism, interdependency, and the influences of external processes (Constantine, Greer, & Kindaichi, 2003). Counselors must respect these influences, consider them in conceptualizing treatment, and collaborate with clients as to the meaning and role of culturally based beliefs, assumptions, and practices in their present situation.

Cognitive–Behavioral Therapy Terminology

Cognitive–behavioral therapies, while sharing a primary cognitive orientation, vary in emphasis, process, techniques, and terminology. The following elements, however, are generally descriptive of the focus of current cognitive–behavioral approaches.

Automatic thoughts are spontaneous ideas, beliefs, images, and memories that flow through people's minds throughout the day (Malkinson, 2007; Padesky & Greenberger, 1995). Automatic thoughts arise from people's underlying assumptions and cognitive schemas and create their emotional reactions. The most common forms of automatic thoughts include all-or-nothing thinking, overgeneralization, mental filter or selective abstraction, catastrophizing or magnification, personalization, labeling, emotion-based reasoning, mind-reading, disqualifying the positive, and should, ought, and must demands (D. Burns, 1999; Malkinson, 2007). Some examples of automatic thoughts include the following: Nothing good ever happens to me; I'll never have an important relationship again; I will never get over this grief; I feel hopeless so things must be hopeless; I cannot handle this; I can't talk about this loss, it is too painful for words; no one needs me anymore; I should be over this by now; I've messed up everything so now I will never get another job; no matter what I do, nothing ever gets better for me. The context, consistency, and consequences of automatic thoughts should be considered carefully in evaluating their functionality; for example, "I can't handle this" or "I can't live without him," expressed in the emotional reactivity of the initial phase of grief, is not necessarily a problematic automatic thought unless it endures and results in certain adverse consequences such as withdrawal or depression.

A belief system is an inclusive term for the cognitions (and their meanings) used by individuals to interpret their experience—that is, what a person thinks. This includes irrational/rational thinking, cognitive schemas, assumptive beliefs, and automatic thoughts.

Cognitive restructuring is the process of amending maladaptive thoughts and replacing them with adaptive thoughts.

Cognitive schemas are the highly personalized core beliefs one holds about self, others, and the world. Maladaptive cognitive schemas are absolute (I am weak), dichotomous (I am totally lovable or totally unlovable), self-perpetuating, and devaluing of self, others, or the world (Malkinson, 2007; Padesky & Greenberger, 1995; J. E. Young, Beck, & Weinberger, 1993). One's cognitive schemas determine what one attends to and what one does not notice. The following are some examples of maladaptive cognitive schemas: I am bad, men are unreliable, the world is dangerous, people will hurt you, the world is always unfair and unjust, I'm worthless, I am powerless to prevent disaster, life is meaningless. In REBT, cognitive schemas are known as "core philosophy." Ellis (1994) described them as "below-the-surface" irrational beliefs (p. 28).

Irrational beliefs are unrealistic, self-defeating, or unreasonable cognitions that lead to problems. The term is identified most strongly with REBT but is often used inclusively to address any maladaptive cognition.

Underlying assumptions are the cross-situational beliefs or rules that guide one's behavior and create one's expectations (Padesky & Greenberger, 1995). They frequently take the form of should, ought, and must demands, make "if, then" conditional statements, and set limits as to distress tolerance. Examples of underlying assumptions commonly encountered in grief counseling include the following: I should have been a better wife; I should not have let him drive that day; I must grieve well; if I don't have the love I want, then I am nothing; life is not worth living without her; I should be able to control my emotions; I deserve this pain because I did not do enough for him; if I love someone, that person will not leave me; if people get to know me, they will find out what a terrible person I really am; if I forget him, then this proves how worthless I am; it is terrible and awful that I should have to endure this; people should behave correctly and should be punished when they do not; I've ruined my children's lives by getting a divorce. Underlying assumptions are seldom expressed out loud or directly, so they must be discovered by tracing back from behavior and emotions. For example, promiscuity or risk-taking behavior following the death of a partner suggests underlying assumptions about self-worth, control, and the meaningfulness of life.

Basic Assumptions of Cognitive–Behavioral Therapies Applied to Loss Adaptation

Grief is a normal and even necessary response to loss. There is, however, a distinction between an emotional response to loss that facilitates healthy loss adaptation and an emotional response to loss that increases and prolongs emotional distress. For example, sadness, sorrow, and pain are functional and normative responses to loss; heightened anxiety, fear, and self-deprecation are dysfunctional emotional responses. The key determinant of this distinction is a person's thinking or belief system (Malkinson, 2007, p. 91). Functional beliefs lead to adaptive emotional and behavioral consequences and to healthy loss adaptation.

Dysfunctional beliefs impair adaptation to loss. Revealed in automatic thoughts, underlying assumptions, and cognitive schemas, dysfunctional beliefs contribute to maladaptive emotional and behavioral consequences. They impair accurate perception; make absolute demands; are devaluing of self, others, and the world; generate negative evaluations (e.g., of grief reactions, for the future); assert low frustration tolerance; and exaggerate or catastrophize circumstances (e.g., awfulizing). The following examples are frequently encountered in loss and grief situations: I can't stand this pain; how dare he leave me like this; I should not have to suffer like this; I deserve the pain for not preventing the loss; I can't stop thinking about her; if I cry I am a weak person; my sadness shows that I am unfaithful; life is not worth living; my life is on hold; I should have done (not done) something; if I think about this loss, I'll go crazy; I'm not handling this loss well; how could this happen (to me)? I'm being punished for my sins; this loss is just another rejection; no one will ever be there for me; I want things to be the way they were.

Beliefs are chosen. In response to loss, people can choose to think in ways that increase or decrease distress. While people generally have no control over the losses that generate grief, they can control how they react and respond in their grieving. In that sense, people choose their consequences.

Secondary symptoms often flow from a client's negative evaluation of his or her reaction to loss. Such "disturbance about the disturbance" takes the form of self-downing messages that reflect the client's core philosophy or personal science and create distressful consequences (Malkinson, 1996, 2007). For example, I am weak for being so overwhelmed; I am bad for feeling angry; I should not be angry at him for dying; it is wrong of me to be so sad because it shows that I lack true faith.

Making meaning of loss is a cognitive endeavor. The experience of loss and grief often challenges the core assumptions, beliefs, and expectations through which a person makes sense of his or her world. Depending on the client and situation, functional loss adaptation is highly likely to involve a process of evaluating and reorganizing those beliefs and assumptions about self, others, the world, and Other (e.g., God). Various cognitive–behavioral strategies can assist clients in this process (e.g., disputing, guided discovery, testing validity). Counselors also provide support when clients cannot discover meaning or make sense of their losses, helping them develop beliefs that allow for this dissonance or ambiguity. For example, "I can't make sense of this right now, and though I don't like it, I can handle it" is more livable than "It is awful that I cannot make sense of this loss and that it will always be meaningless to me."

A collaborative client–counselor relationship is most effective in facilitating loss adaptation. The traditional client–counselor relationship in cognitive–behavioral therapies emphasizes the expertness of the counselor on the client's problems. The counselor identifies underlying assumptions, presents these to the client, then teaches a set of amended beliefs devised largely by the counselor. However, there is more to be gained from adopting a collaborative relationship that honors the expertness of the client on his or her problems and as the "architect of her or his new constructs" (Mooney & Padesky, 2000, p. 151). This calls for altering the traditional counselor's role so that teaching is a matter of facilitating the client's discovery process rather than providing instruction. Client ownership, motivation, and creativity are promoted when the counselor invites clients to lead the way in their own change process.

Grief counseling, from a cognitive–behavioral point of view, assists clients in three ways. This includes (a) revealing the connection between one's beliefs and emotional and behavioral consequences, (b) helping clients identify and evaluate unhelpful or dysfunctional beliefs, and (c) facilitating the development of amended or alternative beliefs that support adaptive grieving.

Implementation of the Cognitive–Behavioral Approach

There are five basic steps in implementing a cognitive–behavioral approach.

Step 1. Collaboratively teach clients that the distressful consequences (or degree of distress) of activating events (e.g., loss) result, to a large degree, from the beliefs they hold about those events rather than from the events themselves.

Step 2. Collaboratively teach clients to identify their beliefs (thoughts, attitudes, self-talk, assumptions, expectations) and the specific emotional, behavioral, and physical consequences of their beliefs.

Step 3. Help clients distinguish between functional (realistic, rational) beliefs that support adaptive grieving and dysfunctional (unrealistic, self-defeating, irrational) beliefs that make for maladaptive grieving.

Step 4. Facilitate evaluating the validity of dysfunctional beliefs (e.g., disputing, Socratic dialogue, hypothesis testing) to support the development of amended or alternative functional beliefs that contribute to adaptive grieving.

Step 5. Support clients in applying amended or alternative functional beliefs, reevaluating their effectiveness, and reconstructing beliefs as necessary.

Using the Cognitive–Behavioral Approach With Loss and Grief

There are some specific concerns and practices relevant to counseling for loss and grief that counselors should consider when implementing a cognitive–behavioral approach.

1. *Encourage a detailed account of the loss and grief experience in the form of telling and retelling the story.* Such exploration gives clues as to the beliefs underlying specific emotional and

PART 2

Counseling Strategies for Loss Adaptation

behavioral consequences, provides information the counselor can use to help the client distinguish between functional and dysfunctional responses, and facilitates cathartic cognitive and emotional expression (Malkinson, 1996). Additionally, the process of telling and retelling the story of loss and grief is critical to the meaning-making process. Investigate the specific circumstances of the current loss, get background information, and identify secondary losses (e.g., loss of relationship, loss of hope, loss of financial security). Remember that the focus of concern is more likely to be a secondary loss rather than the original loss event. For example, a woman who was estranged from her father when he died may grieve the loss of potential reconciliation and future relationship more so than the loss of the current relationship; a divorced man may grieve the loss of an idealized marriage more than the actual relationship itself. In some cases telling and retelling the story is retraumatizing rather than healing, especially for those grieving a loved one's violent death. In this case the counselor should limit retelling about the loss in favor of telling about the grief, keeping the focus on the grieving client rather than allowing too much focus on the lost loved one and the circumstances of the loss. Careful monitoring of client distress is important.

2. *Identify "discomfort anxiety cognitions" that interpret the pain associated with grieving as too distressing, unbearable, or intolerable (Ellis, 1986; Malkinson, 2007).* These usually take the form of absolutist, demanding beliefs. For example: I cannot stand the pain; I cannot think about her because it is too awful; I cannot stand my life without my loved one; life is not worth living without my loved one; since she died, my life is worthless so I don't want to live anymore; nothing can help me. The limits on tolerance of emotional pain set forth in these beliefs, while understandable in the face of many difficult loss circumstances, actually impairs loss adaptation. Use strategies that will challenge the discomfort anxiety cognitions, such as Socratic dialogue, disputing, reframing, and collaborative empiricism

3. *Help clients establish a sense of control to counter being overwhelmed, feeling helpless, or lacking confidence to manage their grief.* Malkinson (2007) recommended thought stopping, cognitive rehearsal, distraction, deep breathing, and creating a dialogue with "why" questions or irrational thoughts.

4. *Pay careful attention to the beliefs that define the grieving client's postloss relationship with a lost object (e.g., the deceased) to determine whether they are consistent with adaptive grieving.* For example, "I must leave him behind and move on" is a *dysfunctional belief* if it invites severance of the relationship and/or avoidance of the pain of grieving. However, this statement is a *functional belief* if it supports acceptance of the reality of permanent loss (e.g., death) while at the same time allowing for a healthy continuing bond. In this case the client might add a clarifying thought, such as "I must leave him behind and move on *knowing he will always be with me in special ways*," to facilitate adaptive grieving.

5. *Detect avoidance behaviors and uncover the beliefs that support them.* Normative grieving involves a natural oscillation over time between a loss focus and a restoration focus that includes some avoidance. However, persistent avoidance of the pain associated with grieving impairs oscillation and is a major complication in loss adaptation (Boelen, 2006; Malkinson, 2007). Avoidance can take several forms. A person might evade conversations, situations, places, or people associated with the loss or that might be reminders of the loss or lost object. This may include, for example, refusing to go by the cemetery, changing the subject in conversation, distancing from friends or family, and

excessively ruminating about grief reactions or why the loss occurred (Boelen, 2006; Malkinson, 2007). Another form of avoidance is allowing or even deliberately seeking out reminders of the lost object so as to deny the reality of the loss and block movement toward restoration. For example, a woman surrounds herself with pictures of her dead child, sets his room up as a living memorial, and talks about him as if he were still alive. Whatever path avoidance takes, clients are operating under the mistaken (irrational, distorted) notion that the pain of loss can be controlled or extinguished through avoidance (Malkinson, 2007). Counselors can help clients face the pain they fear by developing more rational, realistic beliefs that normalize and legitimize the pain and support the client's ability to manage the pain of grieving.

Constructivist Strategies for Loss Adaptation

Postmodern constructivist therapies represent a confluence of psychotherapy traditions, including personal construct psychology, cognitive–behavioral therapies, humanistic–existential psychology, and family systems therapies (Scheer, 2003). Constructivist approaches focus on meaning making—one's interpretations of reality and truth—as the central process of one's life. The meanings people create constitute the beliefs, assumptions, and expectations (meaning structures) through which they view themselves and the world. Loss frequently disrupts those meaning structures, initiating an effort to rebuild, renew, redefine, or reorganize them in a way that make sense. This meaning reconstruction is, according to the R. Neimeyer (2001b), the "central process of grieving" (p. 4).

Constructivism is a major influence on cognitive–behavioral approaches today, challenging the traditional emphasis on correcting "wrong" cognitions by substituting "correct" thoughts, the primacy of the counselor as teacher and guide, the valuing of logic and rationality to the exclusion of intuitive and emotional knowledge, and the preference for an information-processing model (Mahoney, 1993; Malkinson, 2007). Constructivist strategies, especially the constructivist narrative strategies offered in this chapter, emphasize the following:

- a focus on disrupted meanings, deconstruction of meaning, and the reconstruction of meaning
- a therapeutic process focused on client investigation and discovery
- clients, not counselors, as experts on themselves and their experiences
- a collaborative client–counselor relationship
- storytelling or narrative as the primary vehicle for reconstructing meaning
- the value of emotions as important sources and resources, along with cognition, in making meaning
- the influence of sociocultural contexts on meaning reconstruction
- grief as a "personal process, one that is idiosyncratic, intimate, and inextricable from our sense of who we are" (Malkinson, 2007, p. 78)

Further descriptions of constructivist-influenced strategies for loss adaptation are found in Chapter 6, Narrative Therapy Strategies for Loss Adaptation, and Chapter 7, Solution-Focused Therapy Strategies for Loss Adaptation.

Managing Repetitive Thoughts and Ruminative Coping: Three Strategies

Grieving persons sometimes experience being flooded by repetitive thoughts and emotions that are intrusive and distressful. These thoughts and emotions have a runaway, snowball effect that people feel powerless to stop. For example, a woman whose mother recently died has difficulty concentrating on her work because she cannot stop thinking about her mother, aspects of her dying, and the funeral; a man who lost his job cannot stop going over the situation, analyzing and reanalyzing everything in an endless loop that is never productive, never moves toward resolution, and impedes reorienting himself to search for a new job. Unfortunately, these unmanageable repetitive thoughts and emotions further compound the overwhelming sense of loss of control that grieving people often experience, especially in the early phase of loss adaptation. A particularly difficult form of this repetitive thinking is *ruminative coping*, in which grievers focus repetitively on their distress and the meaning and consequences of this distress (not on the loss), for example, "Why do I react this way?" or "I could get a job if I could just snap out of this" (Nolen-Hoeksema, Parker, & Larson, 1994; Stroebe & Schut, 2001a, p. 63).

Three cognitive–behavioral strategies are especially useful in helping clients regain some sense of control in their lives: Refocusing, Thought-Stopping With Refocusing, and Dialogue With a Repetitive Thought. Malkinson (2007) considered these strategies to be an essential part of a "first-aid kit" for grieving persons to help them regain some inner control in the face of the external, uncontrolled experience of loss. Refocusing and Thought-Stopping With Refocusing do not challenge the content of the repetitive thoughts or rumination but instead create distance from the disturbing thoughts. Dialogue With a Repetitive Thought, on the other hand, challenges the repetitive and unproductive "why" question that occurs so often with loss and grief and helps the client search for an answer (Malkinson, 2007).

Refocusing

Refocusing, also called distraction, is simply the act of catching oneself involved in a stream of dysfunctional or distressing thoughts and intentionally redirecting attention to think about or do something else. This interrupts the repetitive inner process by focusing externally on something specific. For example, the client can refocus attention on making a grocery list, singing songs, listening to the radio or iPod, or replaying an activity in slow motion (e.g., baking cookies, throwing a baseball). Attention can also be directed toward noticing and describing colors, smells, shapes, dimensions, and textures in the immediate environment (e.g., cars, buildings, furniture, plants, people, and signs). Refocusing could even involve eavesdropping on a nearby conversation (A. Freeman, Pretzer, Fleming, & Simon, 1990). The idea is to crowd out the repetitive or intrusive thoughts and emotions with other thoughts. Counselors should ask clients what they have been doing to this point to stop the repetitive thinking—they will typically describe Refocusing. In that case, it is a matter of fine-tuning the procedure and encouraging them to "do it more." Additionally, help clients identify other activities that might work best for them in their particular situations. It is useful to caution clients that the technique might not work the first or second time but that practice will raise the probability of success. In-session rehearsal is appropriate.

Thought-Stopping With Refocusing

In Thought-Stopping With Refocusing, the person uses an abrupt, startling action to interrupt the stream of repetitive thoughts or rumination (thought-stopping) and then uses refocusing to switch the thinking in another direction. Usually it is recommended that clients shout "Stop" aloud or to themselves and clap their hands or slap something to dramatically interrupt the stream of thought. This action momentarily stops the stream of thoughts, but refocusing is essential to keep thinking going in a more desirable direction.

Counselors should have clients rehearse Thought-Stopping With Refocusing in-session so that the procedure can be fine-tuned to their particular needs (e.g., alternatives to using the word *stop*). Help clients plan for those circumstances and locations where the repetitive thinking or rumination tends to occur. In-session rehearsal of this strategy enhances motivation. Alternatively, instead of refocusing, clients may prefer switching to a visualization of something pleasant (e.g., walking a beach, watching children play) after the interruptive action to keep their thinking moving in a different direction.

Dialogue With a Repetitive Thought

Sometimes grieving clients experience the difficulty with unproductive, repetitive thoughts centered on "why" or "how could this happen to me" questions. Such questions are in many ways a normal response to loss, generally triggering an examination of beliefs and assumptions disrupted by loss that leads to satisfactory meaning reconstruction. However, in some cases grieving persons can become caught in an endless repetition of "why" questions that never moves toward productive exploration, much less to satisfactory meaning reconstruction. This contributes to the flooding effect of things being uncontrollable (i.e., unanswerable). Malkinson (2007) proposed a Dialogue With a Repetitive Thought to confront the "whys" and, in doing so, enhance a client's sense of control.

In this strategy the counselor encourages clients to stop the cycle of unproductive questioning by entering into dialogue with the repetitive thought—by actually attempting to answer the questions. This interrupts the repetition and redirects clients to the more productive effort of making sense of the loss. There are a number of complicating factors that may appear here. The client may be using the repetitive "why" as a way to avoid the pain of grieving, may be unwilling to question previously held beliefs and assumptions, or may be uncomfortable with the possibility that there is sometimes no satisfactory answer to "why" questions. The counselor continues to work with the client in confronting and working through any of these complicating factors.

Rational Emotive Imagery for Avoidance

Rational Emotive Imagery (REI) is a strategy derived from REBT to help clients change unhealthy or maladaptive emotional reactions into more healthy and adaptive emotional reactions. The strategy involves (a) having clients visualize a disturbing event along with experiencing the unhelpful emotions associated with the event; (b) encouraging clients to push themselves to change or reduce the intensity of those unhelpful emotions; (c) identifying the thinking (beliefs) that allowed them to reduce the emotional intensity; and (d) repeating and practicing the exercise to enhance their skills at changing thinking to modify emotional reactions. *Note.* Counselors must have a solid knowledge of the cognitive therapy and the REBT approach before attempting this procedure.

REI can be used effectively to address a self-defeating pattern of avoidance that may develop following a significant loss. Some avoidance of emotional pain is normative, reflecting the natural oscillation between a loss focus and a restoration focus in the grieving process. However, consistent and excessive avoidance can compromise loss adaptation. Most often this takes the form of avoiding reminders of the loss for fear of experiencing painful emotions. Some examples include not going to movies or visiting the park because these sites are strongly associated with the former spouse or deceased child, not participating in certain social activities or conversing with family or friends because they might mention the deceased, and overrigorous avoidance of any thoughts even remotely connected to the loss or lost object. Malkinson (2007) pointed out that people mistakenly and irrationally believe that avoidance helps them regain control after a loss or that effective grieving means the elimination of pain when, in fact, avoidance creates additional problems (e.g., anxiety, panic attacks, impaired relationships, and work performance). In this case the focus of counseling becomes the secondary symptoms of fear or anxiety (maladaptive emotional reactions) rather than the painful emotions associated with the loss itself (adaptive emotional reactions). For example, the Beliefs–Consequences (B-C) connection for avoidance might look like this:

Client beliefs: I cannot tolerate the pain of thinking about my husband; I will be overwhelmed if I think about my husband; I'll go crazy if I have to remember him.
Consequences of beliefs: anxiety, fear, worry, avoiding the garage where the husband had his tools, avoiding talking to the children for fear they will mention their father, changing the subject whenever anything feels like it might evoke memories, loss of sleep because of fear of dreams and memories.

REI enables clients to recognize the difference between adaptive and maladaptive emotional responses and to alter or control their response to feared painful reminders by modifying their irrational beliefs. Thus the B-C connection for engagement might look like this:

Client adaptive beliefs: This sadness is part of the grieving and, although I would prefer not to experience it, I can tolerate the pain. I miss him but will always have him with me in so many ways. The sadness eases sometimes, if I just face it. I can tolerate this, especially when I share the sorrow with my children. I know that this grief will always be there, but it will ease over time.
Consequences of adaptive beliefs: sadness, sorrow, engagement, participation, growth.

Once clients are successful in modifying their beliefs using the REI procedure, they can then generalize their skills to other problematic experiences.

Implementation of REI

There are three stages in the implementation of REI: preparation, application, and follow-up. The description below is adapted from Malkinson (2007, pp. 115–120).

Preparation
The counseling professional should describe the REI procedure to clients, normalizing anxiety about experiencing painful emotions and reassuring them of their ability to learn to reduce the

intensity of their anxiety and fear. Teach the B-C connection and the 1–10 imaginary scale to measure emotional intensity (where 1 represents *lowest intensity* and 10 represents *highest intensity*). Discuss the clients' readiness to relive a distressful activity or situation. Normalize the fact that the REI procedure is sometimes, but not always, helpful and that further practice is helpful. Finally, discuss any potential obstacles the clients think they might encounter while participating in REI and plan for them.

Application

The actual application of an REI procedure involves six steps. Sample dialogues of counselor directions are provided here for the first four steps.

1. *Build an image.*
   Counselor: Get a vivid image of (e.g., that fear of remembering; that anxiety about having a conversation with your children) . . . then allow yourself to feel the emotions that come from imagining this scene. Try not to avoid them or distract yourself, just let the emotions come; let them upset you. You can choose to open or close your eyes, whatever you want. Nod your head or lift your finger to tell me when you have really got the experience.
2. *Scale the image.*
   Counselor: Think of that 1–10 scale we discussed and tell me where you would rate the intensity of your emotions right now. What number describes how upset you are as you imagine driving past the cemetery? What feelings are you experiencing right now that go with that number?
3. *Reduce image intensity.*
   Counselor: Now concentrate on the emotions and deliberately and intentionally decrease their intensity—make yourself less upset. You're moving that number down. Take as much time as you need to do this and signal me when you think you have been able to reduce the level of emotional upset.
4. *Check in.*
   Counselor: Now, tell me where you rate the intensity of your emotion now. What is the number?
5. *Evaluate client thinking.*
   This step allows the counselor to identify key statements the client can use to manage this problem in the future. There are three possible responses: Clients experience no change, a slight change, or a marked change in the level of emotional intensity. When clients report no change, it is important to find out what they were thinking that prevented change. Malkinson (2007) suggested legitimizing the difficulties encountered and attempting the exercise once again. When clients report only a slight change, this may indicate some bit of success or disappointment that the change is no greater. Again, find out what they were thinking. Reaffirm the positive direction of the change rather than the size of the change. Any change in emotional intensity is examined to ascertain what clients were thinking that facilitated a reduction in the level of emotional intensity (e.g., What did you do or say to yourself that changed the level of upset? What did you say to yourself to lower that number? What made you less tense? What helped? What's the difference between the thoughts that increased emotional upset and those that reduced it?). The counselor helps clients examine the success of their thinking (beliefs) in changing emotional intensity.

6. *Repeat the activity.*

   This step underscores the effectiveness of clients' skills in reducing emotional upset by changing their thinking, emphasizing the B-C connection of REBT, and enhancing the clients' sense of control.

   Follow-Up

Clients are then encouraged to practice the exercise at home, continuing to refine skills at changing thinking (beliefs) to reduce emotional intensity. These efforts should be discussed further in therapy. The counselor can then work with clients to generalize learning to other situations.

REI Combined With In Vivo Exposure

In some cases REI can be combined with in vivo exposure to specific situations. For example, Malkinson (2007) described the treatment of a bereaved mother who avoided driving near the cemetery where her child was buried. An REI procedure and practice was used first to help her modify and manage her anxiety about feeling painful memories, and then gradual exposure was added. First, the client had her husband drive her past the avoided route while she utilized the rational self-statements developed during REI procedure. Later, this client drove herself near the cemetery and was able to further generalize her experience to manage other situations that might evoke painful memories of her child.

Summary Considerations When Using REI

- ✦ The counselor should keep a slow and deliberate pace, adjusting for each client's particular modes of experience and expression. Some clients think before speaking, whereas others express their thinking immediately.
- ✦ It is appropriate to caution clients not to attempt to change the image itself to reduce emotional intensity, because the focus is on changing their responses. Also caution clients not to force a specific emotion or try to feel what they think they should feel. Rather, encourage clients to let the emotions flow spontaneously from the experience (Bernard & Wolfe, 1993).
- ✦ It is helpful to write down client self-statements emerging from REI because they form the basis of future practice. Copies may be made for the client to take home as part of homework rehearsals.
- ✦ Counselors should monitor clients closely during this exercise, especially breathing and pace, and verbally check in with the client throughout.

Telling and Retelling the Story of Obscured Loss

Clients who present with longstanding, unaddressed losses (obscured loss) benefit from a detailed examination of their loss experience with attention to contributing dysfunctional beliefs and efforts at meaning reconstruction. Often such loss experiences involve a long struggle with dissonance between preloss assumptions and beliefs and postloss realities, avoidance of distressing emotions and thoughts, and a failure of the natural oscillation process between loss orientation and restoration orientation.

The strategy of Telling and Retelling the Story of Obscured Loss described here is adapted from the work of K. S. Calhoun and Resick (1993) in treating survivors of sexual assault. Calhoun and Resick's cognitive processing therapy focuses on directly confronting dysfunctional beliefs and conflicts by way of client memories of the assault using written accounts. Telling and Retelling the Story of Obscured Loss builds on the same components: Facilitate a detailed remembrance of loss situations and use that remembrance to reveal, challenge, and alter maladaptive beliefs. In this strategy clients write about their loss experiences, share these written stories in the therapy session, examine their stories for dysfunctional beliefs and dissonance of meaning, challenge the dysfunctional beliefs, develop amended or alternative beliefs, then rewrite their stories to include the more functional beliefs that promote adaptive grieving. This method provides for gradual exposure and reexposure to distressful material that might previously have been avoided and builds on the natural tendency to tell and retell stories of loss and grieving.

Implementation of Telling and Retelling the Story of Loss

Because this strategy requires that clients write about their loss experiences, it is not appropriate for people who cannot read and write, have difficulty with reading and writing, or are not open to written expression. Counselors and clients must collaborate in adapting this strategy to allow clients who are more comfortable writing in their native tongue to do so and to arrange for translation. Because clients may write about distressful and possibly intense emotional material on the homework portions, it is important that counselors carefully assess client coping skills and resources before proceeding with this strategy. Do not attempt to implement this strategy if clients do not have sufficient skills to handle emotionally charged material on their own. Continual assessment of client distress and coping skills is appropriate.

The implementation outlined here is recommended because each step builds on the skills learned in the preceding step. However, counselors may find that more than one session is necessary for each step and should adapt their approach accordingly.

First Session

In the first session the counselor explains the procedures and the approach, emphasizing the reading/writing component, the role of remembrance, the likelihood of emotional experiencing, and the focus on changing dysfunctional beliefs. Ask clients for a commitment to the entire process. Establish plans for coping with uncomfortable material when the client is not in session. Give Assignment 1 in written form and go over it in the session to be sure the client understands.

> *Assignment 1.* Before beginning, establish a time and place where you can fulfill this assignment without interruption and where you will feel comfortable experiencing your emotions. It is strongly recommended that you complete this assignment as soon as possible after today's therapy session. Your assignment has two parts. *Part 1: Write at least one page on what this loss means to you.* Consider the effect this loss has had on your beliefs about yourself, about others, and about the world as well as its impact on your spiritual or religious beliefs. Include some reference to the following topics: self-identity, life purpose, emotions, control, relationships, connections, balance. *Part 2: After you finish writing this account, read it aloud to yourself once a day every day until the next therapy session.*

Second Session

First, counseling professionals should explore clients' experiences by asking, What was it like doing this assignment? Second, invite clients to read their completed assignment aloud. Third, after clients have read the account aloud, ask for their here-and-now feelings and work from there to help them identify and label their emotions, discern the cognitions that create those feelings, and recognize the connection between thinking and feeling. Identify and do some initial exploration of any dysfunctional beliefs but do not move to challenge them yet. Fourth, explore the meaning clients have discovered or, in some cases, the meaning they did not discover. This often takes the form of "why" questions. Listen carefully for stuck places and clarify them but do not move to challenge them at this point. Finally, give Assignment 2 in written form and the A-B-C form (see Figure 4.1) and go over the assignment in the session to be sure the client understands what is required.

Assignment 2. What's going on in your head? Use the A-B-C form to describe your primary and secondary losses, what you have been telling yourself about those losses, and the emotional, behavioral, and physical consequences of those thoughts. Begin this record as soon as possible and work on it at least once daily until the next therapy session.

Third Session

Go over the completed A-B-C form from Assignment 2, underscoring the connection between thinking and consequences and helping clients distinguish functional from dysfunctional beliefs. The focus here is on making certain clients can identify their thinking, feeling, and behavior and understand the correlation between these dimensions. Do not challenge the beliefs yet. Listen

Activating Losses	Belief Directed at the Loss	Consequences
Briefly state your primary loss and all the secondary losses (losses that resulted from the primary loss). For example, loss of childhood, loss of identity, loss of security, loss of hope.	What have you been telling yourself about these losses? Include what you told yourself at the time you became aware of the primary loss.	What feelings and behavior connected with these losses and these thoughts have you experienced? What physical reactions? What did you do or avoid doing?

FIGURE 4.1

A-B-C Form

carefully for automatic thoughts, underlying assumptions, and cognitive schemas. Finally, give Assignment 3 in written form and go over it in the session so that the client understands.

Assignment 3. Tell the story of loss. Before beginning, establish a time and place where you can fulfill this assignment without interruption and where you will feel comfortable experiencing your emotions. It is strongly recommended that you complete this assignment as soon as possible after today's therapy session. *Your assignment is to tell the story of your loss.* Start your account wherever it makes sense to do so (e.g., when you first became aware that a loss would occur or when you were notified of the loss) and bring it forward to today. Tell the story in detail, including information about what you were thinking, feeling, doing, and experiencing physically. Include information about people, places, and things involved in the loss and clearly describe your own experience. Try to write this entire account at one sitting. If you are unable to do so, draw a line where you stopped and pick up at that place when you return to it. If you cannot remember something, draw a line and keep writing. When you have finished this story of your loss, read the account aloud to yourself every day until the next therapy session.

Fourth Session

In this session, the counselor asks clients to read their story aloud. When the client is finished, ask what he or she is feeling, what it was like to do this assignment, and what it is like to read it aloud. From there the counselor helps clients explore their account with special attention to stuck points, dysfunctional beliefs, patterns, and problems with meaning making. Emphasize again the connection between thinking, feeling, and behavior. Do not challenge dysfunctional beliefs but support any challenging initiated by the client. Carefully assess client distress levels and coping skills. Give clients Assignment 4 in written form.

Assignment 4. Your assignment is to write the story of your loss again. Add any information you might have left out of the first account you wrote. Also add any new thoughts and feelings you have, indicating those in parentheses, underlined, or in a different color ink. Again, try to do this in one sitting. When you have finished writing this second account of your loss, read it aloud to yourself every day until the next session.

Fifth Session

Begin by asking what it was like to write the story of the clients' loss a second time. Then have clients read this second account aloud. Explore any new information and note any problematic areas. Work collaboratively with clients to make a list of the dysfunctional beliefs that emerged from the writing and rewriting. (Note: sometimes clients are more receptive to calling their beliefs unrealistic, self-defeating, or unhelpful than calling them irrational or dysfunctional.) At this point begin helping clients challenge their dysfunctional beliefs using preferred cognitive–behavioral methods (e.g., disputing, Socratic questions, guided discovery, hypothesis testing). Help clients develop amended or alternative beliefs that will support functional loss adaptation. Challenging dysfunctional beliefs and developing alternative or amended beliefs may take several sessions. When the counselor believes the client has made sufficient progress in challenging dysfunctional beliefs and developing amended or alternative beliefs that support functional grieving, give Assignment 5 in written form.

Assignment 5. This assignment is a repeat of your first assignment but with the benefit of the hard work you have done since that time. *Part 1: Write at least one page on what this loss means to you.* Consider the effect this loss has had on your beliefs about yourself, about others, and about the world as well as its impact on your spiritual or religious beliefs. Include some reference to the following topics: self-identity, life purpose, emotions, control, relationships, connections, balance. *Part 2: After you finish writing this statement read it aloud to yourself once a day every day until the next therapy session.*

Sixth Session

First, explore the experience by asking clients what it was like to write again about the meaning of their loss or losses. Then ask them to read their account aloud. Help clients explore differences and similarities between Assignment 1 and Assignment 5. Continue to support amended or alternative beliefs that assist clients in making meaning and in functional loss adaptation.

Responsibility Pies and Defense Attorneys Meet Shame and Guilt

Problems associated with guilt (e.g., I did/did not do something that I should/should not have done) and shame (e.g., I am defective, bad, unstable, worthless) are commonly encountered in grief therapy. They are often the source of avoidance and self-punishing behaviors. Clients struggling with shame and guilt often overestimate their personal responsibility for some situation, especially when there are elements that were beyond their control, as is often the case with loss (e.g., sexual abuse, divorce, accidental death, adoption). A careful, objective examination of the circumstances yields a more accurate appraisal of their actual degree of responsibility. This provides the possibility of a shift in perspective that may reduce guilt and shame feelings that are out of proportion to the circumstance. Two strategies for addressing shame and guilt issues are offered here: Responsibility Pie and Defense Attorney. Counselors must be cognizant of the strong influence of culture in determining guilt and shame experiences, especially ethnic background, gender, and spiritual/religious background. This is especially important when working cross-culturally.

Implementation of Responsibility Pie

Step 1. Explore the seriousness of the situation that evokes shame/guilt. The counselor helps clients examine the specific negative event for which they feel responsible and the degree of shame and guilt they attach to the event. Greenberger and Padesky (1995) suggested the following questions:

Do other people consider this experience as seriously as I do? Do some people consider it less serious? Why? How serious would I consider the experience if my best friend was responsible instead of me? How important will this experience seem in one month? One year? Five years? . . . Did I know ahead of time the meaning and consequences of my actions and thoughts? . . . Can any damage that occurred be corrected? How long will such corrections take? (p. 201)

Step 2. Construct a Responsibility Pie. After the seriousness of actions or thoughts have been evaluated, the counselor helps clients consider how much responsibility for actions and thoughts lies solely with them and how much may lie with others. This involves hand drawing a figure, the

Responsibility Pie (see Figure 4.2). Using paper and pencil or whiteboard/poster paper, the clients list all of the people and circumstances (e.g., racism, teacher) that they view as contributing to the outcome of the situation, including themselves. Then the clients draw a large circle or "pie" and, beginning at the top of the list, divide the pie into slices according to the degree of responsibility that each person or circumstance has for the situation. Bigger slices reflect more responsibility and smaller pieces reflect less responsibility. Clients may also be asked to assign a percentage of responsibility for each entity. Erasing and redrawing lines is common here.

Step 3. Weigh personal responsibility. Once the Responsibility Pie is constructed, the counselor asks the client to examine the pie more carefully to see where true responsibility lies. Questions might include: Where does responsibility lie? What do you make of the fact that you are not 100% responsible? What is the impact of this recognition on your feelings of guilt and shame? (Greenberger & Padesky, 1995, p. 205).

It may be helpful to have clients do Responsibility Pies for multiple situations across a lifetime, because different experiences have reinforced maladaptive schemas. The strong visual representation and careful examination involved in constructing a Responsibility Pie facilitates a more realistic appraisal of personal responsibility, contributing to the reduction of shame and guilt feelings.

Self-forgiveness. After thoughtful examinations of situations that generate shame and guilt using a Responsibility Pie, some clients may decide that they do, indeed, bear personal responsibility for doing something wrong (i.e., sins of omission or commission). The issue now becomes one of self-forgiveness. Building on discussions from the previous steps, the counselor helps clients consider their mistakes or "wrong" actions in terms of errors of judgment, perspective, or meaning rather than as evidence of personal defectiveness. For example, a woman who

People/things responsible for *losing my job:*

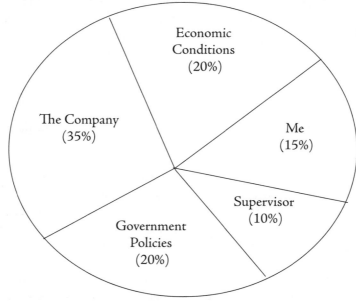

FIGURE 4.2

The Responsibility Pie

considers having had an affair in the context of immaturity, difficulty with relational closeness and distance, poor judgment, and transgression of personal values is more able to accept responsibility, forgive herself, and move on with her life than a woman who sees the affair as evidence of her unchangeable "bad character," which precludes self-forgiveness. Self-forgiveness may also involve making amends or seeking the forgiveness of one's community. The counselor can assist clients in planning for these circumstances and accessing resources that might assist them (e.g., contacting community leaders).

Implementation of Defense Attorney

Leahy and Holland (2000, p. 308) suggested directing the client to "Imagine you have hired yourself as a defense attorney whose job it is to defend YOU. Write out the strongest case you can in favor of yourself, even if you don't believe it much now." This works well as a homework assignment that the client reads aloud in the therapy session. The counselor should encourage the client to play up the defense attorney role during the reading. This "defense" can then be discussed with attention to more objectively appraising responsibility. As an alternative, some clients may prefer making an "oral argument" to writing this assignment.

Loss Experiences Timeline

The Loss Experiences Timeline is a written record of loss events and responses to loss experienced by a client over the course of his or her life. The timeline facilitates both assessment and exploration of multiple variables related to the client's unique history of loss and loss adaptation. Initially prepared by the client as a homework assignment, events and experiences on the timeline are then examined in more depth during therapy sessions. When reviewing a Loss Experiences Timeline, counselors should make special note of the following: cognitive, emotional, and behavioral responses to loss; themes and patterns; lifestyle changes; familial behavior and influences; cultural/social influences; unaddressed or ungrieved losses; dissonance; unfinished business; disrupted meaning constructs and efforts at meaning reconstruction; grieving styles; communication rules; oscillation between loss and restoration processes; developmental factors; exceptions and unique outcomes; different types of loss and grief (e.g., disenfranchised grief, ambiguous loss, sudden loss, multiple losses); primary and secondary loses; concurrent problems; and evidence of client resiliency (e.g., client strengths, resources, and abilities).

Implementation of Loss Experiences Timeline

The recommended approach is to have clients first construct their Loss Experiences Timeline as a homework assignment following written instructions and a form provided by the counselor (see Box 4.1 and Figure 4.3). Alternatively, this initial construction can be done within the therapy session. It is helpful to make a copy of the original completed form and work from copies in session. This allows both client and counselor to make notations, additions, and subtractions or to underline things.

Begin discussion of the completed timeline with the following questions:

- What was it like to construct the Loss Experiences Timeline?
- What feelings came up while you were working on the Loss Experiences Timeline?
- As you worked on your Loss Experiences Timeline, what caught your attention or was especially interesting?

+ Did anything bother you as you review the timeline and, if so, what bothered you?
+ When you look back over your timeline, what things are encouraging or give you hope?
+ What did you notice that you had not noticed before about your life and your loss experiences?

BOX 4.1

Client Instructions for Preparing a Loss Experiences Timeline

---

Step 1: Make a rough timeline of your life

You will need some paper and a pencil. You might use legal size paper but standard notebook paper is OK. Using a pencil allows you to rearrange/erase material easily. Some people find it helpful to do this on the computer.

First, draw a line across a piece of paper lengthwise and label the far left end as "Birth" and the far right end as "Today." Add corresponding dates. This is a timeline of your life.

Think back over your life, noting events and experiences that stand out for you. Insert a mark at the appropriate place on your timeline for each event. Typical markers might include places you lived or people you lived with, jobs, education/school information, and transitional or notable events (e.g., illness, grandfather's death, immigration, military service, birth of a child, first drug use, mother's remarriage, first communion, an injury, an accomplishment, or a move). Label each marker *above the line* and include your date and age. These markers will help you visualize your life's story.

Birth   Today

Using the markers as reference points, recall any events involving loss (death-related and nondeath-related) that occurred and note them on the timeline *below the line*. Go back as far as you can. Include any kind of event in which you experienced loss, *even those that might seem insignificant*; for example, friendship loss; divorce; illness/injury; sister leaving home; lost my doll; sexual/emotional abuse; death of a family member, neighbor, or pet; loss of a prized possession. Describe these events on your timeline with just a few words and include your approximate age. When you have finished go back over your timeline and see if you remember other loss events or need to rearrange things.

Step 2: Explore your unique history of loss

Next you will complete the Loss Experiences Timeline form (see Figure 4.3) using the life timeline you already completed as a reference. List the loss events you remembered in chronological order in the first column along with your approximate age when this experience occurred. Then, answer the questions in the remaining columns. Take your time. Be very honest with yourself and be open to this experience. There is no right or wrong way to do this exercise, so just let things come to you.

Take both your life timeline and your completed Loss Experiences Timeline to your next therapy session. You and your counselor will use it as a basis for discussion.

Loss Experiences Timeline for: _____   **Date:** _____

What loss did you experience and how old were you?	What thoughts and feelings did you experience?	How did you cope at the time?	Who was involved in this experience and how were they involved?	What message did you get about this loss and about grieving?	What impact do you think this loss had on you at the time?	How do you view this loss and its meaning or impact today?
Lost Big Bird doll—5 years old	Angry, upset, betrayed, confused.	Tantrums.	Mom was upset with me and wouldn't go look for it. Then, she gave me another one.	Important things can be replaced.	Not much.	Insignificant.
Grandpa B died—8 years old	Sad, lonely.	Cried, talked about it with Mom.	Mom listened to me and reassured me, but I still felt lonely.	Old people get sick and die.	Felt huge at the time because so many changes happened after that.	Beginning of bad times for us—life would have been better if he had not died.
Dad left and Mom started drinking—9 years old	Abandoned, angry, lonely, confused, and resentful. Sometimes stuffed my anger, sometimes not. My fault my Dad left.	Stayed away and avoided Mom; acted out at school.	No one was there for me; I was absolutely alone.	You cannot count on anyone to be there for you; don't expect anyone to stay; bury your feelings.	Began distancing myself from others. Blamed myself for Dad leaving and life turning to crap.	Have problems with intimacy because I don't trust that anyone I care about will stay around.
Foster placement (lost my family)—10 years old	Rejected, disconnected, angry, sad, and hurt.	Kept my distance; acted out in community; picked fights with foster parents.	Foster parents yelled and disciplined but didn't care; social worker too busy to notice.	No one will be there for you or understand; keep your distance; keep true feelings to yourself.	More distance from others; felt betrayed by Mom's drinking and giving me to foster care.	Same as above.
Mother started drinking again, went to live with uncle and aunt—12 years old	Angry, resentful, disappointed; don't expect much of others.	Distanced myself, busy with school and jobs.	Mom let me down; aunt and uncle tried to love me.	Don't know.	Further distancing from people; even people who loved me.	Don't trust anyone.

FIGURE 4.3

Loss Experiences Timeline

After exploration of the client's responses to these questions, each loss experience noted on the timeline should be discussed individually, preferably in chronological order so as to maintain a developmental perspective.

The Loss Experiences Timeline can be referred to periodically during therapy. Clients often recall loss experiences that they missed when first completing the timeline, so these can be added and discussed further. The timeline can also be paired with therapeutic writing assignments or creation of thematic genograms (discussed below).

This is a flexible strategy that can be incorporated into diverse theoretical approaches and allows the counselor to tailor the intervention to the uniqueness of the clients and their experience. Timelines can be used in family therapy and group therapy. Family members can share their individual timelines with the family, and the family can compose a family timeline either as homework or within the session. Individual timelines can be shared with group members. Counselors must make certain that clients have sufficient skills and resources to cope with any distressing emotions that may arise during the preparation of the Loss Experiences Timeline. Suggesting a time limit on timeline preparation (e.g., 1 hour in one sitting) may enhance motivation for some reluctant clients (James & Cherry, 1988).

Systemic and Thematic Genograms With Loss and Grief

Genograms, a graphic representation of a person's immediate and extended family/social system, are a familiar tool in any professional counselor's repertoire. Originally devised by family therapists in the Bowen family therapy tradition, genograms are now widely used by counseling professionals from diverse approaches, in many different ways, and with endless variations (DeMaria, Weeks, & Hof, 1999; Hardy & Laszloffy, 1995; Kaslow, 1995; Kuehl, 1995; Magnuson & Shaw, 2003; McGoldrick, Gerson, & Shellenberger, 1999). Genograms are useful tools both for assessment and for intervention, allowing the counselor to tailor treatment to clients and their unique needs. They can be used in individual, couple, and family therapy settings. Genograms help to locate loss and the impact of grief in the larger context of family, social network, community, culture, and time; clarify relational patterns, roles, and rules as they interact with the experience of loss and grief; expose unresolved and/or disenfranchised grief; facilitate meaning reconstruction; highlight dissonance in loss adaptation; and reveal cognitive, emotional, and behavioral patterns that assist or undermine loss adaptation. Two types of genograms are described here: Systemic Genograms focus on intergenerational family patterns, how these patterns are transmitted across generations, and their impact on individual and family functioning; Thematic Genograms focus on specific topics (e.g., grief, anger) within the broader context of the family of origin.

When constructing systemic and thematic genograms, the counselor attends especially to various loss events and experiences, soliciting information, reflection, and speculation on these circumstances and their impact on the family. Dates or approximate dates for loss events are useful in tracking the intergenerational impact of loss. Counselors pay particular attention to the secondary losses that flow from primary losses. Types of loss events frequently noted on genograms include those that are defined by loss and those in which loss is a primary component (e.g., sexual abuse), such as the following:

+ Abandonment: spouse, parent, other family members, caretakers, significant others
+ Disappearances: pets, runaways, kidnapping, war/civil unrest
+ Deaths: family members, significant others, pets, perinatal

+ Miscarriage, infertility, and adoption
+ Loss of status: social, economic, religious, vocation/career, cultural
+ Migrations: refugee, immigration, regional/historical movements
+ Relocations: shelter, housing and neighborhood changes
+ Separations: military service, job-related, imprisonment, hospitalization, institutionalization
+ Employment loss, retirement
+ Loss through natural disasters: floods, hurricanes, tornados
+ Child welfare removal and placement, foster care
+ Health-related losses: chronic illness or impairment
+ Abuse: physical, emotional, sexual
+ Addictions: gambling, drugs and alcohol, Internet, compulsive sexual behavior
+ Financial losses, bankruptcy
+ Loss of possessions, homelessness
+ Relationship loss: divorce, separation, estrangement, emotional cutoff, breakup (romantic, friendship, peers, mentors)
+ Cultural loss: loss of cultural memory, history, language, self-rule, resources, traditions; involuntary relocation; migration (Stamm, Stamm, Hudnall, & Higson-Smith, 2003)
+ Lifecycle transitions (family and individual): leaving home, beginning school, retirement
+ Ability/capacity loss: Alzheimer's disease, developmental impairment
+ Spiritual/religious/faith loss, especially changes in affiliation or cessation of accustomed practices
+ Symbolic and fantasy losses (e.g., fantasy that divorced parents will reunite)
+ Loss of expectations and assumptions (e.g., life will unfold in certain ways; I will always live in my native land; colleagues are trustworthy; good things will happen to me)

Systemic Genograms

As stated previously, Systemic Genograms focus on intergenerational family patterns as they are transmitted across generations. Typically, the counselor and client first construct a basic two- or three-generation genogram to include factual information (e.g., identification of family members, relationships, events, dates, cultural and ethnic background, and health, education, and employment information). During genogram construction, special attention is paid to interactional patterns (e.g., distance and closeness, boundaries, triangles, conflict, cutoff) that are noted using prescribed symbols. The counselor uses circular and reflexive questions to identify and track family processes, promote reflection, and encourage realignment of family dynamics. Details on the construction and use of Systemic Genograms should be familiar to all professional counselors and are beyond the purposes of this text. However, the following recommendations concerning loss and grief should be considered when using Systemic Genograms.

+ Maintain a multigenerational perspective, noting that loss often reverberates across the generations.
+ Include quasi-kin relationships in the genogram.
+ Note how loss contributes to raising anxiety in the family system, invoking emotional reactivity.

- Note the impact of loss on family homeostasis.
- Note levels of differentiation of self in the family and the impact of loss on differentiation.
- Track the timing of loss events as they contribute to anxiety and affect family functioning. Problems sometimes occur in reaction to loss or loss may bring longstanding difficulties to a head.
- Note losses in the context of family development and the impact the losses have across the family's lifecycle, especially transitional periods.
- Note the impact of loss on family structure, organization, and leadership functions, especially family roles, rules, boundaries, and alliances. Watch especially for rigidity in roles and rules following loss.
- Compare the preloss and postloss functioning of the family system.
- Note emotional cutoffs, enmeshment, and distancing as complicating factors for grieving families.
- Look for the connection between loss experiences and the emergence of symptoms.
- Recognize that recent losses often activate or reactivate grief from previous losses. It may be most effective to work on previous losses before moving to current losses.
- Identify previously established grieving patterns and their consistency/inconsistency with current behavior.
- Note evidence of any "replacement children" (a child identified closely with a deceased family member).
- Note evidence of family projection process (parental anxiety/problems transmitted to a child) and possible connections with loss and loss adaptation.
- Note evidence of dissonance and how family members respond to dissonance.
- Note the occurrence and impact of ambiguous grief, disenfranchised grief, and stigmatized loss.
- Note myths and secrets that may surround loss events and how these myths and secrets, or decisions made around them, continue to impact the generations.
- Identify adaptive grieving styles and evidence of loss/restoration processes and the impact of these elements on family dynamics (see Chapter 3).
- Note cultural influences (e.g., ethnicity, class, gender, sexual orientation) as they affect family dynamics.
- Note family communication and how this affects the family's adaptation to loss.
- Note rituals or the absence of rituals with deaths (e.g., funerals, memorials) and what that may reveal about family dynamics.

Thematic Genograms

Thematic Genograms, adapted here from the "focused genograms" described by DeMaria et al. (1999), are used to investigate specific issues or topics within the broader context of the family of origin. Unlike Systemic Genograms, Thematic Genograms are not limited to a family systems approach or even to family functioning. Rather, they are adaptable across various theoretical views and can be used in individual and family counseling. Thus, a Thematic Genogram on anger might focus primarily on cognitive distortions and schemas, emotion regulation, cultural and social influences, meaning reconstruction, or some combination of these approaches. The counselor chooses themes according to the unique needs of clients and client families. Common themes when working with loss adaptation include loss events and grieving experiences, addictions, spiritual/religious orientation, attachment, cultural influences (e.g., ethnicity, gender), and specific emotions (e.g., anger, guilt).

Thematic Genograms lend themselves especially to identifying examples of competence and strength, locating inspirational models, and revealing solutions in the families of origin that clients can apply to their own lives. For example, a Thematic Genogram focused on loss events may reveal that great grandmother Mattie, abandoned by her husband and with six children in tow, migrated from Oklahoma to a homestead in rural Idaho at the turn of the century. Helping the client reflect on Mattie's experience and identify the personal traits she might have possessed in dealing with her losses can be meaningful as the client confronts her own losses. A Thematic Genogram focused on emotions might reveal grandparents who, under difficult conditions, demonstrated excellent emotion regulation skills that could serve as a model for their descendents. A Thematic Genogram focused on spirituality/religion in the family of origin might reveal beliefs and practices that are helpful as well as those that might be damaging, providing information that grieving clients might consider regarding their own particular situation.

Thematic Genograms can be used in both individual and family counseling. The basic two- or three-generational genogram is constructed first. Then clients explore the genogram guided by a set of questions developed by the counselor to address the selected themes. The questions may be given as homework, they may be used just within the counseling session, or there may be some combination of these approaches. The initial questions should focus on factual information and then move toward questions that encourage reflection, speculation, and exploration. It is important to include questions that help the client identify functionality, strength, solutions, and competence, not just dysfunction or maladjustment. Suggested questions for frequently encountered themes when working with loss and loss adaptation are offered below. Note that some questions may appear similar but their intent is to encourage elaboration. Counselors should develop questions specific to the needs of their clients rather than just following the suggested questions, but these illustrate the basic design of Thematic Genogram questions.

Loss/Grief Thematic Genogram

This Thematic Genogram is useful for both individual and family counseling focused on loss/grief issues. In preparing clients for a loss/grief Thematic Genogram, the counselor should explain the different kinds of loss events, including the distinction between primary losses (e.g., death, divorce, chronic illness) and secondary losses (e.g., loss of financial security, loss of future, loss of companionship, loss of ability). It is sometimes useful to have clients answer the first question (below) as homework with the genogram and then work through the other questions during the counseling session.

1. What primary losses have occurred for various members in your family of origin? What secondary losses might have accompanied these primary losses?
2. Are there losses that appear to be unnoticed or unrecognized within the family? What has been the impact of that lack of recognition?
3. What was the impact of these various losses on individuals and family members most involved?
4. How did individuals and family members grieve the different loss events? What differences occurred in how members grieved? Were there conflicts over the different ways in which members grieved?

5. Are there any loss events that are clouded by secrets, myths, or misinformation? What has been the impact of this clouding or mythmaking?

6. In dealing with loss and grief, what emotions were experienced and/or expressed by family members? In what specific ways did members manage their grief emotions (e.g., anger, withdrawal, sadness, distraction with work, substance use)?

7. Who seemed to manage their grief especially well? In what ways did they manage their grief well?

8. Who seemed to manage their grief poorly? In what ways did they manage their grief poorly?

9. What assumptions and beliefs did family members have about grieving (e.g., lose yourself in it, ignore it, suck it up, lean on your faith)?

10. In what ways did family members give or fail to give support during grief? What was the impact of giving or failing to give support?

11. How did various cultural factors influence grieving? Consider especially the influences of gender roles, ethnicity, and cultural background. In what ways were these influences helpful or harmful?

12. What stories have emerged around various loss events and what meaning do you draw from these stories?

13. What do you think has been the impact of various losses across the generations of your family?

14. What inner resources and strengths have family members brought to their loss experiences and how can those be helpful to you in your grieving?

15. What do you think has been the influence of various losses and ways of grieving in your family of origin on you today?

16. What models for grieving do you see in your family of origin and how can you use them as inspiration in your own life? What models do you *not* want to follow?

Spirituality/Religious Orientation and Loss Thematic Genogram

It is important to clarify the meanings of spirituality and religious affiliation when preparing these genograms. Frame (2003) suggested that *spirituality* "includes one's values, beliefs, mission, awareness, subjectivity, experience, sense of purpose and direction, and a kind of striving toward something greater than oneself. It may or may not include a deity" (p. 3). *Religion*, on the other hand, can be defined as "a particular set of beliefs, practices, and rituals that have been developed in community by people who share similar existential experiences of transcendent reality" (Hodge, 2001, p. 36). The following questions, adapted from Frame (2001, p. 111) and Hodge (2001, pp. 42–43), are helpful in preparing a spirituality/religious orientation genogram:

1. What types of religious affiliations (e.g., denomination, house of worship, tradition) characterize different members of your family of origin going back through the generations?

2. How have members of your family of origin expressed and practiced their spiritual and religious beliefs? For example, what rituals, traditions, activities, or sayings do you recall as evidence of their spiritual and religious beliefs?

3. How meaningful were family members' relationships with their religious affiliation?

4. In what ways did family members' personal beliefs match or stand in conflict with their religious affiliation or the affiliation of other family members or their community?

5. What spiritually or religiously significant events (e.g., transitions, conversions, affiliations, estrangements, and encounters) have occurred in your family? What was their impact on the individuals involved and on your family?
6. What are the differences and similarities among various family members in their beliefs and practices? How were those differences managed?
7. Who were the spiritual leaders in your family and in what ways did they lead? What do you think has been the impact on the family and on you?
8. How did the spiritual or religious beliefs and practices of family members help them cope with or fail to cope with difficulties?
9. What role did religion/spirituality play in your life when you were growing up and what role does it play, if any, now?
10. What specific religious/spiritual beliefs are important for you now? How are these beliefs a source of connection or conflict between you and members of your family of origin?
11. How do you think the spiritual/religious orientation of individuals in your family of origin influenced their responses to loss and their manner of grieving? What can you learn from their responses?
12. What spiritual/religious beliefs and practices from your family of origin do you find helpful/unhelpful as you adapt to your own losses? What spiritual/religious beliefs and practices of your own are most helpful to you as you adapt to your own losses?
13. What spiritual strengths in your family's history can you draw on to help you deal with your present situation? What insights can you draw from your spiritual genogram that might help you to address your current difficulties?

Anger and Loss/Grief Thematic Genogram

It is often helpful to track particular emotions across generations of a client's family of origin. Counselors should pay particular attention not only to which emotions occur but also to emotion management skills. The first question might be assigned as homework, then the other questions posed within the counseling session.

1. Consider how anger was experienced or expressed in your family, especially among your parents and any siblings. Write down two or three words to describe how each of them handled anger (e.g., withdrawal, lashing out, rarely showed anger). Describe yourself as well.
2. What rules existed in your family regarding feeling anger or displaying anger (e.g., it is not okay to be angry; men can show anger but women cannot; anger must never be violent; anger is always violently expressed)?
3. What did you learn about anger from your family, especially your parents? Who are you most like or unlike when it comes to experiencing anger?
4. Consider the family members who most influenced your parents, especially your grandparents. How did your grandparents handle anger? What do you think was the impact of their way of handling anger on your parents?
5. What stories involving anger have emerged in your family and what meaning do you draw from these stories?
6. In what ways do you think culture has influenced the anger experiences in your family? For example, there may be different expectations about anger for males and females; some ethnic groups limit emotional expressiveness, especially the expression of anger.

7. What do you think has been the impact on you of the various ways of handling anger in your family of origin?
8. How do you think the way in which family members handled anger influenced their responses to loss and their manner of grieving? What can you learn from their responses?
9. What manner of handling anger from your family of origin do you find helpful/unhelpful for you as you adapt to your own losses?
10. Who in your family of origin handled anger in the most effective way and how can you use them as models for yourself as you adapt to loss?

Cultural Influences and Loss/Grief Thematic Genogram

Because loss and grief experiences both shape and are shaped by the cultural contexts in which they occur, it is often helpful to use a Thematic Genogram to reveal various cultural influences on the loss adaptation of individuals and families. These influences include gender, ethnicity, race, age, religion, sexual orientation, and social class. Counselors must be careful to avoid stereotypical assumptions here: People do not always fit neatly into their cultural designations. As always, the most respectful approach in working with cultural material is to invite the clients to educate the counselor about the meaning and influence of culture for them. The following are examples of suggested questions for a Thematic Genogram that focuses on cultural influences and loss/grief.

1. What types of cultural groups (e.g., ethnicity, region, class) characterize different members of your family of origin going back through the generations?
2. How have members of your family of origin expressed and practiced their cultural affiliations? For example, what rituals, traditions, beliefs, activities, or sayings do you recall as evidence of their cultural affiliation?
3. How meaningful were family members' identification with their cultural affiliations?
4. In what ways did family members handle differences or changes in cultural affiliations, and what was the impact of these differences on family members and on your family of origin?
5. What culturally significant events (immigration, cultural loss, and historically significant events) have occurred in your family of origin? In what ways did these events involve loss? What was the impact of these events and losses on individual family members and on the family as a whole?
6. What has been the impact of cultural prejudices or stereotypes in your family of origin?
7. To what degree do you think family members assimilated or accommodated in terms of culture? What has been the impact of that assimilation or accommodation? What has been lost or gained from that assimilation or accommodation?
8. What role did the cultural affiliations of your family play in your life when you were growing up and what role do they play today?
9. How do you think the cultural affiliations of individuals in your family of origin influenced their responses to loss and their manner of grieving? What can you learn from their responses?
10. What cultural practices and beliefs from your family of origin do you find helpful/ unhelpful as you adapt to your own losses? What cultural practices and beliefs of your own are most helpful to you as you adapt to your own losses?

It is recommended that counselors use poster paper or whiteboard when constructing systemic or thematic genograms. The diagram must be easily viewed and provide enough surface to add information without distraction. Poster paper can be rolled up and stored, then reused in future sessions or given to the client. Whiteboard is easily erasable, but a copy of the genogram must be made if it is to be used again.

Early Recollections

The Early Recollections strategy involves exploring specific childhood memories so as to understand their effect on the client's current experience. Originally developed by Alfred Adler as a projective tool for assessing lifestyle and commonly used in Adlerian counseling, the strategy is amended here for a more specific application to loss and grief.

The childhood memories revealed using the Early Recollections strategy are a rich source of information from which the counselor and client can select material most useful for the client's needs and most appropriate to the counselor's theoretical approach. Early recollections can reveal central themes and patterns, dissonance, cognitive schema, emotional content, social interest, behavior, coping skills, historical/developmental influences, sociocultural contexts (e.g., ethnicity, religion, gender), existential themes, characterological traits, and meaning structures. Loss and separation experiences are common in the Early Recollections strategy, often reflecting developmental transitions. Early Recollections expose the client's unique history of loss experiences and suggest their impact over time; for example, an earliest childhood memory of happiness and security in one's family may be followed by later memories, after a parental death, that reveal an emerging view of the world as unjust, chaotic, and insecure.

Implementation of Early Recollections

An *early recollection* is defined as the memory of a single event in childhood. A recollection ("I remember ...") is distinguished from a report ("We used to ..."), which does not focus on a single incident (Powers & Griffith, 1987, p. 87). The recalled event may take the form of a dream or impression if it represents a single incident. In fact, early recollections do not have to be real or provable if they carry a ring of truth for the client or constitute a definitive impression like a memory. The process involves eliciting memories of childhood incidents and exploring each one separately. Generally speaking, three to six early recollections should be gathered (see Box 4.2).

Step 1. Elicit the first recollection. The counseling professional elicits the first client recollection by asking, "Tell me some stories or incidents that stand out in your memory from childhood, starting with the earliest one you can remember" (Powers & Griffith, 1987, p. 88). The counselor should record a brief description of the recollection using the client's own words, preferably on poster paper or whiteboard where both client and counselor can view it together. Note the client's age in the recollection. After obtaining the description, the counselor initiates exploration of the first recollection by asking the following questions and making brief notations of client responses on the poster paper/whiteboard:

+ What is going on in this early memory, especially what behaviors, thoughts, and emotions are occurring?
+ Where you are in this recollection, what are you doing or experiencing? For example, leading, following, passively observing, being victimized, being loved, withdrawing, achieving, failing.

BOX 4.2

Early Recollections of 30-Year-Old Client With History of Intimacy Problems

1. It was winter and it was dark outside and I was in the dining room. I was standing at the window looking through the blinds and I was watching for my Dad. It was Christmas and he brought us presents and took us in the car with him. I was probably 4 or 5 years old.
2. I was standing by a hedge outside school crying because I was late and didn't want to go in. I had wet my pants earlier and gone home. The babysitter scolded me, put on dry pants, and sent me back to school. I was probably 5 or 6 years old because this was after my father left us.
3. I was playing ball with the neighborhood kids and they sent me in to find out what time it was. I didn't know how to tell time and when I got in the house no one was there to ask. I had to go out and tell them that I couldn't tell time. They all laughed at me. I must have been around 7 years old.
4. I remember lying on the bed with my sister, crying, as we listened to my mother and her boyfriend fighting downstairs. I was probably 10 years old.
5. I was doing dishes in the sink and my Mom was mad about something. She came over and started hitting me for no reason. I remember hunching over the sink and just taking it. I think I was 11 years old.

- ✦ If others are involved in the recollection, what are they doing or not doing? For example, helping, rejecting, ignoring, nurturing, blaming, guiding, or hurting.
- ✦ What is the most important or vivid moment in this early recollection? (Seligman, 2004, p. 47).
- ✦ What meaning did this memory hold for you then and what does it hold for you now? (Seligman, 2004, p. 47). For example, the world is unpredictable and unjust; getting close means losing someone; life has difficulties that you accept and work with; family is always there (or never there) for me; men leave; women are manipulative; I'm a good person; God ignores people like me; I am capable of handling things on my own; I need others to take care of me; I am powerless in the face of racism; bad things happen to bad people.

Step 2. Elicit other early recollections. The counseling professional asks clients for their memories of other stories or incidents, proceeding until three to six early recollections are gathered. Counselors should try to obtain the recollections in sequence and avoid recollections around just one period, so that the end result is a set of remembered incidents spanning childhood. Continue to use the poster paper/whiteboard to make brief notations of client responses to the questions. When sufficient recollections have been elicited and explored, ask the client, "Is there any memory that is important to you or we have not had a chance to cover that you would like to include here?" (Powers & Griffith, 1987, p. 88). If there is another recollection, include it. *Note.* Although clients often find these memories interesting and rewarding, the counselor should monitor for potential client distress and especially for traumatic memories.

Step 3. Making the connection. After the early recollections have been gathered and explored and no additional ones are forthcoming, place them in sequence and invite the client to consider the following:

+ What do you think is the connection between the material explored in these early recollections and your experiences of loss and grief?
+ What do you think is the connection between the material explored in these early recollections and your current difficulties?
+ What strengths, abilities, skills, and resources are revealed in your early recollections?
+ What beliefs or assumptions about self, self and others, and self and Other (e.g., Great Spirit) did you develop in your childhood and what has been their impact on you and your life?

The questions proposed here provide a starting point for exploration and are centered on clients' interpretation of their own experiences, not the counselor's interpretation. Counselors can then focus discussion on the specific issues and experiences they think are germane to the therapy, for example, exploration of meaning structures, emotional patterns, cognitive distortions, or existential themes.

According to Powers and Griffith (1987, pp. 89–92) common problems encountered in obtaining early recollections include the following:

+ *Not remembering.* In this case ask clients to start wherever they do have a memory, even if it is not during childhood. Often this will begin to trigger earlier memories.
+ *Absence of feeling.* Do not push the client for feelings and by all means avoid doing the client's work by telling the client what he or she is feeling. Rather than interpreting the absence of feeling for the client, ask the client to do so for himself or herself.
+ *Previously mentioned material.* Include all appropriate early recollections, even if these were described or explored previously in therapy.
+ *Historical accuracy.* Sometimes there is a difference between what the client remembers and the client's sense that it could not have happened or not happened in that way. Because the important thing is the client's impression and how that impression shaped him or her rather than factual truth, include these recollections as if they were reality.
+ *Photographic imagery.* Sometimes, when asked for early recollections, clients may describe a photograph. Ask them to put themselves or something happening in the photograph. If they cannot do so, exclude that from early recollections.
+ *Stories about me.* Sometimes clients have been told a story involving them but they have no specific recall of the event (e.g., being mean to a younger sibling, taking care of others). These stories, like the specific memories, often contribute substantially to the client's self-image and worldview and should be included in early recollections.

Objects of Connection

Grieving clients often use special items as a means of maintaining connection with that which they have lost. More than keepsakes, objects of connection provide a powerful and meaningful ongoing bond with the lost person, relationship, or situation. They are highly unique to the griever and to the various contexts in which the loss occurs. Common examples of objects of connection include the following:

+ clothing (e.g., T-shirt, tie, eyeglasses, shoes, jewelry)
+ "last-minute objects" (Volkan, 1972)—items associated with the moment of death or the time when news of a death was received (e.g., baseball glove, wallet, clothing)

- photographs (e.g., of person, companion animal, accident site)
- personal items associated with the person (or pet) being mourned (e.g., child's drawing, dog collar, toothbrush, rosary, jewelry, pocketknife, lock of hair)
- items associated with the location or experience that was lost (e.g., cattle tags and farm record books from a lost family farm; nametag from former job, stones or feathers from sacred earth)
- hard-copy communication from the person being mourned or associated with the loss (e.g., e-mail, letter, card, obituary, termination notice)
- gifts to the griever from the person being mourned

Objects of connection are often carried with the griever (in a pocket or purse) or placed in a specific place in the griever's environment. Although the object is usually readily accessible, it may be packed away, left in a drawer, or placed in a highly visible place (e.g., a home shrine/altar). Some objects of connection are held more privately, some are shared openly, and some are especially tied to cultural influences (e.g., rosary). Wherever the object may be placed, the grieving person always knows its location. Whereas objects of connection most often serve a positive function in the grieving process, they may also reveal difficulties, especially objects associated with attachment, avoidance of the reality of the loss, resolution of dissonance, or disrupted meaning structures. It is important that counseling professionals explore the existence of objects of connection, help clients discern their functionality in the grieving process, reduce maladaptive use, and enhance adaptive use. There are two types of objects of connection: symbolic objects and linking objects.

Symbolic objects represent some former or current meaning connected to the lost person, relationship, or situation in the griever's life. For example, a 1960s era protest T-shirt may symbolize a time in the griever's life when he or she was at his or her best, something the griever feels is lost; a vacation photograph may symbolize a past moment of closeness for a family now scattered and disconnected; a decorative object purchased by newlyweds, now divorced, may symbolize the lost hope and the deep disappointment of a failed relationship; an airline ticket stub may symbolize the immigrant's continued strong attachment to a former homeland or the ambiguity of allegiance. The actual symbolism of these objects may shift over time, sometimes even coming to represent the grieving experience itself or the life transition flowing from the loss more than the specific loss itself.

Linking objects differ from symbolic objects of connection in that they are used to evoke the presence of the deceased (Volkan, 1972, 1981). This presence is neither symbolic nor just a memory but is an active and real experience of the deceased in the griever's life. Linking objects help bereaved persons create an inner representation of the deceased that often provides great solace (Klass, 1999). For example, a dead child's stuffed toy may be used as a linking object by parents to bring a strong sense of the child present and even interacting with them. It is important that counseling professionals recognize that linking objects often serve a positive function in the grieving experience of some individuals. Having a powerful sense of the deceased's presence is not pathological but an attempt to maintain a meaningful relationship. This contrasts sharply with earlier views associated with Bowlby (1969, 1973) and psychoanalysis (Volkan, 1972) that emphasized detachment, letting go, and severing bonds in bereavement grief. More helpfully, postmodern views (Klass, Silverman, & Nickman, 1996) value the healthy nature of maintaining continuing bonds rather than severing ties with the deceased. Thus, linking objects may help a client develop an altered relationship with the deceased that maintains a meaningful connection while at the same time permitting investment in new relationships and in rebuilding one's life or redefining one's identity. Maladaptive use of linking objects is often associated with an inability to accept the finality of loss, obsessive rumination on the loss or loss circumstances, or excessive dependence.

Implementation of Objects of Connection

There are several steps in working effectively with the strategy of Objects of Connection in grief counseling: ask about them, validate them, explore their meaning and function, and address resolution of problem areas and facilitate transitions.

Step 1. Ask about objects of connection. Whereas many clients will spontaneously disclose the existence of their objects of connection and talk easily about them, often there is some hesitancy about the revelation. They may feel that others will view these objects as inconsequential or as evidence of maladjustment. Clients themselves may worry about being "crazy" because of the power associated with these items, especially with linking objects. Therefore, counseling professionals should ask about objects of connection during the initial assessment and also later in the therapy process after a more secure client–counselor relationship has been established. It is important that the counseling professional convey a normal and matter-of-fact manner when inquiring about objects of connection. For example:

- I've notice that people who are grieving often have some special item that they associate with their loved one. Sometimes they keep those items very close because they are helpful. Do you have anything like that that connects you with Elena?
- When you were describing Shaun's room, I was struck with how important even those everyday things have come to be for you. Which of those things seems to speak the most to you?
- You mentioned the photograph you kept—the one of the two of you together in the village. Where is that photograph today?
- Sissy, what did you do with the beads you found when you went through the house after the hurricane?

Step 2. Validate objects of connection. It is critical that the counseling professional validate the existence and value of objects of connection. This enhances the client–counselor relationship, normalizes the existence of the objects, and facilitates client exploration of their meaning. Ask the client to bring the object to the counseling session so that it can be shown or handled by the client, perhaps even by the counselor. I often ask clients if they have the object with them and if they would be willing to share that with me as we work together.

- I'd like you to bring that baseball glove to the next session, Jorge. It clearly is an important connection with your father and I think it would help you to have it here while we talk.
- Those keys seem to say something important to you about your life as a farmer. Even now, after the farm has been sold and you have started another career, you have the keys to the barn, the tractor, and the storeroom still close by. They say something important to you.
- I think a lot of parents do the same thing when their child dies—keep something special like that stuffed toy. It seems to bring them comfort and connection. It certainly makes sense to me that you would keep this close to you. In fact, I'm glad you have it. Would you consider bringing it to our next meeting?

Step 3. Explore the meaning and function of objects of connection. The counseling professional helps clients explore the meaning they attach to objects of connection and discern their function in adapting to loss. Counselors are interested in the following:

+ Is the object of connection a symbolic object or linking object, and what does it symbolize or who does it link to?
+ How is the object of connection used in day-to-day life?
+ Does it reveal areas of dissonance (e.g., holding on/letting go, love/hate, sorrow/relief)?
+ Is there anxiety attached to the linking object, and how is that experienced (e.g., is losing or misplacing the linking object frequently anxiety-producing)?
+ What problematic behavior, emotions, or cognitions are revealed by exploring objects of connection (e.g., anger, distorted thinking, obsession, helplessness, self-blame)?
+ What function does the object of connection serve in the grieving process (e.g., symbolizes transformation, facilitates restoration of balance or harmony, maintains identity with former status, avoids reality, keeps connection, restricts restoration activities, or maintains dependence)?
+ What is the client's view of the helpfulness or harmfulness of her or his object of connection?
+ How does the linking object provide a continuing bond with the deceased?
+ Does the object symbolize disconnection more than connection? If so, what is the nature of that disconnection?
+ Does using the object evoke feelings of helplessness, self-blame, and disturbed memories or provide solace and comforting memories?
+ Does the object of connection keep the client focused on the loss or the past to the exclusion of the present and future?
+ Does the meaning attached to the object of connection interfere with the client's ability to develop new relationships?
+ Has the value, effectiveness, or symbolism of the object of connection changed over time and in what way?
+ What does the object of connection reveal about what is important for the client?
+ What cultural influences does the object of connection reveal and how do these influences affect grieving and the griever (e.g., reflects culturally prescribed practices, reveals disrupted spiritual beliefs, renews cultural ties, or provides cultural connection)?
+ Is the linking object shared with others or is it held secretly? What is the impact of any secrecy?
+ Does the object of connection, especially a linking object, reveal difficulty accepting the reality of the loss?
+ Do clients believe the function of their linking object is to keep the deceased alive, so that they must at all costs maintain the linking object (anxiety-producing)?
+ Does the use of a linking object in the present actually reflect preloss difficulties with reality testing or relationship dependence?
+ What does the object of connection reveal about clients' sense of self, their worldview, and their relationships with others?

The following questions are examples of ways to explore the meaning and function of objects of connection with clients:

- This note obviously carries great meaning for you, Latoya; help me understand what it means.
- Juanita, what does your Mother's rosary represent for you?
- You mentioned that you often sleep in Robert's T-shirt. Tell me more about what that does for you.
- You said you always keep the picture with you . . . what would happen if you couldn't find it?
- Frieda, does your husband know about Junior's blanket? If not, why not?
- Sometimes the meaning of these kinds of things changes over time; I wonder if that has happened for you? If so, how have things changed?
- You said you keep this just to remind you . . . what do you need to remember?
- What is helpful for me (the counselor) to know about these office keys you keep with you?
- Do you think you will always have the same attachment to this book, or do you think that will change over time? What will bring about the change, if it happens?
- Su-Lin, if your family knew how important this is to you, would they be concerned? If so, what would their concern be?
- You said that most of the time the blanket is comforting, but sometimes more upsetting. Tell me about both sides of that experience.
- You said you were uncomfortable on those occasions when you didn't have this with you . . . help me understand more about that.
- Tell more about this little clay frog, the little Coqui, Rita. What about this reminds you of your life in Puerto Rico before you came to the United States?

Step 4. Address resolution of problem areas and facilitate transitions. Typically, as clients put more energy into the restoration of their lives following a loss, objects of connection become less important or less central in their grieving process. The initial need to maintain continuing bonds via concrete items usually transitions to more abstract means, such as comforting memories (N. P. Field, Nichols, Holen, & Horowitz, 1999). However, in some cases exploring objects of connection reveals more serious difficulties that can be address through various strategies appropriate to the problem (e.g., cognitive restructuring, experiential focusing, anxiety management, chair dialogues, therapeutic rituals, coping imagery, and meaning reconstruction strategies).

Objects of connection can be explored in both family therapy and group therapy settings using the same exploratory processes outlined above. However, some caution should be exercised in family therapy settings. The highly personal and often very private nature of objects of connection may make some people reluctant to share them with family members. It is often better for the counseling professional to wait for some mention of an object of connection before investigating further. Normalizing objects of connection in grief situations, whether or not they are mentioned specifically, is appropriate.

Therapeutic Grief Rituals

Grief rituals are symbolic activities that express the meaning inherent in loss and adaptation to loss for an individual, family, and community. Although such rituals may vary in content and process, they underscore healing and restoration or the establishment of balance and harmony in the lives of the grievers. While the most recognizable form of grief ritual is a funeral, the focus here is on *therapeutic* grief rituals developed specifically by clients in psychotherapy to address their particular needs. The rituals may be simple and brief (e.g., sharing memories at a meal, lighting a candle in remembrance, walking a labyrinth), or they may be more involved (e.g., reading and destroying letters about abuse/recovery; creating a memory box; sharing music, poetry, or other art reflecting the griever's journey and the significance of lost assumptions and fantasies). Therapeutic grief rituals underscore and facilitate the transitional and transformative processes of loss adaptation in the following ways:

- providing a vehicle for meaning making
- promoting resolution of dissonance
- validating losses and relationships
- framing loss and grief as opportunities for growth, reorganization, or evolution
- building and enhancing a sense of community and witness
- clarifying change in the form of separation, leave taking, connection, or disconnection
- clarifying change in the form of continuing bonds, altered relationship, or continuity
- encouraging the experience and expression of emotion in a safe environment
- directing grief into concrete activity
- facilitating forgiveness of self and others
- facilitating the incorporation of loss into emerging client narratives
- providing space and time for remembrance

Therapeutic grief rituals can be used with many death-related and nondeath-related loss circumstances, for example, divorce, death, estrangement, betrayal, illness, sexual abuse, menopause, job loss, migration, and addiction. They may occur within a therapy session or may just as often occur outside the session. They may be performed in public or private, may be carefully scripted or spontaneously enacted, may be repeated or occur only once, and may be religiously or secularly oriented (Castle & Phillips, 2002). Such rituals may reflect the client's own cultural contexts or may be adapted from the practices of other cultures (Parker & Horton, 1996). Grief rituals may be used by individuals, groups, families, or even communities. The timing of therapeutic grief rituals depends on context, client goals, and motivation. Effective therapeutic grief rituals are designed by clients in collaboration with their counseling professional, therefore enhancing ownership, motivation, and meaning reconstruction. Although ritual components may be copied from various sources, it is important that the ritual itself be personalized, tailored to the uniqueness of the client. Adequate preparation for grief rituals is imperative and is, in itself, therapeutic.

Implementation of Therapeutic Grief Rituals

Therapeutic grief rituals are not ends or goals in and of themselves. Instead, they reveal an attitude, orientation, or circumstance already being embraced by the griever—the transitional and transformative experience of adapting to loss. Counselors may recommend therapeutic grief rituals when clients verbalize the positive changes or transitional steps they have made with regard to loss and grief, their narratives include strong elements of revised meaning making, they express a desire to mark or commemorate their loss or their healing, or they spontaneously engage in some form of grief ritual. When introducing this activity, the counselor should (a) explain the rationale and give examples of therapeutic grief rituals; (b) help the client identify themes, issues, acts, or symbols that have been important in the client's therapy and grieving thus far; and (c) encourage the client to investigate cultural, philosophical, spiritual, or religious resources for inspiration.

The following steps are adapted from discussions of bereavement grief rituals by Martin and Doka (2000), Parker and Horton (1996, 1997), Romanoff and Terenzio (1998), and Rando (1993). These steps can be applied to nondeath-related loss circumstances as well.

Step 1. Determine the goal or purpose of the grief ritual. What outcome is desired? What are the client's expectations and how realistic are they? How will this grief ritual contribute to the client's overall adaptation to loss? In what ways does a grief ritual mark transition and/or underscore transformation that is already occurring? How does the grief ritual fit into the client's unfolding life narrative? What one or two words summarize the client's purpose in implementing a grief ritual (e.g., bridge, liberation, leave taking, reconciliation, forgiveness, healing)?

Step 2. Determine what themes, issues, and symbols should be included in the ritual. Most likely these reflect major threads of the grieving process and therapy (e.g., unfinished business, forgiveness, transition, reconciliation). The particular issues of dissonance encountered by a client are frequently included in grief rituals. The ritual may focus on one or two themes, may address the grief journey, may focus on the lost object, or may include a longer life journey or life narrative.

Step 3. Determine which aspects of separation/disconnection/leave-taking and continuing bonds/continuity should be covered and how their integration will be addressed in the grief ritual. Although one aspect may be emphasized more than another, it is helpful when grief rituals reflect the incorporation of both elements of separation and elements of connection. For example, the ritual of a grieving parent may emphasize leave-taking from a dead or estranged child, but it should also mark the bonds that continue as the relationship is reformed. The ritual for a sexual abuse survivor may place emphasis on separation from the past and what was taken (lost), but there should also be some recognition of continuity of self.

Step 4. Select the basic elements and structure of the grief ritual. The elements and structure should create an atmosphere conducive to contemplation and/or celebration and, if including others, enhance a sense of community. The ritual should include reference to the dual dimensions of loss and restoration but may emphasize one more than the other. Therapeutic rituals may reflect the client's own cultural background or may incorporate elements borrowed from other cultural contexts. Encourage clients to investigate various cultural, philosophical, and spiritual/religious resources for inspiration. Basic elements usually include the following:

+ symbols (e.g., labyrinth, sacred circle, photographs, objects of connection, water, fire, a flower)
+ symbolic acts (e.g., reading a letter, scattering ashes, burying something, lighting or extinguishing a candle, planting a tree, erecting a memorial, making a toast, making an offering, eating a meal, sharing stories or memories, singing songs, cleansing)
+ significant people whose roles as participants, witnesses, or observers should be clarified
+ sensation-evoking ingredients (e.g., smoke, incense, colors, dance/movement, bells, drumming, music)

Counselors may or may not be included in therapeutic grief rituals. If they are involved, their role should be minimal and primarily supportive. The ritual structure includes choosing a time, selecting a location, and developing procedures. Very simple, private rituals often are planned for a spontaneous enactment (e.g., "I felt it was time to do this"), whereas more public rituals usually require a set time and location.

Step 5. Consider and plan for the emotional impact of the grief ritual. Rituals elicit, channel, validate, and release feelings (Castle & Philips, 2002; Feinstein & Mayo, 1990; Rando, 1984; Romanoff & Terenzio, 1998). In fact, rituals that are not emotionally meaningful or are overwhelming are not useful (Rando, 1984). What feelings are likely to be encountered in a ritual? Is the client seeking catharsis and, if so, how will the ritual provide that? How will the client manage emotions, especially intense emotions? What coping skills must be developed before undertaking a therapeutic grief ritual? How will the ritual be made safe as a vehicle for emotional experiencing? Scheff (1977) suggested that the griever should be able to move back and forth between the participant and observer role so as to allow emotional distancing. This movement reduces the potential for being overwhelmed and encourages reflection.

Step 6. The client implements the ritual.

Step 7. Review and explore the ritual. What actually occurred? What reactions did the client have during and after the ritual? What feelings were experienced? How did the ritual meet the client's expectations? What did the ritual do for the client, especially in light of the original goal or purpose? What meaning does the client glean from the grief ritual now? How does the ritual fit with the client's emerging narrative of him- or herself and the client's adaptation to loss?

Examples of Items, Activities, and Procedures of Therapeutic Grief Rituals

Items
Bells, chimes, guitars, drums, mantras, meaningful music selections, art, containers, rosaries, herb or sweet grass bundles, flowers, objects of connection, pipes, storytelling stick, containers (e.g., cups, box), ethnic or cultural symbols (e.g., yin-yang, celtic knots, pink ribbons, mandelas), wheel, circle, bridge, herbs for burning/smoking (e.g., sage, cedar, sweet-grass).

Activities
Holding hands, singing, praying, hugging, laying on hands, drumming, walking, dancing, kneeling; visiting places connected with the lost object; displaying photographs or mementos connected with the lost object; establishing a memorial fund or activity; planting gardens or trees; burning herbs associated with ceremonial traditions, preparation, and purification; sharing stories and memories around a celebratory meal; creating a home altar that honors those lost (e.g., deceased, missing, estranged); writing letters about the loss or to people involved in the loss, then disposing of the letters via shredding, burning, or burying; lighting or extinguishing candles; leading or sharing a guided meditation; symbolic cleansing via postritual bath or sweat lodge.

Procedures
+ A man whose father died built a special box using his father's tools and gave the box to his own son.
+ A woman who had a hysterectomy after years of gynecologic problems created a private ritual in which she burned some tampons and danced under a full moon (female symbol).

Another client who had a hysterectomy created a ritual in which she emphasized the loss of fertility and the continuing identity of motherhood via her own prose and photographs; she included her children and her own mother in the ritual.

♦ A group of friends gathered for a special dinner to remember a deceased friend. They shared stories about the deceased and each made a toast in her honor. Another group of friends gathered in the same way to share memories and stories about another friend who had become incapacitated by Alzheimer's disease but had not yet died (marking loss).

♦ A sexual abuse survivor wrote letters to her abusers describing how she had overcome the damage they had done to her. She shared the letters with a group of important friends as they sat in a sacred circle. She then burned the letters and read some poetry about survival and her new identity as she left behind the victim and became a survivor.

♦ A group of friends built a labyrinth path and then walked the path three times: first with a reflection on losses they had endured, second with a reflection on the nature of change and transition, and third with a reflection on gains they had made in adapting to their losses.

♦ A returning war veteran participated in a Native American ceremony designed to restore balance to his life so that he could "walk in beauty."

♦ A woman gathered close women friends and eulogized her anger regarding her husband's infidelity, then later was joined by her husband to celebrate rebuilding their relationship (Winek & Craven, 2003).

♦ A mother and granddaughter sewed a panel for the AIDS Memorial Quilt commemorating their daughter/mother.

♦ Extended family members who fled the genocide in Rwanda gather yearly to mark the event. They share traditional foods, recite the names of family members who died, and tell stories of their lives in Rwanda. They end the meeting with a communal prayer and reminder that they "will always be Rwandans."

♦ A family created a ceremony in which their kidnapped child could be remembered, his absence marked, and the ambiguity of his missing status recognized.

♦ A woman held a mock funeral to mark disconnection from her idealized, fantasy parent (Zupanick, 1994).

♦ A child created a "memory box" of items associated with his dog when this pet died. He shared the items with his school counselor, telling stories about his dog and their life together. The box was kept on a shelf in the counselor's office where he could access it from time to time. He took it home with him at the end of the school year.

♦ A divorcing couple created a leave-taking ritual of stories and affirmations that marked the mutual ending and beginning processes in their divorce. They returned their wedding rings with affirmations of regard, words of regret, and good wishes for the future.

♦ A group of Hurricane Katrina survivors created a ceremony in which members listed the things they had lost and affirmed the things that continued in their lives. They sealed the loss list in a glass bottle and placed it in the waters of the Gulf.

♦ A client raised in years of foster care wrote letters to everyone he remembered who was involved with him in those experiences. He detailed what he had lost and what he had gained in that journey. He read the letters aloud in the therapy session, then buried them as a ritual for letting go of the anger generated in that background.

Cautions for Therapeutic Grief Rituals

Several cautions regarding grief rituals should be noted. Avoid script-driven or literalistic rituals (Parker & Horton, 1996) in favor of client-created rituals because that will enhance motivation and ownership. Establish physical and emotional safety guidelines during and after the ritual. Block symbolic destruction of a person or community as counterproductive to healing (e.g., do not burn effigies). Help clients shape a ritual that fits their grieving style (e.g., oriented toward activity or oriented toward emotional expression).

Recommended Resources

Beck, R., & Metrick, S. B. (2003). *The art of ritual: Creating and performing ceremonies for growth and change*. Berkeley, CA: Celestial Arts.

Farmer, S. D. (2002). *Sacred ceremony: How to create ceremonies for healing, transitions, and celebrations*. Carlsbad, CA: Hay House.

Feinstein, D., & Mayo, P. E. (1990). *Rituals for living and dying: How we can turn loss and the fear of death into an affirmation of life*. San Francisco: HarperSanFrancisco.

Golden, R. R. (2000). *Swallowed by a snake: The fit of the masculine side of healing* (2nd ed.). Gaithersburg, MD: Golden Healing.

Mayo, P. E. (2001). *The healing sorrow workbook: Rituals for transforming grief and loss*. Oakland, CA: New Harbinger.

Parker, R., & Horton, H. S. (1997). Sarah's story: Using ritual therapy to address psychospiritual issues in treating survivors of childhood sexual abuse. *Counseling and Values, 42,* 41–55.

http://www.aidsquilt.org provides information about the AIDS Memorial Quilt and directions for creating a memorial panel.

Therapeutic Writing for Loss: Giving Sorrow Words

The strategy of Therapeutic Writing for Loss and Grief utilizes structured, directed, and spontaneous writing activities to facilitate loss adaptation. Clients may write on topics selected specifically by their counselor, use workbooks, or keep an open-ended journal. Responses may be shared and feedback received from the counselor, or material may be kept private. Writing may take various forms, including journaling, poetry, essays, letters, storytelling, art, or recordings. Therapeutic writing facilitates emotional expression, cognitive processing, problem solving, and meaning reconstruction. It promotes resilience by helping clients identify strengths, abilities, resources, and competencies. Therapeutic writing encourages client self-care, helps clients feel a sense of control in the face of uncontrollable loss and grief, and enhances motivation. It may be used in workshops; in individual, group, or family counseling; and in online psychotherapy. This method can be incorporated into diverse theoretical approaches. The flexibility and adaptability of therapeutic writing allows the counselor to tailor this intervention, respecting the uniqueness of the griever, the course of the griever's loss adaptation, and the multiple contexts (social, cultural, historical, and personal) in which her or his grief occurs. Therapeutic writing is an excellent strategy for loss adaptation when appropriate cautions and guidelines are observed.

> The combination of therapy and writing helps bring out an individual's natural capacities for healing and change. When writing is used as an adjunct to the therapeutic process or as a therapeutic process in and of itself, it is possible to cathart, process, reflect, integrate. (Adams, 1999, p. 2)

Therapeutic writing for loss utilizes *spontaneous writing* and *directed writing*.

Spontaneous Therapeutic Writing

In spontaneous writing clients write whatever comes to mind and work at their own pace. Most often counselors suggest the client undertake spontaneous writing in the form of a journal. This promotes regular use and reinforces the open-ended nature of this format. Spontaneous writing becomes a background experience that feeds the process and contributes to therapy over time, but it is not collected by the counseling professional or used directly during sessions. Clients typically do not share their writing; rather, they share reflections resulting from their writing. The counselor may suggest specific topics from time to time or ask what the client's writing has yielded recently. An important advantage of spontaneous writing is that it is entirely within the control of the client, thus reducing defensiveness and increasing motivation. Clients who already keep a journal or have a positive relationship with writing are most likely to embrace spontaneous writing. Because writing about loss can bring up painful material, it is important that the counselor make certain the client has sufficient coping skills and resources before encouraging spontaneous writing.

Directed Therapeutic Writing

In directed writing the counselor assigns specific topics to the client across the course of therapy. Topics are selected to match client needs, issues, difficulties, and progress in loss adaptation. For example, the assignment may focus mostly on losses early in the process, and then shift to a focus on changes faced by the griever as a result of the losses later in the process (restoration); another assignment might focus only on exploring emotions; yet another assignment might target client resilience. When using directed writing to facilitate loss adaptation, counselors should create the assignments themselves, thus being able to match them to client needs. Commercial workbooks on grief are an excellent resource in this regard (see recommendations below), but it is strongly recommended that the counselor limit the assignments to specific sections or, even better, adapt selected material rather than have the client simply complete the entire workbook. This optimizes tailoring the intervention to client needs, avoids outdated or unhelpful information in some workbooks, and paces the therapy to client progress. The vast majority of commercial workbooks or journals dealing with grief are designed for bereavement, so they are either inappropriate for, or must be adapted to, nondeath-related circumstances.

In directed therapeutic writing, clients share their responses to assignments with the counselor, and this becomes a focus for therapy. This material can be discussed in several ways: (a) The client reads her or his written expressions aloud, then the counselor and client explore this material, or (b) the client shares his or her reflections based on completing the assignment, then the counselor and client explore these reflections. The counselor's role here is to serve as a witness to the unfolding story of loss and loss adaptation, to validate client experiences, to provide feedback on content and process, and to facilitate exploration and reflection. When directed writing is used in a family or group setting, the counselor must also monitor and incorporate the responses of others.

Benefits and Client Concerns About Therapeutic Writing

Many clients respond positively to the suggestion they write about their experiences, especially when some degree of direction is provided. Adams (1999), writing specifically about journaling, noted that the best predictors of success include prior experience with journaling, a positive relationship with writing, high motivation to relieve one's suffering, and a positive relationship with the counselor. Wright and Chung (2001), in a review of the literature on therapeutic writing, noted the following circumstances as benefiting from therapeutic writing: in time-limited, focused, brief therapy; with people who have a self-directed tendency; with people who are or perceive themselves as powerless; with people who are not using their first language in the face-to-face therapy; with people who are silenced by shame, perhaps for cultural reasons; with people who need to externalize and organize their thoughts and feelings; with people who need to disclose and exorcize a specific memory or traumatic experience; and with people at particular life stages associated with strong feelings (e.g., adolescence).

Counselors should be prepared to discuss client apprehension about therapeutic writing. Lattanzi and Hale (1984) noted the following client concerns in writing about bereavement grief: worry that recalling distressful memories would be painful; concerns about increased vulnerability; anxiety about managing painful emotions and distressful memories; fears about the responses of others to writing content; concerns that the writing itself might be awkward, depressing, or just reinforce hopelessness; and concerns about writing skills (e.g., grammar, punctuation, or spelling). There may also be concerns about privacy and security regarding written material. Adams (1999) suggested that therapeutic writing is not appropriate with clients who have thought disorders, impulse control problems, or severe mood disorders. Therapeutic writing is not a fit for every client.

Implementation of Therapeutic Writing for Loss

Successful utilization of therapeutic writing for loss adaptation hinges on the specific topics and issues selected, the manner in which written material is incorporated into therapy, and the key elements of structure, pacing, and containment (Adams, 1999). The counselor should consider the following when introducing therapeutic writing.

1. *Decide what topics or issues might be most useful for particular clients to write about in their experience of loss and grief.* The following are some topics and issues most often beneficial in therapeutic writing for loss adaptation:

   + specific emotions and emotion management (e.g., anger, guilt, shame, regret, confusion, fear, helplessness)
   + dissonance (e.g., ambiguous loss, loss focus vs. restoration focus, life with vs. life without, love vs. hate, resentment vs. guilt)
   + thinking processes (e.g., cognitive distortions, self-defeating thinking, cognitive scripts)
   + meaning structures and meaning reconstruction (e.g., spiritual issues, "why" dilemmas, disrupted assumptions and beliefs)
   + problem solving (e.g., learning new skills, organizing tasks, identifying resources)
   + self-care (e.g., identifying and fulfilling personal needs, physical/health concerns)
   + social support: (e.g., identifying and using social support network, reducing isolation, managing relationships)
   + what grief has taught me

- establishing balance or harmony (especially important in some cultural traditions)
- client strengths and resiliency
- unfinished business
- memories or reminiscences
- cultural influences and issues (e.g., gender, ethnicity, sexual orientation)
- disenfranchised grief
- historical/cultural loss

2. *Determine what type and degree of structure (i.e., topic, format, and complexity) might be most helpful to specific clients.* It is important that clear, concrete directions for assignments be provided in written form. Just suggesting or describing a therapeutic writing assignment is usually a guarantee for failure. Translate the assignment into the client's native language if possible. Emphasize that grammar, spelling, and punctuation are unimportant. Short, structured assignments work best with clients who are unsure about their expressive or writing ability, prefer specificity of topic and a concrete process, prefer writing to topic rather than a disciplined writing schedule, or whose motivation is low. Open-ended assignments (e.g., write whatever comes to mind) work best with highly motivated clients, those who are comfortable with expressive writing and/or their writing ability, and those who prefer a regular writing schedule (Adams, 1999). More instrumental style grievers respond best to a specific, task-oriented structure, whereas more intuitive style grievers would prefer an open-ended structure that underscores their need for expression and connection. The best structure is the most simple. It is important to consult with clients regarding what structure might be most helpful and to revisit that discussion from time to time. Counselors should give clients as much control as possible and be willing to adapt as the client's experience unfolds. Box 4.3 provides one example of therapeutic writing instructions.

3. *Determine what material and assignments would be most beneficial for clients at different times across the course of therapy or across their adaptation to loss (pacing).* Depending on the client and situation, is it better to have the client address emotional, perhaps painful, material early in counseling or later? Should the cultural influences on this client's

---

BOX 4.3

Client Instructions for Writing "My Story of Loss"

Find a place and a time where you can be undisturbed so that you can give your whole attention to this experience. Remember that there are no rules about this writing assignment except one: write naturally. That means you write for yourself and no one else. Grammar and punctuation are unimportant here; feel free to abbreviate, make lists, use phrases; create poetry. You are in charge of what and how you write. Some people find it helpful to set a time limit initially (15–30 minutes), knowing you can return to write more later if you wish. See what works for you.

Your assignment is to write the story of your loss. Tell what happened, what you thought, what you did, and what you felt. Begin your story wherever makes sense to you and bring it up through today. What is the impact of this loss on you and your life?

experience be explored earlier or later? At what point is this client more receptive to exploring difficult or distressing issues? Should there be breaks between writing assignments to facilitate reflection and reduce reluctance or does this client respond better to weekly assignments? If the client reports feeling too pressured or is not completing assignments, then consider a slower or staggered pace. It is important to consult regularly with the client regarding the pacing of therapeutic writing assignments.

4. *Determine what boundaries and limits should apply to therapeutic writing (containment).* It is absolutely critical that the counselor make certain the client has sufficient coping skills to manage emotional material and intensity before making any writing assignments that might trigger catharsis or anxiety. Discuss this situation with clients prior to making any assignments. Consider establishing limits on time, place, and frequency. For example, people who ruminate excessively benefit from limits on time and length. "Five-minute sprints" (writing nonstop for 5 minutes) can help clients set boundaries around emotionally intense material (Adams, 1999). The limits may be relaxed or restricted over the course of treatment. Routinely review the established boundaries and limits to see if they should be amended. R. A. Neimeyer (1999) suggested that clients schedule a transitional activity following a writing episode before moving back into their usual routine, for example, taking a walk, stretching, or breathing exercises.

5. *Determine how material from therapeutic writing will be incorporated into therapy.* In face-to-face therapy, it is best to allow client writings to remain in the hands of clients rather than collecting them or receiving them via mail or e-mail. This keeps the focus on what the client is learning from the assignments, reduces triangling or manipulation (e.g., threatening suicide via e-mail), and decentralizes the counselor's role (clients should be writing for their own benefit, not for the counselor's approval). Remember that therapeutic writing responses should not be included in client files. It is usually best to ask clients to read their written responses aloud or simply share their reflections based on assigned material.

It is important that the counselor avoid commenting on the quality of writing because that will likely distract from the focus on loss and grief (Adams, 1999). The following are some helpful lead-ins for exploration: What do you find interesting or curious as you read over what you have written? I wonder what comes to you now as you reflect on what you have written? It is helpful to select something specific when clients have read their assignments aloud, for example, I am curious about the guilt you expressed in that first paragraph, tell me more about that. You wrote that you see yourself as a cultural misfit; what does that mean for you? I noticed you said that you should not be so angry; where does that message come from?

Suggested Therapeutic Writing Assignments

The following are examples of therapeutic writing assignments that are helpful with clients experiencing loss and grief. They may be utilized in either spontaneous or directed writing.

Captured moment. The client writes brief vignettes describing in detail remembrances of experiences with their lost loved one (Adams, 2007).

Letters to and from Grief. The client writes two letters: one is to Grief and the other one is back to the client from Grief. The letter to Grief is written first and includes the client's current thoughts and feelings. The second letter, from Grief to the client, is written 24 hours later and describes what the client thinks Grief is trying to tell him or her (Deits, 1988; Riordan, 1996). Alternatively, the first letter can be written and shared in-session, then the second letter written and shared at the next therapy session.

Journaling. This assignment is adapted from an investigation on journaling interventions after a stressful or traumatic event described by Ullrich and Lutgendorf (2002). The client is directed as follows:

> Keep a journal of your deepest thoughts and feelings about this loss experience over the next month. How have you tried to make sense of this situation and what do you tell yourself about it to help you deal with it? If you have not been able to make some sense of this loss, describe how you are trying to understand it, deal with it and how your feelings may change about it in the future. (p. 246)

Writing the wrongs and writing the rights. Clients first describe a difficult life experience (e.g., loss and grief event), then "write the situation right" by writing about what they learned or how they benefited from the experience without changing any of the facts (Gladding, 2005, p. 127). Benefit finding is a helpful dimension of meaning reconstruction in grief.

Lists. The client makes lists on various topics, such as: what grief has taught me, things I miss about (my job, my partner, my dog), things that help the grieving, or ways to nurture myself (Porterfield, 2002).

Unsent letters. The client writes a letter to the lost object (e.g., deceased person, absent father, former wife) or persons involved in their loss. The letters typically focus on the expression of thoughts and feelings regarding the loss, the lost object, and their grief. For example, grieving clients may discuss their continuing bond with the deceased. It is important to emphasize that the purpose of the letters is to facilitate the clients' adaptation to loss; therefore they *must not be mailed*. In some cases a farewell letter that facilitates separation without fostering disconnection may be appropriate or in cases in which disconnection is helpful (e.g., breaking bonds with an abusive parent). Do not use this format if there is any concern that the client will act impulsively in mailing these letters. In some cases there may be a formal or ritual disposal of the letter (see Therapeutic Grief Rituals).

Continuous letters. The client writes one letter every day to the lost object (e.g., deceased person) about any topic the client chooses. The letters are shared during the therapy session, usually by reading selected letters aloud. These letters usually are a rich source of material for discussion in therapy and provide an ongoing means of assessment of the client's journey. Typically the intensity of emotions and thinking ebbs as clients reorganize and restructure their world, including, in bereavement, their inner relationship with the deceased (Malkinson, 2007; Van der Hart, 1983, 1988).

Therapeutic workshop. O'Connor, Nikoletti, Kristjanson, Loh, and Willcock (2003) described a 1-day therapeutic writing workshop for bereaved persons. Participants wrote at their own pace on topics related to the exploration and expression of feelings, creating a narrative of their bereavement experience. They met periodically during the day to discuss their activities but were not required to share anything. A trained group leader facilitated the workshop.

Morning pages. The client writes three handwritten pages each day or on scheduled days (e.g., every other day). The topic does not matter as long as the client writes. The exercise is especially helpful when some degree of structure is needed. The approach was designed by Cameron (2002) in *The Artist's Way*, a book about creative writing and spiritual growth.

Life imprint. R. A. Neimeyer (1998) suggested it is often helpful to write about the ways in which a person's life is influenced by the people he or she has lost. This may be positive, may be negative, or may reveal ambivalence.

Biography. The client writes a biography of the person who is the focus of her or his loss. This may involve some research, including interviews with friends, acquaintances, and family. Some clients may want to include pictures, videos, poems, or music as well. Parents of teenagers or adult children find this especially helpful because it allows them to learn about their child's life apart from them. The process and final product are shared with their counselor.

Write the next chapter. Clients are encouraged to envision their own life as a book. They are to write the "next chapter" of their life story as they would like for that life story to unfold postloss (Parry, 1991).

My memoirs. Clients are asked to imagine writing their autobiography or memoirs and, specifically, to actually compose the "last chapter" of these memoirs. This last chapter would allow clients to review and summarize important events in their life (Bacigalupe, 1996).

Letters of advice. Clients are directed to write a letter to an imaginary person who is experiencing a similar loss and grieving process. The letter should express their understanding of what that imaginary person is going through and include their advice about what is helpful in adapting to this type of loss.

20 ways. This is a way of helping clients address problem areas that are inhibiting their adaptation to loss. The client is directed to make a list of "20 ways I can _____." Topics might include: nurture myself, take care of myself, prepare for my future, care for others without sacrificing myself, expand my social support network, and get through a day. Variations include "10 ways" or "50 ways."

Looking forward/looking back. This assignment is helpful when clients have reached an impasse. The client writes a response to the following: Suppose it is 5 years down the road and you have survived all these losses. You look back and say to yourself, "That was a very difficult time for me, especially in the beginning, but I ended up handling it reasonably well." What would you have done to get through this experience so that you could look back in 5 years and say that you handled it all reasonably well?

What remains the same. This assignment helps clients identify those parts of their lives that continue despite their losses. The client writes a response to the following: You have experienced some important losses, but there are also some things you have not lost. What things continue to be a part of your life even though you have experienced these important losses?

Tell the story. This assignment draws on the familiar idea of creating a narrative about one's experiences. Clients are directed to write (or otherwise communicate) a story of their loss and grief as if they were writing a book, an article, a play, or a movie or as though they were telling the story around a campfire.

My Loss Experiences Timeline. Instructions for constructing a timeline of loss experiences are provided elsewhere in this chapter.

Grief as a metaphor. Clients are directed to create a metaphor for their grief experience and to explore all its elements while maintaining the metaphor. The assignment begins with "My grief is like _____" or "My grieving is like _____" or "Living with loss is like _____." For example, one client began her metaphor this way: "My grief is like a back-pack. Early on I could hardly move because it weighed so much and I did not think I could carry it. Gradually I became more able to carry the weight. At times it feels so unbearably heavy, at other times it just seems to be a familiar sensation that I don't notice as much."

Cautions for Counseling Professionals

Adams (1999) noted some special concerns for counselors when they utilize therapeutic writing assignments, including the following: (a) keep the focus on the outcome of client writing, not on style, skills, or effort; (b) manage countertransference; (c) give control to clients in the form of permission to experiment with form, structure, pace, and topic; (d) adapt for cultural differences by encouraging alternative expressions through art, music, dance, storytelling, or movement; and (e) remember that there are multiple truths and multiple layers of truth that are part of the unfolding therapeutic process.

Internet-Based Therapeutic Writing for Loss Adaptation

The Internet provides an excellent vehicle for therapeutic writing. The widespread availability of Internet access to a broad range of people, especially those with limitations (e.g., disabilities, living in remote locations, or lacking adequate professional counseling), greatly enhances delivery of psychotherapeutic services. Certainly the Internet facilitates customizing treatment to fit the uniqueness of clients and their multiple contexts. The activities and procedures of therapeutic writing for loss adaptation outlined here lend themselves well to Internet counseling. Although most appropriate for one-on-one counseling situations, many of these activities can be incorporated into Internet-delivered group therapy or even family therapy. An informative example of Internet-based therapeutic writing for loss adaptation, described by Wagner, Knaevelsrud, and Maercker (2006), involved a 5-week structured writing intervention with clients diagnosed with complicated grief. The cognitive–behavioral intervention consisted of three phases: exposure to bereavement cues, cognitive reappraisal, and integration and restoration. Clients were sent 45-minute writing assignments twice a week and received individualized feedback (on content) from their counseling professional after every second essay. Communication between counseling professionals and clients was entirely by e-mail. Significant improvement was reported on symptoms of intrusion, avoidance, maladaptive behavior, and general psychopathology.

Counselors wishing to provide Internet-based counseling services should follow appropriate ethical and practice guidelines such as those provided by the National Board of Certified Counselors (2007). As with any other counseling strategy, this approach is not necessarily a fit for everyone.

Recommended Resources

Adams, K. (1990). *Journal to the self: Twenty-two paths to personal growth.* New York: Warner Books.

Andreozzi, L. L. A. (2000). *Grief journal.* St. Paul, MN: Good Ground Press.

Hambrook, D., Eisenberg, G., & Rosenthal, H. (1997). *A mother-loss workbook: Healing exercises for daughters.* New York: HarperCollins.

Rich, P. (1999). *The healing journey through grief: Your journal for reflection and recovery.* New York: Wiley.

Rich, P. (2001). *Grief counseling homework planner.* New York: Wiley.

Rich, P., Copans, S., & Copans, K. (1999). *The healing journey through job loss: Your journal for reflection and revitalization.* New York: Wiley.

Rich, P., & Mervyn, F. (1999). *The healing journey through menopause: Your journal for reflection and renewal.* New York: Wiley.

Rogers, J. E. (2007). (Ed.). *The art of grief: The use of expressive arts in a grief support group.* New York: Routledge.

Wolfelt, A. D. (2004). *Understanding your grief journal: Exploring the ten essential touchstones.* Fort Collins, CO: Companion Press.

Cinematherapy With Loss and Grief

Cinematherapy involves using selected commercial films to facilitate discussion and exploration of relevant themes and issues in therapy (Berg-Cross, Jennings, & Baruch, 1990; Hensley & Hensley, 1998, 2001). The strategy builds on people's familiarity and comfort with film and the notion of movie as metaphor: Clients are able to relate themes, characters, situations, and viewpoints from film to their own lives in a manner that facilitates exploration and dialogue of diverse issues in therapy (Hensley & Hensley, 1998; Sharp, Smith, & Cole, 2002). Cinematherapy typically involves the counseling professional assigning a specific movie to be viewed as homework followed by intentional discussion of film material in the therapy session. Clients may rent their own videos/DVDs or counselors may provide loaners.

There are substantial benefits to using cinematherapy. Films provide role models, identify and reinforce internal strengths, facilitate values clarification, suggest possible solutions or steps in problem solving, and show predictable outcomes if dysfunctional behavior continues unchanged (Hensley & Hensley, 1998, 2001). Films raise points for dialogue and reflection that may lead to insight, behavior change, or cognitive restructuring. Discussion of films can reveal client misperceptions, myths, or misunderstandings. Films offer examples of effective and ineffective practices in communication, problem solving, conflict resolution, or decision making. Through films clients can identify strengths and resources they might apply to their current situation. Discussion of films often reveals dominant and alternative narratives. Viewing films also promotes emotional experiencing and expression. Especially important for grief counseling, cinematherapy aids in tailoring treatment to the uniqueness of the client because the counseling professional selects films to match specific client needs and considers distinct personal, familial, social, and cultural influences in assigning those films. Cinematherapy is adaptable across diverse theoretical orientations and is applicable in individual, couple, family, and group counseling.

Guidelines for Selecting and Assigning Films

Counseling professionals should be familiar with a range of films that have potential for cinematherapy and should view these films themselves before assigning them. It is helpful to view films more than once so as to focus on their potential therapeutic value (Sharp et al., 2002). Consider the client's level of interest in film, because some people really have no interest in movies, whereas others have very distinct preferences. Films that reflect client interests (e.g., hobbies, employment) increase the likelihood that the client will identify with film content (Dermer & Hutchings, 2000). Clients derive the most benefit from films whose characters and situations are similar to their own; for example, adolescents relate better to films with adolescent characters (Lampropoulous, Kazantzis, & Deane, 2004). Similarity of culture, race, ethnicity, class, sexual orientation, and gender enhances potential benefits. However, be aware that film content that is too identical to the client's situation may increase defensiveness (Sharp et al., 2002). For example, in working with a client devastated by the death of a parent, the counselor might consider the film *The Horse Whisperer* (Redford, 1998), with its focus on emotional wounds and the healing process, rather than a film that deals directly with parental death.

It is important that counseling professionals be clear about their intentions in using cinematherapy and select films that are consistent with the goals of counseling. What is it exactly that you want this client to see, to understand, or to consider in viewing this film? How does this film address the specific issues and concerns of this client? How might viewing this film help this client move forward in the change process? For example:

> The Benoit family lost their home during Hurricane Katrina. They have had several different living situations since then, including a trailer, sharing a home with relatives, and a motel. The children and parents have lived apart at several different times in different states. Everyone in the family is grieving but doing it in different ways: Some are obsessed with their losses and the emotional toll this has taken while some are unwilling to talk about the losses at all and want to concentrate only on the future; some want to return to their hometown while some do not even want to visit. Conflicts have emerged around these differences. The counselor asks the family to watch *In America* (Sheridan, 2002), a film about a desperately poor family who experienced the death of a child and have recently immigrated to New York City. This film was selected because it includes themes of loss, displacement, and family that the Benoits would find familiar and because the counselor wanted them to explore differences in grieving patterns, the consequences of suppressing emotions, and the challenges of shifting between a focus on loss and a focus on restoration.

It is not necessary to use films about loss when implementing cinematherapy with grieving clients, although this may be helpful. For example, a counselor working with a grieving client's anger problems might assign *Changing Lanes* (Michell, 2002), a film about road rage and anger escalation, to help this client explore cognitive distortions that contribute to anger management difficulties. Although there is some content about loss in the film, this is not a major theme. On the other hand, a client grieving the "living loss" of a parent or partner to Alzheimer's disease may find a film focused on this topic, such as *Iris* (R. Eyre, 2001), especially helpful.

Assigning Films as Homework

Thoughtful preparation of the client for viewing a film as homework enhances the potential benefits. Hensley and Hensley (1998) recommended the following:

+ *Normalize the assignment in the context of therapy.* The counseling professional should present the film-viewing homework as a serious assignment that is part of the overall therapy process.
+ *Provide a rationale.* Explain how viewing the film might address the concerns that brought the client to counseling. Point out themes, problems, strengths, or characters to examine rather than dictate an end result (e.g., "I want you to look at the choices this client makes" works better than "This movie will make you change the way you think").
+ *Describe potentially problematic material clearly* (e.g., violence, sexuality, profanity). Remember that material that is not offensive to the counseling professional may be offensive to a particular client. Discuss the value you see in the film despite the problematic material.

❖   *Assure clients that their responses to the film will be discussed in therapy.* Clients are more likely to comply with a homework assignment if they know the counselor takes the assignment seriously and will address it at a specific time or in a specific session. In family and group counseling, it is helpful to specify a date by which everyone will have viewed the film.

Client Guidelines for Film Viewing

As with most homework assignments used in counseling, specific and brief written guidelines increase the likelihood of compliance and benefit. First, provide practical directions for film viewing, such as minimizing interruptions, replaying scenes, and making notes (Hensley & Hensley, 1998). Second, prepare several focused questions tailored to clients and the films. These questions should be open-ended and fairly broad because they are meant simply to initiate client reflection. Questions might center on characters, situations, or client reactions. For example: What caught your attention or spoke to you in the film and why? What did you like and not like about the film? What reactions do you have to the characters in the film? Which characters or situations in the film did you identify with and in what way? What did you notice about the way certain characters changed or resisted change? What could certain characters have done differently to bring about a different outcome? How do you think this character's spirituality influenced things?

Integrating Film Into Therapy

The manner in which film is integrated into the therapy session depends largely on the goals of counseling, the intention of the assignment, the counselor's theoretical orientation, and the counselor's personal style. Do not focus only on maladaptive or dysfunctional elements; films also provide models of functionality and resilience that are beneficial. Always begin with the focused questions posed in the client's assignment. It is important to capitalize on the metaphorical value of film, so keep the initial dialogue centered on the film—its characters, themes, situations— and avoid moving too quickly to its direct application to the client. This allows the client a comfortable distance from the problem and reduces resistance (Sharp et al., 2002). Use evocative questions to promote client reflection and exploration. For example: What in the film seemed to speak to you and why did you think it did? What losses did the characters experience and how did they respond? What was helpful or unhelpful to them in their grieving? What inner strengths or resources did they discover and what difference did that make to their grieving? In what ways was their response to loss similar or different from that of other characters, and what was the impact of any differences or similarities? What obstacles did different characters encounter and how did they handle those obstacles? Were there turning points for some characters and how did these come about? How did characters change in the film and what do you think brought about that change? Sharp et al. (2002) suggested focusing clients on specific characters. Questions might include "What was this character thinking or feeling? What did the character see as his or her main problems? How did the character resolve his or her issues? What other solutions might the character have used?" (p. 273).

It is best to wait for clients to make the connection between a film's content and their own lives rather than doing that for them. If, however, clients do not make that shift themselves, the counselor may ask more directly. Hensley and Hensley (1998) suggested the following questions:

Which characters did you identify with? In what ways was that character similar to or different from you? What attributes would you like to take from that character? What aspects of that character would you avoid? Are there other characters in the film who present positive options and in what ways? How are they similar to people or situations in your world? How can you use a similar strategy to overcome your own challenges? (p. 70)

Cautions in Using Cinematherapy

There are some important cautions to keep in mind when considering cinematherapy in counseling for loss adaptation. For example, some films portray inappropriate behavior on the part of therapists. Counseling professionals should discuss these situations with clients before they view the film. Hensley and Hensley (1998) offered the following additional guidelines:

- Do not use cinematherapy with clients who have difficulty distinguishing reality from fantasy (e.g., psychotic disorders).
- Consider potential client reactions. It is understood that some films will cause distress for some clients. Discomfort is acceptable, but real distress is not. Discuss potential responses with clients before they view the film. Hensley and Hensley suggested the following rule of thumb: "with clients who are more vulnerable, we describe the films in far more depth than with clients who are more resilient and less emotionally distraught" (p. 37).
- Be certain that clients have sufficient coping skills and support services to handle emotional reactions to the film.
- Do not use films with violence in the home.
- Do not use films with clients who have recently had traumatic experiences similar to those in the film.
- Do not use cinematherapy with clients who do not like movies.

Film Suggestions for Cinematherapy With Loss and Grief

Many films are potential resources for cinematherapy, including animated films. As stated previously, a film does not have to be about grief to be helpful to grieving clients. The following films are recommended because they offer material especially useful in counseling for loss and grief.

- *Always* (Spielberg, 1989): grieving process, continuing bonds
- *Antwone Fisher* (Washington, 2002): multiple losses, foster care
- *Cast Away* (Zemeckis, 1994): developing inner resources
- *Catch and Release* (Grant, 2007): grieving differences, integration of grief
- *Changing Lanes* (Michell, 2002): anger, maladaptive thinking
- *The Color Purple* (Spielberg, 1985): abuse, loss, family, overcoming obstacles
- *Corrina, Corrina* (Nelson, 1994): grieving process, family
- *Da* (Clark, 1988): father–son relationships, loss, aging
- *The Five People You Meet in Heaven* (Kramer, 2004): meaning of life
- *Garden State* (Braff, 2004): guilt, grief
- *Harry Potter and the Sorcerer's Stone* (Columbus, 2001): overcoming obstacles, impact of loss

- *The Horse Whisperer* (Redford, 1998): emotional wounding, loss, grieving differences
- *In America* (Sheridan, 2002): loss, family, grieving differences
- *In the Bedroom* (T. Field, 2001): couple issues, grieving differences
- *Iris* (R. Eyre, 2001): Alzheimer's disease losses
- *Life as a House* (Winkler, 2001): divorce, family, terminal illness
- *Like Water for Chocolate* (Areu, 1993): family, living with/separating from the dead
- *Love Liza* (Louiso, 2002): suicide survivor, spousal grief
- *Marvin's Room* (Zaks, 1999): grieving differences, family, chronic illness
- *Message in a Bottle* (Mandoki, 1999): grief, unfinished business
- *Moonlight Mile* (Silbering, 2002): grieving differences, family, guilt
- *My Life* (Rubin, 1993): terminal illness, family
- *Ordinary People* (Redford, 1980): accidental death, family, guilt, grieving differences
- *Shadowlands* (Attenborough, 1994): grief, spiritual journey
- *Sleepless in Seattle* (Ephron, 1993): grief, father–son
- *Smoke Signals* (C. Eyre, 1998): grief, father–son
- *The Son's Room* (Moretti, 2001): grief, family
- *Soul Food* (Tillman, 1997): family, sibling rivalry, loss
- *Thirteen Conversations About One Thing* (Sprecher, 2001): redeeming self from mistakes
- *An Unfinished Life* (Hallstrom, 2005): unfinished business, forgiveness, family
- *Whale Rider* (Caro, 2002): overcoming loss and disappointment, cultural influences

Recommended Resources

Solomon, G. (2001). *Reel therapy: How movies inspire you to overcome life's problems.* New York: Lebhar-Friedman Books.

Solomon, G. (1995). *The motion picture prescription.* Santa Rose, CA: Aslan.

Wolz, B. (2005). *E-motion picture magic: A movie lover's guide to healing and transformation.* Centennial, CO: Glenbridge.

An excellent, frequently updated, online resource for cinematherapy is provided by B. Wolz at http://www.cinematherapy.com. The Web site includes a film index, film reviews, therapist guidelines, and links to other useful Web sites.

Prescription to Grieve

The Prescription to Grieve strategy provides clients with a structured, time-limited experience to help them gain control over emotionally intrusive grief. This strategy, developed originally by Janson (1985) to address bereavement grief, allows the client to set limits on the time and context of grief expression according to a predictable daily schedule. In this way clients can engage the emotions and thoughts of grieving on their own terms rather than being held hostage by intrusive emotionality, which so often victimizes and disempowers. When clients know that they can attend to their grief exclusively during set daily periods, they often find they are more able to manage emotional intensity at other times (e.g., at work, in class). The Prescription to Grieve is useful when clients (a) have difficulty engaging in normal activities at work and home because of emotionally intrusive grief; (b) have difficulty allowing themselves to express "unacceptable" emotions (e.g., anger, resentment); (c) feel overwhelmed by their grief, especially feeling "out of control"; and (d) have difficulty addressing their grief as a result of delaying or setting their grief aside at the time of loss or by overfocusing on others to the exclusion of attending to themselves.

Implementation of the Prescription to Grieve

In this strategy the counseling professional writes out a "script" for the client, just like a drug prescription from a physician. In the place of the drug name and dosage, the counselor specifies the time, frequency, and location of the assignment to grieve. The Prescription to Grieve can be "refilled" and specific topics appropriate to client needs included at each refilling (see Figure 4.4).

> Consider Daisy's situation. Both of her parents died within the last 2 years; her father died suddenly of a heart attack, then Daisy nursed her mother through a brief illness before her death. During this time Daisy also was laid off from her job and her husband was transferred so that the family relocated to another state. During that 2-year period Daisy put her own grieving aside so that she could focus on meeting her responsibilities to her family. Now things have begun to settle down and Daisy has started a new job. However, she is having difficulty concentrating at work because she suddenly feels overwhelmed with thoughts and feelings about her losses. Daisy is also exhausted from fighting off the emotional surges that seem to come out of nowhere and keep her from concentrating on her work. She worries that if she "gives in" to the grief, then she will be overwhelmed and unable to continue at work. Daisy also worries that something might be wrong with her because she is experiencing these emotions so long after the important losses occurred. She feels helpless and incompetent in trying to handle her grief. Daisy's counselor uses a Prescription to Grieve to help her set aside a daily time to experience her grief. Daisy follows her Prescription to Grieve and gradually experiences a reduction of the unpredictable and intrusive emotionality and gains a reassuring sense of control in her daily life.

---

4 DIRECTIONS COUNSELING CENTER
1951 Trout Road, Rockwall, TX 75087

For: Daisy Beller   **Date:** 10/19/08

Rx: journaling

Once daily × 30 minutes

                              Refill: 3×

Keren M. Humphrey
Dr. Keren M. Humphrey, NCC, LPC, LCPC

FIGURE 4.4

Prescription to Grieve

Note. From "The Prescription to Grieve," by M. A. H. Janson, 1985. *The Hospice Journal*, 1, p. 104. Copyright 1985 by the Inform Healthcare-Journals. Adapted with permission.

Time

Clients select a time of day during which they will focus exclusively on their grief experience. This must be a time when they can be undisturbed. If there is a specific time when the client tends to be most bothered by the grief-connected thoughts and emotions, then that often works well, but the key is that the client be undisturbed. The prescribed "grieving period" is 45 minutes. Janson (1985) noted that 30 minutes is usually insufficient and more than an hour tends to prolong the experience unhelpfully. It is helpful to use a time device (e.g., kitchen timer) with an auditory tone that signals when the time is up. This frees the client to focus on the task at hand and also reinforces the time limit.

Setting

The counselor helps the client select an accessible location, usually at home, where the client feels comfortable, safe, and can be undisturbed. The location may be somewhere closely identified with the loss or the object of the loss (e.g., deceased's bedroom), a place of beauty or quiet (e.g., garden, porch), or simply a familiar place (e.g., one's own bedroom). The setting may include items that generate a sense of closeness or familiarity with the deceased (in the case of bereavement grief) or simply facilitate contemplation. Encourage clients to "set the stage" to enhance the meaningfulness of the setting. For example, clothing belonging to the deceased, photographs, or cultural symbols may be used. Music is sometimes helpful, but it is best to avoid anything with familiar lyrics or melodies because one tends to get distracted with the lyrics. The setting should promote connection with the loss and enhance the experience of thoughts and feelings while not diverting attention.

Activities

The counselor and client collaborate on devising activities that fit the unique needs of the client. The focus may be on facilitating overall adaptation to loss, experiencing and expressing emotion, managing "unacceptable" emotions (e.g., anger), or meaning reconstruction. Two suggested activities are journaling and memory making.

In *journaling*, the clients record their thoughts and feelings regarding their losses and their adaptation to loss. The safety and individuality of a personal journal facilitates meaningful exploration and promotes emotional expression. Clients may write about their experience of challenging emotions, such as anger, guilt, shame, or resentment; they may explore fantasies and dreams connected with their loss; they may write directly to their lost objects (e.g., the deceased, former lover, severed leg) or about the loss event (e.g., immigration). Journals can include symbols, pictures, or other writings as well. Themes and issues that appear during therapy may also be addressed through the personal journal.

In *memory making*, the focus is on reminiscing about one's life and relationship with the loss or lost object. Memories may be evoked by scrapbooks, photographs, objects of connection, cultural symbols, or keepsakes. It is not necessary for clients to record (i.e., write down) the memories; simply allowing the memories to come, be attended to, and released is usually sufficient. Some clients may want to record the memories, although care must be taken that the recording does not simply become a way to avoid engaging fully in the experience.

Closure

At the end of the 45-minute period, the client ends the experience by saying "I am going to return to my daily activities now" or something similar that signals closure.

Decisional Balance and the Possibility of Change

Decisional Balance is frequently identified with cognitive–behavioral therapy and, more recently, with motivational interviewing (Miller & Rollnick, 1991, 2002) and the transtheoretical model (Prochaska, DiClemente, & Norcross, 1992). The purpose of this strategy is to help clients explore their motivation for change, especially the ambivalence that often impedes change. For example, a divorced woman grieving her losses may withdraw from her old friends and resist new relationships, but at the same time desire these connections and feel unable to change her behavior; a parent grieving the death of one child may be unable to resume parenting her surviving children, telling the counselor, "I want to and I know that I should, but I can't"; a widower remains focused on his loss and unable to focus on restoration, telling his counselor, "I want to change, but it means finally losing Fiona and I just cannot do that." The dilemma for these individuals is that there are compelling reasons for *not* changing as well as reasons *for* changing. Such ambivalence undermines the motivation required to make and sustain change. Although some ambivalence is a normative part of grieving that most people resolve on their own, it can become problematic when people get stuck in their adaptation to loss. "Ambivalence is a reasonable place but you wouldn't want to live there" (Miller & Rollnick, 2002, p. 14).

There are several particular circumstances in grief counseling when Decisional Balance might be a especially helpful strategy to use:

- When clients recognize they have reached an impasse in their adaptation to loss. They may mention feeling stuck, "in limbo," or in some way unable to move toward some desired state. These clients may be unable to oscillate between loss-oriented coping and restoration-oriented coping (according to the dual process model) or they may be exhibiting a dissonant response in their adaptive grieving pattern (according to the adaptive grieving styles model).
- When clients verbalize ambivalence regarding their potential for change. Clients may question their ability to make change, mention conflicted feelings/thoughts about the change process, or indicate potential negative consequences of change. For example, a man may recognize the dangers of his alcohol use but may also see drinking as helpful in dealing with his grief; a father grieving the stillbirth of his child may feel ready to engage more fully in work and relationships but may fear this change could adversely affect his wife and their marriage.
- When secondary gain consistently interferes with healthy loss adaptation. Secondary gain occurs when an individual receives reward or value by continuing to focus on loss and grief, even though this may be distressful. Secondary gain rewards in grieving might include distraction from other stressors (e.g., alcohol abuse, making decisions), protection from taking risks, maintaining a crisis mode (e.g., excitement), avoiding personal responsibility, keeping others involved (e.g., counselor), or getting others to take care of them.

Implementation of Decisional Balance

The counselor using Decisional Balance helps clients construct a "balance sheet" that outlines the pros and cons of continuing in their current behavior and the pros and cons of changing their behavior to reach a preferred outcome (see Figure 4.5). The approach relies on systematically eliciting from clients their own distinct list of perceived benefits and disadvantages for each side of the change versus not-change dilemma. It is important that counselors refrain from making their own suggestions or subtly attempting to lead the client to any "right" conclusions. Such coercive and manipulative behavior on the part of the counselor is the quickest way to disaster. Instead, the counselor's role is to respectfully and nonjudgmentally collaborate with the client in exploring the factors that both block change and promote change from the client's perspective.

Effective use of Decisional Balance relies on open-ended questions that evoke "change talk" (Miller & Rollnick, 2002, p. 23), reveal areas of concern, and promote further exploration. Note and underscore self-motivational statements (those that support problem recognition, concern, intention to change, optimism). It is important to help clients elaborate on their answers by using reflection and follow-up directives, such as "Tell me more about X," "What else?" or "Give me an

CONTINUING AS I AM NOW	CHANGING
Benefits/Advantages (Pros)	**Benefits/Advantages (Pros)**
Less responsibility	Improved relationships with family and friends
Easier to deal with people not expecting much from me	See myself as competent and able
As bad as it is, what I know is less scary than what I don't know	Handle emotions better, especially anger
Keep people at a distance	Have some control in my life and of myself
Don't have to face the possibility of failure	Pursue a job/career that I want
Less painful emotionally	Be more independent
Not sure I am ready to make any more changes	Get a life!
	Be happy!
Costs/Disadvantages (Cons)	**Costs/Disadvantages (Cons)**
No end to the emotional pain	Might fail
Friends and family will get fed up and leave me, so I will be more isolated	Might not be able to handle my emotions
Never know if I could make something better out of this	Disappointment—might discover I am not tough enough to handle this problem
Stay in limbo—stuck	Might not be better after all
Hate seeing myself as "disabled"	Might find I am not the man I thought I was
End up a drunk, or in jail, or on the streets	Painful to give up the dreams I had before I lost my leg
More painful emotionally	Might disappoint others if I fail

FIGURE 4.5

Decisional Balance Sheet

Note. This Decisional Balance Sheet was prepared by a man who lost both legs and an arm. The client has made a good physical recovery but remains focused on his losses to the exclusion of a focus on rebuilding his life. Since he mentioned feeling "stuck" several times, the counselor decided to use the Decisional Balance Sheet to help him explore his ambivalence about change.

example." The open-ended questions provided below are illustrative of the approach and not intended as a script (adapted from Miller & Rollnick, 2002, pp. 77–79). Note: Items marked with asterisks are suggested when initiating Decisional Balance as homework.

Questions helpful in exploring the *advantages of not changing* include:

- ✦ *What about the current situation seems to be working for you right now?
- ✦ *What do you like about things as they are?
- ✦ *What is helpful about the current situation?
- ✦ *What is the best that could happen if you do not change?
- ✦ What is helpful about focusing all your energy on what you have lost?
- ✦ What would other people say is beneficial to you about not changing?
- ✦ What is it about your drinking that seems to help you deal with the grief?

Questions helpful in exploring the *disadvantages of not changing* include:

- ✦ *What concerns you the most about the current situation?
- ✦ *What makes you think you need to do something about this situation?
- ✦ *What do you think will happen if you don't change—if you continue as you are?
- ✦ *What is the cost to you of the current situation?
- ✦ *What about the current situation does not seem to be working for you?
- ✦ What exactly are the problems with the current situation?
- ✦ What is it about your current situation that you or others might see as reason for concern?
- ✦ What would other people whose opinions you value say about your continuing to stay at the place you are now?
- ✦ What is the worst that could happen if you do not make some changes?
- ✦ If you continue as you are, what will your life be like in 5 years? In 10 years?

Questions helpful in exploring the *disadvantages of change* include:

- ✦ *What concerns you most about attempting to change this situation?
- ✦ *What might be the cost to you of making these changes?
- ✦ *What might be the impact on others if you make these changes?
- ✦ If you decided to make this change, who might be unhappy about this and why?
- ✦ What is the worst that could happen if you are successful in making these changes?
- ✦ If you did attempt to make some changes, what could go wrong?

Questions helpful in exploring the *advantages of change* include:

- ✦ *How would you like for things to be different?
- ✦ *What would be a good thing about making a change?
- ✦ *If you could make this change immediately, by magic, how might things be better for you?
- ✦ *What do you see as the advantages of making this change?
- ✦ What might be the best thing that could happen if you make these changes?

+ If you were completely successful in making this change, how would things be different?
+ What would other people whose opinion you value say would be good about making this change?

Decisional Balance can be implemented entirely within the therapy session or begun as homework, then discussed in more detail during therapy. When used as homework, it is recommended that the counselor provide a captioned worksheet with a few specific questions tailored to the client's situation. During the more detailed discussion in the therapy session, it is helpful to record the pros and cons on poster paper or whiteboard. Keep the following in mind when implementing Decisional Balance with grieving clients:

+ *Do not attempt to use Decisional Balance too early in the therapy.* The strategy works best when the client indicates some awareness that she or he has reached an impasse and/or states some ambivalence about change.
+ *Do not use Decisional Balance to confront clients with their misbehavior or to force awareness.* This will only foster defensiveness. Rollnick and Miller (1995) noted that client resistance to exploring ambivalence is a sign that the counselor is more invested in change than the client is at a particular point.
+ *Tailor Decisional Balance to the client by posing open-ended questions that are specific to the client's concerns.*
+ *Elicit and use the client's own words.* People are more likely to respond to their own language and their own arguments than to those of their counselor.
+ *Recognize that a completed Decisional Balance worksheet will contain contradictions* (Miller & Rollnick, 2002). That simply underscores the power of ambivalence to impede change.
+ *Do not sabotage the strategy by pushing for a commitment to change.* Focus instead on facilitating the client's exploration of the potential for change and the dimensions of ambivalence. This will allow for what Baumeister (1994) called the "crystallization of discontent" (p. 281) that fuels the motivation to change.

Confronting Secondary Gain

Sometimes a complicating factor in loss adaptation, especially when the grief seems prolonged, is the problem of secondary gain. *Secondary gain* occurs when people receive some benefit, value, or "payoff" by sustaining a focus on their loss and grief to the exclusion of restoration and integration of their loss over time. Their grief thereby serves another function besides grieving. For example, continuing to focus exclusively on loss and grief may

+ Serve as a distraction from other, more distressful issues and concerns (e.g., loneliness, financial worries, family conflicts, parenting challenges).
+ Protect the griever from risk taking, especially interpersonal risk taking (e.g., avoid situations that might yield new relationships).
+ Provide a way to gain attention, social interaction, or importance from others (e.g., display neediness or helplessness).
+ Provide a way to manipulate others for gain (e.g., social services, therapists, family members).

- Provide emotional intensity that may otherwise be absent from a person's life.
- Provide a focus for organizing one's life and lifestyle (e.g., identity or role as griever supersedes all other aspects of identity or roles).
- Serve as an excuse or "permission" to maintain dysfunctional behaviors (e.g., substance abuse/dependence, violence, isolation, and self-punishment).

It is important to distinguish between the usually temporary avoidance that naturally occurs when grieving clients move or oscillate between the dual grieving processes of loss orientation and restoration orientation and the dysfunctional benefit gained from maintaining a focus on loss and grief to the exclusion of restoration and eventual integration. Some exclusive focus on loss and grief is normative and appropriate, including when it distracts temporarily from restoration activities (e.g., adjusting to life without the lost object). That is different from using the loss and grief focus to avoid responsibility for one's actions, gain services, keep people connected, or feel "alive." The key is the functionality or purpose of the behavior and the ways in which that behavior is reinforced. Thus, the counseling professional asks: What does continued focus on loss and grief do for the person and how is that behavior maintained?

A preferred strategy for addressing the problem of secondary gain with loss adaptation is confrontation, in this case, confrontation of the dissonance or conflict between "legitimate" grieving of loss and pseudo-grieving for reward or benefit. Remember that confrontation is not about getting into people's faces or bullying people. The purpose of confrontation is to challenge clients to explore dissonant behavior, emotions, and cognitions. Confrontation simply opens a space in which the client can consider a puzzle. It must be delivered in a manner that clients can hear, that directs attention to specifics, and that blocks avoidance. Unconditional positive regard, genuineness, and empathy on the part of the counselor are essential to effective confrontation. Some counselors worry about the emotional intensity that sometimes accompanies confrontation, but they should remember that such arousal actually propels clients to work toward resolving the dissonance. Begin with mild confrontations; stronger confrontations work best when the client and counselor have established a solid working relationship. Consider that some clients respond to direct confrontation, whereas others, depending on personality and cultural influences, respond better to more indirect confrontations.

Implementation of Confrontation for Secondary Gain

The initial confrontation statement must be sufficiently strong or clear to get the client's attention. It should be phrased as a puzzle or conundrum that invites client reflection and exploration. Let the client "stew" in the puzzle. Silence is usually the best strategy because it invites clients to work. The following are some examples of grief-oriented confrontations:

- I wonder what this is doing for you.
- I wonder if you could keep Claudia interested in you if you get to some resolution of this grief.
- I wonder what life would be like if you stopped organizing it around the grief.
- How does this continued grieving protect you?
- Life would seem pretty boring without this grief as its central focus, wouldn't it?
- I wonder how your grandchildren would relate to you if they could see you without the sackcloth and ashes.

113

- If you stopped focusing so much on Henri's memory, you might have the energy to invest in new relationships but I bet that sounds pretty scary to you.
- When will you be satisfied that you have suffered enough?
- Is there some other more useful way in which you might direct your energies to satisfy your "punisher"? (Joy, 1985).
- Sounds like the only time you really feel alive is when you are expressing the grief.
- What would it look like if you were no longer grieving so intensely? How would your life be different? How would others respond to you?
- It might not be a good idea to resolve this grief, since it would mean you have to then deal with all these other issues.
- So, what's the connection between grieving the infertility and facing the problems in your marriage?
- If you move through this grief and get to the other side, what will it cost you?
- So, if you are not the grieving widower, who are you?
- Some people in your situation would feel that there has been enough time and pain. (indirect confrontation)
- Some say that after a time grieving people must turn their faces once again toward the sun. (indirect confrontation)
- I once had another client who felt that opening herself to life again meant she never really loved her daughter after all. We could all see that this was not true, but she was stuck there. (indirect confrontation)
- The counselor could make the indirect confrontation above more directive by adding "I wonder if your situation is a little similar?"

Often a client's first response to a confrontation is avoidance (e.g., change subject, ignore confrontation, or become defensive). The counselor should block avoidance by restating or refocusing the confrontation. If the client continues to avoid, then either restate again or use immediacy to address the client's here-and-now experience: "What is happening between us right now? You are having a hard time looking at this . . . what is going on right now?" If a client still avoids, then the counselor should consider dropping the confrontation. Continued avoidance or defensiveness suggests the client is not ready to examine this issue at the present moment or it has been delivered in a way that the client cannot "hear." If the issue is important, then the opportunity to address it will come along again.

Once the client responds to the confrontation, recognizes the dissonance, and considers the possibility of change, it is helpful to use strategies, for example, Decisional Balance, that clarify reasons for and against change to enhance motivation. (See also Chapter 5, the Chair Dialogue With Parts section.)

Creating a Resilient Image

Grieving people often encounter periods when they feel overwhelmed by their experiences over the course of loss adaptation. That is, they see themselves as unable to tolerate the demands of grieving. Their distress flows from many sources. There are the powerful emotions of grief (e.g., sorrow, guilt, despair), the exhausting demands of restoration (e.g., rebuilding and reorganizing life), and the process of both facing and avoiding loss. They may be overwhelmed by negative imagery associated with the loss or the lost object (e.g., deathbed scenarios, interpersonal confrontations, hospital room, or violent circumstances). Often the disequilibrium of disrupted beliefs and assumptions is akin to the ground suddenly shifting beneath one's feet. Common responses to feeling overwhelmed include numbing emotions, reactive behavior, excessive rumination, invoking screen emotions (e.g., anger), withdrawal and isolation, avoidance and distraction, and increased helplessness or controlling behavior.

The strategy of Creating a Resilient Image draws on Rynearson's (2001) *restorative retelling* approach with people grieving the violent dying of a loved one, in which he noted the importance of promoting three resilient capacities: pacification (self-calming), partition (self-discrimination), and perspective (self-transcendence). These capacities support one's ability to tolerate the distress associated with grieving, especially feeling overwhelmed. Creating a Resilient Image is a self-directed method for managing or tolerating the distress of feeling overwhelmed that includes self-soothing or self-calming via a safe image; separating one's self from distressful thoughts, emotions, or imagery; and adopting a view of transcending or prevailing over the distress.

Implementation of Resilient Imagery

Clients are asked to create an image that they can call up whenever they feel overwhelmed or see themselves as unable to tolerate the demands of grieving. The image must include the following: (a) the individual alone (promotes self-reliance), (b) in a safe and comfortable setting in which the person is physically separated from distress yet able to view the distress (inside/outside or boundary image), and (c) in which the person is able to visualize a time when the distress has passed by or the person has regained control.

Rynearson's (2001) image provides an example to share with clients: "floating on the surface of a strong tide where I can breathe and remain calm and flow with the current until it has spent itself" (p. 70). Note how this "float and flow" image facilitates self-calming (floating and breathing), self-discrimination (boundary setting), and self-transcendence (visualizing a time when the current has run out). Although clients may wish to adapt this recommended image, it is more useful when the image flows directly from their own experience. It is preferred that the image not include the object of loss (e.g., deceased) or loss environment (e.g., hospital, employment location). The counseling professional asks clients to imagine or recall a circumstance in their life when they felt safe and in control even while there was difficulty or chaos around them. Examples might include snuggling down in a warm bed while a storm rages outside; watching a heavy rain from a secure shelter; walking across a long, sturdy bridge over rapids and waterfalls; or standing on a subway platform, watching the trains go by in different directions, and waiting until the right one comes.

Counseling professionals may work with clients to create the resilient image within the therapy session, or this can be assigned initially as homework, providing specific directions on the necessary components of the image, and then refining it in-session. The image should be simple and vivid, not convoluted. It is often helpful to ask clients to describe the image in one sentence. Assist clients in exploring details of the image with attention to its resilient capacities: How does the image promote self-calming? How does the image allow the client to maintain separation from distress or a boundary between self and distress without running away from it? How does the image encourage a view of transcendence? Finally, discuss the circumstances in which the client might call up the image and check in with the client from time to time to determine whether the image is useful or needs further refinement.

115

For some clients the resilient image becomes more than just a tool for managing distress, instead providing clients with an image symbolic of their overall efforts at adapting to loss. In this case, counseling professionals should explore the symbolism and encourage its application.

The 2 Questions

The 2 Questions is a straightforward strategy that helps clients focus on ways that they can and do help themselves manage distressful feelings and situations related to loss and grief. Proposed originally by Lafond (1994) in her book on grieving mental illness, the questions promote resilience by helping grieving persons recognize and use their own capacities, strengths, and abilities. The 2 Questions (adapted from Lafond, 1994, p. 16) are

1. How can I help myself cope with _____?
2. In what ways can I use my experience of _____ constructively?

Clients are invited to fill in the blanks, typically either with *feelings* (sadness, guilt, anger) or specific *circumstances* (e.g., loneliness, disability, estrangement, illness out of control, family problems, cancer). The questions are phrased in a way that invites specificity, directs attention to what can be done, and implies client efficacy. Question 1 encourages people to identify and label their feelings, a useful skill in emotion management, and to discern what things have already been helpful as well as those that might yet be helpful. Question 2 further empowers people by focusing on what they have learned and then reinforces that self-knowledge by directing them to consider putting it to good use either for themselves or for others.

The questions are most effectively proposed in order, because the second question builds on the answer from the first question. For example, an adolescent grieving her parents' divorce answered the first question in terms of coping with anger at her mother: I can remind myself to chill out and to breathe; talk to my friends; tell my Dad what is going on; work out; talk to my counselor; tell myself that it is my parents' failure and not mine; cry if I need to; take a walk or a run. She answered the second question regarding using the anger at her mother constructively in this way: I can use the energy to motivate me to work out; be understanding of friends who have similar situations; spend time with my little brother even if he is a pain in the neck.

The 2 Questions can be explored effectively within the therapy session or used as a homework assignment. Writing the questions and answers down underscores concreteness rather than abstraction, so it is suggested that the counselor use poster paper or whiteboard (in session) or create a handout to use for homework. Responses can be added to the list from time to time throughout the therapy. The 2 Questions can also be used in family and group psychotherapy. Family members may be encouraged to share their responses with the entire family. Additionally, counseling professionals may encourage family members to consider how they might be supportive of each member's efforts to cope or use experiences constructively. Lafond (1994), discussing group work with grieving clients, encouraged group members to ask the first question ("How do you help yourself . . .?") anytime a member talks about distressing feelings or circumstances.

Breathing Lessons

Deep breathing (abdominal breathing or diaphragmatic breathing) has long been recognized as an effective stress management intervention. When stressed, humans often begin shallow, rapid breathing, which impairs elimination of carbon dioxide and actually makes the lungs and heart work harder, leaving us fatigued and more physically stressed. Deep breathing, on the other hand, brings more oxygen into the lungs, decreases stress on the heart, slows blood pressure, and has an almost immediate calming effect. Most clients benefit from learning to use deep breathing as a self-comforting tool for managing stress. Deep breathing is especially helpful for grieving people because, in addition to self-calming, it gives them a sense of control when they feel overwhelmed. It is recommended as an excellent alternative to the more traditional relaxation exercises because, as Malkinson (2007) pointed out, grieving people find the notion of deep breathing to manage their distress more acceptable than being told to relax in the face of painful and sorrowful loss.

It is recommended that counseling professionals instruct clients in deep breathing early in therapy, inquire regularly as to clients' continued practice of deep breathing, and utilize deep breathing within the therapy session on a regular basis. Simply telling clients to try deep breathing without actually incorporating it into the session is usually a prescription for failure. Some counselors find it helpful to begin and/or end therapy sessions with brief deep breathing exercises. Counseling professionals are also encouraged to use deep breathing forms associated with various ethnic or communal traditions (e.g., Native American, Asian) where appropriate.

Although deep breathing is a safe and healthy practice in most cases, counselors should confer with clients as to their physical and health status before instruction. Deep breathing may not be an appropriate intervention for persons with temporal lobe epilepsy, psychosis, severe respiratory disease, or prior chest surgery (Fried, 1993, cited in J. C. Smith, 2005).

Implementation of Deep Breathing

Deep breathing is best taught by live demonstration during the counseling session. An excellent time to do so is when the client becomes obviously stressed. Whereas there are diverse formats for deep breathing, brief exercises work best as an introduction. Counselors may also recommend books and recordings on deep breathing, as noted below.

Before beginning the exercise, counselors should explain the purpose and potential benefits of deep breathing, especially as it applies to the client's particular situation. The following provides an example of directions for introducing deep breathing to clients:

1. "A number of people in your situation have found deep breathing really helpful in managing times when they feel overwhelmed or stressed. It can really allow you to take control of things. Once you have learned how to do it, you can use deep breathing whenever you encounter especially stressful moments and can also use it daily as an overall stress management technique. [Counselor may provide an example from client's life where deep breathing could have been used.] It takes a little practice, but you will get the hang of it."
2. "When most of us take a deep breath we tend to really pump up our chest, which is not really a helpful way to breathe, especially when we want to calm ourselves. In deep breathing you focus on your abdomen rising rather than your chest expanding, and on exhaling more than you are inhaling."
3. "Place one hand on your chest and the other on your abdomen (over your belly button). Take a slow, deep, soft breath by inhaling through your nose and feel your abdomen rise. If the hand on your chest is rising more than the hand on your abdomen, then you are chest breathing rather than breathing from your abdomen. Try it again until you've got it." [Client practices until he or she has got the concept before counselor proceeds.]

117

4. "Now, once again, take a slow, deep, soft breath by inhaling through your nose and feel your abdomen rise. Inhale for a count of 4." [Counselor counts to 4 out loud.]
5. "Now, purse your lips a bit. Slowly and steadily exhale through your mouth, pushing all the air out. Pretend you are taking a long time to blow out a candle. Exhale for a count of 8. [Counselor counts to 8 out loud.] Always let the exhale be a bit longer than the inhale. It may take a little practice and the count is only a guide; use whatever count works for you. Now, let's do it again."

Repeat this exercise several times, inviting clients to lead the exercise as well. Then work with clients to identify circumstances in which they might use deep breathing and set up a plan for daily practice. It is helpful to provide Steps 2 through 5 to clients in written form. Check in regularly with clients on their daily practice of deep breathing.

Recommended Resources

Lewis, D. (Speaker). (2005). *Natural breathing* [CD]. Louisville, CO: Sounds True.

Weil, A. (Speaker). (2000). *Breathing: The master key to self healing* [CD]. Louisville, CO: Sounds True.

Smith, J. C. (2005). *Relaxation, meditation, and mindfulness*. New York: Springer.

Mindfulness-Based Practices to Manage Distress

Rooted in both Eastern and Western spiritual traditions and contemplative practices, mindfulness-based practices have recently been adapted into Western psychotherapy, especially by cognitive and behavioral approaches such as Dialectical Behavioral Therapy (DBT), Acceptance and Commitment Therapy, Mindfulness-Based Cognitive Therapy, and Mindfulness-Based Stress Reduction (Hamilton, Kitzman, & Guyotte, 2006; Hayes, Follette, & Linehan, 2004; Linehan, 1993a; Sagula & Rice, 2004). These approaches utilize mindfulness to help clients disengage from their thoughts and emotions, thus reducing reactivity (e.g., acting out, ruminating). In contrast to traditional cognitive therapy in which cognitive distortions are replaced with functional and adaptive cognitions, mindfulness-based practices help clients develop a different relationship with their thoughts and feelings. Instead of trying to change cognitive distortions or distressful emotions, clients learn to accept them as part of their experience without needing to do anything with them or about them. In mindfulness, inaction replaces reaction, thus reducing distress.

Put simply, mindfulness "means paying attention in a particular way: on purpose, in the present moment, and nonjudgmentally" (Kabat-Zinn, 1994, p. 4). The following elements of mindfulness practice are most critical to counseling:

+ focusing intentionally, deliberately, and fully on one's present experience and only on the present experience
+ observing in a detached manner one's thoughts, feelings, and physical state in the present moment
+ nonjudgmentally accepting one's thoughts and feelings as part of the landscape of the present moment and no more

Mindfulness-based practices offer an intentional implementation of the time-honored view that effective grieving is a matter of putting one foot in front of the other or, as the widowed father in the movie *Sleepless in Seattle* states, "Well, I'm gonna get out of bed every morning . . . breathe in and out all day long. Then, after awhile I won't have to remind myself to get out of bed every morning and breathe in and out" (Ephron, 1993).

Mindfulness-based practices have proved effective in treating a range of problems, including chronic pain, muscular disorders, hypertension, anxiety, and depression (Kabat-Zinn, Lipworth, & Burney, 1985; Kabat-Zinn et al., 1992; Mills & Allen, 2000; Teasdale et al., 2000). Perhaps most interesting for grief counseling, mindfulness-based practices have been used to improve concentration, enhance emotion regulation skills, and increase tolerance of negative emotions (Hamilton et al., 2006). Mindfulness-based practices can help grieving clients interrupt the repetitive cycles of loss-oriented rumination and manage emotional distress. The goal of mindfulness practices is not to avoid painful emotions but to be okay with them (Kumar, 2005), accepting them as part of the experience of grieving.

Through mindful attention, we discover the fact that grief is not who we are. Grief is not an identity. What feels so solid and real as a grief reaction (or any other reaction) in any moment is merely a combination of reactive habits of thinking, feeling, and physical sensations. Learning to inhabit our awareness and deepen its scope by practicing mindfulness enables us to experience how much larger and more vibrant we actually are—beyond any experience of upset, even grief. And, by inhabiting each moment with compassionate awareness, we discover how capable we are of containing and healing the grief we carry. (Kumar, 2005, p. ix)

An important advantage of using mindfulness-based practices is that these methods are self-help tools utilized in a self-directed manner by the client whenever needed. This has benefits both within and outside of the counseling session. Three selected mindfulness-based practices are recommended especially for grief work: mindful attention, detached acceptance, and mindfulness meditation. Mindful attention and detached acceptance, which can be taught by counseling professionals and used directly within the therapy session, are described below. Mindfulness meditation, which involves daily meditation practice, is recommended as an adjunct strategy.

Cultivating Mindful Attention

A core element of mindfulness involves paying acute attention to and being aware of one's present experience. It is the opposite of multitasking. Mindfulness is not about changing anything other than how one attends to the moment. This mindful attention, or *one-mindedness*, requires a nonjudgmental and compassionate stance that opens people to whatever is happening inside and around them. Cultivating mindful attention involves purposefully focusing on one experience and only one experience at a time, such as washing dishes, driving the car, or even grieving. When the inevitable distracting thoughts and feelings arise that will take away from full attention to one experience, these distractions are simply noted, and then the practitioner refocuses again on the experience at hand.

Do one thing at a time. When you are eating, eat. When you are walking, walk. When you are bathing, bathe. When you are working, work. When you are in a group, or a conversation, focus your

119

attention on the very moment you are in with the other person. When you are thinking, think. When you are worrying, worry. When you are planning, plan. When you are remembering, remember. Do each thing with all of your attention. If other actions, or other thoughts, or strong feelings distract you, let go of distractions and go back to what you are doing—again, and again, and again. Concentrate your mind. If you find you are doing two things at once, stop and go back to one thing at a time. (Linehan, 1993b, p. 113)

Mindful attention requires practice, so it works best if encouraged as a regular activity. Counseling professionals should introduce mindful attention through an initial activity within the session and then follow with homework assignments to build skills. Peeling an Orange is recommended as an in-session introduction useful for individual, family, or group therapy situations (see Box 4.4). Homework assignments should involve the client's regular activities, such as visiting a coffee shop, strolling through a garden, riding a subway, mowing the lawn, doing the laundry, walking the dog, performing job tasks (e.g., filing, factory work), cleaning the house, dancing, swimming, and working out (see Box 4.5 and Box 4.6).

Clients should be encouraged to begin incorporating mindful attention into their daily life. The counseling professional follows up on homework assignments, helping clients fine-tune their practice. In helping clients cultivate mindful attention, it is important to emphasize the client's ability to focus fully and completely on one experience and one experience only; practice nonjudgmental observation of thoughts, feelings, and sensations; handle distractions by naming and then refocusing/shifting attention; and maintain a compassionate attitude toward self. As clients gain some expertise with mindful attention, the counselor may invite them to consider specific points in the day when they might grieve mindfully. Here, clients are encouraged to schedule a time in which they give mindful attention to their grief and then continue with their day. Often clients who do this activity find themselves freed from intrusive rumination and distressful emotions at other times as well. Most clients find it helpful to practice mindful attention to grieving within the therapy session the first time so that the counselor can help them manage the experience. Some counseling professionals have found it helpful to do a mindfulness attention activity with clients at the beginning of a session on a regular basis. In this case clients may be invited to focus mindful attention on whatever is happening for them at that moment.

Detached Acceptance: You Are Not Your Thoughts and Feelings

A critical element of mindfulness practice involves helping clients develop a different relationship with their thoughts, feelings, and sensations. Rather than regarding thoughts as fact and emotions as truth or reality, which leads to *reaction*, mindfulness practice advocates a detached acceptance of one's thoughts and feelings, leading to *inaction* (Marlatt et al., 2004). We all have our thoughts and feelings, but that does not mean we have to do anything about them. We notice them, we observe them, then we accept them nonjudgmentally as part of our experience, but we do not have to analyze, criticize, avoid, deny, judge, defend, identify with, or struggle against them (i.e., react).

It is remarkable how liberating it feels to be able to see that your thoughts are just thoughts and that they are not "you" or "reality." . . . The simple act of recognizing your thoughts as thoughts can free you from the distorted reality they often create and allow for more clear-sightedness and a greater sense of manageability in your life. (Kabat-Zinn, 1990, pp. 69–70)

BOX 4.4

Mindful Attention In-Session Activity: Peel an Orange

Instructions to Counselor: This activity is a good introduction to mindfulness because it emphasizes focusing fully on the present moment. You will need hand towels, a wastebasket, and an orange for everyone (e.g., single client, family or group members, and yourself). Place the oranges on a table and ask everyone to select one, taking yours last, and hold their orange gently in their hand. Give the following directions in a quiet and deliberate manner, breathing slowly and consciously to keep the pace slow.

We are going to use this orange to practice mindfulness in our lives—learning to be fully in the present moment and open to this moment's experience. It sometimes helps to close your eyes during the exercise, but that is up to you. You don't have to talk, just quietly tune in and focus on your senses. There is nothing else to do and nowhere else to be for these few moments. There is no right way or wrong way to anything here and we are not looking for insight or meaning. This is just about being fully open to the present experience. Act as if this activity is the most important thing in your life just for this moment. When you find yourself distracted or not attending, just notice that this is happening, focus on your breathing or the orange, and follow your sensations back to the exercise. Make your actions careful, deliberate, and slow. Be attentive to every moment and take in all the details of this experience.

First, take a soft breath in and out. Slowly, raise the orange to your nose, squeeze it a bit, and breathe in the fragrance. Take another sniff and smile at the pleasantness of it all. Breathe softly in and out. Be mindful of this moment and this moment only.

Now, simply feel the orange in your hand, notice its shape and the way it fits naturally into the curve of your hand. Roll the orange slowly from hand to hand. Run your fingers across the surface of the orange and silently name your sensations of shape and texture. Breathe softly. Now look at your orange, noting the colors of the orange and of your hand holding the orange. Breathe softly. Silently name any sensations that come to you.

Now begin to slowly and carefully peel your orange as you bring all your senses to the moment. Make this like a slow-motion movie. Silently name your sensations as you peel your orange. What do you smell, feel, see, and hear? Take your time. It's your orange and your experience. You have all the time in the world for this. Enjoy! When you are ready, slowly and intentionally eat your orange or as much as you want to eat. It's okay to be messy. Notice the taste on the tip of your tongue and how the orange fills your mouth. Note how the bits of orange deflate as you suck the juice. Enjoy fully the experience of eating an orange in this moment.

When you have finished eating, sit quietly and focus on your breathing. Slowly breathe in and out. Be mindful of this moment and this moment only.

The counselor and client(s) then discuss the exercise, sharing their mutual experience. What was it like to fully attend to a moment? What thoughts, feelings, and sensations were noticed? How was focus maintained? How were distractions handled? Since the point of the exercise is to practice mindful attention, limit any discussion of meaning or insight. Encourage the client to do this exercise at home. You can also use plums, tangerines, or apples (with a peeler or small knife) instead of oranges.

BOX 4.5

Mindful Attention Activity: Wash the Dishes

Wash the dishes slowly, deliberately, and attentively. Be silent and breathe naturally. Treat each plate, cup, and fork as if it is sacred, giving each of them time and individual effort. Act as if washing the dishes is the most important thing in your life at this moment. Open your senses and focus on the details: notice colors, shapes, and textures; notice smells and sounds; notice temperature and movement. Name your sensations silently (e.g., blue, warm, slippery, graceful, sharp). Breathe. When you find yourself distracted by other things or hurrying your task, focus on your breathing to return you to mindfulness. Breathe. Take your time. Attend to the moment. Wash the dishes.

Detached acceptance begins with learning to observe thoughts and feelings while allowing them to exist apart. Maintaining this *observational stance* with negative thoughts and feelings, especially, can enhance tolerance for discomfort and thus improve emotion regulation. It is important to understand that detached acceptance does not mean denying or avoiding one's thoughts and emotions. Instead, by reducing reactivity and building tolerance for negative states, detached acceptance actually frees one to explore uncomfortable or threatening material in a productive manner. One tool for helping clients learn detached acceptance, especially with regard to painful remembering, is to develop their "Watcher Self." The Watcher Self puts psychological distance between the "me" experiencing discomfort and the "me" who is remembering by observing—watching—this experience without being caught up in it (Deatheredge, 1982, cited in Huxter, 2006). Clients are often more willing to approach and explore uncomfortable material when they can use their Watcher Self because it gives them a way of managing the pain itself and, equally important, managing their fear of being overwhelmed by the pain. Counseling professionals should introduce the notion of detached acceptance and the Watcher Self in session and then encourage the client to practice this approach out of the session. When dealing with distressful emotions and thoughts, counselors can ask their clients to talk about what their Watcher Self is observing.

Another tool for developing detached acceptance is Linehan's (1993b, p. 160) steps for letting go of emotional suffering. This material is excellent as a client handout.

BOX 4.6

Mindful Attention Activity: Eat a Meal

Be deliberate in your actions and attentive to each moment. Be silent and breathe naturally. Act as if this meal was the most important thing in your life at this moment and as if you have all the time in the world (you do!). Turn on and tune into all your senses. Notice every detail. Take in your setting. Notice the shapes of your utensils and plate; breathe in the aromas; feast the eyes. Take small bites, chew each bite thoroughly, and take small sips. Notice how food and drink taste, smell, and feel. Savor the moment and all that comes to you. When you find yourself distracted, simply notice this, name the distraction, and follow your sensations back to this moment. Take your time; breathe; attend to the moment; eat a meal.

---

* Observe your emotion: note its presence; step back; get unstuck from the emotion.
* Experience your emotion: as a wave, coming and going; try not to block emotion; try not to suppress emotion; don't try to get rid of emotion; don't push it away; don't try to keep emotion around; don't hold on to it; don't amplify it.
* Remember you are not your emotion: do not necessarily act on your emotion; remember times when you have felt different.
* Practice loving your emotion: Don't judge your emotion; practice willingness; radically accept your emotion.

Detached acceptance is also useful in dealing with distressful thoughts. The "Soldiers in the Parade" exercise, used regularly in Acceptance and Commitment Therapy, is an excellent introduction to using detached acceptance with cognitions. The counselor's script is as follows:

I want to do a little exercise that will help underline the differences between looking at thoughts, versus looking from thoughts. In a moment, I'm going to ask you to let yourself think anything you think. With each thought, imagine that there are little soldiers marching out of your ear and then in front of you, like a parade in front of a reviewing stand. The soldiers are carrying signs, and each thought is printed on a sign in the form of words or pictures. The task is simply this: Watch the parade and see how long you can go letting it flow by. If it stops for any reason—if you join the parade, leave the reviewing stand, become a soldier or whatever—see if you can catch back up just a moment and see what happened right before the observation of the parade stopped. (Hayes, 2004, p. 20)

Many clients from diverse backgrounds find mindfulness-based practices helpful. Even clients who do not see themselves as capable of or interested in meditation often respond positively to mindfulness practice. Whereas the approach described here is derived from Buddhist tradition, variations on mindfulness, contemplation, and meditation are found in many native traditions as well as Jewish and Christian contemplative traditions. It may be helpful to have clients identify any similar practices in their own background. However, the mindfulness approach recommended here is not intended as a spiritual discipline that seeks enlightenment or union with God. Instead, these practices are self-help techniques used only to promote client well-being and facilitate loss adaptation. This addresses the problem of clients using the notion of spiritual quest as a way to avoid uncomfortable thoughts and feelings. Counseling professionals should discuss this important distinction with their clients.

Optimal incorporation of mindfulness-based practices into therapy requires that the counseling professional to be intimately familiar with mindfulness practices. One cannot teach clients what one does not know. The resources below may be helpful to counseling professionals and to clients who are interested in deepening their mindfulness experiences.

Recommended Resources

Germer, C. K., Siegel, R. D., & Fulton, P. R.(2005). (Eds.). *Mindfulness and psychotherapy.* New York: Guilford Press.

Hanh, N. T. (1987). *The miracle of mindfulness: A manual on meditation.* Boston: Beacon Press.

Kabat-Zinn, J. (1990). *Full catastrophe living: Using the wisdom of your body and mind to face stress, pain, and illness.* New York: Delacorte.

Kabat-Zinn, J. (1994). *Wherever you go, there you are: Mindfulness meditation in everyday life.* New York: Hyperion.

Kabat-Zinn, J. (2002). *Guided mindfulness meditation: Series 1, 2, and 3* [CDs and tapes]. Available from http://www.mindfulnesscds.com

Kabat-Zinn, J. (2006). *Coming to your senses: Healing ourselves and the world through mindfulness.* New York: Hyperion.

Kumar, S. M. (2005). *Grieving mindfully: A compassionate and spiritual guide to coping with loss.* Oakland, CA: New Harbinger.

Using Ecotherapy Strategies for Loss and Grief

Ecotherapy, also known as nature-guided therapy and ecopsychotherapy, uses nature-related activities and psychotherapy to promote psychological and physiological well-being. This emerging approach recognizes the connection of mind, body, and spirit with the healing power of nature, focusing on the ways that the experience of nature can alter cognitions, emotions, behavior, and psychophysiology (G. W. Burns, 1998). Ecotherapy is not a matter of sending people out to hug trees or "commune with nature" but is an intentionally client-centered and solution-focused approach to psychotherapy involving specific goals and deliberate plans to reach those goals. However, some strategies derived from ecotherapy can be incorporated into diverse theoretical approaches and tailored to fit the uniqueness of clients and the multiple contexts of their lives. Ecotherapy strategies are especially helpful in the treatment of loss and grief concerns. Meaningful contact with the natural world combined with psychotherapy provides the following:

+ promotes awareness of the here-and-now and aids introspection
+ facilitates meaning reconstruction as clients contemplate themes common to both grief and nature, such as growth and stagnation, symbiosis, seasons of life, interconnection of all things, death and recovery, adaptation, evolution, and regeneration
+ aids stress reduction
+ facilitates the dual grieving processes of loss orientation and restoration orientation
+ encourages resilience
+ promotes a change orientation
+ stimulates emotional experiencing
+ provides helpful distraction or respite from the demands of grieving
+ challenges the numbness of grief by awakening the senses
+ promotes pleasure, harmony, and balance

Two ecotherapy strategies, adapted from G. W. Burns (1998), are suggested here: counselor-initiated sensual awareness and client-sourced sensual awareness. It is assumed that the client and the counseling professional have established therapeutic goals consistent with a change in cognitions, emotions, and behavior prior to implementing these strategies (e.g., establish a sense of control in life, reduce emotional numbness, reduce stress, make sense of loss, build new identity, experience pleasure, or adjust to the environment without the deceased).

Counselor-Initiated Sensual Awareness

In *counselor-initiated sensual awareness*, clients are asked to participate in an activity that directly exposes them to nature, focus fully on sensual awareness of that experience, and then explore that experience in therapy. The counseling professional must first establish what nature-related resources are available to the client, then collaborate with the client as to logistics of the nature encounter (i.e., time, location, accessibility, safety concerns). The activity may involve travel or be locally available, and it can occur as a single experience (observing a sunset on the beach) or be repeated (walking the neighborhood).

Once the setting and logistics are established, the counseling professional directs clients to focus on sensual awareness while participating in the activity. Awareness should focus on sight, sound, smell, taste, and touch, with consideration of variety, intensity, and alterations in these sensations. Clients are encouraged to get up close and fully experience nature. For example, walk barefoot in the grass or on the sand, caress a horse's nose, smell passing aromas, feel the wind, and note differences in color, shape, and form. It is helpful to suggest that clients tune into each sensation separately, and then shift to awareness of the whole. Clients may wish to record their observations but must balance this with being fully aware of their sensual experience; therefore, recording is best done following the activity. If clients find themselves distracted, they should refocus on awareness of their senses. Examples of nature-related activities to promote sensual awareness include walking through a neighborhood, city, or rural area; hiking in a forest; strolling along a beach, river, or lake; visiting a ranch or farm; walking through a park, garden, or arboretum; visiting a farmer's market; observing animals in nature; watching a waterfall; observing a starry night sky; and watching a rainstorm, sunset, or sunrise.

At the next therapy session, the counseling professional asks clients to describe and explore their experience. The counselor helps clients link their experience of nature to their experience of loss and grief. Opening invitations might include the following: Describe your feelings and thoughts while you were participating in this activity. What connections do you see between your experience in nature and your experience of loss and grief? What discoveries did you make or knowledge did you confirm? Did you encounter anything unexpected, and what do you think of that now? What feelings did you experience? What are nature's lessons, and how do they apply to you? In what ways does this experience contribute to thinking, feeling, or behaving differently?

Counseling professionals should customize the sensual awareness activity to client needs and goals. For example, a client who experiences numbness and a general depressed mood might benefit from a particularly stimulating setting (e.g., walking the city), whereas a client who is overwhelmed and overreactive to the demands of grieving might benefit from a more soothing setting (e.g., solitary stroll at dawn). Instead of attending to multiple sensations, counseling professionals may ask clients to focus on one sense experience (e.g., sound) in an activity in one week, then a different one (e.g., sight) the next week and so forth. It is clear that certain locations lend themselves to specific senses. For example, when visiting a public park, the client may be asked to smell flowers, touch grass and trees, listen to specific sounds, and observe people interacting with nature.

Client-Sourced Sensual Awareness

Client-sourced sensual awareness is based on sense-evoking activities in which clients have already participated. The purpose is to enhance the client's sensual awareness as a means of promoting overall well-being, restoration, and integration of grief. Using a Sensual Awareness Inventory (SAI; G. W. Burns, 1998) to elicit a list of sensory experiences that clients find pleasurable, counselors encourage clients to continue, expand, or renew their participation in these activities. There are four steps in implementing client-sourced sensual awareness.

Step 1. The client completes the SAI as a homework assignment (see Figure 4.6).

125

Directions: Under each heading, please list 10–20 items or activities from which you get pleasure, enjoyment, or comfort.

SIGHTS	SOUNDS	SMELLS	TASTES	TOUCH	ACTIVITY
Horses in the pasture	Baby laughing	Honeysuckle	Good wine	Warm pavement	Long, hot bath
Mug of steaming coffee	Mothers cooing to infants	Baking bread	Peanut butter	Massage touch	Gardening
Fireplace fire	Singing birds	Shalimar perfume	Chocolate	Genuine hug	Fishing
My dog curled on the sofa	Sprinkling rain	A salt marsh	Salsa	Spouse caressing my neck	Dancing
Taco stand vendors and customers	Surf	Lavender	Cinnamon	Wool blanket	Shopping for loved ones
	Cat purring		Pretzels		Dinner with friends
	Coffeehouse in the morning		Roasted corn		Bathing my small children
					Family dinner

FIGURE 4.6

Sensual Awareness Inventory

Note. From *Nature-Guided Therapy: Brief Integrated Strategies for Health and Well-Being*, by G. W. Burns, 1998, p. 60, Philadelphia: Brunner/Mazel. Copyright 1998 by the Taylor & Francis Group LLC-Books. Adapted with permission.

Step 2. The counselor and client discuss the SAI, noting any themes (e.g., food, sight, solitude), frequency of participation, and circumstances (e.g., something done in the past in the company of the deceased other). Clients often come up with additional activities at this point. The counselor then poses the questions, moving from "what" to "how" to "when" questions (adapted from G. W. Burns, 1998, p. 68): What did completing the SAI teach you about your own experiences of happiness and pleasure? As you completed the SAI, what did you discover about yourself? What did you learn about how to satisfy your senses? How can you continue gaining pleasure from these sensory activities? When can you start doing these things that give you ongoing pleasure?

Step 3. The counselor and client select a few activities from the list that the client can begin practicing immediately. Clients are encouraged to add activities as therapy progresses. These can be circled on the SAI, which clients take with them. It is helpful to keep a copy of the completed SAI for future reference.

Step 4. At the next therapy session, the counselor and the client discuss the effects of participating in sensual awareness activities and consult about enhancing benefits.

Recommended Resource

The excellent comprehensive resource on ecotherapy is Burns, G. W. (1998). *Nature-guided therapy: Brief integrative strategies for health and well-being.* Philadelphia: Brunner/Mazel.

Client Drawings in Grief Counseling

Client drawings offer an excellent resource in grief counseling because they generate dialogue leading in so many useful directions. Typically taking the form of self-portraits, depictions of grief, or images of relationships, these drawings serve as a focal point for reflection and exploration of the client's experience of loss and grief. Client drawings assist in "telling the story" of loss and grief, facilitate emotional exploration and expression, stimulate self-awareness and introspection, provide a mechanism for expressing the inexpressible (Irwin, 1991), reveal the issues of most concern to clients, facilitate meaning reconstruction especially through symbolism and metaphor, and provide a pleasurable experience that reduces stress and counters sorrow. Additionally, client drawings provide an alternative medium of expression for those who have difficulty processing feelings and thoughts, such as people with learning disabilities (Riches & Dawson, 2000); facilitate gradual exposure to distressful content (Collie, Backos, Malchiodi, & Spiegel, 2006); and allow people to try out different approaches, ideas, and behaviors (Gladding, 1992).

Client drawings can be incorporated into diverse theoretical approaches because they allow the counseling professional to focus on specific areas, for example, cognitive schema, emotional processing, or meaning reconstruction. Drawings are adaptable to individual, family, and group counseling settings. Because client drawings are idiosyncratic, this strategy can be tailored to meet the uniqueness of grieving persons, their particular processes of adapting to loss, and the multiple contexts (e.g., social, cultural) in which grief unfolds.

Implementation of Client Drawings

When using client drawings to generate dialogue, the counseling professional must recognize clients as experts on themselves. Therefore, rather than counselors analyzing and sharing their interpretations (i.e., expert stance), they concentrate on facilitating the clients' own examination and interpretation of their drawings. Minimal structure and direction are important in this regard (Collie et al., 2006; Irwin, 1991). Counselors should supply clients with a mixture of drawing items so that they can select the media they are most comfortable with, such as unlined paper (poster size or letter size), colored markers, pens, pencils, and erasers. A directive might include the following:

> Chia, sometimes it helps to come at all this in a different way. I'd like you to use some of the materials here to draw a self-portrait—a picture showing how you see yourself right now. I'm not looking for high art in this and I'm not going analyze it. I do think it might help us focus on things that are important to you.

Other potential directives include the following:

+ Draw a picture of your grief.
+ Draw a self-portrait or a picture of what you think you are like right now (Carlson, 2000).
+ Draw a picture of where and how you see yourself in relation to your loss or your grief.
+ Draw pictures showing your relationships before and after this loss.
+ Draw a picture that shows your feelings and thoughts [regarding this loss] today.

Avoid overexplaining the directions, and give clients space and time to accomplish the task without hovering over them. Reassure clients who voice concerns about their artistic abilities.

Once the drawing is completed, ask clients, "tell me about the drawing." Do not ask them to "explain" or "interpret" because this tends to predetermine a direction and contribute to client self-consciousness. Often drawings stimulate the telling and retelling of the story of loss, which helps the client accept reality, recall details, and begin organizing memories. Clients may focus initially on the most literal facts (e.g., "this is a picture of me walking on the mountain trail by myself without my partner") and later move to consideration of metaphorical elements (e.g., "I think all this gray area just shows how numb I feel inside"). Resist getting in the way of the client's process by pushing for "aha!" moments. Pose questions designed to facilitate self-reflection, explore meaning, and enhance the process, for example:

+ What do you make of that?
+ What do you think your drawing communicates about you? about your loss(es)? about your relationships? about where you are right now in the grieving process?
+ If I had asked you to do this drawing earlier when this loss occurred, how would it be different than now?
+ What feelings come to you as you talk about this drawing?
+ What would your partner (parent, coworker, friend, teacher) say if he or she saw your drawing?
+ You mentioned just now seeing anger in the picture; tell me more about that.
+ You have mentioned shame several times as we have been discussing your drawing; help me understand what that is about.
+ I heard you say that you did not think it was appropriate for females to express anger; tell me more about that.

The counseling professional can also pose tentative questions that direct attention to specific material in the drawing, for example: The colors you used in the drawing are interesting, tell me about that; I noticed a real difference in the space between you and others in your drawing, what do you think that is about? You've included some symbols here; help me understand those. Be aware that client drawings express cultural and social influences, so look for opportunities to explore these elements.

Client drawings can be initiated any time during therapy to encourage self-reflection and dialogue. It may be beneficial to use client drawings at different points during loss adaptation or therapy, providing points of reference and review. Client drawings are an effective strategy for individual, family, and group counseling. In groups, clients share their individual drawings and respond to questions and feedback from group members. In family therapy, self-portraits can be used or family members may draw pictures of their family in relation to their loss(es). The drawings are then shared with the family, providing a focal point for discussion. Carlson (2000) provided an excellent example of using client drawings in both individual and family therapy:

> An adolescent girl, Misty, in a residential treatment setting completed a self-portrait that revealed a dual face: one side was angry and the other side was smiling. She then shared that self-portrait with her family. Using a narrative therapy approach, the problem of anger was externalized so that Misty could talk about her struggles with "Anger" and family members could discuss the ways in which "Anger" had influenced their lives. In subsequent individual and family sessions, unique outcomes (i.e., times when the problem does not occur) were identified and used to build an alternative narrative in which Misty was overcoming the anger problem with support from her family.

Recommended Resources

Gladding, S. T. (2005). *Counseling as an art: The creative arts in counseling* (3rd ed.). Alexandria, VA: American Counseling Association.

Malchiodi, C. A. (2005). (Ed.). *Expressive therapies*. New York: Guilford Press.

Rogers, J. E. (2007). *The art of grief: The use of expressive arts in a grief support group*. New York: Routledge.

The Association for Creativity in Counseling publishes the *Journal of Creativity in Mental Health* (http://www.aca-acc.org).

A Note About Expressive Therapies

Expressive therapies utilize creative activities, such as art, music, dance/movement, drama, poetry/prose, and play in the context of psychotherapy. They provide an active, experiential, and highly idiosyncratic means of helping clients encounter, express, and explore their issues and concerns. Expressive therapy strategies are typically implemented in-session and often incorporate extra-session homework assignments. In some instances the Internet may serve as a vehicle for sharing.

- Drama therapy uses drama/theater performance and products such as puppetry, improvisation, role-play, pantomime, psychodrama, and theater production.
- Music therapy uses making music, sharing music, or listening to music in various forms.
- Art therapy uses a variety of visual art forms, such as photography, painting, drawing, or sculpting.

- ✦ Dance therapy focuses on creating a performance using various dance forms.
- ✦ Movement therapy focuses on improvisational and intuitive ways of moving in a spontaneous and unrehearsed form (Kampfe, 2003).
- ✦ Literature therapy focuses on exploration of themes, characters, development, and issues through literature, with specific works selected by the counselor. Gladding (2005) characterized two primary forms: poetic and prosaic practices. Poetic practice utilizes exploration of poems. Prosaic practice utilizes novels, biographies, autobiographies, and short stories.
- ✦ Scriptotherapy uses client-generated expressive writing, typically in the form of journals, letters, or stories (see Therapeutic Writing for Loss: Giving Sorrow Words, presented earlier in this chapter).

It is strongly recommended that counseling professionals who wish to use expressive therapies in their practice obtain specialized training in the theories, procedures, and ethics of selected approaches. The following professional associations provide standards, certifications, and resources: American Dance Therapy Association (http://www.adta.org); American Music Therapy Association (http://www.musictherapy.org); American Art Therapy Association (http://www.arttherapy.org); National Association for Poetry Therapy (http://www. poetrytherapy.org); National Association for Drama Therapy (http://www.nadt.org).

Client-Generated Metaphors

When people describe one experience by alluding to another experience, they are speaking *metaphorically* (e.g., grief is like a long and difficult journey, my life is stuck in the mud, I'm keeping a lid on my anger, it's like picking at a scab). Essentially, metaphors are a way to make more describable or concrete those experiences, like grief, that often seem so indescribable or abstract. At first glance the counseling professional may think that these spontaneous expressions merit only an empathetic nod or an automatic reflection of content or feeling. But there is much, much more here. Client-generated metaphors are clues to the meanings clients attach to their experiences—the sense they make of their world—and thus they are vehicles for making new meanings. This is especially important when working with loss and grief because a major source of distress is the disruption of people's taken-for-granted assumptions and beliefs (meaning structures) about their selves and their world.

Client-generated metaphors offer numerous advantages. They reduce resistance, because the indirectness of the metaphor provides a "safe" way of talking about uncomfortable material (Romig & Gruenke, 1991); facilitate the emergence of unexpressed material, especially emotional material (Lyddon, Clay, & Sparks, 2001); reveal dissonance; expose unhelpful or distorted thinking patterns and assist in amending those patterns; offer the client and counseling professional a mutual frame of reference; and strengthen the therapeutic alliance by allowing opportunities for the counselor to validate client experiences (Sims, 2003). Client-generated metaphors are strongly preferred over counselor-generated metaphors because they arise from the client's distinct personal, cultural, and social contexts.

Implementation of Client-Generated Metaphors

A particularly effective approach to working with client-generated metaphors draws from constructivist approaches, especially narrative therapy. The counselor's stance here is one of deep respect for clients' expertness on themselves and abiding curiosity about how they see the metaphor applying to their experience (Anderson & Goolishian, 1992; Monk, Winslade, Crocket, & Epston, 1997). This respectful and curious position precludes interpretation by the counseling professional, who focuses instead on facilitating exploration of the metaphor so that clients arrive at their own interpretations, insights, and conclusions.

It is useful to conceptualize working with client-generated metaphors in terms of four basic steps: recognize the metaphor, underscore the metaphor, explore the metaphor, and extend the metaphor (Bayne & Thompson, 2000; Sims, 2003). Counseling professionals should expect to find some blending of the third and fourth steps (explore and extend) as material emerges, is examined, applied, and then reexamined.

Step 1. Recognize the metaphor. Recognizing the metaphor sounds easy, but metaphors are sneaky, especially the commonplace ones. They are so integral to one's language that they often fly right by without our noticing them. There are, in fact, some metaphors that present so frequently in loss and grief situations that it is helpful to look out for them.

+ *Metaphors that reflect themes of illness, injury, or trauma*: hit in the stomach, cut (rip) my heart out, raped, sick at heart, beat up, killed a part of me, carjacked, sick without expectation of recovery or in a general malaise, drowning, watching a train wreck, under a spell, walking dead, suffering like Job, like a tidal wave, crash and burn, amputation with phantom pain.
+ *Metaphors that reflect themes of journey* (especially of being lost, separated, or alone): living in one room or moving through empty rooms, moving through a tunnel, lost in a forest or desert or city, on an odyssey, climbing up a mountain or out of a hole, living in a strange land, following a path, alone at sea in a boat.
+ *Metaphors that reflect confusion, dissonance, or an impasse*: treading water, untangling knots or fitting pieces of a puzzle together, holding one's breath or breathing slowly, life being on hold, at sea without a compass, paralyzed, unbalanced or out of harmony, being misled by Coyote the trickster, caught in a trap.

Once counseling professionals begin listening more carefully for metaphoric expressions, they will notice them more frequently. This does not mean that counselors should leap on every metaphor their clients utter. Instead, counselors listen for metaphors that have the greatest potential for usefulness. That would include metaphors that are repeated, that allude to difficult or uncomfortable content, that are especially vivid, or that reveal destructive or problematic responses. Counselors should take special note of metaphoric expressions that hint at competence, strengths, or functionality because those are the building blocks of resilience. Also, they should listen for metaphors that reflect the notion of reorganization, assimilation, adjustment, or redefinition, because those speak directly to the healthy adaptation to loss. Counselors can also invite clients to generate metaphors with leading questions, for example: "Estela, fill in the blank: my grief is like _____." "LaShawn, fill in the blank for me: enduring this loss is like _____." "Clive, what would you compare your grieving experience to thus far?"

Step 2. Underscore the metaphor. Underscoring the metaphor involves focusing the client's attention on her or his metaphor as something useful or interesting, then inviting investigation. For example: "Wow, that's a pretty powerful picture. . . tell me more about the divorce being like watching a train wreck." "That's a vivid way of describing things—being kicked in the stomach. I

131

could almost feel that one; let's talk more about that." "Treading water . . . pretty strong image . . . how are you treading water right now? "You mentioned a moment ago that you felt like 'La Llorona, The Weeping Woman.' I am unfamiliar with that character. Tell me more about La Llorona and how you are like her."

It is helpful to indicate by tone, inflection, and body language that the client's metaphor is especially interesting or intriguing (Sims, 2003). This draws the client's interest and encourages participation. Avoid using the word *metaphor* when underscoring because it might deflect attention to the word or concept and away from the metaphor itself. The invitation to explore the metaphor should be open-ended and should not include a reflection of feeling or content (e.g., do not say, "sounds like you feel abandoned") because the reflection points the client in a direction chosen by the counselor rather than allowing the client's meaning making to unfold unhindered. Underscoring the metaphor is like saying to the client, "Hey, look at what just popped up! What you just said is really fascinating; let's stop and look around here for awhile."

Step 3. Explore the metaphor. Here is where the counselor's curiosity comes into play and, it is hoped, engages the client's curiosity as well. The key is to use the metaphor as a vehicle for investigation, so the counselor must keep the metaphor central to the conversation. Ask generative questions that encourage clients to elaborate on what this particular metaphor says about them and their situation. Select details from the metaphor and ask clients to consider their meaning. Highlight the metaphor's visual and sensual nature by asking clients to describe the metaphor's image. Listen for quality terms that merit further examination, for example, *abandonment, guilt, despair, hope, relief*. Note client strengths, competencies, and resources by calling them to clients' attention or asking about them. Detect problematic cognitions as well as particularly helpful cognitions. Ask about client feelings in relation to the metaphor's image. Kopp (1995) suggested inviting clients to examine the connection between the metaphor and their problem (e.g., What are the similarities between this image of a partially healed wound and your experience of grief?). Listen for clues to adaptive grieving styles. Notice any unique outcomes (times when the problems do not exist or are less problematic). The following items provide examples of questions that encourage elaboration:

- Where did the "time bomb" come from?
- What do you think the "time bomb" is about?
- What does it take to keep carrying this "time bomb" around but not let it go off?
- What does it mean for you to have been in a "wreck"?
- In what ways is the "wreck" still happening?
- It sounds like you let some people help you after the "train wreck." How did they help you?
- Paint the scene for me—you treading water.
- What emotions go with "treading water"?
- I'm amazed at the determination it has taken to keep treading water. A lot of folks would just give up and drown, but not you. How have you mobilized that determination day after day?
- What would it mean if you "rested by the side of the road" for awhile?

- What's happening to you when you "hide in plain sight"?
- What does the "untreated broken bone" story say about how you view those old losses?
- What feelings are you aware of when you describe yourself as "walking dead"?
- I wonder what emotions you are in touch with when you say you are like a "motherless child."
- You mentioned the guilt. How does taking down "the wall" make you feel guilt?
- What connections do you see between this story/image and your life?
- You've held onto this "package" for a long, long time. How did you manage to do that?

The exploration stage allows alternative explanations, amended viewpoints, new information, and increased awareness to emerge as different possibilities for consideration by the client (Lyddon et al., 2001; Sims, 2003).

Step 4. Extend the metaphor. Here you help the client to apply the possibilities discovered in the exploration stage to current and future problems. A good way to begin this step is to ask the client what has been useful in the discussion so far or to comment on the material that has surfaced during exploration (e.g., It sounds like some new perspectives are emerging about "carrying around a time bomb"). Particularly vivid imagery with metaphors invites following them out to logical conclusions (e.g., What would happen if you let some air out of that nearly bursting balloon? How could you disarm this time bomb? What will happen if you don't disarm the time bomb?). Kopp (1995) suggested proposing consideration of a change in the metaphor to facilitate extension (e.g., If you could change this image in some way, how would you change it? If you could change this image so it would be better for you, how would you change it?). Help the client build on any unique outcomes noticed during exploration (e.g., You said there were times when you glimpsed light at the end of the tunnel. What is different about those times?). Encourage application of assumptions and beliefs that were examined and amended earlier (e.g., You've said you don't buy the "men are from Mars" stereotype anymore. What difference does that make to how you approach your relationships now and in the future?). Extension is a critical piece in working with client-generated metaphors because it is that place where the insights and awareness of exploration acquire the hands and feet of action.

Sample Dialogue

The client is a 34-year-old recently divorced woman who is immobilized in grieving her losses by her persistent blame of her ex-husband. The counseling process is stuck here as well, so the counselor looks for an opportunity to help the client shift away from her victim stance and begin to construct some sense of ownership in her present and future. A rather commonplace metaphor offers that opportunity.

Client: I feel like someone pushed the "pause" button, you know? Everything's just stopped . . .
Counselor: The pause button—tell me more about that. [Counselor underscores client-generated metaphor.]
Client: Everything's stopped and I'm waiting . . . waiting for something to move forward, but I don't want to move forward. I want to go back to the way it was—everything was OK; I was OK; my child was OK; my marriage was OK . . . but everything is just stopped and I'm left here with it all . . . it's all a big mess.

Counselor: OK. That's pretty vivid. How is it that the pause button got pushed? [Counselor underscores and facilitates exploration of the metaphor.]

Client: [silent a moment, then voice becomes tense] Jerald pushed it. He put my life on hold—and my son's. He didn't say anything to me; he just walked away and left it all. I can't move forward and I can't move back. I'm just stuck . . . and I don't want this—none of this—it's all his fault.

Counselor: Let's keep up with the pause-button thing, it seems like a helpful way of looking at this. I'm curious; what will happen if the pause button never gets released—if everything just stays on pause? [Counselor avoids client's detour into victim stance by maintaining the focus on the metaphor and encouraging further exploration.]

Client: I don't know. I guess things will just stay the same. I'll just stay in limbo.

Counselor: Mmmmm. What else?

Client: I guess I keep hoping someone will come and get me out of this—help me.

Counselor: I've got this image of you standing on this humongous pause button. Does that fit for you, or is it a different image?

Client: Yea . . . that's me; standing there with my arms out hoping that someone will come along and rescue me.

Counselor: With your arms out . . . you don't sound like you are too thrilled with that image.

Client: No—I think that is part of the problem. I want someone to rescue me but that just doesn't work, because people let you down.

Counselor: So you say the pause button means you are waiting for rescue—for something outside of yourself to come along, and you don't like that image. Is that right? [Client nods.] What would happen, do you think, if the pause button was released? [Counselor avoids detour to victim stance by encouraging extension of the metaphor.]

Client: I think it would just turn off after a while or maybe return to play. I don't remember how it works.

Counselor: Mmm. So—if we stay with the story here, let's imagine that the pause button on your life runs its prescribed time and then turns off. Where would that put you?

Client: At least I wouldn't be waiting anymore or hoping someone would come. I would be doing things myself, for myself and for my son. I wouldn't be looking for someone—a man—to take care of things. I wouldn't be thinking about Jerald or looking for others to bail me out. I'd be doing what I need to do. [Client shifts from seeing herself as hopelessly stuck and dependent on others to seeing herself as taking action on her own.]

Counselor: Wow! It sounds to me like the "play" button just got pressed. [Counselor highlights this shift while retaining the metaphor and its extension.]

Client: [smiling] Ha—I guess so. I'd like to think I could do that. It's hard . . . but that's what I have to do.

One advantage of working with client-generated metaphors is that they provide an ongoing reference point—a convenient linguistic vehicle—for therapy. For example, the pause-button metaphor described above may be invoked by either counselor or client at other times during the course of treatment as new understandings continue to unfold. Thus the exploration and extension of the metaphor continues to illumine the therapy.

Metaphors in Group Counseling and Family Counseling

Client-generated metaphors can also be used effectively in group counseling. The group leader might follow the steps above with an individual group member, then ask for the reactions of other group members (e.g., What struck you about what Juan has been saying? Why did that resonate with you?). Or group members, once familiar with generative questions, can be directly involved in exploration and extension of the metaphors of other members, rather than relying on the group leader. It is useful for group leaders to link the metaphors of group members where commonalities occur. For example, when two members of a divorce recovery group both present "journey" metaphors, the leader might use a fishbowl structure (the two group members in the middle with the leader surrounded by other group members) to facilitate their mutual exploration and extension of this metaphor. Reactions and feedback from group members in the outer circle can be requested as appropriate. Whatever approach is utilized, it is important that the group leader maintain the focus on the metaphor, facilitate generative questions, and emphasize the client's expertness on themselves.

The same steps apply in family therapy (e.g., recognize, underscore, explore, extend). When metaphors are mentioned, the counseling professional may ask family members for their reactions (e.g., meanings, feelings) to the metaphor and then facilitate exploration and extension. Ask family members where they see themselves in another member's metaphor. Highlight linkages between metaphors (e.g., I'd like to understand more about what is going on in a house where Twyla is "walking on eggshells" and Aaron hears a "ticking time bomb"). Ask individual family members about what changes they would make in the metaphor's image if they could, then explore with the entire family how that change might affect their relationships. Alternatively, the counselor can ask the entire family for a metaphor that would express their preferred way of functioning.

Recommended Resources

Kopp, R. R. (1995). *Metaphor therapy: Using client-generated metaphors in psychotherapy.* New York: Brunner/Mazel.

Neimeyer, R. A. (2001). The language of loss: Grief therapy as a process of meaning reconstruction. In R. A. Neimeyer (Ed.), *Meaning reconstruction and the experience of loss* (pp. 261–292). Washington, DC: American Psychological Association.

Wisdom Chronicles

Wisdom Chronicles are collections of writings *by clients* for the benefit of *other clients* experiencing similar problems. The strategy is based on the concept of "creating an audience" from narrative therapy, in which selected people act as witnesses and provide support for the efforts of clients to live out more preferred ways of being (Ingram & Perlesz, 2004). Clients who have experienced some measure of improvement in their concerns as a result of their own efforts are asked to draw on their knowledge and experience—their wisdom—to provide information, support, and advice to other clients in the form of an open letter. Authorship is anonymous. Other forms, including notes, stories, or journal entries, may also be used. These writings are then archived by the counseling professional/agency and made available to clients. Wisdom Chronicles benefit the clients who create these documents by reinforcing their personal agency and influence over their difficulties, honoring their stories, underscoring the specific changes they have made, and encouraging continued change. There is the additional benefit of helping others. Clients who read these documents receive understanding from people who have experienced the same or similar problems, support and encouragement for their personal journey, and practical knowledge about what is helpful and not helpful in dealing with their particular difficulties. This strategy is adaptable to the unique needs of clients and can be incorporated into theoretical approaches other than narrative therapy. Wisdom Chronicles can be used with individuals, couples, families, or groups. The format for wisdom letters described here is based on the Wisdoms Project, an approach developed at the Bouverie Centre in Melbourne, Australia (Ingram & Perlesz, 2004).

Creating Wisdom Letters

Wisdom letters are created by clients themselves in the first person or "ghostwritten" by counseling professionals in first or third person or using a pseudonym (Ingram & Perlesz, 2004). In both cases a collaborative revision process occurs before arriving at the final document.

Client-Generated Wisdom Letters

These letters are assigned as homework and then shared during the therapy session (see Box 4.7 for client instructions). Clients read their letters aloud during the therapy session. The revision process may occur over several sessions, especially because the letters offer an opportunity for further exploration of client concerns and their change process. The counselor might make suggestions about the inclusion of certain material, especially noting how the client accessed strengths and skills, altered certain perspectives, or initiated change. Counselors should avoid overattending to grammar or style, because this is unrelated to the purpose and might undermine the process. It is helpful to keep the focus on the client being of service to others and on the client's hard-earned wisdom. Revising the original letter is a collaborative effort, and the final result must be satisfactory to the client.

Of course, other difficulties can be substituted for the reference to loss and grief (e.g., anger, guilt, estrangement, conflict) and different starter questions can be suggested (e.g., those relevant to cognitive therapy or an existential approach). In family therapy, wisdom letters can be written by individual family members about their own journeys or that of their family, then revised as a family. In group therapy, the letters can be shared with the group and revised with their assistance. Whereas there are many benefits for clients in creating wisdom letters, it is important to keep the focus on the changes involved in the new story and on being of service to others rather than on the client seeking catharsis: "it is not the same as vomiting or getting a poison out of the body . . . invite the person to consider other metaphors, such as painful wounds which need to be left alone to heal" (White, 1995, p. 85).

Ghostwritten Wisdom Letters

These letters are used when clients are either unable or unwilling to create wisdom letters themselves (Ingram & Perlesz, 2004). Once the client has indicated her or his willingness to participate in the process, the counselor writes the letter in first person or third person or using a pseudonym. The wisdom letter is then read aloud to the client, and she or he is invited to collaborate in revising the document. Counselors should consider the suggestions provided above in creating a wisdom letter on behalf of a client. Be certain to highlight client strengths, knowledge,

BOX 4.7

Client Instructions for Writing a Wisdom Letter

You have made some significant changes since you began therapy and acquired some very specialized knowledge—wisdom—about dealing with loss and grieving. Other clients experiencing loss would find your wisdom very, very beneficial, especially when they are just starting therapy or at times when they get discouraged about things. So, we ask you to write a letter to other clients in which you share your specialized knowledge. We will add this letter to our collection—our Wisdoms Archives—where it will be available in our waiting room. Please be assured that your letter will remain anonymous and will not be included in any official file.

How to write a wisdom letter? Most folks find it helpful to think about things this way: There is the "old story" of your struggle, with loss and grief having control in your life, and there is the "new story" in which you are living with the grief in a way that allows you to enjoy your life and your relationships—to be in control of your life. Your wisdom letter would talk about your journey from the old story to the new story, sharing your understanding and knowledge so as to help another person along the way. Feel free to do this in any way that feels right to you. Here are a few things you might think about to help you get started:

1. Briefly tell the old story of how loss and grief influenced your life.
2. What is the difference between the old story and the new story?
3. How did the changes between the old story and the new story come about?
4. What do you do or say to yourself that allowed you to begin the changes in the new story?
5. What steps did you take to get on track to changing things?
6. Since we know that grief never goes away (it changes), what do you do to manage those times when it threatens to take you back to the old story?
7. How do you think differently or behave differently now that you are attempting to live the new story?
8. What do you think is important for someone who is also grieving to know that will help them in their journey?

You might ask your counselor for any thoughts about things he or she has noticed that might be included in your wisdom letter. When you bring your letter to the next counseling session, you and your counselor will go over it together. Thank you so much for sharing your hard-earned wisdom about loss and grief in a way that helps others. Your kindness is deeply appreciated.

and skill in managing the problems and making change. Ghostwritten letters can be done on behalf of one family member, then shared with all, or written on behalf of the entire family.

Counselors using this strategy must adopt a collaborative approach if the revision process is to be successful. The client, the client's story, and the client's personal agency in bringing about change must be at the center of this process and not the counselor, the counselor's expertise, or the counselor's agenda. Be careful to work with clients to obscure information that would make them too identifiable. This is, of course, even more imperative in smaller communities.

Using Wisdom Letters

Wisdom letters can be collected into an archive of similar documents that is then made available to clients. The waiting room of the agency or private practice is a recommended location. Letters can be protected with clear sleeves and placed in a notebook. In creating an archive, it is helpful to obtain wisdom letters from other sources (e.g., professional colleagues; http://www.narrativeapproaches.com) to mix in with locally prepared letters. Whereas handwritten letters make this more personable, typed letters can further obscure identity.

Counselors might also select letters from an agency archive or their own files to share with selected clients during therapy. These letters are chosen for their resonance with client experiences to facilitate discussion and exploration and provide encouragement. For example, C. Ingram (personal communication, August 30, 2007) tells of sharing a wisdom letter from a mother who had experienced domestic violence with a mother and daughter who were also dealing with the consequences of domestic violence. Reading such letters aloud to clients is particularly effective as is making copies for them to take with them.

Counselors can use wisdom letters anytime, but there are specific situations when it seems most appropriate, especially when clients are discouraged or overwhelmed or when they are stuck in the change process. Generally speaking, the letters are not as helpful early in therapy (when they can be dismissed) as later, when some progress is being made. Counselors may read the letter aloud and then ask for a response, for example: What do you hear in this letter that strikes a note with you? What did you find interesting or made you curious? The situation described in this letter is not exactly like yours, but there are some similarities; I wonder what we could get from this that might be helpful to both of us?

Recommended Resources

Ingram, C., & Perlesz, A. (2004). The getting of wisdoms. *International Journal of Narrative Therapy and Community Work, 2,* 49–56.

The Web site http://www.narrativeapproaches.com provides a collection of client-generated narratives on a range of topics (e.g., sexual abuse, anorexia, and bulimia) as well as additional information about the Wisdoms Project at Bouverie Centre, Melbourne, Australia.

Brief Homework Assignments to Promote Change

Counseling professionals can use the time between therapy sessions to enhance client change through brief homework assignments. The six assignments described here are designed to increase awareness of specific ways in which clients can help themselves manage the problems associated with grieving. The assignments are especially helpful with clients who do not recognize their own ability to influence their grieving experience or who see grief as something that is more to be endured than to be managed. These assignments are adaptable to individual, family, and group counseling settings. In group situations everyone may be asked to complete the assignment before the next therapy session, or several members at a time may do so. Family members may complete homework activities separately, then share their results during the family session.

Notice What Stays the Same

This assignment challenges the view that "all is lost" by focusing clients on those things (e.g., relationships, identity, beliefs) that remain constant in their lives. It is often helpful in the early phases of counseling. The directive is as follows:

In the time between today and our next appointment notice the things in your life that remain unchanged by your experience of loss and grief, especially relationships, habits, attitudes, or behaviors. Start a list today that you can add to periodically and bring the list to your next counseling session.

Notice What Is Helpful

This assignment, adapted from McNeilly (2000), helps clients recognize that they are already doing things to manage their grief. It is often most helpful early in therapy, perhaps within the first three sessions. The directive is, "Notice those things that you are doing that are helpful to you in managing this grief and write them down. Bring your notes to the next counseling session."

Notice What Is Different

This assignment also helps clients recognize that change is already happening and that they themselves are already doing things to make change. The directive is as follows:

Begin paying attention to those times when things are going well or just better—when you seem to be managing your grief. What is different about those times? How are you different? What do you notice different about others? Consider these questions at least every other day and write down your thoughts. Bring your responses to the next counseling session.

When discussing the completed assignment, the counselor must keep the focus on what the client is thinking, feeling, and doing *differently* to influence change. This assignment is particularly useful early in therapy.

Changing Unhelpful to Helpful

This assignment is especially useful when clients are stuck or engaging in unhealthy or counterproductive activities. The directive is as follows:

Make a list of those things that you find yourself doing that are *unhelpful* to you. For each item you describe, think of what you can do instead and try doing some of these more helpful things. Bring your list with you to the next session.

When using this activity in family therapy, ways in which family members may be able to assist each other in changing unhelpful behaviors can be discussed.

Letter to Myself

This assignment raises awareness of change by recognizing improvement, no matter how small that may be. In family situations the counselor may have the entire family undertake the assignment as a whole or may have individual members complete the assignment separately, and then share with the family during the therapy session. The directive is, "You have acquired some expertise in managing grief. Write a letter to yourself describing the steps you have taken and the skills and resources you have used to manage your grief. Bring the letter to the next session." It is most effective when people read their letters aloud.

You Will Know What to Do

This assignment, adapted from McNeilly (2000, pp. 125–126), helps clients gain clarity on the obstacles to integrating grief or resolving issues and identify what changes could improve their situation. There are two parts. First, the counselor instructs the client to "Look around and find something that symbolizes your problem that you could carry around with you. Bring it to the next session so we can discuss it." At the next session, following discussion of the symbolism attached to the object, the counselor gives the client the following deliberately ambiguous assignment: "Carry this symbol around with you for awhile and, when you are ready, you will know what to do with it." Counseling professionals should refrain from suggesting symbolic objects, providing further clarification of the assignment, or asking what action clients have taken with their objects so that clients do their own work.

Shared Reminiscence

One of the most common aspects of grieving is reminiscence—the act of recalling past experiences and events associated with the loss and lost object. It takes many forms, for example, repeating details associated with the story of loss, describing last encounters or last moments, or remembering isolated incidents connected with the lost object. Reminiscing seems to help most people bridge the gap between the unreality of loss and the reality of loss's impact; begin placing the loss in the context of past, present, and future; assist with meaning reconstruction; and channel emotional responses. Recalling past experiences and events is especially helpful to families, enabling them to share their grief and build a coherent narrative for the immediate family and in the generational life of the family. Counseling professionals encourage reminiscence in therapy to promote these advantages and also to reveal potential problems areas (e.g., guilt and shame issues).

Reminiscences are sometimes disjointed or fragmented, reflecting limited aspects of the loss or lost object or reinforcing unrealistic perspectives (e.g., the marriage was perfect, the lost job was ideal, Uncle Josef was a saint, life in the native country was idyllic). This partial view is particularly unhelpful to grieving children who must rely on the memories of others to formulate their view of a deceased or an absent parent. Parents grieving the loss of a child are often left with the fragmented view, drawing largely on their own memories and remaining ignorant of their child's life apart from them (e.g., how playmates or adult friends experienced the child). Fragmented views frequently result from difficult circumstances, such as suicide, incest, estrangement, or divorce. In these cases the lost object often becomes a caricature rather than a living person.

Implementation of Shared Reminiscence

Counseling professionals can suggest that clients engage in Shared Reminiscence (Cooke & Dworkin, 1992), in which they obtain additional or alternative information, stories, perspectives, and memories associated with the lost object from other individuals, for example, childhood friends, college roommates, work colleagues, or fellow soldiers. The counseling professional encourages clients to seek out people and gather their reminiscences as a homework assignment, the results of which can be explored further in therapy. Alternatively, these individuals might be invited to a therapy session (individual or family) focused on sharing their memories so as to aid construction of a more coherent image of the lost object. Cooke and Dworkin noted that clients seeking shared reminiscences may encounter information or situations that are disturbing to them (e.g., discovering one is adopted or of uncertain parentage). Counselors should discuss this possibility with clients before encouraging this activity.

Loss Characterization to Address Fragmented Identity

Loss Characterization, a strategy suggested by R. A. Neimeyer (2000a), is designed to help clients explore the impact of loss and grief on their personal identity. Along with sense making and benefit finding, identity change is one of the three activities of meaning reconstruction often involved in grief (Gillies & Neimeyer, 2006). In challenging the core beliefs and assumptions on which people live their lives, loss sometimes disrupts people's self-narratives about who they are and how they are in the world so that they experience a kind of fragmentation of their sense of self. As one bereaved parent said,

> I failed as a mother; I was useless as a wife. . . . What kind of mother lets her child get killed? Nothing made sense anymore. I couldn't stand my husband near me. I went through the motions with the other children. I just felt I wasn't there. (Riches & Dawson, 2000, p. 12)

The process of adapting to loss involves rebuilding or reorganizing this sort of fragmentation in a way that integrates loss and grief into a life-affirming and coherent self-narrative.

In the Loss Characterization strategy, clients create a portrait or "character sketch" of themselves, including their experience of loss and grief, as if they were the major character in a book, play, or movie. This narrative or storytelling vehicle is recommended for addressing identity changes brought about by the loss experience (R. A. Neimeyer et al., 2007). It is particularly useful in helping grieving clients enlarge or shift their perspective, focus specifically on different aspects of their identity and how their identity has changed, and reconstruct their self-story to incorporate loss in life-affirming ways.

Implementation of Loss Characterization

The client is given the following written instruction as a homework assignment:

> Imagine you are writing a book, movie, or play and you want to lay out a detailed description or "character sketch" of the main character to guide your writing. This character sketch should reveal an intimate and sympathetic knowledge of the main character, as if you were writing about a good friend. This is actually a character sketch of YOU *in light of your loss experiences*. Be sure to write this character sketch in the third person, so begin by saying "_____ [your name] is . . ." (adapted from R. A. Neimeyer, 2000a, p. 154)

At the next therapy session, the client reads the character sketch aloud, and the counseling professional helps the client explore the story with a focus on how loss is shaping his or her personal identity. In doing so, the counselor and client should attend especially to sources of meaning (e.g., values, faith, beliefs); ways of explaining loss and its impact; repeated terms, themes, or patterns; fragmentation or conflicting parts (e.g., competent vs. incompetent); dissonance (e.g., ambivalence, incongruence); and sources of validation (e.g., family, friends).

It is helpful to maintain a third-person reference (i.e., the client's name instead of "you") when discussing the person in the character sketch and to maintain the framework of evolving story or narrative. Because the purpose of this strategy is to explore the impact of loss on a person's identity and promote reorganizing fragmentation into a coherent self-narrative, it is inappropriate to focus on things such as maladaptive thinking or neurotic behavior (R. A. Neimeyer, 2000a). Neimeyer suggested that this activity can also be incorporated into a personal journal or repeated at various times (e.g., loss-connected anniversaries). Some clients may prefer to respond orally rather than in written form or even make a recording of their response. The counseling professional should collaborate with clients in identifying a format that works best for them.

Whereas this strategy is most appropriate for individual treatment, it may also be useful in family or group therapy settings. Individuals may read their character sketch aloud while other group or family members listen without interrupting. The counselor then asks follow-up questions or invites group or family members to ask questions, keeping the focus on the individual's experience and not on that of other group or family members. Alternatively, the character sketch can focus on a family or relationship instead of the individual's experience. In that case, the homework directive is as follows:

> Imagine you are writing a book, movie, or play about a family and you want to lay out a detailed description or "character sketch" of the family to guide your writing. Write this character sketch from the perspective of someone who really knows this family intimately and sympathetically, perhaps better than anyone else. This is actually a character sketch of YOUR FAMILY *in light of the loss experiences* it has endured. Be sure to write this character sketch in the third person, so begin by saying, "The _____ _____ Family is . . ." (adapted from G. J. Neimeyer & Neimeyer, 1994, p. 99)

These sketches can be read aloud by individuals within the family session, with the counselor asking follow-up questions or inviting family members to ask questions. It is important to maintain the narrative or storytelling form and the third-person viewpoint during the family or group discussions.

Recommended Resource

Neimeyer, R. A. (2000). *Lessons of loss: A guide to coping*. Memphis, TN: Center for the Study of Loss and Transition. This book describes a number of recommended counseling strategies.

Using Photographs to Facilitate Meaning Reconstruction

Viewing and discussing photographs and similar visual representations in therapy is a helpful method for addressing loss and grief. Photographs provide both a factual record and a symbolic reference point around which people can investigate the concerns and issues related to their specific experience of loss. Counselors can use these photographs to help clients tell the story of their loss and grief in a restorative manner, including consolidating positive memories. Using photographs also facilitates emotional processing, assists meaning reconstruction, exposes maladaptive thinking, uncovers dissonance, supports the revelation and resolution of unfinished business, reveals dominant and alternative narratives, exposes family structure and dynamics, and encourages remembrance and family communication (Klass, 1999; Riches & Dawson, 1998, 2000).

Exploring photographs assists in the construction of personal, familial, and communal narratives by anchoring the loss and lost object in the continuing story of relationship. This is especially helpful in circumstances of death, estrangement, disappearance, and emotional cutoff because photographs attest to the fact of existence, identity, and relationship. Riches and Dawson (1998), reporting specifically on their work with bereaved parents, pointed out four ways that exploring photographs and similar artifacts can be helpful: (a) Photographs confirm the existence of a child and the fact of parental identity with this specific child; (b) photographs help parents explore places and situations associated with their child's death; (c) photographs help parents relive events and experiences associated with the child's life (remembrance); and (d) photographs help parents construct a public, postbereavement identity that recognizes their parental status and their continuing bond with their child.

Helen and Oscar have not seen or heard from their only child, Chelsea, since she joined a religious cult and expressed an intention to cease any contact with her parents 11 years ago. Initially, they hoped that Chelsea would reestablish contact, but as the years have accumulated with no word from her, their hope has turned to despair. In therapy Helen and Oscar deal with their losses, especially the loss of hope for reunion and the loss of their image of themselves as successful parents. They confront and manage the blame and guilt that have at times driven them apart. When invited by their counselor to share photographs, they come loaded with family albums, a stuffed animal, and childhood drawings. As each item is reviewed and memories are recalled across Chelsea's childhood and adolescence, the counselor helps Helen and Oscar construct a narrative that reaffirms their identity as parents and embraces their life with Chelsea as a family. Gradually Helen and Oscar become less focused on loss and more focused on this celebratory narrative of relationship, family, and a continuing, revised, bond with their daughter.

Implementation of Photography for Meaning Reconstruction

The invitation to clients to share their photographs should emphasize the counselor's interest in knowing more about the "lost" person or imply a desire for relationship (Klass, 1999). For example: "I wonder if you would be willing to bring any photographs you have of Shawna that would help me understand more about her; it would help me to get to know Pablo better if you would bring in some photographs—maybe even a family album; I'd like to get to know Klaus as well as I can, would you be willing to share your photographs with me?" The counselor should be open to other visual representations, such as a child's artwork, awards, or stuffed animals. In some cases this might also include autopsy reports, police reports, obituaries, or even medical statements.

Counselors should handle the photographs or representational objects themselves, looking at them together with clients and handing them back and forth. Invite clients to select where to start with the photographs. It is important to allow sufficient time and avoid rushing the process so that relevant material can emerge. Klass (1999), in his work with bereaved parents, provided an excellent description of the manner in which the counselor should approach these photographs.

I give the photographs the same attention I give to art on a museum wall. I try to let the photographs speak to me. I sit beside the parent on the sofa slowly going through the photographs. I note the developmental changes; note the similarity in build, facial features, or expression to other people in the photos. I look intently at photographs that show the child in the family group or with a group of peers; because I often find that I get a sense of the child from the body postures and the physical relationships of the people in the picture. As thoughts occur to me, I make comments and the parent confirms or clarifies what I see. . . . I take the task at hand very seriously. I want to get to know that child. By the end of one or two sessions I usually have. (p. 184)

In family therapy situations, the counselor involves all family members in viewing and discussing the photographs. Pictures should be passed around while soliciting observations and comments from individual members. The photographs may even be placed on empty chairs to symbolize the presence of an absent or lost person.

It is important to recognize that while photographs certainly provide some factual or objective reality, their real therapeutic value lies with the meanings ascribed to these images by clients— their constructed meaning. As Weiser (1999) noted, "each viewer's response is based on unique individual perceptions, the meaning of the photograph therefore exists as an unobservable, though not necessarily random, combination of possibilities that occurs only in the interface *between* that person and the image itself" (p. 3). Recognizing this, counselors help clients encounter these images anew by examining them more critically so as to arrive at their own interpretations of meaning. The counselor's role is facilitative and collaborative, making observations and raising questions that explore assumptions and beliefs, encourage reflection, and honor client expertness. The following are examples of the types of questions or observations that can be used initially to open photograph exploration:

+ What is happening in this picture?
+ What does the picture say about the people in it and the person taking the picture?
+ What feelings come to you now as you look over these photographs?
+ This photograph doesn't seem to fit with how you described Yolanda to me; let's talk about that some more.
+ What do you see now, as you look over these photographs from the perspective of wisdom and experience?
+ What here surprises you or makes you more curious?

Once the initial exploration of photographs has occurred, counselors can then work more specifically on areas of concern (e.g., maladaptive thinking, emotional processing, meaning reconstruction, dominant and alternative narratives, or family dynamics) using the photographs as a reference point. For example, the parent with unfinished business regarding a stillborn child may be invited to share items from the "treasure box" supplied by the hospital (containing a lock of hair, a photograph, and nail clipping). The counselor may then facilitate confrontation with previously avoided emotions or assist exploration of any irrational thinking relating to guilt and shame that may be revealed.

Other Considerations on Using Photographs

+ The counselor may want to schedule a therapy session in the client's home where photographs may be more readily available, or in the case of regular home visits, the counselor may simply utilize any photographs that might be displayed.
+ Viewing photographs associated with loss can be distressing, so the client's emotional reactions must be monitored and appropriate regulation and containment facilitated.

Counseling professionals also must prepare themselves to work with distressing or even disturbing photographs (e.g., terminally ill children, bodies in caskets, stillborn babies, mass gravesites).

+ Be sensitive to cultural backgrounds that discourage or limit images of the deceased. In some cases clients may have other representational items that can be used in place of photographs. When in doubt on this matter, always ask the client.

+ Work with what you have. Some people have access to many photographs and others will have virtually no photographs. Sometimes it is helpful to encourage people to solicit photographs from others (e.g., family members). In some circumstances people can describe photographs that they recall but no longer have (e.g., lost in a flood or house fire).

+ Do not allow clients to retraumatize themselves by using the photographs to reenact distressful death and dying circumstances repetitively. Although some discussion of the death/dying circumstances may be appropriate, viewing the photographs is restorative only if it helps to activate memories of the living person to replace distressful death/dying memories. This is especially important in cases of violent death (e.g., murder, suicide). Rynearson (2001) suggested refocusing away from such reenactment by stating, "I want you to interrupt your thoughts of their dying with thoughts of their living" (p. 72).

Recommended Resources

Riches, G., & Dawson, P. (1998). Lost children, living memories: The role of photographs in processes of grief and adjustment among bereaved parents. *Death Studies, 22,* 121–140.

Weiser, J. (1999). *PhotoTherapy techniques: Exploring the secrets of personal snapshots and family albums* (2nd ed.). Vancouver, British Columbia, Canada: PhotoTherapy Centre.

Dr. J. Weiser's Web site, http://www.phototherapy-centre.com, provides excellent introductory material, notice of training events, reading and resource lists, and a discussion group.

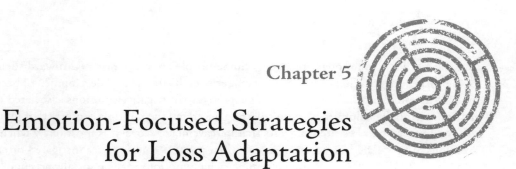

Chapter 5

Emotion-Focused Strategies for Loss Adaptation

This chapter presents counseling strategies that focus primarily on emotional processing rather than on cognitive or behavioral experiences in adaptation to loss. Working effectively with client emotions is often an integral part of counseling for loss and grief. In fact, the traditional notion of grief work emphasizes the value of emotional processing to facilitate functional grieving. Emotional processing involves experiencing one's emotions, perceiving and labeling emotions accurately, analyzing and understanding emotions, and outwardly expressing the inner emotional experience. The following are the potential benefits of emotional processing with loss adaptation:

- Emotions tell the griever that something is going on that requires further attention. In that sense emotions act as "hot cognitions" (Greenberg & Safran, 1988) that invite exploration of meaningful cognitive material, especially underlying assumptions and beliefs. Exploration of emotions often uncovers issues that are otherwise obscured. People are in a better position to appraise, understand, and act once they have information from their emotions as well as their cognitions.
- Emotional processing may establish a direction for therapy. A client's feelings about something, more so than what the client thinks, frequently signals potentially important material.
- Beliefs, attitudes, and assumptions are often more amenable to change when people are emotionally aroused (Frank & Frank, 1991). Experiencing feelings in the here-and-now, especially the distressing emotions associated with grief, motivates people toward actions that modify and relieve their distress.
- Emotional experiencing can relieve distressful symptoms. Much like slowly letting the air out of a balloon, ventilation or catharsis of emotional intensity makes people feel better. Catharsis is, in and of itself, not a cure, but it can relieve the intensity of emotional distress.
- Emotional processing enhances the counselor–client relationship. Clients are then encouraged, on the basis of this supportive relationship, to take more risks in experiencing and exploring their emotions (M. E. Young, 2001) and addressing the cognitive challenges of loss adaptation.

Respecting Client Differences in Emotional Processing

It is important that counseling professionals recognize the substantial differences among grieving people regarding the nature of their emotional experiences, their manner of emotional expression,

147

and their skills in emotional processing. Some people are more oriented toward their feelings than others as a reflection of personal characteristics, historical and developmental background, and cultural influences. Expressing or not expressing the negative emotions associated with grief may or may not be helpful, depending on the griever and the multiple contexts that influence the griever. In fact, some research suggests that bereavement recovery "is most likely when negative emotions are regulated or minimized and when positive emotions are instigated or enhanced" (Bonanno, 2001, p. 493). Culture determines what emotions may be socially acceptable in grief and often prescribes "display rules" that guide what emotions may be expressed or suppressed (Ekman, 1993; Rosenblatt, 1988).

Additionally, people vary significantly in their command of the basic skills associated with emotional processing. For example, one person may not be able to accurately recognize and label her feelings, another person may lack awareness even of the physiological experience of his feelings, and another person may not recognize variations in affect intensity. *It is not the purpose of grief counseling to force people to experience and express their emotions.* Emotional experiencing and expression, if pursued, is only one adaptive strategy and is generally insufficient on its own to promote change. Such a demand or overemphasis is deeply disrespectful, unprofessional, and unproductive. Instead, counseling professionals must carefully assess the nature of a client's experience and understanding of his or her emotions, emotion management skills, and the relevance of emotional processing for a specific client along with other adaptive strategies (e.g., cognitive, behavioral, spiritual). Intervention must then be tailored to the uniqueness of clients and their specific needs in adapting to loss.

Create a Holding Environment for Difficult Emotions

The single most important element in helping grieving clients with emotional processing is the creation in therapy of a *supportive holding environment*. The distressing, painful, and often threatening emotions of grief are most likely to be experienced, expressed, addressed, and resolved or integrated when therapy occurs in a safe and accepting place. It is the counseling professional's responsibility to create such an environment. The counselor must be able to communicate in depth the core conditions of empathy, unconditional positive regard, nonjudgmental acceptance, respect, and genuineness. It is here that grieving clients may speak the unspeakable and express the inexpressible. An effective holding environment is essential in providing a corrective emotional experience for clients who present difficult relational templates and interpersonal models (Teyber, 1997). Moreover, a necessary ingredient of a supportive holding environment for grieving persons is the communication of hope: that these distressing feelings can be endured, that the aching pain will subside, that value will come from experiencing their emotions, and that change for the better is possible.

It is difficult, if not impossible, to create a beneficial supportive holding environment for grieving clients from a one-up position. The counselor–client relationship must be one of collaboration with clients fully recognized and respected as experts on themselves. Counseling professionals should consult with clients regarding the direction, pace, depth, breath, and intensity of their emotional processing rather than forcing clients to go where counselors want them to go. This means fully advising clients as to the risks and potentials of counseling strategies that focus on emotional processing, checking in with clients regarding their emotional experiencing, and providing support and resources for emotion containment and regulation.

Emotional Processing Challenges in Loss Adaptation

Counseling professionals working with grieving clients should take special note of the following challenging situations regarding emotional processing.

Avoidance of Emotions

People are understandably reluctant to experience and address the distressful emotions that accompany grieving. After all, most people choose to avoid pain if they can. Some avoidance can be helpful at times; for example, staying busy or steering clear of certain situations or topics are effective temporary means of emotion management. The problem occurs when the avoidance is used consistently to deny legitimate feelings (e.g., blocking, minimizing, distracting, suppressing). There are many reasons that grieving persons may avoid emotions. They may not believe that anything can be better if they experience and express emotion. This is often the case in the early phases of grief, when it is difficult to see that anything can ever be different, especially emotional pain. People may fear that experiencing and expressing emotions will reveal them as inadequate, weak, or disturbed. They may be concerned about their own reactions as well as the reactions of others (e.g., their counselor). They may fear rejection or criticism from others (e.g., their counselor) because they judge some feelings as unacceptable. They may fear that experiencing and expressing their emotions will cause them to lose control. This is common for clients grieving losses that are often beyond their control and in situations in which control was taken from them (e.g., rape). They may lack affective awareness and experiencing skills. In this case the counseling focus shifts toward helping clients develop these basic skills in experiencing, expressing, and understanding their emotions.

It is important to explore the reasons for client avoidance of emotions. Counselors often refer to this as "talking about the wall" rather than attempting to break down the wall: Why avoid? What is the client worried about? What if the emotions were approached? What will happen if these emotions are not approached? What is the worst and best that could happen? What helps? Is emotional avoidance tied only to the current loss or is this a consistent pattern? What are the origins of reluctance to experience and express feelings? Additionally, counseling professionals should help clients develop coping skills to reassure them about managing emotional distress. Perhaps most importantly, clients are reassured by the counselor's consistent acceptance and empathy, competence, unhurried presence, willingness to approach distressful emotions, and confidence that emotional processing is beneficial.

Screen Emotions

The function of screen emotions is to hide deeper, more threatening emotions. Even though the selected screen emotion may be painful, problematic in relationships, or unproductive, it is preferable in the client's mind to experiencing a more threatening emotion. For example, a person may be more willing to experience intense guilt than to deal with deeper feelings of resentment. A common screen emotion in loss adaptation is anger, which may hide sadness, fear, helplessness, despair, depression, or guilt. This is particularly unhelpful because the anger causes conflicts with others, pushing away potential sources of social support, thus isolating the griever. Screen emotions require a great deal of energy to maintain because the unaddressed threatening emotions continue to assert themselves. It is important to help clients who are using screen emotions to approach, feel, explore, and resolve the feared underlying emotions.

149

Talking About Versus Experiencing Emotions

Talking about rather than experiencing emotions is a common way of defending against feeling specific emotions or simply feeling at all. For example, the counselor notices that when Tonya describes her loss history—a brother murdered, a sister's drug use, an absent father, and a mother too overwhelmed by poverty and stress to provide care—she is disconnected emotionally from the experience. It is as if she is reading a news report concerning someone else; her affect does not match her narrative. Counselors can assist clients who engage in such avoidant behavior by encouraging them to feel their emotions, providing a supportive environment, and helping them develop adequate coping skills.

Old Loss Wounding

When the griever's emotional response seems inconsistent with or out of proportion to the current loss event, it may signal unresolved feelings from previous loss experiences. It is as if the scab of a long-ago wound has been picked open and begins to bleed. This is especially true in the case of relationship losses. Current relationship endings touch prior relationship endings, most notably the formative relationships. For example, unresolved feelings from father loss and mother loss (e.g., abandonment, rejection, hurt, resentment) are evoked by a present breakup, estrangement, or divorce. The focus of therapy should then shift to the old loss wounding. Once the unresolved material from the prior losses is addressed and the client reaches some satisfactory closure or resolution on that matter, then the current loss can be fully grieved.

Absence of Emotion

Counseling professionals must be careful about their assessment of the absence of emotion in grieving clients. The affective bias of most counselors and the traditional emphasis on emotional expression as essential to functional grieving fail to recognize the considerable individual differences among grievers. Minimal or absent emotion, or even being unaware of emotion, is not an automatic sign of dysfunction. Rather, it should be viewed as a point to be assessed in light of the uniqueness of the griever and the multiple contexts (e.g., cultural) that influence a person's grieving. Is this person's satisfactory adaptation to loss impaired by an absence of emotion or emotional awareness? Does the apparent absence of emotion signal denial of reality (repression) or a refusal to attend to one's needs, or is it simply an expression of minimal distress? Does the absence of emotion reflect a temporary phase, especially conserving of energy to deal with grief? Would the experience and expression of emotion be helpful to this person and, most importantly, in what way would it be helpful? Is the counselor's judgment of absence of emotion biased by cultural and personal assumptions? Is the absence of emotion or minimized emotion in this loss consistent with or an exception to an individual's customary functioning and/or his or her cultural background? If an exception, then this would suggest that the absence of emotion might be problematic. If consistent, then further assessment can determine the functionality of the absent emotion.

Characterological Affect

The experience of loss and grief sometimes highlights a recurrent emotion that pervades a person's life—the characterological affect. In this case the sadness, anger, self-blame, or shame that seems at first glance to be connected to a current loss experience (behavioral and situational) is, in fact, more a reflection of low self-esteem (characterological). In this situation the focus of counseling shifts away from loss adaptation to this recurrent emotion and what it reveals about the client's sense of self (Teyber, 1997).

Emotion Management Through Substance Use or Abuse

Some people manage the distressful emotions that accompany grief through use or abuse of alcohol, prescription drugs, and nonprescription or illegal drugs. Substances may be used to anesthetize emotional pain, to avoid painful feelings, or even to provoke emotional expression. Substance abuse may be part of a larger problem and an established pattern (e.g., alcoholism), or it may be a consequence of the grieving experience itself. Some increased alcohol intake for people who do drink is not necessarily problematic. However, the counselor and client must evaluate whether substance use or abuse is contributing in unhelpful ways to consistent avoidance of emotions or denial of the realities of loss and restoration. In most cases a substance abuse problem should be addressed before attempting to work on processing the emotions of grief.

Mixed or Dissonant Emotional Reactions

One challenge to loss adaptation occurs when people have difficulty resolving the mixed or dissonant feelings regarding a loss experience. For example, a person's reaction to losing a job may be both relief and anger; when a relationship dissolves, a person may experience a mix of guilt, sadness, and relief; the adult child may experience both love and hate at the death of an abusive parent. Intervention should focus on the different reasons for difficulties managing mixed or dissonant feelings in loss adaptation. Some people have a minimal ability to experience and recognize any feelings, much less mixed or conflicting feelings regarding the same event. Intervention here is appropriately geared toward raising basic awareness of emotional reactions, recognizing feelings, and labeling emotions. Sometimes people are only aware of one emotion while another emotion remains influential (and often recognizable to others) but out of their awareness. Intervention then focuses on recognizing feelings, exploring variations of emotional intensity, and accepting the possibility of mixed or dissonant emotions. At other times people are aware of dissonant emotions but find one of these emotions unacceptable. Intervention should then focus on normalizing all emotions, developing coping skills, giving permission or encouraging self-permission to experience and express unacceptable emotions, examining polarities (e.g., guilt and resentment), and exploring the reasons for rejecting specific emotions.

While the overall goal with mixed or dissonant emotional reactions is integration, that is not always possible with loss and grief experiences. Sometimes the best outcome is simply clarification of mixed or dissonant emotions along with the development of skills for managing ambivalence. For example, the adult who experienced sexual abuse in childhood from a parent may not be able to fully integrate the conflicting feelings of love, hate, resentment, guilt, sadness, and relief upon the death of that parent, but he or she may be able to accept and live with those dissonant emotions in a way that promotes healing.

Here-and-Now and There-and-Then

The primary work of emotional processing focuses on the client's present experience. However, counseling for loss and grief sometimes moves back and forth between here-and-now experiencing and there-and-then reflection. It may be helpful for clients to revisit the feelings attached to old loss wounds and connect these to present emotional reactions, especially to more current losses.

General Guidelines for Emotional Processing With Loss Adaptation

1. Attend to Nonverbal Expression

Counselors must attend carefully to nonverbal expressions of emotions (e.g., body language, facial expression, posture) and paralanguage (e.g., sounds, voice tone and volume, speech pace). Watch especially for changes or incongruence between verbal and nonverbal behavior. Remember that eye contact is heavily influenced by culture, so is not necessarily a good gauge of emotional reaction. It is usually helpful to call attention to nonverbal expressions and explore the emotions attached to them. However, be careful to avoid overfocusing or interrogation because this provokes self-consciousness.

2. Teach the Language of Emotions

Counselors should help clients acquire a language for describing their emotions. This increases awareness, reduces confusion, and assists in meaning making. Clarity in labeling feelings inhibits ruminative coping, often a problem in loss adaptation (Salovey, Bedell, Detweiler, & Mayer, 1999). Labeling should go beyond broad categories to finer distinctions of feelings; for example, irritation, frustration, and rage are more accurate descriptors and provide much better information than "anger." Naming physical sensations is a starting point for some people (e.g., my shoulders are tense). Remember that people must have awareness that they are experiencing an emotional reaction before they can label that reaction (Brems, 2001). It is often helpful to introduce a Feelings List to clients, have them consult the list in the session, and use the list outside of session (see Table 5.1). Counselors should avoid labeling feelings for clients (e.g., you feel insecure) because this is counterproductive to clients learning to label for themselves. This is especially problematic when counselors overuse reflection techniques. Instead, counselors encourage clients to do their own work of identifying and labeling emotions (e.g., What feelings are you aware of right now?).

3. Address Fear of Emotions

Counselors should intentionally address client fears of being overwhelmed by feelings. This is often a challenge in loss situations because grief emotions tend to be strong, distressing, sometimes unfamiliar; often invoke underlying beliefs and assumptions; and may have been strengthened via suppression or avoidance. In the midst of grief people often do not see that anything can be different, especially that their painful emotions can diminish. They see themselves as on the edge of being overwhelmed and fear going over that edge. Counseling professionals can reassure clients that they can manage their emotions, that their counselor will monitor their emotional status, that they will be consulted and not pushed inappropriately to experience their feelings, and that they will never be allowed to leave a session in an emotionally reactive state.

4. Establish Emotion Management Skills Early

Counselors should assist clients in establishing emotion containment and regulation skills before asking them to address deeper and more painful emotions. Assess what skills a client may already have

TABLE 5.1

Feelings List for Loss and Grief Experiences

AFRAID	irked	quiet	mystified	alarmed
alarmed	irritated	relaxed	perplexed	discombobulated
apprehensive	livid	relieved	pessimistic	disconcerted
awed	mad	serene	puzzled	perturbed
cautious	outraged	soothed	stagnant	rattled
desperate	patronized	tranquil	stuck	restless
defensive	peeved	unmoved	torn	shocked
dread	perturbed	unruffled	trapped	startled
fearful	pissed (off)		troubled	surprised
foreboding	provoked	**CONFIDENT**	uncertain	troubled
frightened	rebellious	able	undecided	uncomfortable
guarded	resentful	able-bodied	uneasy	uneasy
intimidated	sabotaged	bold	unsettled	unnerved
mistrustful	steamed	certain	unsure	unsettled
nervous	stifled	competent		upset
panicked	upset	complete	**DISCONNECTED**	
petrified	used	empowered	alienated	**EXCITED**
reluctant	vengeful	fulfilled	alone	amazed
scared	vindictive	hopeful	aloof	astonished
shy		open	apathetic	eager
stunned	**ANXIOUS**	positive	bored	energetic
suspicious	apprehensive	proud	cold	enthusiastic
terrified	concerned	safe	detached	invigorated
timid	disquieted	satisfied	distant	lively
overwhelmed	distressed	secure	distracted	passionate
vulnerable	disturbed	steady	indifferent	vibrant
wary	fearful	sure	lonely	
worried	ill at ease		numb	**FATIGUED**
	nervous	**CONFUSED**	perplexed	beat
ANGRY	perturbed	ambivalent	removed	burnt out
abused	restless	awkward	ungrounded	depleted
agitated	stressed	baffled	uninterested	exhausted
aggravated	tense	bewildered	upset	lethargic
annoyed	tormented	bothered	withdrawn	listless
boiling	troubled	caught	worked up	sleepy
cranky	uneasy	conflicted		tired
enraged	worked up	dazed	**DISINTERESTED**	weary
exasperated	worried	directionless	bored	worn out
exploited		disorganized	cold	
frustrated	**CALM/GOOD**	distracted	indifferent	**GRATEFUL**
fuming	at ease	distrustful	insensitive	appreciative
furious	at peace	doubtful	lifeless	moved
harassed	balanced	dull	neutral	thankful
hateful	collected	flustered	preoccupied	touched
hostile	composed	foggy	reserved	
humiliated	contented	hesitant	tired	**GUILTY**
incensed	harmonious	immobilized	weary	ashamed
indignant	in harmony	indecisive		chagrin
infuriated	in balance	lost	**DISTURBED**	condemned
irate	peaceful	misunderstood	agitated	conscience-stricken

(Continued on next page)

153

TABLE 5.1 *(Continued)*

Feelings List for Loss and Grief Experiences

GUILTY	HURT	callous	restored	fidgety
(Continued)	aching	chilled	pacified	frazzled
contrite	agonized	dazed	soothed	irritable
convicted	aggrieved	dead		jittery
culpable	alienated	drugged	SAD	nervous
criminal	anguished	empty	abandoned	overwhelmed
embarrassed	cut	hardened	alienated	restless
illegitimate	battered	inured	defeated	stressed out
mortified	bereaved	insensitive	dejected	tense
penitent	bruised	paralyzed	demoralized	
punished	crushed	shocked	depressed	STRONG
remorseful	damaged	stunned	despondent	able
resentful	devastated	uninterested	devastated	capable
shame	grief-stricken	unemotional	disillusioned	certain
sinful	heartbroken		disappointed	competent
wicked	humiliated		discouraged	earnest
	injured	PLEASURE	disheartened	enduring
	lonely	amused	dismayed	firm
HAPPY	miserable	bliss	down	fixed
alive	pained	contented	drained	hardy
appreciated	punished	delight	empty	invulnerable
cheerful	stabbed	ecstacy	forlorn	keen
confident	tortured	enjoyment	gloomy	mighty
delighted	traumatized	euphoria	heavy-hearted	muscular
ecstatic	wronged	glad	helpless	prepared
elated	wounded	happy	hopeless	secure
encouraged		joyful	hurt	sound
energized		jubilant	lonely	sturdy
enthusiastic	LOVE	satisfaction	melancholy	sure
excited	acceptance	thrill	miserable	unyielding
fulfilled	adoration	tickled	mournful	unbeatable
grateful	adulation		pessimistic	
gratified	affinity	REGRETFUL	pitiful	VULNERABLE
hopeful	agape	ashamed	rejected	empty
joyful	attachment	apologetic	sorrowful	fatigued
jubilant	closeness	bitter	tearful	fragile
optimistic	connection	disillusioned	unappreciated	guarded
pleased	devotion	guilty	uncared for	helpless
relieved	fondness	humbled	unhappy	hesitant
satisfied	friendliness	remorseful	unwanted	incapable
thrilled	infatuation	sorrowful	wounded	inferior
uplifted	intimacy	sorry	wretched	insecure
	kindness/kindly			leery
HOPEFUL	liking	RELIEVED		overwhelmed
eager	passion	appeased	STRESSED	paralyzed
expectant	regard	calmed	anxious	pathetic
encouraged	trust	comforted	cranky	sensitive
optimistic		consoled	distressed	shaky
positive	NUMBNESS	freshened	distraught	weak
upbeat	apathetic	rested	edgy	

(Continued on next page)

TABLE 5.1 (*Continued*)

Feelings List for Loss and Grief Experiences

WEAK	incompetent	OTHER HELPFUL WORDS
anemic	lame	_____
debilitated	limp	_____
dismayed	insecure	_____
engulfed	overcome	_____
faint	overpowered	_____
feeble	overwhelmed	_____
flaccid	sensitive	_____
fragile	shaky	_____
guarded	spineless	_____
helpless	swamped	_____
hopeless	wimpy	_____
incapacitated	wishy-washy	_____

in this regard and the functionality of those skills (e.g., distraction is a skill that can be used in a functional or dysfunctional manner; substance abuse is usually an unhelpful emotion regulation method). Teach emotion regulation skills where appropriate. These might include distraction, thought-stopping, or imagery (e.g., putting feelings under lock and key, envisioning relaxing scenarios, or rational emotive imagery). The ability to label emotions accurately is helpful with emotion regulation because it improves recognition of differing levels of arousal. Mindfulness-based practices are highly recommended in this regard. Many counseling professionals regularly introduce grieving clients to mindfulness procedures early in therapy so that they can practice these before moving into more distressing emotional material. Counselors also can help clients build their tolerance for emotional discomfort by encouraging them to "stay with the feeling" whenever some emotion is approached.

5. Connect Emotions, Thoughts, and Behavior

Sometimes clients do not see the connection between their emotions, thoughts, and behavior. It may be painfully obvious to everyone else that Terry's angry acting out is connected to the multiple losses he has recently endured (e.g., family members displaced, homelessness, illness of primary caretaker), but Terry may not have a clue. People may also not understand that their emotional reactions in the present loss situation are more reflective of prior loss experiences— old wounds. Identifying a pattern of emotional reactions and linking these to thoughts and behavior facilitate functional loss adaptation.

6. Promote Acceptance of All Emotions

Grieving clients sometimes avoid their feelings because they fear "unacceptable" emotions or subscribe to myths about emotions (e.g., anger is depression turned inward). Normalizing and legitimizing all emotions, both positive and negative, enhance self-understanding and facilitate client motivation for change. Counselors encourage clients to view emotions as rich sources of information distinct from truth or personhood.

7. Allow Time for Emotional Processing

Counselors should carefully consider the time element when assisting clients with emotional processing. Rushing through emotional material or disrupting the process because of time constraints is counterproductive. A slow and steady pace encourages more depth. The counselor must never initiate an intervention designed to arouse emotions (e.g., chair dialogues) near the end of a session. Consider the time needed for clients to recover their balance and prepare themselves to resume their daily routine.

8. Attend to the Influence of Culture on Emotion

A counselor must be aware of the cultural influences likely to affect a client's experience and expression of emotion. Counselors should consult research, colleagues, and other sources to enhance their knowledge of different cultural influences, but the most important action is to ask the experts—the clients. This involves a collaborative approach that enlists the client and counselor in a mutual investigation: What expectations or rules for expressing emotions do you hold and where do those expectations come from? How does your ethnic background impact the way you experience and express anger? What emotions do you feel most uncomfortable with (or most comfortable with), and where did you learn about handling emotions? Help me understand how your Japanese American background affects the way you express your emotions. What does being an Hispanic male have to do with experiencing and expressing emotions, especially crying or anger? What emotions are not acceptable for women (men) to express? Counselors must be diligent in avoiding stereotypes—people often do not reflect the expected norms. This is another reason to seek clients' advice on their understanding of cultural influences on their lives.

9. Respect Client Differences Regarding Emotions

Counseling professionals must consider carefully whether or not and to what extent a focus on emotions is beneficial to specific clients, being certain that the affective bias of the psychotherapy field, especially regarding grief, does not blind them to the uniqueness of clients. People vary tremendously in their capacity for emotional processing. Counselors should ask themselves: What is the goal of facilitating emotional expression with this client? Does this client express emotional content more through behavior and cognition than "emoting"? Is this client having difficulty with emotional processing and, if so, how will this or that strategy address that? In what ways should emotional processing strategies be adapted for this particular person and her or his unique situation?

Recommended Resources

Brems, C. (2001). *Basic skills in psychotherapy and counseling*. Belmont, CA: Brooks/Cole. (Note especially Chapter 10.)
Teyber, E. (2006). *Interpersonal process in therapy: An integrative model* (5th ed.). Belmont, CA: Brooks/Cole. (Note especially Chapter 5.)

Using a Feelings List for Grief Experiences

Accurately identifying one's emotional reactions is a beneficial emotional processing skill. Labeling emotions increases awareness, enhances communication, reduces confusion, assists in emotion regulation, reduces avoidance of feelings, and contributes to meaning reconstruction. There is also some evidence that clarity in labeling feelings inhibits the ruminative coping that is often problematic in loss adaptation (Salovey et al., 1999). A list of words describing emotional states commonly encountered in loss adaptation assists clients in developing a vocabulary for their inner affective experience. While physiological awareness may yield some descriptors (e.g., knot in the stomach, tension in the shoulders, tense jaw), labeling the inner experience with emotion descriptors—a higher skill level in emotional processing—enhances accuracy and distinguishes emotional states. Even people who already have some proficiency in recognizing and labeling their emotions often find Feelings Lists beneficial. An additional benefit of a Feelings List is that it invites clients to name and describe their own emotional states rather than relying on the counselor to do the work for them.

Implementation of a Feelings List

A good time to introduce a Feelings List to clients is when they exhibit some difficulty labeling emotions during the therapy session. The counselor provides clients with the Feelings List (see Table 5.1) and asks them to search out words that might describe their feelings or moods. The Feelings List can then become a standard reference used in and out of the therapy session to enhance emotional processing. It is advisable to have copies on hand for consultation during the session and with homework. Clients are encouraged to add words to the list as they see fit. Counselors should supply translations of emotions on the Feelings List if appropriate. However, languages do not always have equivalent expressions, especially for emotions. Counselors must be open to incorporating language-specific words for emotions where that serves the client's needs.

The Feelings List assists clients in making increasingly finer distinctions in their emotional experience. Simple descriptors such as angry or sad are a first step for many but do not provide sufficient clarity about the intensity, range, or depth of feelings. The Feelings List helps a client move beyond "anger" to more accurate descriptors such as irritation, rage, or exasperation, and beyond "sad" to descriptors such as discouraged, blue, wounded, or devastated. Once these finer distinctions are made, it is sometimes useful to propose a scale in which the affective variations are visualized. For example, on a scale of 1 to 10 regarding anger, 1 may represent *mild annoyance*, 5 may represent *aggravation*, 8 may represented *boiling*, and 10 may represent *enraged*. This scale then provides the counselor and client with a common understanding of the client's emotional state.

Some form of Feelings List is an essential part of any counseling professional's toolkit. The Feelings List provided in this chapter (Table 5.1) is geared toward the emotions most commonly experienced in working with grieving people in therapy.

Chair Dialogues

Chair Dialogues, most often associated with psychodrama and Gestalt therapy, are useful strategies in grief counseling, especially for emotional processing. The basic approach involves clients talking to the imagined presence of some significant person or perceived part of the self (e.g., absent parent, amputated leg, deceased partner, anger) represented by a vacant chair. Unlike role-plays, which involve preparation and practice for real encounters, Chair Dialogues use an imagined encounter with an imagined other to facilitate emotional experiencing and expression, enhance awareness, and promote steps to resolution of key issues associated with loss and grief. The versatility and adaptability of Chair Dialogues allow the counseling professional to tailor this intervention to meet the unique needs of clients and the multiple contexts of their loss. Thus, Chair Dialogues can be used with diverse types of loss (e.g., symbolic, death-related, ambiguous), grief (e.g., disenfranchised grief, obscured grief), and experiences (e.g., unfinished business, polarities). Chair Dialogues help clients confront avoidance so as to bring hidden or obscured issues and emotions into awareness. While the primary emphasis of Chair Dialogues is on emotional processing, the strategy often reveals meaningful cognitive material, such as mistaken beliefs, maladaptive schemas, unrealized or unrealistic expectations, and irrational beliefs. Additionally, Chair Dialogues can be used to reveal meaning structures (e.g., beliefs, assumptions, expectations) that have been disrupted by loss, and then serve as a vehicle for revising and amending those meaning structures.

Implementation of Chair Dialogues

Chair Dialogues actually begin with a *monologue* (one-way) in which the client addresses a significant person or perceived part of self (represented by a vacant chair), followed by reflection and exploration on the encounter. However, the process may then evolve from a monologue to a *dialogue* (two-way) in which the client imagines a response from the significant person or perceived part of self. This may even include switching chairs to facilitate the "conversation" between client and imagined other or part (enacted by the client). Reflection and exploration of material from the dialogue then follows. Two forms of Chair Dialogues commonly used in grief counseling are described here: *empty-chair dialogue* and *chair dialogue with parts*.

Empty-Chair Dialogue
An empty-chair dialogue is used to address *unfinished business*. Unfinished business is the intrusion of unresolved material from the past into the present that compromises one's ability to form new attachments or fully participate in new experiences. For example, a woman may use distancing and controlling behavior in a current relationship to avoid feelings of abandonment and rejection associated with a former relationship. She cannot fully participate in the new relationship because she is continually looking over her shoulder at the disconnections from her "lost" relationship (old wounds). Unfinished business is frequently a complication of loss and grief. In fact, E. W. L. Smith (1985) suggested that unfinished business is created by avoidance of the emotional pain of grieving. Continued avoidance, in the form of repressed or denied feelings, prolongs the unfinished business. An empty-chair dialogue is used to confront the avoidance by arousing and intensifying emotions as the individual "converses" with the imagined person most associated with one's unfinished business (e.g., father, former partner, deceased friend). This process removes blocks to awareness, revealing the specific nature of the client's unfinished business (e.g., guilt, betrayal, shattered assumptions). The counseling professional coaches clients through the process, helping them to remain fully present in the here-and-now, feel their emotions deeply, and explore whatever is revealed so as to resolve or "finish" the business of the past. According to Greenberg, Rice, and Elliott (1993), intense emotional arousal, statement of needs, and a shift in viewpoint of the imagined other are critical elements in resolving unfinished business. Resolving or finishing unfinished business related to loss often includes reconstructing one's narrative of the past, the loss, the lost object, and relationships; recognizing and accepting the difference between what one can and cannot change or control; disconnecting from anger; reorganizing one's view of self and others; and learning to trust one's feelings.

Because empty-chair dialogues usually generate intense emotional arousal and distress, it is important that counseling professionals plan implementation thoughtfully, prepare clients for the procedure, and carefully monitor the unfolding process. Traumatization, especially that associated with posttraumatic stress disorder, should be addressed before attempting an empty-chair dialogue to avoid retraumatization. An effective empty-chair dialogue occurs within a supportive holding environment characterized by a collaborative and respectful client–counselor working relationship. The counseling professional should note the following:

* Make sure the client has appropriate emotional containment and regulation skills before attempting this strategy.
* Consider the appropriateness of promoting emotional intensity in view of the client's personal and cultural influences.
* Collaborate with the client to identify potential issues and topics to be addressed before attempting the procedure. Note that resentment is a frequent component of unfinished business (Greenberg et al., 1993).
* Describe the procedure before obtaining permission to implement, including the likelihood of emotional distress and the client's choice to stop the procedure.
* Allow sufficient time for the empty-chair dialogue to occur, including time for postdialogue reflection and emotional recovery. Never introduce an empty-chair dialogue in the last moments of a therapy session.

When setting up an empty-chair dialogue, place the vacant chair close enough to the client to facilitate connection or relationship. The counselor moves to the side of or slightly behind the client so as to facilitate the client's focus directly on the empty chair (e.g., the imagined person), discouraging avoidance via eye contact or conversing with the counselor instead of the lost object. The counselor's role in an empty-chair dialogue is as facilitator and coach, encouraging clients to experience and express their thoughts and feelings in an unrestricted manner in the here-and-now. The counselor helps clients remain grounded in reality and assists them in managing avoidance. The following steps are suggested (see Figure 5.1).

Step 1. Imagining presence. The counselor directs clients to imagine the significant other who is the focus of their unfinished business sitting across from them in an empty chair. The counselor helps clients make the imagined presence more real by asking them to describe the person or entity: What do you notice about him? What does her face look like? What is she wearing? How is he sitting? What form do you imagine the other taking [if the entity is not human]?

Step 2. Experiencing presence. The counselor encourages clients to quietly experience being present with this significant other at this moment. Moving slowly, the counselor directs clients to attend first to their overall sensations, then to their emotions, and, after giving time for awareness to come, encourages them to name their feelings. The emphasis on feelings rather than on cognition at this point helps the client become aware of the present moment. If clients avoid emotion (e.g., changing the subject, discussing thoughts instead of emotions), the counselor simply redirects them to attend to what it feels like to sit across from this significant other. The counselor should be physically still so as to encourage a slow pace and inner directedness. At this point it is helpful to ask open-ended questions that promote clients fully sensing the imagined entity in the empty chair in the present moment. For example: What is it like to sit here with her after all this time? What feelings are you aware of as you experience his presence? What's happening with you right now? What feelings lurk at the edge of your awareness? Bring them in closer and really feel them. The counselor should encourage clients to look at the empty chair or close their eyes to tune into the experience as they answer these questions; they should not look at the counselor.

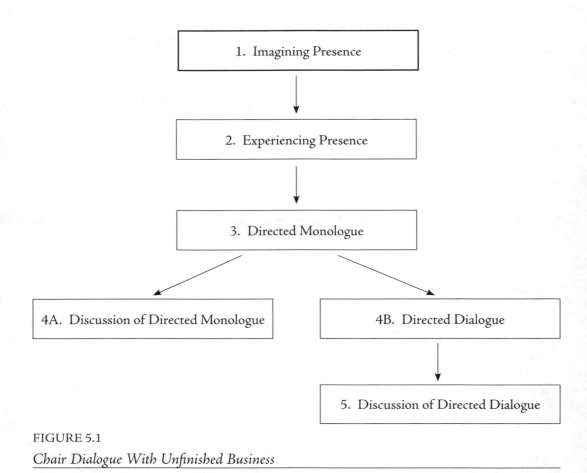

FIGURE 5.1

Chair Dialogue With Unfinished Business

Step 3. Directed monologue. Next, the counselor directs clients to greet the imagined person sitting in the chair and express whatever they are thinking and feeling at that moment to this significant person. The one-sided conversation that now unfolds is minimally directed by the counselor, keeping in mind the following guidelines:

- Direct clients to use "I statements" (e.g., I feel guilty; I resent you; I hate what you did to me). Intercede to have clients restate in "I statement" form if necessary.
- Encourage clients to experience and express their feelings without restriction (e.g., stay with the feeling; tell him what you are feeling; look her in the eye and tell her what this is like for you; let the resentment be present). Careful pacing and direction helps clients move beyond surface layers to deeper experiencing of emotions (e.g., go deeper; feel what is underneath the anger).
- Notice any physical movements and direct clients to express verbally what that movement indicates (e.g., let that fist speak; give that swinging foot a voice). Draw on the client's previous description of experiencing the presence of the imagined other to encourage expression (e.g., allow that tension in your shoulders to speak; let that resentment bubble up from your middle). Pay attention to any discrepancy between verbal and nonverbal actions, directing the client to "give voice to" the nonverbal.

+ Block avoidance by redirecting clients to their emotions or to the imagined presence (e.g., he is listening to what you have to say; tell her how you feel). "The points of avoidance are the points of therapeutic intervention" (E. W. L. Smith, 1985, p. 77). Move slightly out of the client's line of sight if there is a tendency to shift focus to the counselor instead of the imagined other; do not collude with avoidance by engaging directly with the client at this point. Do not let the session degenerate into invective and accusation.

+ Help clients stay in the present moment, not relive traumatic and critical encounters. Make certain clients remain grounded in reality. It is all right to talk about the past but only as that relates to what is happening now. For example, if clients begin speaking about past incidents, direct them to talk about what that means to them now as they sit with their significant other. Allow the directed monologue to unfold naturally and spontaneously, following its own course as much as possible. Pace slowly and speak minimally, keeping directions as brief as possible. Sometimes it helps to direct the client to "look at her" or "see the expression on his face" to make the imagined presence more real during the directed monologue.

+ Counseling professionals may encourage clients to take a moment to gather themselves and silently focus on sensing their innermost feelings before continuing the conversation with the imagined other. This can facilitate moving to deeper levels of feeling and awareness or a shift in direction. This moment of "gathering self" should not take the client out of the process, because that would foster avoidance.

+ Direct clients to the feelings that accompany any distorted thinking (e.g., irrational thoughts, schemas, underlying assumptions, maladaptive beliefs) that may arise so as to raise awareness.

+ Help clients express the unexpressed wants and needs that are often an ingredient in unfinished business. E. W. L. Smith (1985) suggested that bereaved clients be encouraged to fully express the following: appreciations (good memories, positive feelings), resentments (unpleasant memories, negative feelings), and regrets (acknowledgment of things not being as one would like). "A good clean grieving seems to require expression of all three. Otherwise, some piece of unfinished business remains" (p. 77). There is a tendency for clients with unfinished business to focus exclusively on unpleasant memories and feelings. Healing is usually associated with a more balanced view, so it may be helpful to encourage clients to recall good times and pleasant memories if they can. For example, a man whose empty-chair dialogue with his mother focused on neglect and abuse as a child may be encouraged to recall some positive feelings and memories of good times as well. The goal here is a more balanced perspective. However, the counselor must be careful that such recollections do not deny or obscure the more difficult feelings and issues.

Step 4. Option: discussion or directed dialogue. When no new material is forthcoming in the directed monologue, the counseling professional may select from two options: initiate a discussion of the monologue experience (Option 4A) or move into a directed dialogue (Option 4B).

Option 4A. Discussion of directed monologue. The counselor engages clients in an exploration of their experience in the directed monologue. It is useful at this point for the counselor to move the vacant chair away and reposition himself or herself for a more direct conversational connection. This helps the client recover from emotional intensity and focus exploration. It is important to discuss any avoidance, how the client resisted and/or confronted the avoidance, and what that means for the client. The counselor helps the client link experiences, especially the connections between old wounds and current situations. The discussion may remain focused on emotions for a time but eventually should move to more cognitive elements so as to promote resolution and integration of the unfinished business.

Option 4B. Directed dialogue. Rather than discussion of the directed monologue, the counseling professional may instead encourage the client to "become" the imagined other and "speak" from that role/position. Thus, the client who spoke to her deceased mother now imagines herself as her mother speaking back to her daughter (the client). This is facilitated by having the client move to the vacant chair formerly "occupied" by the imagined other: "Geri, just move over here into your mother's chair and imagine being your mother speaking to you." Direct the client, in the role of imagined other, to respond to what was said in the directed monologue. This provides the opportunity to explore different perspectives, consider the weaknesses and limitations of others, and clarify actions. The counselor continues to remind the client, even in the role of imagined other, to experience and express feelings.

Becoming aware of the weaknesses and limitations of people who, in the clients' minds, have caused pain or loss is often a critical ingredient in finishing unfinished business. Understanding the wrongdoer's motives and background can help clients make sense of the loss. This is not to say that wrong behavior is acceptable or excusable but that it is more understandable given the context in which it occurred. The wrongdoer thus becomes more human and less of an object or stereotype (Brandsma, 1982; Denton & Martin, 1998). In some cases a measure of empathy or compassion for the wrongdoer occurs, but this is certainly not required and should not be a goal.

Do not allow clients to make false or baseless statements in the imagined role but to be realistic in their ideas of what the imagined person might actually say to them. Such realism does not exclude hopefulness about desired responses. For example, a client doing an empty-chair dialogue with her mother expresses how difficult and hurtful the mother's unavailability and unpredictability had been during the client's childhood. Because the counselor knows that the client's mother had been severely depressed, the counselor directs the client to switch roles and "sit in the chair and become your mother, talking to her adult daughter today about the mother she wanted and hoped to be but could not be because of the burden of mental illness." The idea here is not that the imagined other is somehow miraculously transformed into someone unrecognizable spouting feel-good platitudes, but that the potential for responding differently once an impediment is removed offers another perspective.

The counselor continues to encourage the client to address important issues and themes and to work through uncomfortable emotions. This might include acceptance of an unsatisfactory or disappointing response from the imagined other. Sometimes this process is facilitated by having the client switch back and forth between self and imagined other. When switching parts, have the client move from her or his own chair to the chair representing the imagined other. The counselor also can shift position so as to inhibit client avoidance by engaging directly with the counselor instead of the imagined other. When no further new information is forthcoming from the directed dialogue, have the client say "goodbye for now" to the imagined other so as to underscore the end of the experiential part of the procedure.

Step 5. Discussion of directed monologue and dialogue. If the empty-chair dialogue has included both directed monologue and directed dialogue, the counselor then engages clients in an exploration of their dialogue experience. As suggested previously, the counselor should move the vacant chair away and reposition himself or herself for a more direct connection with the client (signaling the end of the experiential segment of the strategy). Help the client to link old wounds and current situations, examine responses, and explore avoidance and ways in which the client managed the avoidance. What meaning does the client attach to the unfinished business now? Is there anything the client did not or could not say? Did something come up that surprised the client? Counseling professionals may also share, in a collaborative manner, their own observations of the client's experience in the chair dialogue. There should be a gradual shift from emotional processing to a cognitive focus as the client considers any newly revealed material.

Additional Consideration for Empty-Chair Dialogue

Some additional points to be considered in implementing an empty-chair dialogue include the following:

+ It is important that clients understand that the purpose of the empty-chair dialogue is to facilitate emotional processing and raise awareness and is not intended as preparation for real encounters. Avoid referring to this strategy as a role-play and reiterate that this is not a rehearsal for action.
+ Remember that awareness that may result from emotional processing is a means to an end and not an end in itself. Awareness is only useful when the client can transform it into change.
+ Empty-chair dialogues are especially useful in addressing anger, resentment, shame, guilt, and the resultant desire for revenge, retaliation, or self-punishment. This strategy helps clients become aware of the sources of these emotions, the energy that they consume, and the damage they do, especially to the client. It can then serve as a means for disconnecting from or letting go of these negative states. This is a necessary condition of forgiveness (Denton & Martin, 1998; Malcolm & Greenberg, 2000), which some clients may find useful in functional adaptation to loss.
+ Awareness and understanding that contribute to altered beliefs, assumptions, attitudes, or narratives may not occur in one session, but the empty-chair dialogue can be an effective means of furthering the process of awareness and resolution of unfinished business. Sometimes minimal discussion at the time of the dialogue generates more depth of discussion in later sessions.
+ Take steps to ensure client safety and resource availability before the clients leave an empty-chair dialogue therapy session. Help clients recover sufficiently from emotional intensity. Review client emotion management, self-care skills, and contingency plans to establish client safety and resources (e.g., emergency contacts).
+ Remember that catharsis, while it may temporarily relieve distress, is not the goal of an empty-chair dialogue. Emotional processing must be accompanied by enhanced awareness and understanding to promote meaningful change.
+ The imagined other in an empty-chair dialogue is most often a known significant person but may also represent a less familiar person (e.g., drunken driver), a nonhuman entity (e.g., cancer, amputated leg, drug abuse, the farm), or a collective identity (e.g., dominant culture, the military, managed care, university administration).
+ The counseling professional's role in an empty-chair dialogue is facilitative. The counselor should focus on creating a space in which the client experiences and works. Often the

most useful things the counselor can do are to help the client remain in the here-and-now and avoid intruding on the client's process by becoming overly directive. Remember that the more the counselor talks, the less the client works.

- Do not overdramatize the setup for doing an empty-chair dialogue because that can raise client anxiety and even resistance. Move simply and naturally into the procedure.
- Do not use an empty-chair dialogue with clients who cannot maintain contact with reality (e.g., delusional) or have cultural taboos regarding "contact" with the deceased or ghosts.
- Some clients may express an initial reluctance for chair work by alluding to feeling silly talking to an empty chair. The counselor can encourage them with a matter-of-fact attitude to "try it anyway, just to see what happens." Further reluctance should be explored with consideration that this may not be the time or format that most serves the client's needs.
- The empty-chair dialogue can be extended for clients who would benefit from a ritualized way of underscoring their resolution or "finishing" of unfinished business. The client is invited to reenter the presence of the imagined other and talk to that entity about the experiences they shared (remembrances) and the things the client learned from or was given by the imagined other. The client then might shift chairs to inhabit the role of the imagined other, sharing what that entity learned or gained from the client. Blatner (2005) proposed this approach specifically for bereaved persons, but it clearly may be used for nondeath-related circumstances.

Chair Dialogue With Parts

A chair dialogue with parts is used to address a person's inner sense of fragmentation, conflicting parts, differing aspects, or splitting. In the Gestalt view, this fragmentation takes the form of polarities, which represent unexplored, disowned, or opposing aspects of a person's experience. The idea is that people tend to be aware of or overemphasize one dimension and avoid the opposite dimension. From a constructivist viewpoint, the fragmentation of identity reveals a disrupted self-narrative in that previously accepted assumptions about one's self no longer hold true . Such fragmentation causes emotional distress, impedes reality-testing, impairs meaning reconstruction, and drains energy, thus complicating the integration of loss and grief into the whole fabric of one's life. For example:

> Fritz exhibits intense resentment toward the staff of the nursing home where his mother died. Even 2 years later and following dismissal of his legal proceedings aimed at the nursing home, Fritz is so consumed by anger that he is unable to integrate his loss. It is only when his counselor helps him begin to address the opposing polarity of his resentment—his guilt at placing his mother in the nursing home—that Fritz becomes aware of the real source of his anger.

> Serena, who developed chronic fatigue syndrome and fibromyalgia several years ago, feels she has steadily lost parts of herself. Once an independent, self-motivated, and active career woman, she has become more dependent on her family, struggles physically to get through the day, experiences some cognitive confusion ("fibro-fog"), and can no longer hold a job. Serena's illness has robbed her of some core aspects of her identity, leaving her with a disrupted and disorganized sense of self.

The specific nature of fragmented parts that may complicate loss adaptation varies across people, their losses, and the multiple contexts of their lives and their grief. However, the following parts, splits, or polarities present frequently in loss adaptation: love/hate, guilt/resentment, victim/survivor, connection/distance, control/passivity, controlled/out of control, powerfulness/powerlessness, strength/weakness, acceptance/rejection, numbness/pain, growth/stagnation, wholeness/brokenness, good person/bad person, self-blame/other-blame, should/should not, success/failure, loser/winner, sorrow/relief, faithful/faithless, hopeful/hopeless, overresponsible/underresponsible, holding on/ letting go, dependence/independence/interdependence, moving on/staying, and broken bonds/ continuing bonds. The purpose of a chair dialogue with parts is to facilitate awareness, understanding, acceptance, and reconciliation of the fragmented parts through emotional processing. The emphasis is on arousing and intensifying emotions to confront and move through the avoidance that blocks full awareness, making eventual reconciliation of the fragmented parts possible.

The chair dialogue with parts (Figure 5.2) is similar to that of the empty-chair dialogue except that the imagined entity in the vacant chair is now a fragment (aspect, part, or polarity) of the client's inner experience rather than a significant other representing unfinished business. There are two primary variations of the chair dialogues with parts in working with loss adaptation. In the first variation, the client "converses" directly with the imagined, fragmented parts. For example, Patricia, a woman with conflicting feelings of anger, affection, and disappointment toward her dying mother, is encouraged to "talk" to each feeling (i.e., part) as she imagines each inhabiting a vacant chair. The counselor may then direct Patricia to switch chairs and respond back in the role of each of those feelings (e.g., disappointment speaks to Patricia). In the second variation, the

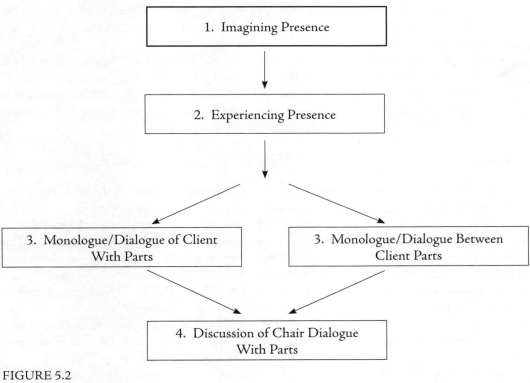

FIGURE 5.2
Chair Dialogue With Parts

client "becomes" a fragmented part speaking to another part, and then switches roles to continue the conversation. For example, Rodney, inhabiting the part of him that wants to stop drinking, talks to the part of him that fears he cannot handle his emotions without alcohol; he then switches chairs to respond from the opposite perspective.

The counseling professional then follows the same basic steps outlined above in the description of an empty-chair dialogue. The emphasis is on emotional processing: Arouse and intensify emotions to confront and move past avoidance so as to raise awareness of all the fragmented parts. The counseling professional, as facilitator, helps clients explore the fragmented parts so as to gain clarity and understanding. The overall goal is not the elimination of parts but acceptance and reconciliation of the parts or a revision and reorganization of identity.

Additional Considerations for Chair Dialogue With Parts

In addition to the considerations for implementing an empty-chair dialogue outlined above, several other considerations specific to a chair dialogue with parts include the following:

- The counseling professional and client should clearly identify the fragmented parts (splits, polarities, aspects) before beginning the procedure.
- Clients, not counselors, should name their fragmented parts.
- Clients who are reluctant to consider certain fragmented parts may be encouraged to participate in the dialogue "just to see what material comes up."
- Previously unidentified material, especially other fragmented parts, are often revealed in a chair dialogue. The counseling professional should note and include them in the unfolding process.
- Multiple parts can be differentiated by placing index cards with the part name on the vacant chair(s) and/or using objects (e.g., pillows) placed in a chair.
- Parts sometimes take the form of screen emotions, such as anger. The underlying emotions (e.g., hurt, rejection) that feed the screen emotion are usually revealed in a chair dialogue and should also be addressed as another fragmented part.

Focusing: Moving Deeper With Feelings to Awareness

Focusing, also called experiential focusing, is a particularly helpful intervention when clients are disconnected or distanced from their emotions. Developed by Eugene Gendlin (1981), the strategy of Focusing is designed to help people move through emotional blocks to a deeper experience of their emotions, facilitating emotional release and enhancing client awareness. This is, of course, especially useful with issues of loss and grief. Grieving persons may intellectualize or talk around emotionally laden issues; externalize feelings; feel overwhelmed, numb, or "blank"; or report some vague sense that something is dissonant or "not right" but be unable to identify or express whatever is bothering them. Gendlin called this last situation the *unclear felt sense*. The counselor uses Focusing to help clients attend to this unclear felt sense via internal awareness of bodily sensations, imagery, emotion, and cognition so as to reveal their *felt sense*, a clarification of their difficulty. This strategy is a highly experiential, here-and-now process.

Focusing is more effective with clients with a capacity for imagery and abstraction and is less effective with clients with a high need for concreteness. It is not recommended for clients with delusions or hallucinations. Focusing is useful in helping people enhance their ability to tolerate emotional discomfort, but counselors must carefully monitor their client's level of emotional arousal and feelings of safety through inquiry and observation (Greenberg et al., 1993). Once Focusing is introduced, counselors and clients can invoke this process whenever it seems helpful in the therapy. Additionally, once clients learn Focusing, it becomes a self-directed skill that clients can use independent of the therapy session.

The counselor's role in Focusing is facilitative rather than overly directive. Counselors demonstrate their respect of clients' expertness on themselves by allowing clients the space and effort to do their own work. It is important that counselors trust the process and the client's evolving experience. This means believing that useful material will emerge as long as the client (and the counselor) do not detour the process with interpretation, analysis (Greenberg et al., 1993), or intrusive reflections of feelings or content. Silence, especially allowing clients time and space to reflect inwardly before responding, is essential in this strategy.

Implementation of Focusing

In Focusing, the counselor provides a framework within which clients experience their own process and explore their own content. It is important to go slowly. Focusing is generally presented as a six-step process, adapted here from Gendlin (1981) and Greenberg et al. (1993).

Step 1. Clearing a Space

The counselor first encourages the client to assume a comfortable position, breathe quietly, and relax. Then the counselor invites the client to imagine a room or an inner space that could contain her or his problems, concerns, and feelings. Have the client describe the room so as to make it more real, vivid, and here-and-now. After obtaining this description, the counselor encourages the client to attend to her or his inner experience in the present moment (focus) and allow any concerns or feelings to come into awareness by asking, "What is going on with me right now? What is the main thing for me?" The counselor encourages the client to name each concern or feeling as it emerges and push each one aside into the room. It is important that the counselor not allow the client to analyze, judge, or censor the material at this point but rather to simply let the problems surface and be named one by one until no more problems emerge. Encourage the client to quietly attend to his or her sensations (physical, emotional, cognitive) and allow things to come forward. Reassure the client that he or she does not have to do anything with these feelings or concerns right now other than to let them present themselves and be placed in the inner space. When no more concerns emerge, the counselor invites the client to visualize a cleared area in the middle of this inner space or room filled with problems or feelings.

Counselor: Elena, I want you to imagine a room or some other inner space that can hold the problems and emotions that are troubling you right now. This is called *clearing a space*. I want you to visualize the room, but not the concerns, and, when you are ready, describe the room to me. [Client describes room or inner space.] OK, I can almost see that room myself. Now, listen inwardly to yourself—to your whole inner self. You are going to fill your room or inner space with all these things that are bothering you. To do this, ask yourself, "What is going on with me right now? What is the main thing for me? What feelings or concerns come forward to my awareness right now?" As each feeling or concern comes to your attention, just name it out loud and push it into the room. You don't need to do anything with these feelings or concerns right now, so just let them come forward, name them, and imagine placing them in the room.

Client: OK . . . anger . . . loneliness . . . confusion . . . distance from Kevin . . . my Dad's death.

Counselor: [Repeats each concern or feeling as it is expressed, directs the client to return her or his attention to that inner awareness to see what else might come up, then tells the client to "push it into the room." This continues until no more material is forthcoming.]

Counselor: Now consider that inner space or room filled with these concerns and feelings and visualize a cleared area in the middle of the room. All these concerns and feelings are pushed along the edges of the room and you can see that cleared area right in the middle of the room. Let me know when you can visualize that cleared middle space. [The metaphor of "the middle" is frequently used in Focusing. Clients may be asked to imagine a middle space or attend to how something makes them feel in the middle of their body.]

Step 2. Getting a Felt Sense

The counselor directs the client to select one problem as a focus. The client is encouraged to get a sense or feel of the problem by focusing on it without trying to elaborate or explore it. This is called "getting a felt sense." It is important to go slowly here, allowing time and space for the client to reflect inwardly. Clients may mention several things before settling on one. If the issue selected seems tentative, ask clients to recheck their inner experience.

Counselor: Elena, as you gaze around your inner space, I want you to pick one thing for us to focus on. Ask yourself these questions: Which of these is bothering me the most right now? Which one needs my attention right now? Stand back from these issues and feelings in the room, scan them, and allow something to move itself into your awareness. Take your time and try not to force it—just allow the thing that most needs your attention today to emerge into your awareness.

Client: Well, several things are coming up. I'm not sure which one I should choose.

Counselor: That's OK. Just focus inwardly. Sift through these things. Ask yourself, "What needs my attention right now?"

Client: Mmmm . . . probably the distance from Kevin [client sighs] . . . that's causing me the most problems.

Counselor: OK, the Distance from Kevin. Check again, does that feel like it is the thing most important to attend to right now? [Client nods.] OK. Locate the Distance from Kevin along the sides of your inner space and pull it out into the middle where you can see it clearly. OK? Now, Elena, I want you to feel that Distance from Kevin and everything that is involved in that. Don't think about it too much; just try to be aware of the feelings and sensations that go with the Distance from Kevin. Feel it in your body, in that inner space. Take your time and really touch it—get a sense of what that Distance from Kevin is all about. This is what we call your felt sense.

It is helpful to note that the felt sense is not just about emotion or emotional release. "It is a sense of your total emotional situation, a feel of many things together, in which an emotion can be embedded or from which an emotion is produced" (Gendlin, 1981, p. 101). Thus, the counselor helps clients consult their inner sense of being, directing their attention to awareness from emotion, imagery, body sensation, and cognition. The client moves from the unclear felt sense to a felt sense.

Step 3. Labeling

While remaining in touch with the felt sense of the selected problem, the client is encouraged to label it in a way that conveys its quality (e.g., heavy, stabbed in the heart, confused). Some useful questions include the following: What is the quality of that felt sense? What one word, phrase, or image comes out of this felt sense? What word, phrase, or image really conveys what this is about? The more descriptive the label, the better.

> *Counselor:* As you allow yourself to get a sense of Distance from Kevin and feel the emotions that go with that, what word, phrase, or image comes to you that captures what you are feeling? Just let it come . . . wait for it to reveal itself.
>
> *Client:* Mmmm . . . that's hard. It hurts . . . aches.
>
> *Counselor:* Tell me more about the ache—what it feels like.
>
> *Client:* It's my heart; it's just aching—like it's bruised. Yes, that's it. I can feel the bruising.
>
> *Counselor:* Tell me more about the bruising. What does it look like . . . feel like? [Counselor continues to help client explore the emotions while maintaining connection to the felt sense (Distance from Kevin) and the label (bruising, bruised).]

Step 4. Checking or Resonating

The client is directed to examine or check to see whether the felt sense of the problem and the label/descriptor actually are in agreement. If not, the client is directed to attend to the felt sense again until another, more accurate, label emerges. It is important to go slowly here, allowing clients to reflect and attend to their felt sense. The emphasis is on allowing material to emerge rather than forcing or directing something.

> *Counselor:* Elena, we've been looking at the aching, then the bruising that goes with the Distance from Kevin . . . I want you just to check something here to be sure we are on the right track. Allow yourself to go to the feeling—the sense you have—about all the stuff that goes with Distance from Kevin, then feel that bruising you described. Go back and forth between the two if that helps; take your time . . . Is bruising still the thing that comes to you? Let's just check to see if that still applies or if something else has begun to emerge here.

Step 5. Asking

At this point the counselor helps the client move more deeply into the emotional experience by focusing exploration on the label/descriptor: What is it about the whole problem that makes me feel so bruised? What makes the problem so bruising? What is at the core or heart of the bruising? What is most important about the bruising? Notice the movement from a problem description (Distance from Kevin), toward an initial emotion (aching), to a deeper feeling (bruising), then to a deeper awareness of underlying difficulty.

> *Counselor:* OK, stay with that feeling—the bruising—a bit longer. I wonder what is really at the heart of that feeling? There is something important about that bruising sense you have; I wonder what that is? Feel the bruising . . . hold on to it . . . what's the bruising tell you?
>
> *Client:* It's the same thing that happened with my dad, and with Juan, and with Sergio. I loved them all and they all left me. I'm so afraid Kevin is going to leave . . . I'm afraid to love him . . . [silence while client reflects on her statement]. I'm afraid if I love him, then he will leave me . . . so I try not to love him.

Gendlin (1981, p. 174) suggested the following if the client is having difficulty in the asking phase: What is the worst of this feeling? What's really so bad about this? What does it need? What should happen? Don't answer; wait for the feeling to stir and give you an answer. What would it feel like if it was all okay?

Step 6. Receiving

The client considers the felt sense about a problem on the basis of new information gained from the Focusing process. Elaboration and exploration (not interpretation) follows as the client continues to be in touch with the felt sense. Again, forcing or directing at this point (on the part of the counselor or the client) is counterproductive. Gendlin (1981) cautioned especially against blocking any critical voice that may intrude in this phase. The receiving phase ends with the counselor asking the client if she or he is ready to stop the process; then the counselor facilitates movement out of emotional intensity.

> *Counselor:* OK, let's just stay with that for a moment—that fear of being left and trying not to love him. The bruised feeling, too. Listen to that inner sense you have about those things. Take your time . . . what comes to you?
>
> *Client:* I'm afraid to love him . . . I'm afraid to lose him . . . But what if I can't get over this?
>
> *Counselor:* Hold on . . . stay with that inner sense—the fear of loving and losing Kevin. Don't do anything with it or try to censor it . . . just receive it—hold it there.
>
> *Counselor:* [After allowing client to quietly reflect and if no other useful material is forthcoming] OK, you might want to stop focusing right now? [Client agrees.] Just close the door on all of this . . . we can come back and pick it up another time if we need to. [Counselor allows time for client recovery.]

When clients are trying too hard or report feeling nothing, Gendlin (1981, p. 126) recommended asking: What is that feeling of "I need to try harder" or What is that nothingness feeling? The counselor assists recovery from emotional intensity by asking clients to take a few breaths and stretch themselves, helping them talk "about" the experience rather than continuing to be "in" the experience, and making eye contact if that is appropriate for this client.

Once introduced, Focusing can be invoked whenever more clarity, direction, or depth is needed. The counselor simply asks clients to focus inwardly (to get at the felt sense) and consider what needs their attention right now. Greenberg et al. (1993) noted the helpfulness of Focusing when the client or counselor has the experience of going in circles or not getting at real issues. Although Focusing is proposed here as a strategy for emotional processing, it often reveals meaningful cognitive material as well. Counselors unfamiliar with Focusing should practice this strategy themselves before attempting to use it in therapy.

Recommended Resources

Gendlin, E. T. (1981). *Focusing* (2nd ed.). New York: Bantam Books. (Still in print and remains the essential reference for Focusing.)

http://www.focusing.org, the Web site of the Focusing Institute, is an excellent resource, providing newsletters, handouts, examples of diverse applications and adaptations, and training information.

Mapping Loss and Grief: Focus on Feelings

Mapping Loss and Grief is a client-directed method for raising awareness of diverse and multiple elements in one's experience of loss and grief. The strategy is derived from a visual system for generating and organizing ideas called *mind mapping* (Buzan, 1991; Margulies, 2002). Clients compose a visual diagram of thoughts and feelings related to their loss and grief experience. Mapping stimulates the client's intuitive processes in which thoughts and feelings trigger other thoughts and feelings, revealing information and relationships previously obscured. It is presented here specifically to facilitate emotional processing but can be adapted to focus on cognitions. Mapping is a simple, client-directed procedure that is adaptable to the uniqueness of the client and multiple contexts of loss and grief.

Implementation of Mapping: Focus on Feelings

The counseling professional goes over the directions for mapping as a homework assignment, being especially certain that the client understands the difference between emotions and thoughts (see Box 5.1). Clients should be encouraged to take their time with this assignment and to focus on their emotions. Some clients may also find a Feelings List (see Table 5.1) beneficial. At the next session, the counselor invites clients to share their homework (maps), with special attention to the questions from Step 7 (see Box 5.1), and then facilitates further exploration and emotional processing. Alternatively, the counselor may expand the assignment to focus on specific secondary losses. Figure 5.3 provides an example of Mapping: Focus on Feelings.

Mapping for loss and grief can also be used with families and groups. Clients complete the homework individually, then share their maps with their family or group within the therapy session.

Recommended Resource

Margulies, N. (2002). *Mapping inner space: Learning and teaching visual mapping*. Tucson, AZ: Zephyr Press.

How My Dark Emotions Have Made Me Strong

In this strategy, clients are invited to write or tell a story that details how the distressing emotions of their grief have made them strong or transformed them. The focus here is not so much on provoking an emotional experience as considering one's emotions in light of loss. This strategy, called How My Dark Emotions Have Made Me Strong, underscores the value of emotions, promotes acceptance of one's emotional world, and facilitates integration of behavioral, cognitive, emotional, and spiritual dimensions of the client's personal journey through grief. Creating this narrative helps clients recognize the good that can come out of a bad situation (e.g., loss). This benefit finding, sense making, and identity change constitute important components of meaning reconstruction. The strategy offered here is adapted from one described by Greenspan (2003, p. 278) in her book, *Healing Through the Dark Emotions*.

171

BOX 5.1

Client Instructions for Mapping Loss and Grief—Focus on Feelings

Supplies: unlined legal size paper or poster paper, pencils or felt-tipped markers (various colors if you wish); optional: highlighting markers. *Context:* find a quiet place where you will not be interrupted for at least 30 minutes while you do this exercise. Take as much time as you need and feel free to take a break and come back to it after the initial 30 minutes if you wish.

1. Draw a circle in the middle of a page and write the title of your *primary loss* in capital letters in the middle of the page (e.g., amputation, job loss, divorce, abortion, health crises, death).
2. Consider all the thoughts and feelings that are included in your grief. Write them down, separately, somewhere on the page. Feel free to spread out and use the entire page for this exercise.
3. Draw a line connecting each thought and feeling to the primary loss circle. The lines can be crooked or straight—however it strikes you.
4. Now focus on the thoughts you have recorded and consider what feelings go with the thoughts (e.g., the thought "I can't go on" might bring feelings of despair or hopelessness). Write down the feelings that go with the thoughts somewhere close to the thought and then draw a line connecting that thought with those feelings.
5. Go back and underline or encircle each feeling. Think about the underlined feelings, listen inwardly to yourself, and write down any other feelings or thoughts that bubble up. Then draw a line connecting those thoughts and feelings to the underlined or encircled feeling. Keep doing this for each thought and feeling until nothing else comes to you.
6. Now look over your map. Add or move something if you wish. Add colors, attach extra pages, and draw pictures . . . just be open to whatever comes to you. Make connections between feelings and thoughts as they make sense to you.
7. Consider the following: What do you notice about the feelings that you have recorded? What do you think are the most important and least important feelings recorded? Did anything here surprise you? Are there feelings about feelings (e.g., ashamed of feeling angry)? Are there connections that you had not thought of before?
8. Now, share your Loss and Grief Map with your counselor at your next therapy session.

Implementation of How My Dark Emotions Have Made Me Strong

This strategy is most appropriately used when clients have gained some degree of perspective on their experience of loss that allows them to consider and reflect without becoming overwhelmed. It is not appropriate early in loss adaptation when people are more emotionally reactive. It is particularly useful when people seem stuck in their grieving journey or when they have difficulty recognizing that grief and its accompanying emotions can, indeed, transform them in positive ways. The following assignment is provided to the client as homework:

> Write the story of your dark emotions that highlights how your experience of grief has made you
> strong or transformed you. Begin by considering what dark emotions you have encountered in your

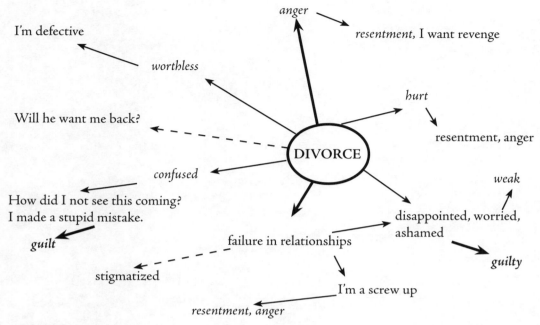

FIGURE 5.3

Mapping of Loss and Grief: Focus on Feelings

Note. Map of a 28-year-old woman grieving a divorce. While most of the feelings and thoughts expressed on her map were familiar, she was surprised that "guilt" popped up twice on her map.

grieving, for example, despair, sadness, guilt, fear, helplessness, or anger. What have those emotions helped you discover about yourself and about your life? What strengths have come from experiencing these dark emotions?

At the next therapy session, clients share what they have written, usually reading their stories aloud. Alternatively, the counselor invites clients to create the story entirely within the therapy session. Clients from cultural traditions that value storytelling are especially responsive to this alternative. This strategy can also be beneficial with groups and families. In those situations the counselor facilitates discussion among group or family members after each individual shares his or her story.

Chapter 6

Narrative Therapy Strategies for Loss Adaptation

Narrative therapy, a postmodern, social constructionist approach to counseling and community work, originated primarily in Australia and New Zealand in the late 1980s and 1990s with the work of Michael White and David Epston (Freedman & Combs, 1996; Monk, Winslade, Crocket, & Epston, 1997; White, 1989). It emphasizes the stories or narratives of people's lives and how telling and retelling these stories in a particular manner creates a different perspective on life experiences. Using particular language devices, narrative therapists help clients challenge the underlying beliefs and assumptions (meaning structures) of dominant narratives, amending these beliefs and assumptions to support an altered narrative leading to more preferred ways of being and living. Narrative therapy can be used with individuals, families, children, groups, and distinct communities (e.g., homeless persons, native peoples, hospice patients). The term *narrative practices* describes the application of narrative therapy in varied settings and with diverse populations.

Narrative therapy is especially helpful in addressing issues of loss and grief in counseling. Its emphasis on meaning making and sociocultural influences directly addresses important facets of loss adaptation. Telling and retelling the story of grief, a common experience in loss adaptation, dovetails nicely with the attention in narrative therapy to dominant and evolving stories. This therapeutic approach helps clients challenge deficiency descriptions of themselves (e.g., weak, broken, failed, unable) that are often a complicating factor in loss adaptation. Remembrances, a common and powerful experience in grief, are utilized as important resources for healing in this approach. Incorporating lost relationships into one's personal history, especially stressing their potential as resources to support more preferred life stories, is consistent with the notion of continuing bonds in loss adaptation. Finally, narrative therapy's appreciation of the idiosyncratic nature of each person's life experience, unknowable by another, is consistent with valuing the uniqueness of each client's experience of loss and grief.

This chapter does not attempt to provide an exhaustive explanation of narrative therapy but only to suggest ways in which narrative practices can be applied to issues of loss and grief. In doing so, I hope to (a) provide illustrative material concerning the application of narrative therapy to issues of loss and grief and (b) encourage professionals who are less familiar with narrative therapy to recognize the advantages of using this approach. Further study and training, especially a solid grounding in the theoretical constructs of narrative therapy, is strongly recommended. Suggested resources are provided at the end of this chapter.

Narrative Therapy Terminology

The following are some terms commonly used in narrative therapy.

Alternative story or narrative. A story that contradicts the dominant or pervasive story and leads to preferred ways of living. Narrative therapy focuses on developing alternative stories.

Deconstruction. The process of taking apart and examining the assumptions and beliefs that support client stories and "masquerade as reality" (Monk et al., 1997, p. 302).

Dominant story or narrative. A pervasive story based on assumptions and beliefs that are so widely accepted that the story appears to represent truth or reality (Monk et al., 1997). Narrative practices challenge the underlying assumptions of dominant stories via deconstruction.

Externalizing conversation. A way of speaking in which people and their difficulties are differentiated and problems spoken of as distinct entities (Winslade & Monk, 1999). Thus, a specific difficulty is referred to as the "Problem" or given a name (e.g., Intrusive Memories).

Mapping the influence. A process of exploring the relationship between clients and their problems. Mapping explores the influence of the Problem on the person as well as the influence of the person on the Problem.

Restorying or reauthoring. A process by which clients begin to notice and recount those events, actions, and behaviors that best suit them, as opposed to those that currently accompany the dominant story (Zimmerman & Dickerson, 1996, p. 93).

Story or narrative. Selected elements arranged in a sequence, "a unit of meaning that provides a frame for lived experience. . . . We enter into stories; we are entered into stories by others; and we live our lives through these stories" (Epston, White, & Murray, 1992, p. 96). The coherence and continuity of people's personal life stories or narratives are disrupted by loss and grief, thus disorganizing their evolving autobiographies (R. Neimeyer, 2001a). Loss adaptation involves reauthoring one's personal life stories to account for and integrate loss and grief into a coherent narrative.

Unique outcome. An aspect of one's experience that contradicts the problem-saturated story (Monk et al., 1997); an exception to normal expectations.

Basic Assumptions of Narrative Therapy

1. *"We live our lives according to the stories we tell ourselves and the stories that others tell about us"* (Winslade & Monk, 1999, p. 2). There is no single story; rather people's lives are multistoried, made up of dominant and less influential stories that are constantly evolving. Sometimes the dominant stories create problems. A person can develop her or his less influential stories into substantial, alternative stories that amend or contradict the dominant stories and bring more preferred ways of being and living in the world.

2. *Alternative stories are already happening, but they are inadequately developed and supported.* Discovering, exploring, and enhancing these stories is a major goal of narrative approaches.

3. *People tend to note things that confirm a dominant view or story and tend not to recognize those things that run counter to the dominant view.* Narrative therapy uses those experiences that do not fit the dominant story—that are unique or aberrant as opposed to expected—by enlarging or "thickening" them to form alternative or preferred stories.

4. *The Problem is the problem; the person is not the problem.* Separating the person from her or his difficulty (the Problem) opens up a space that allows for more objective viewing of difficulties, makes them more manageable, decreases self-blame, and enhances hope. Problems, not people, are the focus of change in narrative therapy.

5. *People are the experts on the stories of their lives, and their expertness is central to the therapy process.* Thus the counselor's stance in narrative practices is one of "respectful curiosity" (Winslade & Monk, 1999, p. 6), "deliberate ignorance" (Hoffman, 1992, cited in Monk et al., 1997, p. 302), or "not knowing" (Anderson & Goolishian, 1992, p. 29).

    The not-knowing position entails a general attitude or stance in which the counseling professional's actions communicate an abundant, genuine curiosity. That is, the therapist's actions and attitudes express a need to know more about what has been said, rather than convey preconceived notions and expectations about the client, the problem, or what must be changed. The therapist, therefore, positions himself or herself in such a way as to always be in a state of "being informed" by the client. (Anderson & Goolishian, 1992, p. 29)

6. *Cultural, social, and political factors influence the problems seen in counseling.* Narrative therapy helps people challenge the sociocultural depictions that limit their more preferred ways of being and living in the world (e.g., showing emotions is unmanly, women are too emotional).

7. *The problems people bring to therapy often reflect a view of themselves as deficient or defective.* For example, people may see themselves as codependent, incompetent, sick, not good enough, or mentally ill. Unfortunately, these "totalizing descriptions" are often supported by the larger culture, including traditional psychotherapy. Narrative therapy encourages clients to question and reject such one-dimensional and disempowering views.

8. *People have skills, abilities, knowledge, competencies, values, beliefs, and strengths that can help them manage their difficulties* now. Narrative practices help people recognize and use these resources to build up their alternative stories and bring about preferred ways of living.

9. *There are always times when problems do not occur or occur minimally.* These occurrences or contradictions to the usual story provide the basis for constructing alternative stories about people's lives that move them toward preferred ways of living.

10. *Counselors using narrative approaches attend carefully to the words clients use and how they use them.* "Narrative therapy pays particular attention to language because it can blur, alter, or distort experience as we tell our stories, it can condition how we think, feel, and act and can be used purposefully as a therapeutic tool" (White, 1995, cited in Besley, 2001, p. 82).

11. *Narrative approaches challenge clients to examine their beliefs, assumptions, and attitudes.* In this way they can discover if these adequately account for the contradictions and dissonance of events and experiences in their lives. This is especially helpful when counseling for loss and grief, because disruption of meaning—the shattering of one's taken-for-granted assumptions—is often a source of great distress. Meaning reconstruction is a primary task in adapting to loss.

Narrative Style Questioning and Externalizing Conversation

Narrative Style Questioning

Asking questions is the core strategy of narrative practices. The narrative questioning style is not so much about getting specific answers or gathering information; rather, it is more about exploring assumptions, encouraging reflection, and making meaning (Monk et al., 1997). Questions are designed to help people view their personal, family, or communal stories from a different perspective, to loosen the hold of dominant stories, and to consider different possibilities. Narrative authors often invoke the metaphor of an archeologist or anthropologist when describing the narrative style of questioning: sifting through the evidence, looking for things that might have been missed, listening for what was not said, and investigating the unusual so as to challenge conventional wisdom. It is important for traditionally trained counseling professionals to understand that narrative style questions are not designed to persuade or lead clients to "acceptable" conclusions or behaviors (e.g., to think rationally, to behave functionally, to live congruently). Such leading is disrespectful (and not a little arrogant) because it is about the expertness of the therapist rather than the expertness of the client. There are no trick questions in the narrative therapy approach: The counselor asks clients about things they already know (M. Payne, 2006). Consider the following examples of narrative style questioning:

- How have you managed to keep Depression from getting worse?
- In what ways does obsessive ruminating affect your daily work? your relationships?
- How do you think you have responded to society's message that older people should not be sexual?
- If your partner was here, what would he tell me he knows about you that makes him willing to hang in, even when you push him away or mistreat him?
- How does that feeling that other people view you as "just another poor, incompetent Black person" affect your idea of yourself as a survivor or a victim?
- In what ways does homophobia affect your life and your goals?

In narrative practices, questions are followed by more questions, then by more questions, as the counselor and client work together to broaden and deepen examination, exploration, and reflection. Questioning should move from the general to the specific, for example:

Counselor: How has Paralyzed by Grief kept you from doing something?
Client: My daughter asked me to go with her to a cooking class the other day and I begged off.
Counselor: What made you beg off?
Client: I just couldn't make myself go into something that was so unfamiliar—going downtown, a room full of strangers. We had talked about doing this before Rolando died but now I just cannot do it. I know she was upset with me and I hated to disappoint her.
Counselor: So, Paralyzed by Grief is keeping you from doing things you want to do and even interfering in your relationship with your daughter. Tell me more about how it is able to make you do that?

Counselors must be careful not to allow the questioning process to become an interrogation. Questions arise naturally from dialogue and remain in the context of exploration, not conclusions. In fact, Monk (1997) warned clients that if they feel that he, as the counelor, is asking too many questions, they can tell him they are "questioned out." Narrative style questioning is always done in a respectful manner, reflecting the current flow of conversation and characterized by a genuine interest in people and curiosity about the varied stories of their lives.

Externalizing Conversation

Externalizing is a particular way of speaking that separates the person from her or his problems. In contrast to internalizing conversation, in which clients present their problems as if there is something wrong with them, externalizing conversation frames problems as if they are a distinct entity or even a personality that causes difficulties for the client (Winslade & Monk, 1999). Internalizing conversation typically conveys a sense of "I am," whereas externalizing conversation conveys an "It is" perspective (Morgan, 2000). For example:

> Internalizing language: I am a worrier, especially when confronted with new things.
> Externalizing language: Worry stops you from trying new things.
> Internalizing language: I'm bipolar you know.
> Externalizing language: So a bipolar situation influences your life in significant ways.

In narrative therapy, counselors must be intentional and consistent in using externalizing conversation, which takes practice. Morgan (2000) suggested thinking of a difficulty (the Problem) as a thing sitting in the corner of the room. The Problem can also be personified (e.g., Angry Mother, Dutiful Daughter). Counselors also listen for and adopt client-generated externalizations when possible. For example, when the client speaks of "what alcoholism does to me," he or she is externalizing the Problem (as opposed to the internalized "I am an alcoholic"). Some languages even lend themselves to externalized speech. Sued and Amunategui (2003) pointed out that various Mexican expressions use externalizations for troubles or difficulties and that many expressions in Spanish are natural externalizations (e.g., "the washing machine is refusing to wash").

Some counselors may be concerned that externalizing conversations do not hold people accountable and responsible for their actions. In fact, the opposite is true. Externalizing frees people from the self-blame that disempowers and, therefore, impedes accepting responsibility. Externalizing does not change difficulties; it shifts the perspective so that one can see other possibilities for responding to those difficulties. M. Payne (2006) clarified that abusive or selfish actions are not externalized (e.g., you were abused; you deliberately hurt him). Rather, the assumptions and beliefs behind them are externalized (e.g., you were dominated by a belief that hitting was an acceptable way to handle things). Externalization is simply a rhetorical device that facilitates the process of exploration and shifting of perspective. It is a means to an end. There is something infinitely more hopeful about a problem that exists outside of a person than a problem being a deficient person.

Implementation of Narrative Practices

The narrative therapy field is diverse, with variations of emphasis or structure while sharing common assumptions. The procedures suggested here illustrate a narrative approach and should be viewed as guidelines rather than prescriptions. In fact, the collaborative nature of narrative therapy and the emphasis on dialogue require that the therapeutic structure be adaptable to the needs of clients and the evolving process of therapy. Experienced narrative therapy practitioners often move across and in and out of phases and steps, constantly amending and adjusting to explore the varied dimensions of client narratives. The basic format involves identifying and taking apart (deconstruction) dominant, problem-saturated narratives, then reauthoring (reconstruction) alternative, preferred narratives. These steps are just that, steps. They are not intended as a recipe nor tied to number of sessions. Instead, they are sensitive to the client and his or her evolving stories.

Deconstruction phase
    Step 1.   Listening to the problem-saturated story
    Step 2.   Naming the Problem
    Step 3.   Mapping the influence of the Problem on the person
    Step 4.   Mapping the influence of the person on the Problem
    Step 5.   Deconstructing unique outcomes
Reconstruction phase
    Step 6.   Building and extending an alternative story/preferred narrative

Step 1. Listening to the Problem-Saturated Story

Clients are invited to share the concerns that have brought them to therapy. Typically they relate problem-saturated descriptions that reveal assumptions about their difficulties and about themselves, including who is to blame (e.g., my son is rebellious; I'm not strong enough to handle this loss). The counselor's role here is that of "double-listening" (White, 2004): listening to the unfolding stories while at the same time listening to the client's beliefs, values, hopes, and dreams. It is helpful to allow clients to describe their difficulties without interruption because that may obscure certain nuances in the stories and in the telling. The counselor should take in the difficulties without comment, remembering that what is being presented is one viewpoint, one take on reality, one truth, and one story among multiple stories (M. Payne, 2006).

When the initial presentation winds down and there is that inevitable pause, the counselor begins asking questions to flesh out details and reveal more about how the problems came about, their history, and their effect on the client's life. The counselor uses externalizing language that begins to separate problems from the person by using words such as "it," the "problem," or the "difficulty," for example: When did you first notice this difficulty? How long has it been going on? What were things like before this problem entered your life? Tell me more about how grief has invaded your life.

Step 2. Naming the Problem

Once the problem-saturated stories have been explored with sufficient detail, the counselor invites clients to name their problem. At this point "problem" become the "Problem." Naming the Problem further separates it from the person so that it can be examined more objectively, subtly suggests taking control of the Problem, and reduces blaming (especially helpful with couples). Names are given to attitudes, strategies, perspectives, feelings, thoughts, and behaviors. Naming also helps the client to pinpoint exactly what the major issues are. Families and couples must agree on the Problem's name, which should not lay blame but instead reveal how this is a problem for everyone (e.g., Worries, Anger Management, and Perpetual Conflict). There are different ways the counselor can solicit naming of the Problem.

+ Sometimes it is helpful for people to give their concerns a name so that we can talk about them as if they were something separate—like a monkey on your back. What name do you think really gets at the heart of these problems?
+ If you were to give these problems a name, what do you think it would be?
+ Do you have a particular name for what you're going through at the moment? If you could imagine boxing up all of these concerns and labeling them for storage, what name would you write on the label?
+ I wonder if you two could come up with a name for this problem that you've been describing? Something that you both can agree on and that describes how this is a problem for both of you.
+ What is your main feeling when this problem is around? . . . Anger and frustration? OK, I wonder if that's what we ought to call it or can you think of a better name?

Naming problems is not necessarily an easy task and is, after all, an unexpected direction for most clients. The counselor may need to ask again. Go slowly here. If clients have difficulty naming their problem, the counselor's first response is simply to wait for them to do so. Some people are in the habit of letting others take charge (be experts), so it is important that the counselor not jump in too quickly to do this for them. If clients still cannot come up with a name, then counselors may tentatively review some of the storied experiences presented initially: "As I listened to you, I heard you talking about the fear, the worry, and the loneliness that has intruded on your life since Hurricane Katrina. I wonder if any of those experiences suggest a name for all this?" Alternatively, just continue to refer to the difficulty as "the Problem" or "It." A name may be forthcoming, just as it is acceptable to change the name later if something better seems to fit. Here are some examples of problem names:

+ difficulties with grieving—Victim of Loss, Stuck in Grief, Intrusive Memories
+ difficulties with anger—The Demon, The Anger Queen
+ couple/family conflict—Fighting, Bickering, Pushing and Shoving
+ difficulties with discouragement—Hopeless in Seattle
+ problematic relationship style—the Rescuer, the Doormat
+ difficulties with guilt—The Preacher, Convicted
+ difficulties with gender expectations—Be a Man, Only a Woman
+ difficulties with cultural expectations—The Outcast

Problems associated with loss and grieving may or may not include those labels, depending on the nature of the difficulties. Help clients ascertain whether grieving is actually the problem or if it is something else (e.g., excessive rumination, anxiety). Remember also that grief is not an abnormal state or something to be eliminated; it is a natural response to loss and is appropriately assimilated, not extinguished. Therefore, when naming does involve grief, it is helpful to attach a descriptive term that clarifies the way in which grief is problematic (e.g., Paralyzing Grief) or is complicated by a problematic attitude or belief (e.g., Victim of Loss).

Step 3. Mapping the Influence of the Problem on the Person

Naming problems reveals the dominant story operating in the client's life. Next, the counselor, using questions and externalizing conversation, facilitates more detailed investigation of the dominant story in a way that further separates the person from the Problem. Exploring or "mapping" the influence of the Problem on the person helps clients recognize what their difficulties have cost them and the ways in which they have been manipulated by their views of the Problem. A most helpful tool for externalizing at this point is to personify the Problem—speaking of it as if it were a living entity. The counselor helps clients explore the many ways in which the Problem impinges on their lives: the Problem's tricks, tactics, ways of operating, ways of speaking (i.e., voice, tone, content), intentions, beliefs, plans, likes and dislikes, rules, purposes, lies, desires, motives, allies (who stands with it or beside it; who supports it), techniques, and dreams (Morgan, 2000). The items below provide examples of entry-level externalizing questions useful in mapping the influence of the Problem on the person or family. These questions are examples only; they should not be viewed as predetermined or as presenting a fixed order. Remember that questions facilitate exploration, which facilitates more questions, more exploration, and more questions ad infinitum. Follow the dialogue. Get details about what the client thinks, feels, and does. Use "tell me more" and "help me understand" to extend and clarify exploration. Go slowly. Remain conversational. *Keep externalizing.* Be genuinely interested in your clients, in being informed by them, and in understanding everything about how the Problem affects their lives.

- What does Angry Husband make you do?
- How do Intrusive Memories affect you? your life? your relationships? your work? your family?
- What does Always a Victim do to your sense of self?
- What does Resentful demand of you when it seems to be in charge of things?
- How does the Anger Queen just take over sometimes?
- When Fear makes an appearance, how does it affect how you get along with others and how others treat you?
- How does Worry convince you that it is no use resisting it?
- Whenever you try to resist, to not listen to the demands of Paralyzing Grief, what does it do to make you give in and give up?
- The Preacher sounds pretty devious, almost like it sneaks up behind you and whispers in your ear. . . what does it whisper in your ear when it is sneaking up on you like that? What tone does it use?
- So, how has Surviving Sibling convinced you that you should alienate yourself from those who care about you?
- How does Manly Man affect your grieving?

During exploration of the Problem's influence on the person, it is often helpful to play up the personification angle by using a voice, tone, and attitude that portrays the Problem as devious or tricky. This further supports the goal of separating the person from the Problem. A helpful homework assignment at this stage is to ask clients to look for evidence of those times when the Problem influences them and report that at the next therapy session.

Step 4. Mapping the Influence of the Person on the Problem

Once problems have been thoroughly examined in terms of their effects on the client, it is time for a slight alteration in course to introduce an important new direction. Instead of looking at how problems have affected the client, the focus now shifts to how the client has affected his or her problems. This new direction is aimed directly at loosening the grip of the dominant story (the Problem) by poking holes in it. Mapping the influence of the person on the Problem seeks out "unique outcomes"—times when the Problem does not occur or occurs minimally. For example, a woman whose dominant story is that she never stands up to her husband in fact does at times stand up to him; a man who says he is grieving intensely all the time actually does experience moments when his grief is less intrusive. Mapping the influence of the person on the Problem enables clients to notice that which they tend to ignore in the shadow of the dominant story: At times they do prevail, they are not overwhelmed, they get along, they cope, and they have some control. Unique outcomes include actions, thoughts, feelings, relationships, experiences, or events that contradict or deny the dominant story. It is always assumed that unique outcomes exist. They may go largely unnoticed and they are often dismissed as coincidence or chance. More recent unique outcomes are generally more helpful than those from a most distant time, but these tend to be harder to get at (McKenzie & Monk, 1997). Nevertheless, there are "sparkling moments" (White, 1992, cited in Monk, 1997) when the problems do not occur.

When mapping the influence of the person on the Problem, the counselor continues to use externalizing conversation to separate the person from his or her difficulties, especially personifying them. Metaphorical language that casts the client as the one who resists and struggles against the Problem is commonly used. However, White (cited in M. Payne, 2006, p. 75) cautioned against overdoing the notion of "fighting back" because that may further oppress people in difficult circumstances and tends to overemphasize Western values of individualism that might be unhelpful. Remember that grief should not be viewed as something to resist or fight against as much as something to experience, manage, and integrate. Overdoing personification of grief is counterproductive. Grieving clients may be hard pressed to relate a time when they were not grieving. In that case the counselor helps the client focus on times when the grieving was less painful, more manageable, or somehow less problematic.

The items listed below provide entry-level examples of externalizing questions useful in mapping the influence of the person on the Problem. As stated previously, these questions are examples only. The counselor continues to operate from the stance of not knowing and respectful curiosity in order to collaborate with the client in exploration and reflection. Move from the general to the specific by posing a question and then getting the details, for example, "Tell me more," "Help me understand," and "How did you do that?" When clients explain the occurrence of a unique outcome as accidental or chance, continue to investigate by asking what the client might have thought about or done differently in those circumstances (Winslade & Monk, 1999). The goal here is to uncover evidence of unique outcomes. Obtain as many unique outcomes as possible; the more unique outcomes there are, the less likely the client will dismiss them as accidental. The counselor's role is comparable to that of a miner panning for gold: patiently kneeling by the creekside to shake the pan, looking for shiny flecks amid the gravel, picking those flecks out of the pan, then holding them up to the light so as to examine them closely, setting some aside, then returning to the pan to search for more shiny flecks that might be gold.

- ✦ Do you recall a time when you could have given in to the Anger Queen but you did not? Tell me how you did that.
- ✦ I noticed that you said there were a few times when Worry did not get in the way—things were different. Tell me about those times.
- ✦ Tell me about those times when Intrusive Memories have been less of a problem for you. When was that and how were you able to do that?
- ✦ What is different about those times when Paralyzing Grief is not so much of a problem for you? How are you different?
- ✦ Tell me about a time when you have been stronger than Worry.
- ✦ You've indicated that sometimes you have been able to push Angry Man away—to resist it. Tell me how you are able to do that.
- ✦ You mentioned that sometimes things are okay. What happens when the Preacher takes a vacation so that things are okay?
- ✦ What happens when you are able to defeat Depression, even for a little while? How does that happen?
- ✦ I'm curious about those times when Coyote's tricks backfire and he is unsuccessful in getting you to cut yourself off from people.
- ✦ How have you managed to keep Resentment from getting worse?

Sometimes there is little evidence of unique outcomes. Alternatively, ask about times when the client *tried* to act or even just *intended* to act. For example, "I can see that Intrusive Memories have been pretty darn strong in your life for awhile. I'd be discouraged, too. I wonder if you could tell me about a time when you *tried* to push Intrusive Memories away, even though you were unable to do so?" The counselor then follows up on the intention and attempt. A helpful homework assignment at this stage is to ask the client to look for evidence of those times when the client has been able to influence the Problem and report that at the next therapy session.

Step 5. Deconstructing Unique Outcomes

Once a number of unique outcomes have been identified, the therapy zooms in to explore them in more depth by taking them apart—deconstructing them. Deconstructing unique outcomes has a number of functions. It uncovers clues to a potential alternative story that is already happening to some extent. It highlights client competence in the form of strengths, abilities, skills, and talents. It robs the dominant, problem-saturated story of its power and makes meaning or gives significance to those experiences that are exceptions to the dominant story. Deconstructing can be thought of as "adding meat to the bones" of unique outcomes uncovered earlier when mapping the influence of the person on the Problem.

The process of deconstructing unique outcomes continues to use questions and externalizing conversation. The idea is to gather information so as to create a vivid picture of everything involved in each unique outcome. What happened before, during, and after? Who was involved? How did this unique outcome come about? What meaning or significance does the client attach to different elements of the unique outcome? What does the unique outcome reveal about the client? It is especially important to highlight any evidence of competence. Narrative therapists typically liken this effort to analyzing the elements of a story: plots and subplots; characters and themes; sequencing of events (history); thoughts, feelings, and actions; story structure; and meanings (values, beliefs, assumptions, attitudes). Typically, exploration of each unique outcome begins with the basic details using landscape-of-action questions. These are followed by a mixture of other question types as appropriate to the evolving story. Remember to move from general to specific as you facilitate reflection and exploration for more depth and breadth. The items given below are examples of entry-level questions used to deconstruct unique outcomes.

Landscape-of-Action Questions

Landscape-of-action questions establish the basic details (e.g., who, what, where, when, and how) of unique outcomes and, most important, anchor them in the client's history or personal narrative.

+ Where were you when this happened?
+ Were you on your own or with someone else?
+ When did it happen?
+ How long did it last?
+ What happened just before and after?
+ How did you prepare yourself? How did you get yourself ready to take those steps?
+ Have you done this before or was this the first time you were able to pull this off?
+ How did you arrive at the decision to resist Guilt? Did you make that decision on your own or did you consult with someone?
+ What have you experienced so far in your life that tells you that it is possible to get through this difficult time of grieving?
+ What have you witnessed in your life up to now that gives you some hint that something else or some other way of being is possible for you?

Landscape-of-Identity Questions

Landscape-of-identity questions ask clients to reflect on the meanings of their unique outcomes in terms of their desires, intentions, beliefs, preferences, hopes, values, strengths, commitments, abilities, and purposes (Morgan, 2000, p. 61).

+ You have told me how disillusioned you became with the military and the direction of things in Afghanistan. Despite that, you kept your focus, did your job, honored your fellow soldiers. I wonder what that says about the core values and beliefs you hold?
+ What do you think doing this says about your (strengths, skills, abilities)?
+ You said you regret staying away from your daughter after the divorce but that you hoped to spare her being caught in the middle of such a mess. What does that say about you that you were willing to do that despite the emotional pain it cost you?
+ It seems to me that all these times when you have managed to resist the Victim stance reveal something important about who you are and what you value. What do you think that is?
+ What does this history of struggle with Depression tell you about what Trini believes is important and what she stands for in her life?
+ The things that have happened to you and your family in your journey to this place have been so difficult and have clearly taken their toll, but you've shown me that there have been times when you have been able to, in your words, "rise above" the pain. I wonder what that says about you and your family—about the values, hopes, and dreams that you hold?

- Considering the abuse you both suffered as children, what does that say about you that you are both so committed to ensuring a different experience for your own children?
- If LaToya was in the room with us right now and I could ask her what it is about you that makes her stay, what do you think she would say?
- Tell me how, despite the powerful influence of Drugs in your life, you made a decision to come for therapy and you managed to get yourself here today? What did that take?

Experience-of-Experience Questions

Experience-of-experience questions encourage people to see themselves through the eyes of others. The counselor invites elaboration and expansion on their answers.

- Of all those people who have known you, who would be least surprised that you have been able to really challenge Anger's influence on your life?
- If I had observed you when you were younger, what do you think I would have seen you doing that might help me understand how you have been able to overcome so many losses more recently?
- If your husband was here today, what would he tell me about how you have faced up to challenges like this in the past?
- Who would be least surprised to see you take this step, and what would that person say that this indicates about you?

Questioning Practices of Power

Questioning practices of power encourages people to examine and challenge the opinions and expectations of others (e.g., friends, family, community, society, counselors).

- You lost your job when your company moved its operations overseas. I wonder how society has influenced your feeling guilty about not having a job?
- Where do you think your friends and family got the idea that you should "move on" with your life?
- "You say you've been grieving since your son told you he is homosexual. I'd find it really interesting if we could talk about the use of that word 'grieving' in this situation; would that be ok?" (M. Payne, 2006, p. 86).
- "Your letter from the hospital has lots of abbreviations and initials, which you don't understand. I don't understand them either! Does the letter reveal anything about the attitudes of the person who wrote it and the persons who authorized it? Could its style have any connection with your feeling dismissed and intimidated?" (M. Payne, 2006, p. 87).
- Where does that idea come from that to deal well with grief, one must cut oneself off from the one who died?
- How do you think religion contributes to those ideas about what women [men] should do and how they should be in these situations?

Effectively deconstructing unique outcomes reveals hitherto hidden or overlooked evidence, yields new information, and suggests a different perspective on problems that contradicts the conclusions of the old dominant story. What emerges are the thoughts, feelings, and behaviors of other stories that are already occurring but have been obscured from view. Before, there was just the overarching shadow of the dominant story; now other, more preferable stories reveal themselves.

Step 6. Building and Extending an Alternative Story or Preferred Narrative

Now it is time to put together all the bits and pieces of the preferred stories uncovered during the deconstruction of unique outcomes and arrange them into a coherent narrative called the *alternative story*. This alternative story is a contradiction to the problem-saturated, dominant story. Remember that the alternative story is already happening to an extent but needs more clarification and depth to be effective and fully operational. This step begins with an invitation to the client to name the emerging, alternative story. Naming increases the distinction from the dominant story, emphasizes authorship and agency, and provides a literary device and framework for reference (i.e., the old story vs. the new story). The following are some suggested ways of asking for a name for the alternative story:

+ You talk about "finding a new direction;" would that be a good name for us to use for what you want more of in your life?
+ Is "holding on to hope" a fair way of describing this other way of doing things, that is, resisting depression's grip on your life? (Morgan, 2000, p. 70).
+ We've been talking a bit about how you have been "facing up to things" since Hurricane Katrina. I wonder if this would be a good name for us to use as we continue to talk about the changes you have begun to make? Maybe there is another name that you think would describe this better.
+ You called that old story "Hopeless in Seattle" and we've been seeing a new story evolve for you. What would you call that new story?

As with the earlier naming of the dominant story, it is important that the client, not the counselor, name the alternative story. There may be some negotiation of the name in the context of the collaborative relationship, but in the end the client symbolically takes control of the emerging story by naming it. If there is difficulty with naming, the counselor might tentatively suggest something by highlighting important components uncovered during the deconstruction of unique outcomes, or the alternative story may be referred to as "It" or "the New Story" or "the Better Story."

Once the alternative story has a name, the counselor helps the client explore it so as to create a richly detailed and realistic picture of a preferred way of being. This is called *thickening the story*. The medium of externalizing conversation continues, primarily with use of landscape-of-action, landscape-of-identity, and experience-of-experience questions. Once again, gathering details is essential. Keep the emphasis on how and what will be different when the alternative story is being lived; how clients will recognize this difference; and what the client will be doing, thinking, and feeling when this occurs. The following examples suggest entry-level questions for building an alternative narrative. Remember to facilitate exploration and reflection to get more details.

+ What will be different in your life if Walking in Harmony was in charge—was running things?
+ What happens when One Step in Front of the Other defeats Paralyzed by Grief and does not let it mess things up?
+ In what ways can you make Standing Up for Myself happen?
+ When Supportive Partner is operating, what will other people notice about you?
+ How can you remind yourself that Survivor is in charge of your life now?

- If there is a slip and it looks for a moment like Worry is going to take hold again, what can Confident do to get back on track? . . . What else?
- What will life look like in 5 years when Connected is firmly operating in your life?
- When you are living out the story of Survivor, how will you handle the tough moments when Victim tempts you back into old ways?
- How will living the story of Standing Up for Myself help you when you deal with the people in the hospital?

In fleshing out the details of the alternative story, it is important for counselors not to get ahead of clients by focusing on what they need to do in the future. Instead it is better to "stay behind" clients, exploring what has happened or is happening now (Monk, 1997). Also, when the client gets stuck on the old problem-saturated dominant story, it is useful to refocus by asking, "Is this the old story or the new story?"

As the alternative story gains detail and substance, it becomes increasingly clear that therapy has reached a turning point: The client can continue to embody the problem-saturated, dominant story or begin intentionally living out the alternative story on the basis of new information and new perspectives (M. Payne, 2006). At this point, the counselor "raises the dilemma" (White's original term, cited in M. Payne, 2006, p. 75) and facilitates exploration, especially of the meanings attached to this turning point: "Where do you want to go from here?" There may be legitimate reasons for not embracing an alternative story at this point, and only the client can make that determination. The following questions might be used as a homework assignment, then discussed thoroughly within the therapy session:

- "Is this the right time for me to take new directions, or do I need more time to consider the possibilities?" (M. Payne, 2006, pp. 14–15)
- "Is the Problem still too much in charge of my life right now for me to challenge it safely? If so, when might its power be reduced? How might I recognize that development?" (M. Payne, 2006, pp. 14–15)
- Is it advisable for me to continue down this road of change right now?
- What would it mean for me to make more changes? What would it mean if I keep going in the old way instead of following this new direction we have been talking about?
- What are the advantages and disadvantages of moving in a different direction right now?

It is important that the counselor not pressure, lead, or manipulate clients with regard to taking a position. Most clients will move forward with their alternative story at this point. Making that decision on their own, besides being respectful, reinforces their commitment (M. Payne, 2006). If, however, clients are not ready to move forward, their reasons and situations can be explored further.

Therapy continues to facilitate telling and retelling of the client's alternative story, extending its application to current life experiences. The goal is to help the client create a richer, deeper inhabiting of the alternative story. In the case of grief, the goal is not the elimination of grief but the assimilation of loss and grief into the alternative story. Therapy ends when this alternative story—now the client's self-story—sustains her or his preferred way of being in the world (M. Payne, 2006).

Strategies for Supporting the Alternative Story

Narrative therapists recognize that attempting to live out the preferred, alternative story is a challenging task. One way of doing this is to enlist the support of significant others as witnesses, cheerleaders, and resources. "A good story needs an audience before it can be appreciated as a good story. A counselor may be the first audience. But there is a need for the deliberate searching out of a wider audience" (Winslade & Smith, 1997, pp. 188–189). A narrative approach helps clients create an audience for their alternative narratives using the following strategies: imaginary audience, re-membering conversations, outsider witnesses, and narrative letters.

Imaginary audience. Clients are asked to imagine the responses, opinions, ideas, and even advice of someone from their lives regarding their emerging alternative story. This might include the client himself or herself. A common form is to ask clients who would be surprised or not surprised at their efforts. The following are some examples of questions designed to invoke the contributions of an imaginary audience:

- Who from your past do you think would be most surprised at your determination to make Hopeful in Seattle happen?
- Who would be least surprised to learn of the changes you are making?
- What do you think Sergeant Giles would say about your commitment to this new direction for your life?
- Who else knows about your determination to be a good parent, and what would they think about the efforts you have been making to parent effectively despite your illness?

Follow up these invitations by getting at details that make the contribution of this imaginary audience more real, vivid, and substantial, for example: What expression would Sergeant Giles have on his face? What would be his tone of voice? What exactly would he say, and how would he say it? What would make you believe what he says? What else would the Sergeant say? What would his words mean to you?

Re-membering conversations. Re-membering is a process by which clients metaphorically consult with significant people in their lives to support living the preferred, alternative story. The figures comprising one's "club of life" (White, 1997) may be living or dead, related or unrelated, and from the past or present. Membership is elected; clients may include or exclude people from their lives into their club of life. Counselors help clients engage in re-membering conversations in which they imagine the reactions and responses of club-of-life members. Re-membering conversations have several advantages: They decentralize the position of the counseling professional, link the client's alternative story to their past, access "forgotten knowledge," and provide access to alternative viewpoints and resources (M. Payne, 2006). Re-membering is an especially healthy and useful means of facilitating a continuing bond with people the client has lost. Below are two excellent examples of re-membering conversations that center on establishing continuing bonds with the deceased.

White (1989) related working with John, a 39-year-old man whose longstanding self-esteem difficulties were evident in his need for the approval of others and a highly critical attitude toward himself. An important issue in John's history was his mother's death when he was 7 years old. No one around John handled the loss well, and even his father was unavailable at the time. His mother's death marked an important transition, after which "things were never really the same again." White helped John reclaim this lost relationship with his mother in a way that informed construction of a more self-accepting alternative narrative. White's powerful questions included the following:

> What did your mother see when she looked at you through her loving eyes? How did she know these things about you? What is it about you that told her about this? What can you now see in yourself that had been lost for many years? What difference would it make to your relationship with others if you carried this knowledge [his mother's image of him] with you in your daily life? How would this make it easier for you to be your own person, rather than a person always accommodating to others? What could you do to introduce others to this new picture of yourself as a person? How would bringing others into this new picture of your person enable you to nurture yourself more? In what way would such an experience of nurturing yourself affect your relationship with yourself? (White, 1989, p. 31).

White also worked with Mary, a 43-year-old woman whose husband had died suddenly 6 years ago. Mary presented herself as "going through the motions of life." Clearly believing the view of experts that she should work to sever her relationship with the deceased, Mary wondered if she would ever be able to say goodbye. White speculated aloud about the value of saying goodbye and suggested instead that it might be better to "say hello." After getting Mary's consent to experiment with "saying hello," White (1989) posed the following questions:

> If you were seeing yourself through Ron's eyes right now, what would you be noticing about yourself that you could appreciate? What difference would it make to how you feel if you were appreciating this in yourself right now? What awakening would occur to bring alive the enjoyable things that Ron knew about you? What difference would it make to you if you kept this realization about yourself, alive on a day-to-day basis? How could you let others know that you have reclaimed some of the discoveries about yourself that were clearly visible to Ron, and that you personally find attractive? How would this new awareness after six years enable you to intervene in your own life? What difference would knowing what you now know about yourself make to your next step? In taking this next step, what else do you think you might find out about yourself that could be important to know? (p. 30)

The club-of-life metaphor emphasizes the client's prerogative in excluding and including people. It is also important to encourage clients to select other names more reflective of their background and views, for example, witnesses, sacred circle, wise ones, or consultants.

Outsider witnesses. Significant or especially helpful people may be invited by the client to participate in the client's therapy as *outsider witnesses* to the emerging alternative story. In addition to providing support and feedback, outsider witnesses can often identify situations that might have been overlooked or undervalued. Usually only one or two outsider witnesses are involved in a given therapy meeting. Outsider witnesses are drawn from friends, family, a particular group or community, or other counseling professionals (referred to as a reflecting team), for example:

- A grieving Native American person might select other members of his or her tribe to serve as outsider witnesses.

- A grieving lesbian individual or partners might select other lesbians as outsider witnesses.
- A man grieving the child he gave up for adoption might select other individuals who did the same and might also include adults who were given up for adoption by their fathers as outsider witnesses.
- A woman grieving an abortion might select other women who have had abortions as outsider witnesses.
- An adolescent whose sister died might ask other adolescents in the community who have experienced the death of a sibling to be outsider witnesses.
- A soldier who experienced disabling wounds might select other recovering soldiers or even family members of other recovering soldiers to serve as outsider witnesses.

Outsider witnesses attend the therapy meeting and observe the therapy (via one-way mirror, closed-circuit television, or in fishbowl fashion) without commenting. First, they observe the counselor and client discussing the emerging alternative story—what it involves, the hopes and dreams associated with it, and particular challenges to living the alternative story. Then the outsider witnesses join the counselor and client to discuss their observations. It is critical that outsider witnesses understand their role: They are to observe the discussion of the alternative story and share their observations *relative to the client and the alternative story* from their unique position. Everything they say must be for the benefit of the client. They are not to give advice or opinions, make judgments, or give praise and empathetic responses. There is no hypothesizing, interpreting, or analyzing—they are *not* doing therapy (M. Payne, 2006; White, 1997). It is the responsibility of the counselor to make this role clear and to keep the process focused appropriately. The following are some examples of questions the counselor might use with outsider witnesses: What did you hear that caught your attention? What did you hear that revealed something of the client's values? What are you curious about? What particular expressions struck you as interesting? What in the client's alternative story or new direction resonates with your own life? (White, 2006, pp. 34–36).

A more extensive use of outsider witnesses involves a four-stage *definitional ceremony* (Morgan, 2000; White, 1995, 1997). Here, outsider witnesses first observe the therapy session (as above), then switch places with the client and discuss their observations with the counselor while the client observes. Next, the outsider witnesses and client swap places again, and the client discusses her or his observations of the previous observed conversation. Finally, all join together for a final conversation, which includes asking the counselor for his or her observations. As one can imagine, a definitional ceremony requires careful planning. It is strongly suggested that counselors wishing to use outsider witnesses prepare themselves by further study of narrative therapy, particularly in the use of definitional ceremonies or reflecting teams.

Narrative letters. Narrative practices use a variety of therapeutic documents to record, support, and extend the embodiment of alternative stories outside of the therapy session. Typically, therapeutic documents, including letters, certification/awards, and statements of knowledge or affirmation, are a mainstay of narrative therapy (Morgan, 2000; White, 1995; White & Epston, 1990). One specific type of therapeutic documentation, *narrative letters*, is especially useful in counseling for loss and grief.

The counseling professional composes a letter to the client that intentionally and specifically addresses the client's efforts to uncover and live out a preferred, alternative story.

191

What distinguishes a narrative letter is that it is literary rather than diagnostic; it tells a story rather than being expository or explicatory. The letter engages the reader not so much by developing an argument to a logical conclusion as by inquiring what might happen next. Structured to tell the alternative story that is emerging along with the therapy, it documents history, current developments, and future prospects. (J. Freeman, Epston, & Lobovits, 1997, p. 112)

The client is, essentially, reading his or her own story—an extraordinarily empowering experience.

Most often letters are sent following a therapy meeting and may be used intermittently across the therapy or timed for special occasions (e.g., prior to anniversary of a loss event). The letters usually summarize the session with attention to the main ideas discussed, all in the context of a narrative approach using questions and externalizing conversation. Narrative letters may allude to unique outcomes, raise questions for reflection, or note areas where further exploration is needed. They commonly point out client strengths, abilities, values, beliefs, and skills as these characteristics support the alternative story. Narrative letters also raise questions for the client to consider before the next therapy session (e.g., "At our next meeting we might talk more about those times when you have been able to keep Anger and Resentment from sabotaging things, especially when you are dealing with the police and the court system"). The following tips for letter writing are based on White's (1995) recommendations (cited in J. Freeman et al., 1997):

+ Quote verbatim from notes taken during the session.
+ Pose questions to encourage the client's thinking of preferred ways of being, for example, "What will it look like when you are managing your grief more effectively?"
+ Use reflexive verbs to imply acting on self, for example "Hyong, does this mean you are *taking control of your responses?*" instead of "Hyong was in control."
+ Use gerunds (verbs used as nouns, ending in "ing"), for example, "Serena, you said that worrying makes you get really down on yourself."
+ Use subjective mood (e.g., might, may), for example, "Do you think you *might* be acquiring new skills in handling difficult situations?"
+ Be willing to use humor.

The narrative letter below summarizes the first meeting of the counselor (David Epston) with a 15-year-old boy, Ray, whose older brothers were killed in a car accident. Ray had become increasingly distressed as the time approached for a ceremonial unveiling of his brothers' tombstone, and his family had referred him for counseling. Note here the value of summarizing the meeting from a narrative therapy approach (i.e., externalizing, addressing strengths and resources, noting unique outcomes, thinking about other possibilities). Note also how the counselor used the client's own words to support the implied alternative story of Managing Grief.

Dear Ray,

The death of your beloved brothers, Kerry and Brian, would have been a great shock and sadness to you. No wonder, only recently, have you come out of shock and are now experiencing your sadness. You have no need to fear this, as it is easily understandable that your brothers' deaths both upset and saddened you. But remember the law of grief: "crying on the outside means that you are no longer crying on the inside. And crying on the inside drowns your strength." I would imagine that you have some crying to do but you know now that that is right and proper. And if you didn't, it could only mean that your brothers meant nothing to you, and I know that is surely not so. However, you have many people to turn to if you require calming down: your mother, Mrs. Blair, Angela, and Shane. Each and every one of them has his or her own particular way of doing that: your Mum and Mrs. Blair "talk lovingly" to you; Angela knows "how to cheer me up"; and Shane and you "talk over the things we all (including Kerry and Brian) used to do."

Now you are over your shock, you may be ready to think about ways to keep your brothers' memories alive. You told me that Brian wanted to be a strong person because strength would contribute to your happiness. And here I imagine Brian meant personal strength rather than physical strength. Brian was a caring person and particularly protective of you, perhaps because you were the youngest. He was the eldest and a very responsible person. As you put it, he "set an example for us." He was an excellent sportsman in both cricket and rugby. But "just being a big brother" probably was the major accomplishment of his too short life. You told me that you could keep their memories alive by "carrying on growing up in a manner that would please them." Well, Ray, I guess that that won't be very hard for you to do.

Your brothers' unveiling is in a month's time. An unveiling is a special time to lay to rest your sadness and grief but also a time to think about ways to remember them. I suggest we meet again before then and talk about this. I want you to know, Ray, that even though you have suffered a great loss in your life, you struck me as a young man who is already almost everything your brothers would have hoped for.

Best wishes,
D.E.
(White & Epston, 1990, pp. 105–106)

Narrative letters can also be brief and address a specific issue. The following example demonstrates a narrative letter used to support a client's determination to challenge the dominant narrative.

Dear Jake,

When we were discussing what your problem required of you in order to guarantee its survival, your participation in the application of special techniques for blaming others seemed essential.

So you decided that you would refuse to be an instrument of the problem, went on strike against it, and dismissed these techniques for blaming others from your life.

At a meeting, I mentioned this to some colleagues and they were eager to know how this had affected the attitudes of others towards you. We decided to send you a couple of questions that we were preoccupied with in our discussion: How do you think this strike has affected the picture that others have of you as a person? What, in turn, has this helped you discover about yourself that you can appreciate? I look forward to hearing about what you turn up.

M.W.
(White & Epston, 1990, p. 119)

It is important to negotiate with clients regarding the delivery of letters from counselors and the location to which they will be sent so as to protect client privacy. Letters are typically mailed or e-mailed within a few days of a counseling session. Additionally, there should be discussion about what clients might do with these letters when they are received, because they may disregard them as administrative or even as a bill!

Narrative letter variations. Adaptations of narrative letters include clients writing letters to themselves or even to other clients. These are especially useful in loss and grief situations. *Rainy day letters* (M. A. Murray, 2002) are written on those days when clients feel things are going well, especially that they are living their alternative story, to be read at times when things are not going particularly well. The letter should point out the ways in which the alternative story is already happening, ways of increasing its power, and the values, strengths, and abilities that can be applied to the task. Suggested "tricks" for defeating the old dominant story and encouraging words might also be included. *Letters from the future* (M. A. Murray, 2002) are written from the perspective of 5 years or many years in the future. The client's point of view from the future is that she or he was able to fully live out the alternative story, assimilating loss and grief into its fabric, and has continued to do so. The letter would point out just what steps were taken, how challenges were overcome, and what strategies were used.

Clients can also be asked to write letters, anonymously, to other clients experiencing similar problems. These letters might include the author's personal story, suggested strategies, and encouragement regarding the move from dominant story to alternative story. The letters are collected by the counseling professional and made available to other clients. Further description of this type of narrative letter is found in Chapter 4, Wisdom Chronicles.

Recommended Resources

Freeman, J., Epston, D., & Lobovits, D. (1997). *Playful approaches to serious problems: Narrative therapy with children and their families.* New York: Norton.

Kropf, N. P., & Tandy, C. (1998). Narrative therapy with older clients: The use of a "meaning-making" approach. *Clinical Gerontologist, 18*(4), 3–16.

Monk, G., Drewery, W., & Winslade, J. (2005). Using narrative ideas in group work: A new perspective. *Counseling and Human Development, 38*(1).

Morgan, A. (2000). *What is narrative therapy? An easy-to-read introduction.* Adelaide, South Australia, Australia: Dulwich Centre Publications.

Payne, M. (2006). *Narrative therapy: An introduction for counsellors* (2nd ed.). London: Sage.

Excellent Web sites that provide articles, downloads, and training opportunities include http://www.narrativeapproaches.com, http://www.dulwichcentre.com.au, and http://www.harleneanderson.org.

The *International Journal of Narrative Therapy and Community Work* and the *Dulwich Centre Newsletter* are both published by Dulwich Centre Publications in Adelaide, South Australia, Australia.

Chapter 7

Solution-Focused Therapy
Strategies for Loss Adaptation

Solution-focused therapy offers some especially helpful strategies when counseling for issues of loss and grief. The approach draws primarily from Solution-Focused Brief Therapy, developed by Steve de Shazer, Insoo Kim Berg, and associates at the Brief Family Therapy Center in Milwaukee, Wisconsin (De Jong & Berg, 2002; Lipchik, 2000), and Solution-Oriented Therapy or Possibility Therapy, developed by Bill O'Hanlon (2006; O'Hanlon & Weiner-Davis, 2003). The emphasis on promoting client strengths and competence, deemphasizing pathology, tailoring treatment to match the uniqueness of clients and their context, the collaborative client–counselor relationship, the inevitability of change, and the co-construction of meaning is consistent with effective grief counseling practice. This approach helps people figure out how to meet life's difficulties (e.g., grief, guilt, anxiety) by emphasizing the elements that would be in place when a problem is resolved (solutions) and utilizing their own agency in bringing about resolution. It is important to recognize that solution building in grief counseling is not about the absence of grief or ignoring grief but about assimilating, integrating, or effectively managing grief.

Basic Assumptions of Solution-Focused Therapy

The following are some basic assumptions of solution-focused therapy applied to grief counseling:

1. *Clients have strengths, abilities, and resources, often unrecognized, to help them manage their grief.* An important element of therapy is helping clients realize and apply these personal assets to manage their grief in more effective ways.
2. *Focus on what works, not what does not work.* If clients managed their grief (or anger, rumination, guilt) effectively or coped better 1 day out of 5 days, then what they did, thought, and felt on that 1 day is more useful for recovery than what did not happen on the other 4 days. If clients controlled their anger appropriately for a few moments before exploding unhelpfully, then the skills, attitudes, and strengths brought to those few moments of managed anger are more useful for promoting change than what happened when the anger was no longer controlled.
3. *Clients are already doing some things to manage their grief (or guilt, anxiety, hopelessness).* These successes or "exceptions" should be explored and enhanced as critical components of change. Even if the exceptions seem minimal or did not last, they still suggest client attitudes, strengths, resources, and skills that can be applied to handling grief and its components. This is a matter of harnessing resilience.

4. *Small changes lead to larger changes.* Focusing clients on small steps or successes enhances motivation, leads to self-efficacy, and promotes more change. If clients can do one thing differently in managing their grief, then they can build on that success and do more things differently until they are managing in a more satisfactory manner.

5. *The person is not the problem; the Problem is the problem.* Grief becomes more manageable, more normal, and less overwhelming when viewed as a problem existing outside of the client rather than something that is "wrong" or "pathological" within the client. As personal as grief is, it is still an experience, not the sum of the individual.

6. *Clients are experts on themselves.* It is the client's grieving experience and not that of the counselor; therefore, the counseling professional respects the client's viewpoint and works in a collaborative manner that promotes client competence and self-discovery.

7. *There are many possible solutions to client problems, not just one.* Clients and their difficulties are unique, requiring solutions that reflect that uniqueness. What works in one situation may not work as well in another situation or at another time for the same client. Therefore solution-oriented counselors not only help clients develop diverse strategies for grieving but also help them develop flexibility in the application of those strategies in various contexts.

Implementation of Solution-Focused Therapy

Although solution-focused therapy usually follows a formulaic structure, it is often more useful in grief counseling to incorporate specific solution-focused strategies than to follow a predetermined structure. The counseling professional must judge those times when following a solution-focused structure or simply using solution-focused questions is most appropriate to the content and process of therapy. For example, counselors may use solution-focused therapy coping questions early in therapy to address the immediate feelings of being overwhelmed or out of control and use a miracle question later, after those initial responses have been experienced and become more manageable.

A critical element of the solution-focused therapy approach is clients' detailed exploration of possibilities in resolving their problems via exceptions—those times when the problems did not occur or occurred less intensely. Berg and her associates (Berg, 1994; Berg & Reuss, 1998; De Jong & Berg, 2002) devised the acronym EARS to guide the counseling professional in facilitating this exploration:

E = *eliciting* exceptions and successes (current and potential) in handling or resolving problems

A = *amplifying* the exceptions with details that illuminate client competence, control, and efficacy

R = *reinforcing* client strengths, abilities, and resources revealed by the exceptions

S = *starting* again by getting more details and emphasizing differences

The question forms below provide examples of solution-focused therapy strategies applied to grief counseling. Most of these are eliciting (E) questions and should be followed with questions that amplify client competence (A) and reinforce client strengths and abilities (R). No ordering of questions is intended here, nor should all the questions be asked. They are simply examples of ways solution-focused strategies can be applied in grief counseling.

Coping Questions

Coping questions promote competence by helping clients recognize ways in which they already manage their difficulties and increasing awareness of the strengths, abilities, and resources they can bring to bear on their problems. Coping questions are especially helpful when clients feel overwhelmed, devastated, or hopeless, as is often the case with grief.

+ With all you have endured, how did you manage to get out of bed today?
+ With all you have been through, how did you manage to get yourself here to the session?
+ How are you managing to get through each day, considering all that has happened?
+ How are you managing to get yourself to work (or class)?
+ What has been helpful in coping with the grief (anger, hopelessness) so far?
+ When you have encountered difficult things before, you somehow managed to get through. How did you do that? What did it take to handle those difficult circumstances?
+ How can you use those abilities to cope now?
+ You've had to make a lot of changes since the accident. How have you done that?
+ I can tell that the divorce has really forced you to make some difficult decisions. How have you managed to handle all of that?
+ A lot of people who have gone through what you have would have dropped out of school by now. What keeps you coming to school?
+ It's clear that something inside of you is at work here, helping you keep on despite the discouragement. What is it inside of you that keeps you going?
+ What have you been doing to take care of yourself during this time?
+ How is it that things are not worse than they are?
+ How are you managing to keep things from getting worse?
+ How did you learn to do that—to stop a moment, take a breath, and think about what you are doing?

Exceptions Questions

Exceptions questions are used to discover times when clients are deliberately or spontaneously handling difficulties, even to a small degree. These questions reveal ways in which clients can be in control of their problems rather than their problems controlling them (e.g., managing the grief rather than the grief controlling them). Counselors should be prepared to build on client comments that reveal success in managing their problems and/or specifically introduce exception questions. The counselor must keep the focus of exploration on client efficacy (what the *client* is doing when the grief is more manageable, not what others are doing) and on teasing out client strengths and abilities in controlling the problem or its symptoms.

+ Tell me about times when the grief seems more manageable.
+ Tell me about times when you feel you are more a survivor and less a victim of the grief.
+ Tell me about the moments when you forget you're grieving.
+ You mentioned that yesterday was a better day for you. What was different about yesterday in terms of managing all of this?

- OK, you said you didn't think you were doing anything; it was just a better day. I'm curious as to how you kept that good day going. After all, you could have sabotaged it, but you did not. You let it be a better day. What did you do to keep that good day going?
- You said a few moments ago that you held off giving into the grief until you could get home from work. How were you able to do that?
- I'm sure you have already found that grief has its own ebb and flow. I wonder about times when you have found it more bearable. What did it take for you to bear the grief better in those times?
- You said a little while ago that realizing your anger wasn't really about the nurses helped you calm down. I'm curious about that. How were you able to use that realization to calm yourself?

On-Track Questions

On-track questions help clients identify specific evidence of change. Such questions are especially useful in getting direction for the session, revealing differences, helping clients become more specific about what they want or need, preventing relapse, and enhancing motivation. Generally, on-track question are phrased to emphasize client competence in a future circumstance that will take place—not *if* a change occurs but *when* a change occurs.

- Suppose you were on the right track to handling this grief well. What would tell you that you are on track?
- You sound pretty discouraged. I wonder what is one thing you might see that would tell you that you are on track to resolving this—to moving on with your life? . . . What else might you see?
- When you get a little off track in making these changes, what will get you back on track again?
- What would be different about you when you are on the way to resolving the loss of this fantasy that your mother will one day realize what she has done?
- We've talked a lot about the sadness and emptiness you feel about all these losses. Exploring and expressing those feelings has been important. Now, as you consider things, what would tell you that you are on track to the next step in mourning these losses?
- What could we work on today that would tell you that we are on track in this therapy?
- What needs to happen here today that would tell you that the therapy is on track? What needs to happen next?

Relationship Questions

Relationship questions expand client perspective, flesh out details, and reinforce progress by focusing on interactional aspects of change. They are especially helpful in moving around "I don't know" responses. The focus of relationship questions is not on the other person but on expanding perspective, so counselors must keep the focus on the client and his or her behavior. Notice that relationship questions reinforce the potential for a satisfactory outcome by using positive, future-oriented language. Relationship questions are most useful for amplification and reinforcement following exception questions.

- What would your roommate say he notices when you are handling things better?
- What would your girlfriend say that she notices when you are able to control the anger?
- What would your friends say they see you doing when you are coping better with the breakup?
- How would your friends react differently to you if you were coping better with the breakup?
- What would your mother see that would tell her that things are better and that you are coping better?
- What will I notice is different about you in therapy when you are ready to move on to the next phase of life?
- Suppose you are no longer withdrawing and isolating yourself. What will you be doing instead?
- Suppose, once you make the changes you spoke about, you meet a complete stranger who knows nothing about your loss experiences. How would she or he describe you?

The counselor identifies referential people to use in relationship questions by listening carefully to clients' descriptions of their world, especially noting significant others. The counselor might also solicit that information directly. For example: Who is important in your life? Who has an investment in your managing this grief effectively? What people would be most likely to notice any changes in you or your behavior? If we made a film about your grieving experience, who would be in the film?

Scaling

Scaling, one of the most flexible counseling techniques from solution-focused therapy, is used to search for exceptions, evaluate progress, reduce vagueness, identify feeling states, explore potential solutions, prioritize issues, and assess client motivation (Berg & Miller, 1992; De Jong & Berg, 2002; de Shazer, 1994). Scaling is a visual metaphor that provides a common reference point that helps counselors and clients talk about things that are difficult to describe by making them more concrete (de Shazer, 1994). The counselor tells clients to imagine a scale running from 0 to 10, with 10 representing the most desired state and 0 representing the least desired state. The counselor asks clients to select a number that represents their current state and describe what that means. The numbers themselves on a scale are insignificant. What the numbers represent (i.e., meaning) and how they are used are what is important. Using the selected number as a reference point, the counselor helps clients to envision what improvement (e.g., from 8 to 9) or continued coping (holding at 5) would look like and what it would take to implement that improvement or coping. The counselor uses small steps (e.g., from 4 to 5; from 3 to 3½; from −1 to 0; from 75% to 70%) followed by elaboration and amplification of each point on the scale via "what" and "how" questions. Drawing the scale facilitates the visual metaphor. The following are examples of scaling applied to common grief circumstances:

- On a scale of 1 to 10 where the number 10 represents you are managing this grief exceptionally well and the number 1 represents the worst it has been, where would you put yourself today? . . . Help me understand what that number X represents for you?

After clarification, the counselor can direct the client toward improvement (What would it take to move up one number on the scale?) or maintenance (What are you doing to keep things from going lower on the scale?). Further amplification and expansion of the answer then follows.

+ [Addressing a grief counseling group] "On a scale of one to ten with the number ten being where life is picking up, and you feel yourself 'moving on,' and the number one is where things are as bad as you imagine they can get, how would you rate last week compared to this week?" (Gray, Zide, & Wilker, 2000, p. 22). After the client selects a number and clarifies the meaning attached to that number, the counselor may suggest a future focus that emphasizes moving ahead, "It sounds like it's been really tough for you these past few months . . . what would have to happen for you to go from a score of three to a score of four?" (p. 23), or a present focus to keep things from getting worse, "It sounds like you've been working really hard in dealing with your memories and loss of Joe. What do you notice you've been doing that keeps your score at a three, and not going lower, to maybe a two?" (p. 23). Further amplification and expansion of the answer then follows.

+ You've talked about recognizing the importance of forgiving yourself at some point, but it's been really difficult to do that. On a scale of 1 to 10, with 10 representing forgiving yourself enough so that you can move on and 1 representing being absolutely unable to even consider forgiveness, where would you put yourself today? After the client selects a number and clarifies the meaning attached to that number, the counselor may suggest a future focus to help the client envision improvement (What would need to happen, in terms of this forgiveness issue, for you to move from the current level 3 to a level 4?) or keep a present focus to emphasize maintenance (What have you been doing to keep yourself at that Level 3?). Further amplification and expansion of the answer then follows.

Miracle Questions

Miracle questions are designed to shift clients' perspective toward consideration of what they would be doing, thinking, or even feeling when their problems are solved. In the case of grief, a miracle question shifts the focus away from clients' present pain toward a picture of recovery when the grief is more manageable. Expansion and exploration of the answers to a miracle question helps clients identify more specifically the changes they want and the possibilities for resolution of their concerns (De Jong & Berg, 2000).

There are many variations of miracle questions, but all use a "miracle" or "magic" as a mechanism for forcing a perspective shift toward an imagined future when the problem does not exist or exists minimally, and when the client is thinking, feeling, and doing things differently. The shift is from problem saturation toward solution building. Counselors must remember to keep the focus on client efficacy and what, specifically, a client will be thinking, feeling, and doing differently. Client strengths, abilities, and competence should be promoted. If exceptions have been identified earlier, these should be incorporated into amplification and exploration that follow answers to the miracle question. The following are examples of miracle questions applied to grief situations:

+ Suppose a miracle occurred tonight while you were sleeping and you were suddenly able to cope very well with the grief you are experiencing. You still feel the loss and grieve—but the miracle is that you are able to handle it very well. However, you don't know a miracle has occurred because you were sleeping. What would be the first thing you notice when you wake up that would tell you that this miracle has occurred and you are coping effectively with this grief? What would others notice is different about you? *Note.* Explore the answer for specific persons separately (e.g., parent, partner, children, work colleague). What would be the next thing you notice?

+ If we had a magic wand and could make this problem (e.g., grief, guilt, hopelessness) disappear, what would you be doing (thinking, feeling) differently?

+ If a miracle happened tonight and the difficulties and concerns associated with the loss that prompted you to come to the bereavement group were resolved while you were asleep, what would be different when you woke up in the morning? What would be some of the first things you would notice that were different about how the day would go? (Gray et al., 2000, p. 21)

+ Suppose a miracle happened tonight while you were sleeping and you found, on waking tomorrow morning, that you had survived these losses and were experiencing a satisfying life. What would be different? What would you notice is different about you? What would your children notice is different about you? What would your work colleagues notice is different? What things are you doing to take care of yourself when you have survived these losses and have this more satisfying postloss life?

+ Let's say there are two movies about your life. Movie A is about your life if things continue as they have been. Movie B is about your life when you find ways to adapt to these losses and build a satisfying and full life again. We know a lot about what happens in Movie A. What would Movie B look like? What would you be doing differently if Movie B was running? Who would be in it? How would your relationships with those people be different? What would Movie B show us about how you would handle this grief in a way that permits you to live fully?

The counselor should pose the miracle question in a way that draws the client into the story, with the curious (and freeing) notion of miracle, delivered "deliberately and dramatically" (De Jong & Berg, 2000, p. 85). Be prepared to redirect some typical unhelpful client responses, for example:

+ A client may focus initially on an unrealistic miracle (e.g., my partner will not be dead; I would never have had to leave my native land; I would still have my job; I never had the abortion). The best response to this is, "That would be nice, but the miracle is based on what you are really dealing with. So, the miracle is about how things will look when you are, for example, managing this grief well, no longer angry, guilt-free, moving on."

+ A client may focus on what others will be doing differently or on changed circumstances that are out of the client's control (e.g., someone will give me another job, nothing reminds me of her that day; he doesn't make me angry anymore). It is important to refocus the client on differences within her or his own control. For example: "Let's say you have not yet gotten another job, what would you be doing differently when you are coping effectively with losing your job?" "That would be nice, but people are the same, it is you who are different now, so things will still happen that make you angry. What will be different after the miracle about how you handle that?"

Timing is critical when using miracle questions with grief circumstances. Miracle questions move the client deliberately toward change and tend to emphasize behavior and cognition. If the client is at that point in his or her process at which experiencing and expressing emotion or exploring the meaning of loss in the context of past and present is more appropriate, then a miracle question is counterproductive.

Looking Forward/Looking Back Questions

Looking forward/looking back questions help clients expand the possibilities for thinking, feeling, and doing in their present situation by shifting the time perspective. Clients are directed to imagine an improved future but must look backward from that stance to identify possibilities for change. In grief counseling, the imagined future is either of a time when the client is no longer grieving or, more realistically, of a time when the grief is being handled satisfactorily. Shifting perspective by looking backward from the future helps the client recognize mechanisms that create change (e.g., effective coping strategies). These questions are especially helpful for grieving clients who often have difficulty envisioning a change in their grieving—a time when they will not experience the intense distress of the present.

- Suppose it is 5 years down the road and you have survived these losses. You look back and say to yourself, "That was a difficult time for me, especially in the beginning, but I ended up handling it pretty well after all." What would you have done to get through this experience so that you could look back in 5 years and say you handled it well?
- If you could look back in 5 years, what inner resources would you say you were able to draw on to help you?
- If you could look back in 5 years, what would have been the turning point in your ability to handle this? What would have happened to make that a turning point?
- Suppose it is just a year from now and you look back on losing this job and you find yourself thinking, "Well, I wish it had not happened or had not happened the way that it did, but I've managed to turn things around." What would you have done to turn things around?
- I've noticed that people who have experienced loss sometimes get to the place where they can say, "I wish this had not happened; it was awful and I miss what (or who) I have lost, but I am a better person for having survived this." What would it take for you to be able to say that about yourself someday?

The time period specified with these questions certainly can vary based on the counselor's judgment. Adolescents respond better to shorter time periods (6 months, 1 year, 5 years), whereas adults are usually responsive to longer time periods (5 years, 10 years, 20 years). When a client cannot envision a particular time period, ask the question again with a shorter time period. If a client can successfully envision some changes at one time period, the counselor might push the time further to encourage envisioning even more change (e.g., what will be different in 1 year, in 5 years, in 20 years?).

People Potential

Webb (1999) suggested that clients should consider how others have approached similar problems and identify human resources that might assist them in their grieving experience. This is an excellent way to help clients develop an effective support system of family, friends, and organizations. "Potential people" also might be completely imaginary or based on a character from theater or literature. Grieving clients might imagine the advice of the deceased or someone who is otherwise inaccessible (e.g., birth parents of adoptee). Here are some questions designed to identify potential people.

+ What would your Tia Maria tell you to do to handle this situation?
+ What advice would your mother/father give you in this situation?
+ What suggestions would the other guys in the unit have about handling the grief (stress, anger)?
+ Where else could you look for help in managing this grief (guilt, anger, anxiety), and how would you get that support from them?
+ What have you seen other people do to manage their anger in similar situations?
+ You said you thought that Lavon seemed to manage his discouragement about losing his job pretty well. What does Lavon know that you don't know?
+ You said you were impressed with how that character in the film handled the challenges. If she were a real person and could advise you right now, what would she tell you?
+ How do other people your age deal with similar situations?
+ What do you think other parents of murdered children can tell you about what helps them manage at this point in their grieving?
+ You said earlier that the foster mother at your second placement was really great; you said she was wise. Imagine that you could consult her about the best ways to get these losses into perspective—what do you think she would tell you?
+ You mentioned how difficult it is for you to ask for help sometimes. Imagine that you are overcoming this difficulty and asking for help. Tell me what that would look like?

Clarifying/Defining Goals

Goal clarification and definition provides direction and motivates change. Useful goals must be specific, realistic, achievable, and stated as the presence of or beginning of something, not the absence of something. Goal measurability should be defined by the client. The following are examples of goals appropriate to grief counseling:

+ To manage grief effectively.
+ To develop and use skills for handling this grief.
+ To practice self-care during grieving.
+ To adapt to the ebb and flow of life.
+ To reorganize my life around the loss in a way that allow me to continue to invest in life.
+ To incorporate losses into my life and reinvest in life-affirming ways.
+ To develop a continuing bond with my (deceased) daughter that is healthy and functional.
+ To effectively manage the anger (anxiety, loneliness) involved in this grief.
+ To mourn while continuing to parent successfully.

Sufficient exploration of the answers resulting from the solution-focused strategies described above will suggest goals appropriate to particular clients and their contexts. Additionally, the following questions are helpful in setting goals with grieving clients:

+ How will you know when you have sufficiently integrated this grief?
+ How will you know that you are managing your grief effectively?
+ What evidence will exist that reveals you are handling the grief in a meaningful and helpful way?
+ What will be happening regarding your grief that is different from what is happening now when it is sufficiently resolved?
+ What will it look like when the grieving is integrated or assimilated for you?
+ What signs will you see that tell you that you have come to terms with these losses?
+ What will be different about you when you have resolved these losses in a way that allows you to reinvest in a satisfying life?

As stated previously, timing is important in using solution-focused therapy with grief issues. Counselors should not rush to develop goals. In grief situations especially, it is important to facilitate clients in telling their stories, exploring the meaning of their losses, implementing coping skills, and experiencing and expressing emotions before directing them toward change through goal clarification. Counselors should trust that potential goals appropriate to the uniqueness of clients and their context will emerge after sufficient exploration. Exception questions and the miracle question are especially helpful in leading directly to goal clarification.

Recommended Resources

Gray, S. W., Zide, M. R., & Wilker, H. (2000). Using the solution-focused brief therapy model with bereavement groups in rural communities: Resiliency at its best. *Hospice Journal, 15*(3), 13–30.

Lipchik, E. (2000). *Beyond technique in solution-focused therapy: Working with emotions and the therapeutic relationship*. New York: Guilford Press.

O'Hanlon, B., & Beadle, S. (1997). *Guide to possibility land: Fifty-one methods for doing brief, respectful therapy*. New York: Norton.

Web sites providing diverse resources on solution-focused therapies include http://www.billohanlon.com and http://www.brief-therapy.org.

Chapter 8

Adjunctive Strategies for Loss Adaptation

There are a number of activities that can be used alongside conventional face-to-face psychotherapy for loss and grief. These activities are not intended as substitutes for psychotherapy but provide added benefit to clients, their adaptation to loss, and the therapeutic process. The adjunctive strategies suggested here recognize the interconnectedness of body, mind, and spirit and how each of these dimensions affects the others. The focus is on the whole person and accessing resources that provide support, facilitate a change orientation, and promote balance and harmony. They reflect a respect for clients as knowledgeable experts on themselves and the multiple contexts of their lives.

Clients may participate in these activities according to their own needs and preferences, thus allowing counseling professionals to further customize treatment to the uniqueness of their clients and their particular adaptation to loss. Although some elements of these adjunctive strategies may be incorporated directly into the therapy (e.g., mindfulness meditation, support groups, walking a labyrinth), these are primarily voluntary, self-directed activities that occur independent of therapy sessions and may be utilized by clients long after therapy ends. Engaging in extra-therapy activities empowers clients by encouraging them to nurture themselves and increase their sense of control. The rationale given when recommending that clients explore these activities should be deliberately ambiguous. This encourages client ownership and openness to whatever experience and benefit may result. The counselor might say, "Some people who also experienced grief have found this helpful," "I think you might find this an excellent way to take care of yourself during this difficult time," or "There are some things that you might do on your own outside of therapy that will benefit the work we do together in therapy." Counseling professionals should provide specific resources or help their clients plan how to obtain information as appropriate.

Client Self-Care

It is appropriate for counseling professionals to inquire as to client self-care and encourage attitudes and activities that promote personal health. The benefits of a balanced diet and regular exercise are well known; however, they are especially important when people are coping with difficult transitions such as loss and grief. Counseling professionals do not put people on diets, but they should encourage clients to examine their lifestyles and plan ways in which they can sustain a healthy lifestyle that will support them during the grieving process. This may also include assistance with abusive or addictive behaviors, such as drug abuse, compulsive sexual activity, or gambling. Self-care also involves self-nurturing activities, such as a soaking in a warm bath, listening to special music, shopping, having breakfast in bed, visiting or working in a garden, going fishing, eating comforting foods, or taking a day off from work to "do nothing." Some clients may need assistance with devising such activities or may even need "permission" to enjoy themselves when they are grieving. Clients may prefer to do public activities (e.g., dining out, shopping) alone at locations where they are unlikely to see people they know as a break from dealing with loss-related explanations and inquiries (i.e., "I can just be a normal person."). A further benefit of many self-care activities is that they provide momentary and necessary distractions from both the loss and restoration functions of grieving.

Therapeutic Massage

Massage therapy contributes to emotional and physical well-being by reducing tension, increasing relaxation, easing physical discomfort, and encouraging self-nurture. All of these promote the overall well-being of the whole person, providing physical and emotional support during the grieving process. An equally important aspect of therapeutic massage is the healing power of caring touch. This is often helpful for grieving people and particularly so when their losses deprive them of regular human touch (e.g., widowhood). The most prevalent types of massage include Swedish massage, deep tissue massage, trigger point massage, and Shiatsu massage. Most qualified massage therapists provide more than one type of massage. When recommending massage, counseling professionals should encourage clients to seek out licensed or certified massage therapists or practitioners who meet established training and practice standards and abide by ethical and legal guidelines. Many, but not all, states regulate massage therapy, and national certification is provided by the National Certification Board for Therapeutic Massage and Bodywork (http://www.ncbtmb. org). Counseling professionals who recommend massage should, of course, have first-hand experiences of its benefits and know the resources in their area.

Massage therapy may not be appropriate for people who have cultural objections or who have been traumatized, especially in cases of sexual abuse. However, abused persons may also find massage a significant aid to healing when the timing and conditions are right (e.g., when they are less reactive to physical touch, by using a same-sex massage therapist, or by applying restrictions on body parts available for massage). Counseling professionals should work with such clients and sometimes directly with massage therapists to establish conditions that will promote healing.

Compassionate touch, an intentional touch and gentle massage practice especially designed for those in eldercare, hospice, and palliative care settings, is a recommended resource. Counseling professionals may utilize this method themselves or encourage ill or dying clients and their families to seek out caregivers who are trained in this method. Training is provided by the Center for Compassionate Touch (http://www.compassionate-touch.org).

Labyrinth Walking

A labyrinth is an enduring symbol of the cycle of life, sacred space, or healing common to many ancient cultures, most notably Celtic, Cretan, Mayan, Greek, and Native American (e.g., Hopi, Pima, and Tohono O'odham peoples). It has also been associated with mystical Judaism and Christianity. It has many forms, such as the Man in the Maze or Medicine Wheel (Native American), although the best-known example today is found inlaid on the floor of Chartres Cathedral in France (1201 CE). The labyrinth consists of a single, circuitous path winding to a center. Unlike a maze, in which there are dead ends and hidden turns where one may become disoriented or lost, a labyrinth is fully visible, with one clear path leading inward and outward with a single entrance/exit. Labyrinths are typically structured as walking paths and found in hospitals, hospices, churches and spiritual centers, prisons, psychotherapy and rehabilitation centers, public gardens, community centers, and private settings. They may be formed from turf or rocks, drawn on the floor, or even drawn on canvas for portability. Finger or lap labyrinths, made of wood, paper, or metal, allow the user to trace the labyrinth path with a finger. There are even online labyrinths. Eleven-circuit, seven-circuit, and three-circuit labyrinths are the most common forms.

Walkers follow the labyrinth path in a quiet yet purposeful manner to its center, pause, then retrace their steps outward to the place where they began. People walk the labyrinth at their own pace, pausing to meditate, pray, experience, or center themselves according to their needs. The labyrinth metaphor is one of "shedding and releasing distractions and negative thoughts, going to the center where one gets nourishment and healing, going out again marking return, rejuvenated, to the world" (Kennedy, 2007, p. 12). Labyrinth walking is useful for people going through difficult transitions in their lives such as loss and grief. It facilitates introspection, encourages focus, respects the inner experience, and quiets the mind and emotions. In walking the labyrinth people metaphorically "walk" the grieving journey between loss and restoration. Following the path inward focuses the person's mind on loss and its meaning; at the center the individual pauses to consolidate resources and shift perspective; then following the path outward focuses the person's mind on restoration and its meaning. Walkers may enter the labyrinth with particular questions or problems to explore, or they may simply open themselves to the experience on their own terms. This exercise is especially helpful when clients are at an impasse in therapy or in loss adaptation. Sometimes clients find it useful to walk the labyrinth just before or just after a therapy session as a way of concentrating or relaxing. An important advantage of labyrinth walking is its flexibility and adaptability, so that people use it in ways and at times that are most helpful to them. Counseling professionals should emphasize that the process of walking the labyrinth is more important than arriving at some specific outcome.

Lap or finger labyrinths can be utilized within the therapy session to enhance relaxation and stimulate exploration. Neil Harris, a professional counselor, uses a double-finger labyrinth that allows client and counselor to trace the labyrinth path simultaneously at the beginning of the session (Curry, 2000; Harris, 2008). Peel (2004) described using a labyrinth in family therapy. Family members are asked to construct a labyrinth together, allowing for assessment and exploration of family dynamics, such as communication, leadership, reactivity, and boundaries. Later members utilize the family labyrinth as a means of mutual problem solving.

The following labyrinth resources are recommended:

+ The Web site http://www.labyrinthos.net, maintained by Caerdroi, the *Journal of Mazes and Labyrinths*, provides information as well as templates, patterns, and instructions for creating and using labyrinths.
+ A worldwide labyrinth locator is found at http://wwll.veriditas.labyrinthsociety.org/.
+ An online finger labyrinth is found at http://www.gracecathedral.org/labyrinth/interactions.
+ An excellent introductory book including drawing directions, history, and suggested meditations is Curry, H. (2000). *The way of the labyrinth: A powerful meditation for everyday life*. New York: Penguin.

The Nature Cure

A valuable adjunctive strategy for many clients who are dealing with loss and grief is participation in nature-related activities. Such activities aid relaxation and reduce stress, promote introspection, and provide helpful distraction. Mother Nature often symbolizes a place of refuge and solace when one is dealing with life's difficulties. The lessons of nature can facilitate meaning reconstruction for grieving individuals. The nature-related themes of changing seasons, cycles of birth, death and rebirth, damage and recovery, wounding and healing, transformation, adaptation, and regeneration offer symbolic application to the experience of loss and grief. The sensual richness of the outdoors challenges the numbing internal focus of grieving. Nature-related activities are adaptable to the needs and preferences of the individual. Some activities, such as hiking, bird watching, or visiting a public garden, are well suited to the griever's fluctuating desire for solitude or society. Some activities provide opportunities for focused activity (e.g., recording observations), some may require learning new skills (e.g., fly fishing), and other activities simply provide in-the-moment experiencing.

Nature-related activities could include hiking, camping, bird watching, visiting parks and public gardens, walking the neighborhood or a beach or along a stream, boating, gardening, weather-watching, fishing, or collecting natural items. Anything that gets people outdoors and aware of their natural surroundings is beneficial, and many nature-related activities cost nothing. However, this is not just a matter of telling clients to take a walk or go outdoors. Counseling professionals should be intentional about helping clients explore their impressions and experiences by linking nature's lessons to their grieving journey. One way to introduce clients to nature-related activities is to dedicate a therapy session to a joint outside walk designed specifically to enhance sensual awareness. The walk may be conducted largely in silence so as to focus on sensations. At the end of the walk the counselor engages the client in an exploration of what she or he noticed during the walk, shifting the focus externally or internally as appropriate, and helps the client make linkages to her or his grieving experience.

An excellent resource for using nature-related activities in psychotherapy is Burns, G. W. (1998). *Nature-guided therapy: Brief integrative strategies for health and well-being*. Philadelphia: Brunner/Mazel.

Tai Chi and Yoga

Tai chi and yoga are gentle exercise practices derived from Eastern philosophy and spirituality that emphasize the balance of body, mind, and spirit. Both practices use movement, breathing, and meditation to enhance physical and emotional well-being. Their well-known benefits include reducing stress, increasing flexibility, improving muscle coordination and balance, increasing energy, and enhancing overall well-being. Tai chi and yoga can be performed by most people in various physical conditions with appropriate adaptations, including persons with disabilities. Counseling professionals may recommend tai chi or yoga to their grieving clients for the physical benefits, especially promoting relaxation (feeling better physically generates feeling better emotionally). Meditation and deep breathing can assist in centering and calming the mind. The deliberate attending and focusing (posing, breathing) aspect of tai chi and yoga practices also provides relief in the form of distraction from the sometimes all-consuming aspect of grieving and can help clients improve concentration. Participation in classes or groups aids socialization, whereas solitary practice can be self-nurturing. The act of learning tai chi or yoga encourages a change orientation.

Tai chi, a Chinese martial art form most commonly practiced for its health benefits, consists of slow, deliberate, prescribed movements and postures combined with deep breathing and meditation. Each movement flows into the next in a graceful manner. It draws especially on the harmonizing principle of yin-yang: forward and backward, movement and calm, soft and hard, push and pull, square and round. Tai chi can be practiced alone, and many people also enjoy participating in groups at informal "meet-ups." Classes and meet-ups are offered in many communities.

Yoga, originating from India, consists of assuming various specific postures or poses (*asanas*), combined with stretching, synchronized breathing, and meditation. Like tai chi, yoga focuses on the balance of opposites: flexing then tensing, rounding then arching, lifting then settling, movement then stillness. There are various types of yoga, with Hatha yoga being the most common in the United States. Many people incorporate yoga into their daily routine either as a solitary practice or in groups. Yoga instruction is available in many communities.

Counseling professionals should stress the importance of finding trained and/or certified instructors when recommending tai chi or yoga to their clients.

Creative Activities

Many clients dealing with loss and grief may benefit from participation in creative activities, such as painting, photography, sculpting, poetry, woodworking, rapping, or dancing. Such creative endeavors facilitate emotional expression, assist with meaning reconstruction, increase self-awareness, provide pleasure, promote problem-solving and organizational skills, encourage empowerment, foster a sense of control, and stimulate a change orientation. Participation in creative activities can provide a means of integrating the various threads of grieving, for example, establishing a continuing bond, finishing unfinished business, or confronting and avoiding the dual grieving dimensions of loss focus and restoration focus. "Art provides a balance for feelings, thoughts, and experiences. It is this balance which provides hope and nurturing" (Raymer & McIntyre, 1987, p. 35).

Creative activities may specifically address the loss and grieving experience (e.g., grief poetry) or may simply provide an expressive outlet and activity. Some creative endeavors may take the form of memorials (e.g., roadside memorial, garden bench). Counseling professionals may encourage clients to learn new creative ways or to revive former activities. Clients who have reservations about their "artistic" abilities should be reassured that the process is far more important than the product. Examples of creative activities include photography, writing plays or poetry, woodworking, playing or composing music, choreographing a dance, cooking or cooking lessons, sculpting, drawing, painting, basket making, collecting objects (e.g., rocks, shells, and stamps), creating a Web page, making a film, papermaking, design and construction, storytelling, and making jewelry. A recommended resource for creative activities and grief is http://www.recover-from-grief.com.

Another facet of using creative activities to address grief is encouraging clients to expose themselves to art. Clients may visit art galleries and museums, attend arts and crafts fairs, explore exhibits, or even observe artists at work. Many such activities are free or low cost. These activities provide helpful distraction from distress but can also increase self-awareness and facilitate emotional processing. Grieving persons may visit an art gallery alone or with others depending on their need for solitude or socialization. Counseling professionals should engage client in discussion of these experiences, facilitating connections to grief and adaptation to loss.

Mindfulness Meditation

Mindfulness meditation, the most widely known mindfulness practice, is a useful strategy in counseling for loss and grief. It incorporates all of the critical components of the mindfulness approach: intentional focus on the moment-to-moment experience; detached observation of thoughts, feelings, and sensations; and nonjudgmental acceptance of one's experience. Also called insight meditation or Vipassana, mindfulness meditation is one of several Buddhist meditation practices that have been adapted to the West (Hamilton, Kitzman, & Guyotte, 2006). The Mindfulness-Based Stress Reduction (MBSR) program developed by Jon Kabat-Zinn at the University of Massachusetts Medical Center is the basis for numerous applications (e.g., treatment of anxiety, depression, chronic pain) and is widely available across the United States.

Essentially, MBSR involves an 8-week introductory program inclusive of didactic instruction and daily meditation practice. Participants are taught the basics of mindfulness meditation, including the body scan technique, mindfulness of breath, and yoga postures, and then assisted with application of their learning to daily life (Hamilton et al., 2006; Kabat-Zinn, 1990, 1994; Sagula & Rice, 2004). Counseling professionals can locate MBSR programs in their area and facilitate client referrals to this program. Alternatively, if no MBSR programs are locally accessible, counselors should work with other professional colleagues to develop a mindfulness meditation program that will meet local needs. It is absolutely critical that such an alternative program be led by persons who are knowledgeable and experienced practitioners of mindfulness meditation. The Center for Mindfulness in Medicine, Health Care and Society at the University of Massachusetts Medical School maintains a list of trained practitioners at http://www.umassmed.edu/cfm/mbsr/.

Grief Support Groups

Grief support groups are voluntary *nontherapy* associations that provide education and emotional support for grieving persons. They offer acceptance, practical information, social connection, and an outlet for altruism. Grief support groups reduce social isolation, decrease disenfranchisement, and promote effective coping. They are offered in many communities through churches and synagogues, hospital/hospices, funeral homes, and social service or mental health agencies. More recently online support groups have emerged. Leadership is typically provided by trained volunteers or sometimes by counseling professionals. Most support groups are focused solely on bereavement grief and often are specific to circumstance, for example, groups for parents of murdered children, survivors of a loved one's suicide, and friends of persons with HIV/AIDS. Divorce recovery groups are increasingly common. There is tremendous variation in approach and activities in grief support groups. Some may emphasize socializing opportunities, others may emphasize religious or spiritual support, and yet others may emphasize social activism (e.g., changing drunk driving laws). Bereavement grief support groups are typically unhelpful to people who have experienced nondeath-related loss. Do not refer people to bereavement grief support groups immediately following a death, because this tends to overwhelm and retraumatize them.

Instead, suggest the support groups after the initial, most intense distress has eased and when there is evidence of sufficient coping skills.

Counseling professionals should acquaint themselves with local and national grief support group resources. Local leadership of these groups often changes, and the quality of leadership and accuracy of information vary. Some clients find that attending a group outside of their local area, where they are not known, is most comfortable. Group situations are not a fit for everyone, especially those who are more reserved about expressing their emotions, so clients should never be pressured to attend. Online support groups offer excellent opportunities for support but present some challenges as well. Like face-to-face support groups, leadership and quality of online support groups vary, with some clearly designed to sell products and services and many providing outdated or incorrect information. Counseling professionals should discuss the pros and cons of using online support groups when referring clients and regularly check in with clients regarding online experiences. Bereavement support groups arising from national organizations are generally most reliable (e.g., Compassionate Friends, Survivors of Suicide, and Parents of Murdered Children). Internet search engines (e.g., Google, Yahoo) are a starting point for exploring online support resources.

The Counseling Professional
Working With Loss and Grief

This chapter describes preferred counselor roles in working with loss and grief and provides recommendations for effective professional and personal practices.

Three Essential Counselor Roles

Working effectively with grieving clients in the 21st century requires professionals to embrace counseling roles that prioritize the uniqueness of clients, their experiences, and the multiple contexts of their lives; recognize the normality of grief; empower clients to be actively involved in their own loss adaptation; support clients without attempting to cure or fix them; and respect clients as experts on themselves. This calls for some expansion and adaptation of more traditional counseling roles and discerning which roles are most appropriate at various times and with different clients. The three essential roles for working with loss and grief are *witness*, *facilitator*, and *collaborator*.

In the *witness role*, counseling professionals join one of the most ancient of healing practices: to observe, to listen, to hear, to remember, and to understand at the deepest level the powerful narratives of loss and grief. To witness is to be fully and intentionally present to clients without fixed agendas or needing to do anything other than be "with" the client. The counselor in the witness role creates a safe space within which the stories of loss and grief can emerge and reemerge. From this stance, counselors bear witness to sorrow, despair, guilt, relief, hopelessness, determination, and yearning. They listen intuitively with the "third ear" (Reik, 1972) to unspoken fears, long-held secrets, disrupted beliefs, broken dreams, and suppressed emotions. As witnesses, counselors demonstrate their willingness to walk together with clients into uncharted territory, even into painful, frightening, or shameful places; provide validation of the loss and the griever; and acknowledge the significance of these experiences in the life of the individual, the family, and the community. In the role of witness, counseling professionals

+ listen more than they talk.
+ employ respectful silence as a primary intervention.
+ fully attend to clients rather than listening selectively with preconceived notions and labels (e.g., stages, diagnoses, stereotypes) or robotic responses (e.g., reflection of feeling).
+ exhibit comfort with their clients' strong or distressing emotions and thoughts.

213

+ allow clients to experience their grief without attempting to fix, cure, or solve it, even when clients request rescue.
+ demonstrate a respectful and nonjudgmental attitude.

In the *facilitator role*, counseling professionals provide a therapeutic framework conducive to functional loss adaptation. This framework consists of *focus*, which directs client attention to potentially usefully material, and *structure* (e.g., procedures, strategies, experiments), which enables the client's own unique process. The facilitator continually checks in with clients and makes adjustments regarding focus and structure based on client feedback (e.g., How can I be of help to you? How is the session going thus far? Is this where we should be focusing or is there somewhere else? Where should we be spending our time?). The counselor as facilitator does not so much make the client's path easier as make it more constructive. The most important factor is respecting client ownership: The counselor facilitates the client's work but does not presume to do the client's work. In the role of facilitator, counseling professionals

+ provide only the degree of structure appropriate to client needs, goals, and preferences.
+ direct client attention to useful or likely issues and experiences.
+ pose questions that encourage exploration, examination, clarification, elaboration, and amplification.
+ tailor treatment to the client rather than attempting to tailor clients to treatment.
+ refrain from giving answers or making interpretations and pronouncements.
+ select therapeutic strategies consistent with client style and preferences.
+ recognize that the more responsibility the counselor assumes, the less responsibility the client assumes.
+ encourage recognition and use of client strengths, resources, and abilities.
+ respect the natural ebb and flow of the grieving journey, including periods of disorder, impasse, resistance, and confusion as part of the loss adaptation process.
+ consult with clients regularly as to the direction of therapy and the usefulness of various therapeutic activities, making adjustments where appropriate.
+ assist clients where they are and not where the counselor wants them to be.

In the *collaborator role*, counseling professionals consult and confer with clients, recognizing them as experts on themselves and their own experiences. In fact, collaborative counselors are more interested in client perspectives than they are in preconceived notions about grief based on the expertness of others. Neither directive nor nondirective, the counselor as collaborator is a fellow explorer who shares thoughts, contributes ideas, and raises questions in a manner that respects the client as "leader of the expedition" through grief's territory. Recognizing clients' knowledge and expertise, collaborative counselors invite clients to inform and educate them (the counselors) regarding the factors and influences of their lives. For example: Help me understand how this loss fits into your experience as an African American. How are your faith beliefs and practices important to who you are? What does not having children mean for you as individuals, as a couple, and within your community? What does this job loss mean to you as a man? A client–counselor relationship defined by collaboration emphasizes dialogue and conversation as the means of exploring and integrating the myriad aspects of loss and grief experiences. In the role of collaborator, counseling professionals

+ respect clients as central narrators of their own stories.
+ are abundantly curious, encouraging in clients an attitude of exploration and discovery.
+ rely on "what" and "how" questions to encourage reflection and ownership.
+ utilize a flexible and adaptable therapeutic style that optimizes work with diverse clients.
+ teach more in the manner of sharing information than bestowing expert advice.
+ invite client ideas rather than making assignments (e.g., What might help you manage your anxiety about this during the coming week?).
+ provide a social context in which clients may make meaning of their loss.
+ empower change by recognizing client expertness and ownership.
+ encourage divergent thinking.
+ actively seek evidence of and promote client resiliency.

Practical Suggestions for Counseling Professionals

Recognize Grief Is a Natural Process

Counselors must recognize that grief is not an illness or problem to be cured or fixed but a process to be experienced. Clients do not need to be "rescued" from their grief. Grieving may be distressful and may even compound other difficulties, but it remains a normative, natural human experience that merits facilitation, not elimination. Counseling professionals must resist the incredible pressure from managed care to "fix it in five" (sessions) and from clients who may wish to circumvent what is often a difficult and painful process. The counseling goal is not the extinction or short-circuiting of grief but the management of symptoms and promotion of functional loss adaptation.

Be Theoretically Grounded

Whether counseling professionals subscribe to a single theoretical system, several related systems, or an integrated/eclectic system, a sound theoretical grounding is absolutely necessary for effective, competent, and ethical psychotherapy practice. Strategies alone are insufficient. One challenge for counseling professionals is to integrate their selected theoretical orientation with current research, concepts, and theories of grief and loss. A second challenge is to be open to new theoretical models and evolving knowledge. "Good clinicians are flexible and good theories are widely applicable . . . theories being adapted for use in a variety of contexts and clinicians borrowing heavily from divergent theories" (Prochaska & Norcross, 1999, p. 5).

Instill Hope

Clients seeking therapy for issues related to loss and grief are often discouraged or demoralized about their experiences and their efforts to manage their grief. It is important that counseling professionals nurture hope in these clients, not that their losses can be erased or their distress eliminated, but that their distress can be eased, something can be done to survive the experience, and a life-affirming future is possible. According to Frank and Frank (1991), all effective psychotherapies share four essential elements that combat client demoralization: (a) an emotionally charged, confiding relationship with a helping person; (b) a healing setting; (c) a conceptual approach that provides plausible explanations and procedures; and (d) interventions that both client and counseling professional believe will deliver desired results. Additionally, client hopefulness is stimulated by their sense that their counselor believes in them, not just in the fact that things can get better for them but specifically in their capacity to bring about change. Discouragement abates and hope grows when people can imagine the possibilities of living beyond and through their losses to a satisfying future. Counseling professionals facilitate this hope by intentionally presuming a focus on the future, posing questions that create a vision of what clients can move toward, such as: What will it look like when you are fully embracing life again? What will be different when you are managing this grief (distress) well? How will you know when things are better? What will it look like when you are remembering but also moving forward? How will your relationship look when you grieve for Salome but also live fully as a couple?

See the Client as a Whole Person

Counseling professionals sometimes lose sight of the client as a whole person, allowing labels and descriptions to define individuals and equating people with their problems or diagnoses (e.g., depressive, resistant, dysfunctional, codependent). These totalizing descriptions dehumanize people and undermine therapy. Counselors who see the whole person recognize a separation between clients and their problems and concerns: People are not their problems. Clients encounter or deal with problems associated with grief, such as despair, anxiety, anger, dissonance, shattered assumptions, or maladaptive schemas, but they are never "the" problem. Seeing clients as whole persons also means recognizing the multidimensional nature of their lives and the impact of loss and grief across those dimensions. Therefore, effective intervention that takes the whole person into account considers cognitive, emotional, physical, behavioral, spiritual, and social (e.g., ethnicity, gender) aspects of their experience.

Emphasize Resilience

An important element in functional adaptation to loss is the individual's ability to establish resilience, "relatively stable, healthy levels of psychological and physiological functioning" (Bonanno, 2004, p. 20). This does not mean the absence of distress or problems, rather it means adjusting to and negotiating difficulties in a life-affirming way. "Resilience is directional—it points toward living" (Rynearson, 2001, p. 18). Counseling professionals emphasize resilience by helping clients with the following:

+ identify and utilize their own strengths, skills, and abilities
+ uncover evidence of competence from their past and shape that competence to meet the challenges of loss adaptation
+ utilize diverse resources (e.g., support groups, online information, religion, cultural traditions)
+ determine to "act resilient" even when they are not feeling resilient (Rynearson, 2001)
+ develop "hardiness" beliefs: life has meaning and purpose, one can influence outcome and surroundings, and it is possible to learn and grow through negative life experiences such as grief (Bonanno, 2004)
+ embrace a positive view of self
+ formulate an outlook that situates loss and grief in a long-term perspective
+ seek out people and opportunities that generate positive emotions and experiences (e.g., love, laughter, acceptance)

216

Utilize Homework

Purposefully selected and timed homework that reflects thoughtful tailoring of treatment to the uniqueness of the client enhances client progress. Counselors should adapt content and procedures to optimize utility and motivation. It is usually best to provide written instructions and forms. However, make adjustments according to client literacy, preferred language, or relevant disabilities before doing so. By storing homework materials on the computer, the counselor can tailor instructions and documents for specific clients, even including the client's name or the name of the deceased on a homework document. Rather than directing clients to do assignments ("I want you to do this"), a more collaborative approach invites client participation, for example, "I have something that I think might be useful; let me describe it and see what you think." It is often useful to simply ask clients what they could do or think about between sessions that would be beneficial and then turn that into a specific activity.

Always discuss homework assignments, usually early in the session. Failure to do so is disrespectful of clients, undermines confidence in the counselor's competence and goodwill, and impedes progress. If the client and counselor are not interested in the results of a homework assignment, then it probably was a poorly conceived or poorly timed effort. It is best to ask clients to share their responses or read them out loud in the session so as to promote reflection. Do not simply accept an assignment as if it was schoolwork. If clients fail to complete assignments, there is usually a good reason. For example, they did not understand the directions or assignment, they forgot (especially likely when they are not given documents), they are not ready to explore this material, the method is inconsistent with their needs (e.g., keeping a journal for someone who dislikes writing), or they lack confidence in their counselor. It is important that counselors invite clients to discuss any reservations about doing homework and explore ways in which to improve compliance and utility. However, counselors must recognize that specific between-session homework, while a valuable strategy, is not a fit for everyone.

Let Clients Do Their Own Work

Counseling professionals sometimes use practices that actually interfere with clients doing the work that brings about change. One of the most common examples is intruding on silence. This is usually due to the counselor's discomfort with client distress, inexperience, impatience, disregard for the client, or the need to do something instead of being present to the client. Another bad habit is constantly telling clients what they (clients) think and feel instead of encouraging clients to own, identify, and explore their thoughts and feelings. Overusing reflections of content and feeling is most damaging in this regard (e.g., you feel betrayed; you feel . . . because . . . ; you are confused by her reaction). Instead counselors should more often facilitate the work of clients by asking for their thoughts and feelings and encouraging clients to label their own thoughts and feelings. For example: How does that feel? What emotions go with that? What feelings are you aware of right now? What do you think about that? What conclusions do you reach? What does that mean for you? What sense do you make of that? What is underneath that feeling (thought)? Clients who have difficulty identifying and labeling their emotions begin to acquire this skill when they are asked for their feelings rather than told what they are feeling by their counselors.

Making summary reflections more tentative also invites client contribution. For example, instead of "I heard you say . . . ," the counselor can say "I'm not sure I've got this right, but let me tell you what I think you just said." Counselors should also recognize that overusing reflections can actually encourage client avoidance. Many clients learn that if they just wait long enough, the counselor will bail them out of the hard work of self-awareness and exploration by telling them (clients) what they think and feel. It is not that reflections of content and feeling should never be used, but counselors should attend closely to overusing them or using them in a way that undermines client ownership and process.

Another practice that interferes with clients doing their own work involves setting goals for clients rather than collaborating with clients to define their goals. Managed care demands and some psychotherapy models contribute most to this problem. This is a disrespectful practice that ignores the obvious: Clients are more likely to embrace therapy, invest in change, and remain motivated if they set their own goals. Rather than selecting goals and objectives from preapproved "laundry lists," counseling professionals should collaborate with clients in establishing therapeutic goals appropriate to their needs, not the needs of others.

Master the Art of Silence

The single most useful intervention when counseling for loss and grief is silence. Respectful silence is the primary means of bearing witness to stories of loss and grief. Counseling professionals use silence to punctuate salient moments, prompt reflection, and provide support. Therapeutic silence often creates moments of decision for clients, for example, whether or not to go deeper, to hold on or let go, to avoid or confront, to feel or numb feelings, and to fight, flee, or freeze. Silence is not a matter of doing nothing but of creating a space where clients can do something. Counseling professionals who master the art of silence must be self-aware, able to tolerate client distress, patient, respectful of client choices and expertness, and confident in the therapeutic process.

The Person of the Counseling Professional: Know Thyself

Working with clients concerning issues of loss and grief is among the most challenging and rewarding endeavors a counseling professional will ever encounter. Self-knowledge is critical to the work. Counselors must be aware of and able to manage loss and grief concerns in their own lives so that these do not intrude on the client's therapy. One place to start is by critically evaluating one's own experience of loss and grief. Counselors should ask themselves:

+ Am I able to recognize and accept differences between my clients' grief experiences and my own?
+ Am I able to recognize differences in grieving styles and adaptive strategies between my clients and myself and among my clients?
+ Do I recognize and value the uniqueness of each person and his or her experience of loss and grief?
+ Am I aware of any unresolved material or unfinished business from my own loss experiences that might impair my work with grieving clients?
+ Do I attempt to rescue my clients from their grief?
+ Do I avoid certain grief-related issues, topics, or emotions with clients because of my own discomfort?
+ Do I spend so much energy managing or controlling my own emotions that I cannot fully attend to my clients?

- ✦ Do I have difficulty with client terminations because I am uncomfortable with loss?
- ✦ Do I try to save my grieving clients from the pain of grief by avoiding distressful topics?
- ✦ Does the topic of death and dying make me apprehensive or anxious?
- ✦ Is my own loss adaptation process too new or too raw to allow me to work effectively with grieving clients at this time?

It is important that counseling professionals explore their own loss histories to enhance their understanding of the nature and impact of loss and grief in their lives. Every counselor should complete a loss experiences timeline, a systemic genogram focused on loss events, and a loss/grief thematic genogram (refer to Chapter 4). Then ask a trusted professional colleague, your own counselor, or your clinical supervisor to help you explore loss-related material revealed in these activities, especially noting any evidence of unfinished business, avoidance, dissonance, disrupted meaning structures, emotional inhibition, and cognitive maladaptions. Other strategies detailed in this book might also be helpful in increasing self-awareness.

Many counseling professionals who work regularly with clients experiencing loss and grief difficulties find mindfulness practices, especially mindfulness meditation, to be helpful. In addition to the personal benefits (e.g., stress reduction), mindfulness helps the counselor maintain focus and attention more effectively with clients, "being completely present in every thought, spoken word, and movement. If the therapist cannot be mindful, the patient will not feel cared for" (Duran, 2006, p. 46).

Self-care is essential for counseling professionals working with client issues of loss and grief. Counselors must be intentional about engaging in activities that nourish creativity and promote physical and psychological well-being. Counselors should maintain healthy personal and professional relationships, including establishing appropriate boundaries between their personal and professional lives. Spiritual/philosophical practices reflective of life-affirming meaning structures contribute substantially to counselor self-care.

The most important tool the counselor brings to the practice of therapy is herself or himself. Just as working with client loss and grief requires appreciating the uniqueness of clients, counseling professionals must recognize and respect their own uniqueness. "Embrace your strengths and limitations into a unique style that becomes a portrait of oneself as a counselor and as a human being" (Wolfelt, 1998).

References

Adams, K. (1999). Writing as therapy. *Counseling and Human Development, 31*, 1–16.

Adams, K. (2007). *Managing grief through journal writing*. Retrieved March 7, 2007, from http://www.journaltherapy.com/articles/cjtsec08_i.htm

American Psychiatric Association. (2000). *Diagnostic and statistical manual of mental disorders* (4th ed., Text Revision). Washington, DC: Author.

Anderson, H., & Goolishian, H. (1992). The client is the expert: A "not knowing" approach to therapy. In S. McNamee & K. J. Gergen (Eds.), *Therapy as social construction* (pp. 25–39). London: Sage.

Areu, A. (Director). (1993). *Like water for chocolate* [Motion picture]. United States: Miramax Films.

Aros, J. R., Buckingham, P., & Rodriguez, X. (1999). On machismo, grief abreactions, and Mexican culture: The case of Mr. X, the counselor, and the curandera. *Journal of Personal and Interpersonal Loss, 4*, 85–93.

Artlet, T. A., & Thyer, B. A. (1998). Treating chronic grief. In J. S. Wodarsky & B. A. Thyer (Eds.), *Handbook of empirical social work practice* (Vol. 2, pp. 341–356). New York: Wiley.

Attenborough, R. (Director). (1994). *Shadowlands* [Motion picture]. United States: Savoy Pictures.

Attig, T. (1996). *How we grieve: Relearning the world*. New York: Oxford University Press.

Bacigalupe, G. (1996). Writing in therapy: A participatory approach. *Journal of Family Therapy, 18*, 361–373.

Baumeister, R. F. (1994). The crystallization of discontent in the process of major life change. In T. F. Heatherton & J. L. Weinberger (Eds.), *Can personality change?* (pp. 281–294). Washington, DC: American Psychological Association.

Bayne, R., & Thompson, K. (2000). Counsellor response to clients' metaphors: An evaluation and refinement of Strong's model. *Counselling Psychology Quarterly, 13*, 37–49.

Berg, I. K. (1994). *Family-based services: A solution-focused approach*. New York: Norton.

Berg, I. K., & Miller, S. D. (1992). *Working with the problem drinker: A solution-focused approach*. New York: Norton.

Berg, I. K., & Reuss, N. H. (1998). *Solutions step by step: A substance abuse treatment manual*. New York: Norton.

Berg-Cross, L., Jennings, P., & Baruch, R. (1990). Cinematherapy: Theory and application. *Psychotherapy in Private Practice, 8*, 135–156.

Bernard, M., & Wolfe, J. L. (Eds.). (1993). *The RET resource book for practitioners.* New York: Institute for Rational-Emotive Therapy.

Bertolino, R. A., & O'Hanlon, B. (2001). *Collaborative, competency-based counseling and therapy.* Boston: Allyn & Bacon.

Besley, T. (2001). Foucauldian influences in narrative therapy: An approach for schools. *Journal of Educational Inquiry, 2*, 72–93.

Blatner, A. (2005, February 19). *Some principles of grief work.* Retrieved October 20, 2007, from http://www.blatner.com/adam/psyntbk/grief.htm

Boelen, P. A. (2006). Cognitive–behavioral therapy for complicated grief: Theoretical underpinning and case descriptions. *Journal of Loss and Trauma, 11*, 1–30.

Bonanno, G. A. (2001). Grief and emotion: A social-functional perspective. In M. Stroebe, R. O. Hansson, W. Stroebe, & H. Schut (Eds.), *Handbook of bereavement research: Consequences, coping, and care* (pp. 493–515). Washington, DC: American Psychological Association.

Bonanno, G. A. (2004). Loss, trauma, and human resilience: Have we underestimated the human capacity to thrive after extremely aversive events? *American Psychologist, 59*, 20–28.

Bonanno, G. A., & Kaltman, S. (1999). Toward an integrative perspective on bereavement. *Psychological Bulletin, 125*, 760–776.

Bonanno, G. A., Keltner, D., Holen, A., & Horowitz, M. J. (1995). When avoiding unpleasant emotions might not be such a bad thing: Verbal-autonomic response dissociation and midlife conjugal bereavement. *Journal of Personality and Social Psychology, 69*, 975–989.

Bonanno, G. A., Moskowitz, J. T., Papa, A., & Folkman, S. (2005). Resilience to loss in bereaved spouses, bereaved parents, and bereaved gay men. *Journal of Personality and Social Psychology, 88*, 827–843.

Bonanno, G. A., Wortman, C. B., & Nesse, R. M. (2004). Prospective patterns of resilience and maladjustment during widowhood. *Psychology of Aging, 19*, 260–271.

Boss, P. (2001). *Ambiguous loss: Learning to live with unresolved grief.* Cambridge, MA: Harvard University Press.

Boss, P. (2006). *Loss, trauma, and resilience.* New York: Norton.

Bowlby, J. (1969). *Attachment and loss: Vol. 1. Attachment.* New York: Basic Books.

Bowlby, J. (1973). *Attachment and loss: Vol. 2. Separation: Anxiety and anger.* New York: Basic Books.

Bowlby, J. (1980). *Attachment and loss: Vol. 3. Loss: Sadness and depression.* New York: Basic Books.

Braff, Z. (Director). (2004). *Garden state* [Motion picture]. United States: Fox Searchlight Pictures.

Brandsma, J. M. (1982). Forgiveness: A dynamic theological and therapeutic analysis. *Pastoral Psychology, 31*, 40–50.

Brave Heart, M. Y. H., & DeBruyn, L. M. (1998). The American Indian holocaust: Healing historical unresolved grief. *Journal of American Indian and Alaska Native Mental Health Research, 8*(2), 60–82.

Brems, C. (2001). *Basic skills in psychotherapy and counseling.* Belmont, CA: Brooks/Cole.

Burns, D. (1999). *Feeling good: The new mood therapy.* New York: HarperCollins.

Burns, G. W. (1998). *Nature-guided therapy: Brief integrative strategies for health and well-being.* Philadelphia: Brunner/Mazel.

Buzan, T. (1991). *The mind map book.* New York: Penguin.

Calhoun, K. S., & Resick, P. A. (1993). Post-traumatic stress disorder. In D. H. Barlow (Ed.), *Clinical handbook of psychological disorders: A step-by-step treatment manual* (2nd ed., pp. 48–98). New York: Guilford Press.

Calhoun, L., & Tedeschi, R. (2001). The positive lessons of loss. In R. A. Neimeyer (Ed.), *Meaning reconstruction and the experience of loss* (pp. 157–172). Washington, DC: American Psychological Association.

Cameron, J. (2002). *The artist's way: A spiritual path to higher creativity.* New York: Penguin Putnam.

Carlson, T. D. (2000). Using art in narrative therapy: Enhancing therapeutic possibilities. *American Journal of Family Therapy, 25,* 271–283.

Caro, N. (Director). (2002). *Whale rider* [Motion picture]. United States: Newmarket Films.

Carter, B., & McGoldrick, M. (1999). *The expanded family life cycle* (3rd ed.). Boston: Allyn & Bacon.

Cass, V. C. (1979). Homosexual identity formation: A theoretical model. *Journal of Homosexuality, 4,* 219–235.

Castle, J., & Phillips, W. (2002). Grief rituals: Aspects that facilitate adjustment to bereavement. *Journal of Loss and Trauma, 8,* 41–71.

Cheston, S. (2000). A new paradigm for teaching counseling theory and practice. *Counselor Education and Supervision, 39,* 254–269.

Chwalisz, K. (1998). Brain injury: A tapestry of loss. In J. Harvey (Ed.), *Perspectives on loss: A sourcebook* (pp. 189–200). Philadelphia: Taylor & Francis.

Clark, M. (Director). (1988). *Da* [Motion picture]. United States: FilmDallas Pictures.

Collie, K., Backos, A., Malchiodi, C., & Spiegel, D. (2006). Art therapy for combat-related PTSD: Recommendations for research and practice. *Art Therapy: Journal of the American Art Therapy Association, 23,* 157–164.

Columbus, C. (Director). (2001). *Harry Potter and the sorcerer's stone* [Motion picture]. United States: Warner Brothers.

Conarton, S., & Kreger-Silverman, L. (1988). Feminist development through the life cycle. In M. A. Dutton-Douglas & L. E. Walker (Eds.), *Feminist psychotherapies: Integration of therapeutic and feminist systems* (pp. 37–67). Norwood, NJ: Ablex.

Constantine, M. G., Greer, T. M., & Kindaichi, M. M. (2003). Theories of cultural considerations in counseling women of color. In M. Kopala & M. Keitel (Eds.), *Handbook of counseling women* (pp. 40–52). Thousand Oaks, CA: Sage.

Cooke, A. S., & Dworkin, D. S. (1992). *Helping the bereaved: Therapeutic interventions for children, adolescents, and adults.* New York: Basic Books.

Corr, C., & Doka, K. (2001). Master concepts in the field of death, dying, and bereavement: Coping versus adaptive strategies. *Omega, 43,* 183–199.

Cross, W. E. (1971). The Negro-to-Black conversion experience: Toward a psychology of Black liberation. *Black World, 20,* 13–27.

Cross, W. E. (1991). *Shades of Black.* Philadelphia: Temple University Press.

Curry, H. (2000). *The way of the labyrinth: A powerful meditation for everyday life.* New York: Penguin.

Davis, C., & Nolen-Hoeksema, S. (2001). Loss and meaning: How do people make sense of loss? *American Behavioral Scientist, 44,* 726–741.

De Jong, P., & Berg, I. K. (2002). *Interviewing for solutions* (2nd ed.). Pacific Grove, CA: Wadsworth.

de Shazer, S. (1994). *Words were originally magic.* New York: Norton.

Deits, B. (1988). *Life after loss: A personal guide to dealing with death, divorce, job change, and relocation.* Tucson, AZ: Fisher Books.

DeMaria, R., Weeks, G., & Hof, L. (1999). *Focused genograms: Intergenerational assessment of individuals, couples, and families.* Philadelphia: Brunner/Mazel.

Denton, R. T., & Martin, M. W. (1998). Defining forgiveness: An empirical exploration of process and role. *American Journal of Family Therapy, 26,* 281–292.

Dermer, S. B., & Hutchings, J. B. (2000). Utilizing movies in family therapy: Applications for individuals, couples, and families. *American Journal of Family Therapy, 28,* 163–180.

Doka, K. (Ed.) (1989). *Disenfranchised grief: Recognizing hidden sorrow.* Lexington, MA: Lexington Books.

Duran, E. (2006). *Healing the soul wound: Counseling with American Indians and other native peoples.* New York: Teachers College Press.

Ekman, P. (1993). Facial expression and emotion. *American Psychologist, 48,* 384–392.

Ellis, A. (1986). Discomfort anxiety: A new cognitive behavioral construct. In A. Ellis & R. Grieger (Eds.), *Handbook of rational emotive therapy* (Vol. 2, pp. 105–120). New York: Springer.

Ellis, A. (1994). *Reason and emotion in psychotherapy: A comprehensive method of treating human disturbances* (Rev. ed.). New York: Birch Lane.

Ephron, N. (Director). (1993). *Sleepless in Seattle* [Motion picture]. United States: TriStar Pictures.

Epston, D., White, M., & Murray, K. (1992). A proposal for re-authoring therapy: Rose's revisioning of her life and a commentary. In S. McNamee & K. J. Gergen (Eds.), *Therapy as social construction* (pp. 96–115). London: Sage.

Evans, N. J., Forney, D. S., & Guido-DiBrito, F. (1998). *Student development in college.* San Francisco: Jossey-Bass.

Exline, J. J., Dority, K., & Wortman, C. B. (1996). Coping with bereavement: A research review for clinicians. *In Session: Psychotherapy in Practice, 2*(4), 3–19.

Eyre, C. (Director). (1998). *Smoke signals* [Motion picture]. United States: Miramax Films.

Eyre, R. (Director). (2001). *Iris* [Motion picture]. United States: Miramax Films.

Feinstein, D., & Mayo, P. (1990). *Rituals for living and dying: How we can turn loss and the fear of death into an affirmation of life.* San Francisco: HarperSanFrancisco.

Field, N. P., Nichols, C., Holen, A., & Horowitz, M. J. (1999). The relation of continuing attachment to adjustment in conjugal bereavement. *Journal of Consulting and Clinical Psychology, 67,* 212–218.

Field, T. (Director). (2001). *In the bedroom* [Motion picture]. United States: Miramax Films.

Folkman, S. (2001). Revised coping theory and the process of bereavement. In M. S. Stroebe, R. O. Hansson, W. Stroebe, & H. Schut (Eds.), *Handbook of bereavement research: Consequences, coping, and care* (pp. 563–584). Washington, DC: American Psychological Association.

Foote, C., & Frank, A. (1999). Foucault and therapy: The discipline of grief. In A. Chambon, A. Irving, & L. Epstein (Eds.), *Reading Foucault for social work* (pp. 157–187). New York: Columbia University Press.

Fowler, J. W. (1981). *Stages of faith.* New York: Harper & Row.

Fowler, J. W. (1991). Stages in faith consciousness. *New Directions for Child Development, 52,* 27–45.

Frame, M. W. (2001). The spiritual genogram in training and supervision. *The Family Journal, 9,* 109–115.

Frame, M. W. (2003). *Integrating religion and spirituality into counseling: A comprehensive approach.* Pacific Grove, CA: Brooks/Cole-Thomson Learning.

Frank, J. D., & Frank, J. B. (1991). *Persuasion and healing: A comparative study of psychotherapy* (3rd ed.). Baltimore: Johns Hopkins University Press.

Frantz, T. T., Farrell, M. M., & Trolley, B. C. (2001). Positive outcomes of losing a loved one. In R. A. Neimeyer (Ed.), *Meaning reconstruction and the experience of loss* (pp. 191–209). Washington, DC: American Psychological Association.

Freedman, J., & Combs, G. (1996). *Narrative therapy: The social construction of preferred realities.* New York: Norton.

Freeman, A., Pretzer, J., Fleming, B., & Simon, K. M. (1990). *Clinical applications of cognitive therapy.* New York: Plenum.

Freeman, J., Epston, D., & Lobovits, D. (1997). *Playful approaches to serious problems: Narrative therapy with children and their families.* New York: Norton.

Gendlin, E. T. (1981). *Focusing* (2nd ed.). New York: Bantam Books.

Genia, V. (1995). *Counseling and psychotherapy of religious clients: A developmental approach.* Westport, CT: Praeger.

Gilbert, K. (1996). "We've had the same loss, why don't we have the same grief?" Loss and differential grief in families. *Death Studies, 20,* 269–283.

Gilbert, K., & Smart, L. (1992). *Coping with fetal or infant loss: The couple's healing process.* New York: Brunner/Mazel.

Gillies, J., & Neimeyer, R. A. (2006). Loss, grief, and the search for significance: Toward a model of meaning reconstruction in bereavement. *Journal of Constructivist Psychology, 19,* 31–65.

Gilligan, C. (1991). Women's psychological development: Implications for psychocounseling. In C. Gilligan, A. G. Rogers, & D. L. Tolman (Eds.), *Women, girls and psychocounseling: Reframing resistance* (pp. 5–32). New York: Haworth Press.

Gilligan, C. (1993). *In a different voice: Psychological theory and women's development.* Cambridge, MA: Harvard University Press. (Original work published 1982)

Gladding, S. T. (1992). *Counseling as an art: The creative arts in counseling* (2nd ed.). Alexandria, VA: American Counseling Association.

Gladding, S. T. (2005). *Counseling as an art: The creative arts in counseling* (3rd ed.). Alexandria, VA: American Counseling Association.

Glass, R. M. (2005). Is grief a disease? Sometimes. *Journal of the American Medical Association, 293,* 2658–2660.

Grant, S. (Director). (2007). *Catch and release* [Motion picture]. United States: Sony Pictures Entertainment.

Gray, S. W., Zide, M. R., & Wilker, H. (2000). Using the solution-focused brief therapy model with bereavement groups in rural communities: Resiliency at its best. *Hospice Journal, 15*(3), 13–30.

Greenberg, L. S., Rice, L. N., & Elliott, R. (1993). *Facilitating emotional change: The moment-by-moment process*. New York: Guilford Press.

Greenberg, L. S., & Safran, J. D. (1988). *Emotion in psychotherapy*. New York: Guilford Press.

Greenberger, D., & Padesky, C. (1995). *Mind over mood: Change how you feel by changing the way you think*. New York: Guilford Press.

Greenspan, M. (2003). *Healing through the dark emotions: The wisdom of grief, fear, and despair*. Boston: Shambhala.

Hallstrom, L. (2005). *An unfinished life* [Motion picture]. United States: Miramax Films.

Hamilton, N. A., Kitzman, H., & Guyotte, S. (2006). Enhancing health and emotion: Mindfulness as a missing link between cognitive therapy and positive psychology. *Journal of Cognitive Psychotherapy: An International Quarterly, 20*, 123–134.

Hardy, K., & Laszloffy, T. A. (1995). The cultural genogram: Key to training culturally competent family therapists. *Journal of Marital and Family Therapy, 21*, 227–237.

Harris, N. (2008). *Effective, short-term therapy utilizing finger labyrinths to promote brain synchrony*. Retrieved April 16, 2008, from http://www.relax4life.com/articles.html

Harvey, J. (Ed.). (1998). *Perspectives on loss: A sourcebook*. Philadelphia: Taylor & Francis.

Hayes, S. C. (2004). Acceptance and commitment therapy and the new behavior therapies: Mindfulness, acceptance, and relationship. In S. C. Hayes, V. M. Follette, & M. M. Linehan (Eds.), *Mindfulness and acceptance: Expanding the cognitive–behavioral tradition* (pp. 1–29). New York: Guilford Press.

Hayes, S. C., Follette, V. M., & Linehan, M. M. (Eds.). (2004). *Mindfulness and acceptance: Expanding the cognitive–behavioral tradition*. New York: Guilford Press.

Helms, J. E. (1990). Toward a theoretical model of the effects of race on counseling: A Black and White model. *Counseling Psychologist, 12*, 153–165.

Hensley, J. W., & Hensley, J. G. (1998). *Rent two films and let's talk in the morning: Using popular movies in psychotherapy*. New York: Wiley.

Hensley, J. W., & Hensley, J. G. (2001). *Rent two films and let's talk in the morning: Using popular movies in psychotherapy* (2nd ed.). New York: Wiley.

Hodge, D. (2001). Spiritual genograms: A generational approach to accessing spirituality. *Families in Society, 82*(1), 35–48.

Holland, J. L. (1992). *Making vocational choices: A theory of vocational personalities and work environments* (2nd ed.). Odessa, FL: Psychological Assessment Resources. (Original work published 1985)

Humphrey, K. (1993). Grief counseling training in counselor preparation programs in the United States: A preliminary report. *International Journal for the Advancement of Counselling, 16*, 333–340.

Huxter, M. (2006). *Grief and the mindfulness approach: Death, dying, and bereavement*. Retrieved July 22, 2006, from http://www.buddahnet.net/psygrief.html

Ingram, C., & Perlesz, A. (2004). The getting of wisdoms. *International Journal of Narrative Therapy and Community Work, 2*, 49–56.

Irwin, H. J. (1991). The depiction of loss: Uses of clients' drawings in bereavement counseling. *Death Studies, 15*, 481–497.

James, J. W., & Cherry, F. (1988). *The grief recovery handbook*. New York: Harper & Row.

Janoff-Bulman, R. (1992). *Shattered assumptions: Towards a new psychology of trauma*. New York: Free Press.

Janson, M. A. H. (1985). The prescription to grieve. *The Hospice Journal, 1,* 103–109.

Joy, S. S. (1985). Abortion: An issue to grieve? *Journal of Counseling & Development, 63,* 375–376.

Kabat-Zinn, J. (1990). *Full catastrophe living: Using the wisdom of your body and mind to face stress, pain, and illness.* New York: Delacorte.

Kabat-Zinn, J. (1994). *Wherever you go, there you are: Mindfulness meditation in everyday life.* New York: Hyperion.

Kabat-Zinn, J., Lipworth, L., & Burney, R. (1985). The clinical use of mindfulness meditation for the self-regulation of chronic pain. *Journal of Behavioral Medicine, 8,* 163–188.

Kabat-Zinn, J., Massion, A., Kristeller, J., Peterson, L. G., Fletcher, K., Pbert, L., et al. (1992). Effectiveness of a meditation-based stress reduction program in the treatment of anxiety disorders. *American Journal of Psychiatry, 149,* 936–943.

Kampfe, C. (2003, March). *Parallels between creative dance and creative counseling.* Paper presented at the annual convention of the American Counseling Association, Anaheim, CA.

Kaslow, F. (1995). *Projective genogramming.* Sarasota, FL: Professional Resource Press.

Kastenbaum, R. (1969). Death and bereavement in later life. In A. H. Kutscher (Eds.), *Death and bereavement in later life* (pp. 27–54). Springfield, IL: Charles C Thomas.

Kennedy, A. (2006, February). Tribal training: Inupiat Eskimo counselor helps to bridge the multicultural gap. *Counseling Today,* 8–9.

Kennedy, A. (2007, August). A mindful maze. *Counseling Today,* 12–13.

Kissane, D. W., & Bloch, S. (2002). *Family focused grief therapy.* Philadelphia: Open University Press.

Klass, D. (1999). *The spiritual lives of bereaved parents.* Philadelphia: Taylor & Francis.

Klass, D., Silverman, P., & Nickman, S. (Eds.). (1996). *Continuing bonds: New understandings of grief.* Washington, DC: Taylor & Francis.

Kohlberg, L., & Hersh, R. H. (1977). Moral development: A review of the theory. *Theory Into Practice, 16,* 53–59.

Kopp, R. R. (1995). *Metaphor therapy: Using client-generated metaphors in psychotherapy.* New York: Brunner/Mazel.

Kramer, L. (Director). (2004). *The five people you meet in heaven* [Motion picture]. United States: American Broadcasting Company.

Kubler-Ross, E. (1969). *On death and dying.* New York: Macmillan.

Kuehl, B. P. (1995). The solution-oriented genogram: A collaborative approach. *Journal of Marital and Family Therapy, 21,* 239–250.

Kumar, S. (2005). *Grieving mindfully: A compassionate and spiritual guide to coping with loss.* Oakland, CA: New Harbinger.

Lafond, V. (1994). *Grieving mental illness: A guide for patients and their caregivers.* Toronto, Ontario, Canada: University of Toronto Press.

Lampropoulos, G., Kazantzis, N., & Deane, F. P. (2004). Psychologists' use of motion pictures in clinical practice. *Professional Psychology: Research and Practice, 35,* 535–541.

Lattanzi, M., & Hale, M. E. (1984). Giving grief words: Writing during bereavement. *Omega, 15*(1), 45–52.

Lazarus, A. A., & Beutler, L. E. (1993). On technical eclecticism. *Journal of Counseling & Development, 71,* 381–385.

Leahy, R. L., & Holland, S. J. (2000). *Treatment plans and interventions for depression and anxiety disorders.* New York: Guilford Press.

Linehan, M. M. (1993a). *Cognitive–behavioral treatment of borderline personality disorder.* New York: Guilford Press.

Linehan, M. M. (1993b). *Skills training manual for treating borderline personality disorder.* New York: Guilford Press.

Lipchik, E. (2000). *Beyond technique in solution-focused therapy: Working with emotions and the therapeutic relationship.* New York: Guilford Press.

Litz, B. T. (2004). *Early intervention for trauma and traumatic loss.* New York: Guilford Press.

Louiso, T. (Director). (2002). *Love Liza* [Motion picture]. United States: Sony Pictures Classics.

Lyddon, W. J., Clay, A. L., & Sparks, C. L. (2001). Metaphor and change in counseling. *Journal of Counseling & Development, 79,* 269–274.

Magnuson, S., & Shaw, H. E. (2003). Adaptations of the multifaceted genogram in counseling, training, and supervision. *The Family Journal, 11,* 45–54.

Mahoney, M. J. (1993). Introduction to special section: Theoretical developments in cognitive psychotherapies. *Journal of Consulting and Clinical Psychology, 61,* 187–193.

Malcolm, W. M., & Greenberg, L. S. (2000). Forgiveness as a process of change in individual psychotherapy. In M. McCullough, K. Pargament, & C. Thoresen (Eds.), *Forgiveness: Theory, research, and practice* (pp. 179–202). New York: Guilford Press.

Malkinson, R. (1996). Cognitive behavioral grief therapy. *Journal of Rational-Emotive and Cognitive–Behavioral Therapy, 14,* 155–171.

Malkinson, R. (2007). *Cognitive grief therapy: Constructing a rational meaning to life following loss.* New York: Norton.

Malkinson, R., & Rubin, S. S. (2007). The two-track model of bereavement: A balanced model. In R. Malkinson (Ed.), *Cognitive grief therapy: Constructing a rational meaning to life following loss* (pp. 23–43). New York: Norton.

Mandoki, L. (Director). (1999). *Message in a bottle* [Motion picture]. United States: Warner Brothers Pictures.

Margulies, N. (2002). *Mapping inner space: Learning and teaching visual mapping.* Tucson, AZ: Zephyr Press.

Marlatt, G. A., Witkiewitz, K., Dillworth, T. M., Bowen, S. W., Parks, G. A., Macpherson, L. M., et al. (2004). Vipassana meditation as a treatment for alcohol and drug use disorders. In S. C. Hayes, V. M. Follette, & M. M. Linehan (Eds.), *Mindfulness and acceptance: Expanding the cognitive–behavioral tradition* (pp. 261–287). New York: Guilford Press.

Martin, T., & Doka, K. (2000). *Men don't cry . . . Women do: Transcending gender stereotypes of grief.* Philadelphia: Brunner/Mazel.

Martin, T., & Wang, W. (2006). A pilot study of the development of a tool for measuring instrumental and intuitive styles of grieving. *Omega, 53,* 263–276.

McGoldrick, M., Gerson, R., & Shellenberger, S. (1999). *Genograms: Assessment and intervention* (2nd ed.). New York: Norton.

McKenzie, W., & Monk, G. (1997). Learning and teaching narrative ideas. In G. Monk, J. Winslade, K. Crocket, & D. Epston (Eds.), *Narrative therapy in practice: The archeology of hope* (pp. 82–117). San Francisco: Jossey-Bass.

McNeilly, R. B. (2000). *Healing the whole person: A solution-focused approach to using empowering language, emotions, and actions in therapy.* New York: Wiley.

Michell, R. (Director). (2002). *Changing lanes* [Motion picture]. United States: Paramount Pictures.

Miller, W. R., & Rollnick, S. (1991). *Motivational interviewing: Preparing people to change addictive behavior.* New York: Guilford Press.

Miller, W. R., & Rollnick, S. (2002). *Motivational interviewing: Preparing people for change* (2nd ed.). New York: Guilford Press.

Mills, N., & Allen, J. (2000). Mindfulness of movement as a coping strategy in multiple sclerosis: A pilot study. *General Hospital Psychiatry, 22,* 425–431.

Monk, G. (1997). How narrative therapy works. In G. Monk, J. Winslade, K. Crocket, & D. Epston (Eds.), *Narrative therapy in practice: The archeology of hope* (pp. 121–157). San Francisco: Jossey-Bass.

Monk, G., Winslade, J., Crocket, K., & Epston, D. (Eds.). (1997). *Narrative therapy in practice: The archeology of hope.* San Francisco: Jossey-Bass.

Mooney, K. A., & Padesky, C. A. (2000). Applying client creativity to recurrent problems: Constructing possibilities and tolerating doubt. *Journal of Cognitive Psychotherapy: An International Quarterly, 14,* 149–161.

Moos, R. H., & Schaefer, J. A. (1986). Life transitions and crises: A conceptual overview. In R. H. Moos (Ed.), *Coping with life crises: An integrated approach* (pp. 3–28). New York: Plenum Press.

Moretti, N. (Director). (2001). *The son's room* [Motion picture]. United States: Miramax Films.

Morgan, A. (2000). *What is narrative therapy? An easy-to-read introduction.* Adelaide, South Australia, Australia: Dulwich Centre Publications.

Murray, J. (2001). Loss as a universal concept. A review of the literature to identify common aspects of loss in adverse situations. *Journal of Loss and Trauma, 6,* 219–241.

Murray, M. A. (2002). Passing notes: The use of therapeutic letter writing in counseling adolescents. *Journal of Mental Health Counseling, 24,* 166–176.

Nagel, J. K. (1988). Unresolved grief and mourning in Navajo women. *American Indian and Alaska Native Mental Health Research, 2*(2), 32–40.

National Board of Certified Counselors. (2007). *The practice of Internet counseling.* Retrieved June 1, 2008, from http://www.nbcc.org/webethics2

Neimeyer, G. J., & Neimeyer, R. A. (1994). Constructivist methods of marital and family therapy: A practical précis. *Journal of Mental Health Counseling, 16,* 85–104.

Neimeyer, R. A. (1997). Meaning reconstruction and the experience of chronic loss. In K. J. Doka & J. Davidson (Eds.), *Living with grief when illness is prolonged* (pp. 159–176). Washington, DC: Hospice Foundation of America.

Neimeyer, R. A. (1998). Can there be a psychology of loss? In J. H. Harvey (Ed.), *Perspectives on loss: A sourcebook* (pp. 331–341). Philadelphia: Taylor & Francis.

Neimeyer, R. A. (1999). Narrative strategies in grief therapy. *Journal of Constructivist Psychology, 12,* 65–85.

Neimeyer, R. A. (2000a). *Lessons of loss: A guide to coping.* Memphis, TN: Center for the Study of Loss and Transition.

Neimeyer, R. A. (2000b). Searching for the meaning of meaning: Grief therapy and the process of reconstruction. *Death Studies, 24,* 541–558.

Neimeyer, R. A. (2001a). The language of loss: Grief therapy as a process of meaning reconstruction. In R. A. Neimeyer (Ed.), *Meaning reconstruction and the experience of loss* (pp. 261–292). Washington, DC: American Psychological Association.

Neimeyer, R. A. (Ed.). (2001b). *Meaning reconstruction and the experience of loss*. Washington, DC: American Psychological Association.

Neimeyer, R. A., Holland, J. M., Currier, J. M., & Mehta, T. (2007). Meaning reconstruction in later life: Toward a cognitive-constructivist approach to grief therapy. In D. Gallagher-Thompson, A. M. Steffen, & L. W. Thompson (Eds.), *Handbook of behavioral and cognitive therapies with older adults* (pp. 264–277). New York: Springer.

Neimeyer, R. A., Prigerson, H. G., & Davies, B. (2002). Mourning and meaning. *American Behavioral Scientist, 46*, 235–251.

Nelson, J. (Director). (1994). *Corrina, Corrina* [Motion picture]. United States: New Line Cinema.

Nolen-Hoeksema, S., Parker, L. E., & Larson, J. (1994). Ruminative coping with depressed mood following loss. *Journal of Personality and Social Psychology, 67*, 92–104.

O'Connor, M., Nikoletti, S., Kristjanson, L. J., Loh, R., & Willcock, B. (2003). Writing therapy for the bereaved: Evaluation of an intervention. *Journal of Palliative Medicine, 6*, 195–204.

O'Hanlon, B. (2006). *Frequently asked questions about possibility therapy.* Retrieved May 29, 2006, from http://secure.webvalence.com/williamohanlon/brieftherapy/faq/whatis.htm

O'Hanlon, B., & Weiner-Davis, M. (2003). *In search of solutions: A new direction in psychotherapy* (Rev. ed.). New York: Norton.

Ortiz, A., Simmons, J., & Hinton, W. L. (1999). Locations of remorse and homelands of resilience: Notes on grief and sense of loss of place of Latino and Irish-American caregivers of demented elders. *Culture, Medicine, and Psychiatry, 23*, 477–500.

Oser, F. K. (1991). The development of religious judgment. In F. K. Oser & W. G. Scarlett (Eds.), *Religious development in childhood and adolescence* (pp. 5–25). San Francisco: Jossey-Bass.

Ossana, S. M., Helms, J. E., & Leonard, M. M. (1992). Do "womanist" identity attitudes influence college women's self-esteem and perceptions of environmental bias? *Journal of Counseling & Development, 70*, 402–408.

Padesky, C. A., & Greenberger, D. (1995). *Clinician's guide to mind over mood.* New York: Guilford Press.

Parker, R., & Horton, H. S. (1996). The typology of ritual: Paradigms for healing and empowerment. *Counseling and Values, 40*, 82–97.

Parker, R., & Horton, H. S. (1997). Sarah's story: Using ritual therapy to address psychospiritual issues in treating survivors of childhood sexual abuse. *Counseling and Values, 42*, 41–55.

Parkes, C. M. (1971). Psycho-social transition: A field of study. *Social Science and Medicine, 5*, 101–115.

Parkes, C. M. (1972). *Bereavement: Studies of grief in adult life.* New York: International Universities Press.

Parry, A. (1991). A universe of stories. *Family Process, 30*, 37–54.

Payne, M. (2006). *Narrative therapy: An introduction for counsellors* (2nd ed.). London: Sage.

Payne, S., Jarrett, N., Wiles, R., & Field, D. (2002). Counselling strategies for bereaved people offered in primary care. *Counselling Psychology Quarterly, 15*, 161–177.

Peel, J. M. (2004). The labyrinth: An innovative therapeutic tool for problem solving or achieving mental focus. *The Family Journal, 12,* 287–291.

Phinney, J. (1989). Stages of ethnic identity development in minority group adolescents. *Journal of Early Adolescence, 9,* 34–49.

Porterfield, K. M. (2002). *Journaling the bereavement journey.* Retrieved March, 6, 2007, from http://www.kporterfield.com

Powers, R. L., & Griffith, J. (1987). *Understanding life-style: The psycho-clarity process.* Chicago: Americas Institute of Adlerian Studies.

Prigerson, H. G., Shear, M. K., Jacobs, S. C., Reynolds, C. F., Maciejewski, P. K., Davidson, J., et al. (1999). Consensus criteria for traumatic grief. *British Journal of Psychiatry, 174,* 67–73.

Prochaska, J. O., DiClemente, C. C., & Norcross, J. C. (1992). In search of how people change. *American Psychologist, 47,* 1102–1114.

Prochaska, J. O., & Norcross, J. C. (1999). *Systems of psychotherapy: A transtheoretical analysis.* Pacific Grove, CA: Brooks/Cole.

Rando, T. A. (1984). *Grief, dying, and death: Clinical interventions for caregivers.* Champaign, IL: Research Press.

Rando, T. A. (1993). *Treatment of complicated mourning.* Champaign, IL: Research Press.

Rando, T. A. (2000). Foreword. In T. Martin & K. Doka, *Men don't cry . . . women do: Transcending gender stereotypes of grief* (pp. xi–xiv). Philadelphia: Brunner/Mazell.

Raymer, M., & McIntyre, B. B. (1987). An art support group for bereaved children and adolescents. *Art Therapy, 4,* 27–35.

Redford, R. (Director). (1980). *Ordinary people* [Motion picture]. United States: Paramount Pictures.

Redford, R. (Director). (1998). *The horse whisperer* [Motion picture]. United States: Buena Vista Pictures.

Reik, T. (1972). *Listening with the third ear.* New York: Arena.

Riches, G., & Dawson, P. (1998). Lost children, living memories: The role of photographs in processes of grief and adjustment among bereaved parents. *Death Studies, 22,* 121–140.

Riches, G., & Dawson, P. (2000). *An intimate loneliness: Supporting bereaved parents and siblings.* Philadelphia: Open University Press.

Riordan, R. J. (1996). Scriptotherapy: Therapeutic writing as a counseling adjunct. *Journal of Counseling & Development, 74,* 263–269.

Rollins, J. (2008, February). A matter of trust. *Counseling Today, 1,* 36–37.

Rollnick, S., & Miller, W. R. (1995). What is motivational interviewing? *Behavioral and Cognitive Psychotherapy, 23,* 325–334.

Romanoff, B., & Terenzio, M. (1998). Rituals and the grieving process. *Death Studies, 22,* 697–711.

Romig, C. A., & Gruenke, C. (1991). The use of metaphor to overcome inmate resistance to mental health counseling. *Journal of Counseling & Development, 69,* 414–418.

Rosenblatt, P. C. (1988). Grief: The social context of private feelings. *Journal of Social Issues, 44*(3), 67–78.

Rubin, B. J. (Director). (1993). *My life* [Motion picture]. United States: Columbia Pictures.

Rynearson, E. K. (2001). *Retelling violent death.* Philadelphia: Brunner-Routledge.

Sagula, D., & Rice, K. G. (2004). The effectiveness of mindfulness training on the grieving process and emotional well-being of chronic pain patients. *Journal of Clinical Psychology in Medical Settings, 11,* 333–342.

Salovey, P., Bedell, B. T., Detweiler, J. B., & Mayer, J. D. (1999). Coping intelligently: Emotional intelligence and the coping process. In C. R. Snyder (Ed.), *Coping: The psychology of what works* (pp. 141–164). New York: Oxford University Press.

Sanders, C. (1989). *Grief: The mourning after*. New York: Wiley.

Scheer, J. (2003). *The Internet encyclopedia of personal construct psychology*. Retrieved June 1, 2008, from http://www.pcp-net.org/encyclopaedia/const-psther.html

Scheff, T. (1977). The distancing of emotion in ritual. *Current Anthropology, 18,* 483–490.

Schlossberg, N. K., Waters, E. B., & Goodman, U. (1995). *Counseling adults in transition: Linking practice with theory* (2nd ed.). New York: Springer.

Seligman, L. (2004). *Technical and conceptual skills for mental health professionals*. Upper Saddle River, NJ: Pearson.

Sharp, C., Smith, J. V., & Cole, A. (2002). Cinematherapy: Metaphorically promoting therapeutic change. *Counselling Psychology Quarterly, 15,* 269–276.

Sheridan, J. (Director). (2002). *In America* [Motion picture]. United States: Fox Searchlight Pictures.

Sheskin, A., & Wallace, S. (1976). Differing bereavements: Suicide, natural, and accidental death. *Omega, 7,* 229–242.

Silbering, B. (Director). (2002). *Moonlight mile* [Motion picture]. United States: Buena Vista Pictures.

Sims, P. (2003). Working with metaphor. *Journal of Psychotherapy, 37,* 528–536.

Smith, E. W. L. (1985). A Gestalt therapist's perspective on grief. In E. M. Stern (Ed.), *Psychotherapy and the grieving patient* (pp. 65–78). New York: Harrington Park Press.

Smith, J. C. (2005). *Relaxation, meditation, and mindfulness*. New York: Springer.

Spielberg, S. (Director). (1985). *The color purple* [Motion picture]. Los Angeles: Warner Brothers Pictures.

Spielberg, S. (Director). (1989). *Always* [Motion picture]. United States: United Artists.

Sprecher, J. (Director). (2001). *Thirteen conversations about one thing* [Motion picture]. United States: Sony Pictures Classics.

Stamm, B. H., Stamm, H. E., Hudnall, A. C., & Higson-Smith, C. (2003). Considering a theory of cultural trauma and loss. *Journal of Loss and Trauma, 9,* 89–111.

Stroebe, M., Gergen, M., Gergen, K., & Stroebe, W. (1996). Broken hearts or broken bonds? In D. Klass, P. Silverman, & S. Nickman (Eds.), *Continuing bonds: New understandings of grief* (pp. 31–43). Washington, DC: Taylor & Francis.

Stroebe, M., & Schut, H. (1999). The dual process model of coping with bereavement: Rationale and description. *Death Studies, 23,* 197–224.

Stroebe, M., & Schut, H. (2001a). Meaning making in the dual process model of coping with bereavement. In R. A. Neimeyer (Ed.), *Meaning reconstruction and the experience of loss* (pp. 55–69). Washington, DC: American Psychological Association.

Stroebe, M., & Schut, H. (2001b). Models of coping with bereavement: A review. In M. S. Stroebe, R. O. Hansson, W. Stroebe, & H. Schut (Eds.), *Handbook of bereavement research: Consequences, coping, and care* (pp. 375–429). Washington, DC: American Psychological Association.

Stroebe, M., Schut, H., & Stroebe, W. (1998). Trauma and grief: A comparative analysis. In J. Harvey (Ed.), *Perspectives on loss: A sourcebook* (pp. 81–96). Philadelphia: Taylor & Francis.

Stroebe, M., Schut, H., & Stroebe, W. (2005). Attachment in coping with bereavement: A theoretical integration. *Review of General Psychology, 9,* 48–66.

Stroebe, M., & Stroebe, W. (1991). Does "grief work" work? *Journal of Consulting and Clinical Psychology, 59,* 479–492.

Stroebe, M., van Vliet, T., Hewstone, M., & Willis, H. (2002). Homesickness among students in two cultures: Antecedents and consequences. *British Journal of Psychology, 93,* 147–168.

Sue, D. W., & Sue, D. (1990). *Counseling the culturally different: Theory and practice.* New York: Wiley.

Sued, E., & Amunategui, B. (2003). A Mexican perspective on teaching narrative ideas. *International Journal of Narrative Therapy and Community Work, 4,* 42–44.

Super, D. E. (1985). Validating a model and a method. *Contemporary Psychology, 30,* 771.

Teasdale, J., Segal, Z., Williams, J., Ridgeway, V., Soulsby, J., & Lau, M. (2000). Prevention of relapse/recurrence in major depression by mindfulness-based cognitive therapy. *Journal of Consulting and Clinical Psychology, 68,* 615–623.

Tedeschi, R., Park, C., & Calhoun, L. (Eds.). (1998). *Posttraumatic growth: Positive changes in the aftermath of crisis.* Mahwah, NJ: Erlbaum.

Teyber, E. (1997). *Interpersonal process in therapy: A relational approach* (3rd ed.). Belmont, CA: Brooks/Cole.

Thomason, T. C. (1991). Counseling Native Americans: An introduction for non-native American counselors. *Journal of Counseling & Development, 69,* 321–327.

Tillman, G. (Director). (1997). *Soul food* [Motion picture]. United States: Twentieth Century-Fox Film Group.

Troiden, R. R. (1989). The formation of homosexual identities. *Journal of Homosexuality, 17,* 43–73.

Ullrich, P. M., & Lutgendorf, S. K. (2002). Journaling about stressful events: Effects of cognitive processing and emotional expression. *Annals of Behavioral Medicine, 24,* 244–251.

Van der Hart, O. (1983). *Rituals in psychotherapy.* New York: Irvington.

Van der Hart, O. (1988). (Ed.). *Coping with loss: The therapeutic use of leave-taking rituals.* New York: Irvington.

Viorst, J. (1986). *Necessary losses.* New York: Ballantine Books

Volkan, V. (1972). The linking objects of pathological mourners. *Archives of General Psychiatry, 17,* 215–221.

Volkan, V. (1981). *Linking objects and linking phenomena.* New York: International Universities Press.

Wagner, B., Knaevelsrud, C., & Maercker, A. (2006). Internet-based cognitive–behavioral therapy for complicated grief: A randomized controlled trial. *Death Studies, 30,* 429–453.

Walter, T. (2005). What is complicated grief? A social constructionist perspective. *Omega, 52,* 71–79.

Washburn, M. (1988). *The ego and the dynamic ground.* Albany: State University of New York Press.

Washington, D. (Director). (2002). *Antwone Fisher* [Motion picture]. United States: Fox Searchlight Pictures.

Webb, W. (1999). *Solutioning: Solution-focused interventions for counselors.* Philadelphia: Accelerated Development.

Weiser, J. (1999). *PhotoTherapy techniques: Exploring the secrets of personal snapshots and family albums* (2nd ed.). Vancouver, British Columbia, Canada: PhotoTherapy Centre.

Weiss, R. S. (1998). Issues in the study of loss and grief. In J. Harvey (Ed.), *Perspectives on loss: A sourcebook* (pp. 343–352). Philadelphia: Brunner/Mazel.

White, M. (1989). *Selected papers*. Adelaide, South Australia, Australia: Dulwich Centre Publications.

White, M. (1995). *Re-authoring lives: Interviews and essays*. Adelaide, South Australia: Dulwich Centre Publications.

White, M. (1997). *Narratives of therapist's lives*. Adelaide, South Australia: Dulwich Centre Publications.

White, M. (2004). Working with people who are suffering the consequences of multiple trauma. *International Journal of Narrative Therapy and Community Work, 1*, 45–76.

White, M. (2006). Working with people who are suffering from the consequences of multiple trauma: A narrative perspective. In D. Denborough (Ed.), *Trauma: Narrative responses to traumatic experiences* (pp. 25–86). Adelaide, South Australia, Australia: Dulwich Centre Publications.

White, M., & Epston, D. (1990). *Narrative means to therapeutic ends*. New York: Norton.

Winek, J. L., & Craven, P. A. (2003). Healing rituals for couples recovering from adultery. *Contemporary Family Therapy, 25*, 249–266.

Winkler, I. (Director). (2001). *Life as a house* [Motion picture]. United States: New Line Cinema.

Winslade, J., & Monk, G. (1999). *Narrative counseling in schools: Powerful and brief*. Thousand Oaks, CA: Corwin Press.

Winslade, J., & Smith, L. (1997). Countering alcoholic narratives. In G. Monk, J. Winslade, K. Crocket, & D. Epston (Eds.), *Narrative therapy in practice: The archeology of hope* (pp. 158–192). San Francisco: Jossey-Bass.

Wolfelt, A. D. (1998, March). *Companioning vs. treating: Beyond the medical model of bereavement caregiving*. Keynote address given at the annual conference of the Association for Death Education and Counseling, Chicago, IL.

Worden, J. W. (1982). *Grief counseling and grief therapy: A handbook for the mental health professional*. New York: Springer.

Worden, J. W. (1991). *Grief counseling and grief therapy: A handbook for the mental health professional* (2nd ed.). New York: Springer.

Worden, J. W. (2002). *Grief counseling and grief therapy: A handbook for the mental health practitioner* (3rd ed.). New York: Springer.

Wortman, C., & Silver, R. (1989). The myths of coping with loss. *Journal of Consulting and Clinical Psychology, 57*, 349–357.

Wortman, C., & Silver, R. (2001). The myths of coping with loss revisited. In M. Stroebe, R. O. Hansson, W. Stroebe, & H. Schut (Eds.), *Handbook of bereavement research: Consequences, coping, and care* (pp. 405–429). Washington, DC: American Psychological Association.

Wright, J., & Chung, M. C. (2001). Mastery or mystery? Therapeutic writing: A review of the literature. *British Journal of Guidance and Counselling, 29*, 278–291.

Young, J. E., Beck, A. T., & Weinberger, A. (1993). Depression. In D. H. Barlow (Ed.), *Clinical handbook of psychological disorders* (2nd ed., pp. 240–277). New York: Guilford Press.

Young, M. E. (2001). *Learning the art of helping: Building blocks and techniques.* Upper Saddle River, NJ: Merrill Prentice Hall.

Zaks, J. (Director). (1999). *Marvin's room.* [Motion picture]. United States: Miramax Films.

Zemeckis, R. (Director). (1994). *Cast away* [Motion picture]. United States: Twentieth Century-Fox Film Group.

Zhang, B., El-Jawahri, A., & Prigerson, H. (2006). Update on bereavement research: Evidence-based guidelines for the diagnosis and treatment of complicated bereavement. *Journal of Palliative Medicine, 9,* 1188–1202.

Zimmerman, J. L., & Dickerson, V. C. (1996). *If problems talked: Narrative therapy in action.* New York: Guilford Press.

Zupanick, C. E. (1994). Adult children of dysfunctional families: Treatment from a disenfranchised grief perspective. *Death Studies, 18,* 183–195.

Index